CONFESSIONS OF A THUG

CONFESSIONS OF A THUG

MEADOWS TAYLOR

GYAN

Published by

GYAN

Gyan Publishing House
5, Ansari Road
Daryaganj, New Delhi-110002
Phone: 011-47034999, 9811692060
E-mail: books@gyanbooks.com

Distribution Network
gyanbooks.com
India, USA, Canada, UK, Australia, France

ISBN : 9788121232715 (PB)
First Published, 1839

2nd Impression 2020

Printed at: Gyan Press, Delhi.

Confessions of a Thug
Author: Meadows Taylor

TO
THE RIGHT HONOURABLE
GEORGE, LORD AUCKLAND, G.C.B.,
GOVERNOR-GENERAL OF INDIA
WHO IS VIGOROUSLY PROSECUTING THOSE
ADMIRABLE MEASURES
FOR THE SUPPRESSION OF THUGGEE
WHICH WERE BEGUN BY THE LATE
LORD WILLIAM CAVENDISH BENTINCK,
G.C.B. AND G.C.H.,
HIS PREDECESSOR
THESE VOLUMES
ARE, BY PERMISSION, AND WITH GREAT RESPECT,
DEDICATED

CHAPTER I

You ask me, Sahib, for an account of my life; my relation of it will be understood by you, as you are acquainted with the peculiar habits of my countrymen; and if, as you say, you intend it for the information of your own, I have no hestitation in relating the whole; for though I have accepted the service of Europeans, in my case one of bondage, I cannot help looking back with pride and exultation on the many daring feats I have performed. Often indeed does my spirit rise at the recollection of them, and often do I again wish myself the leader of a band of gallant spirits, such as once obeyed me, to roam with them wherever my inclination or the hope of booty prompted.

But the time is past. Life, Sahib, is dear to every one; to preserve mine, which was forfeited to your laws, I have bound myself to your service, by the fearful tenure of denouncing all my old confederates, and you well know how that service is performed by me. Of all the members of my band, and of those with whom chance has even casually connected me, but few now remain at large; many have been sacrificed at the shrine of justice, and of those who now wander broken, and pursued from haunt to haunt, you have such intelligence as will lead to their speedy apprehension.

Yet Thuggee, capable of exciting the mind so strongly, will not, cannot be annihilated! Look at the hundreds, I may say thousands, who have suffered for its profession; does the number of your prisoners decrease? No, on the contrary they increase; and from every Thug who accepts the alternative of perpetual imprisonment to dying on a gallows, you learn of others whom even I knew not of, and of Thuggee being carried on in parts of the country where it is least suspected, and has never been discovered till lately.

It is indeed too true, Ameer Ali, said I; your old vocation seems to be as flourishing as ever, but it cannot last. Men will get tired of exposing themselves to the chance of being hunted down like wild beasts, and hung when they are caught; or what is perhaps worse to many, of being sent over the Kala-Panee[1]; and so heartily does the Government pursue Thugs wherever they are known to exist, that there will no longer be a spot of ground in India where your profession can be practised.

[1] Transported.

You err, Sahib; you know not the high and stirring excitement of a Thug's occupation. To my perception it appears, that so long as one exists, he will gather others around him; and from the relation of what I will tell you of my own life, you will estimate how true is my assertion.

How many of you English are passionately devoted to sporting! Your days and months are passed in its excitement. A tiger, a panther, a buffalo, or a hog, rouses your utmost energies for its destruction—you even risk your lives in its pursuit. How much higher game is a Thug's! He is man: against his fellow-creatures in every degree, from infancy to old age, he has sworn relentless, unerring destruction.

Ah! you are a horrible set of miscreants, said I: I have indeed the experience, from the records of murders which are daily being unfolded to me, of knowing this at least of you. But you must begin your story; I am prepared to listen to details worse than I can imagine human beings to have ever perpetrated.

It will even be as you think, said Ameer Ali, and I will conceal nothing; of course you wish me to begin my tale from as early a period as I can recollect.

Certainly; I am writing your life for the information of those in England, who would no doubt like to have every particular of so renowned a person as yourself.

Well, then Sahib, to begin; the earliest remembrance I have of anything, and until a few years ago it was very indistinct, is of a village in the territories of Holkar, where I was born. Who my parents were I know not; I suppose them to have been respectable, from the circumstances of my always wearing gold and silver ornaments, and having servants about me. I have an indistinct recollection of a tall fair lady whom I used to call mother, and of an old woman who always attended me, and who I suppose was my nurse; also of a sister, who was younger than myself, but of whom I was passionately fond. I can remember no other particulars, until the event occurred which made me what I am, and which is vividly impressed on my mind.

From an unusual bustle in the house, and the packing up of articles of clothing and other necessaries, I suppose we were on the eve of departure from our home. I was right in my conjecture, for we left it the next morning. My mother and myself travelled in a doolie[1], old Chumpa was mounted on my pony, and my father rode his large horse. Several of the sons of our neighbours accompanied us; they were all armed, and I suppose were our escort.

On the third or fourth day after we left our village, after our march of the day, we as usual put up in an empty shop in the bazaar of the town we rested at. My father left us to go about his own business, and my mother, who could not show herself outside, after repeated injunctions that I was not to stray away, lay

[1] A kind of palankeen.

down in an inner room and went to sleep. Finding myself at liberty as Chumpa was busy cooking and the juwans[1] were all out of the way, I speedily forgot all my mother's orders, and betook myself to play with some other children in the street. We were all at high romps, when a good-looking man of middle age addressed me, and asked me who I was. I must have been remarkable from the rest of the ragged urchins about me, as I was well dressed, and had some silver and gold ornaments on my person. I told him that my father's name was Yoosuf Khan, and that he and my mother and myself were going to Indore.

'Ah, then,' said he, 'you are the party I met yesterday on the road: your mother rides on a bullock, does she not?'

'No indeed!' retorted I angrily, 'she rides in a palankeen, and I go with her, and father rides a large horse, and we have Chumpa and several juwans with us. Do you think a Pathan like my father would let my mother ride on a bullock, like the wife of a ploughman?'

'Well, my fine little fellow, it shall be as you say, and you shall ride a large horse too, one of these days, and wear a sword and shield like me. But would you not like some sweetmeats? See how tempting those julabees[2] look at the hulwaee's[3]; come with me, and we will buy some.'

The temptation was too strong to be withstood by a child, and after a fearful look towards the shop where we stayed, I accompanied the man to the hulwaee's.

He bought me a load of sweetmeats, and told me to go home and eat them; I tied them up in a handkerchief I wore round my waist, and proceeded homewards. This transaction had attracted the notice of some of the ragged urchins I had been playing with, and who had longingly eyed the julabees I had been treated to; and as soon as the man who had given them to me had gone a short distance, they attacked me with stones and dirt, till one more bold than the rest seized me, and endeavoured to get my prize from me. I struggled and fought as well as I could; but the others having fairly surrounded me, I was mobbed, and obliged to deliver up my treasure. Not content with this, one big boy made a snatch at the necklace I wore, on which I began to bellow with all my might. The noise I made attracted the notice of my acquaintance, who running up soon put the troop of boys to flight, and taking me under his charge, led me to our abode, where he delivered me up to Chumpa; at the same time telling her of the scuffle, and cautioning her not to let me out of her sight again.

I was crying bitterly, and my mother hearing a strange voice called me to her. Asking me what had happened, I told my story, and said that the person who had saved me was speaking to

[1] Juwan, lit. *a young man*, applied in a general sense to soldiers.

[2] A kind of sweetmeat.

[3] Sweetmeat seller.

Chumpa. She addressed him from behind the cloth, which had been put up as a screen, and thanked him; and added, that my father was absent, but that if he would call again in an hour or two, he would find him at home, and she was sure he would also be glad to thank the person who had protected his child. The man said he would come in the evening, and went away. My father returned soon afterwards, and I received an admonition in the shape of a sound beating, for which I was consoled by my mother by a quantity of the sweetmeats from the hulwaee's, which had been the cause of my trouble, and I may add also of my present condition. You see, Sahib, how fate works its ends out of trifling circumstances.

Towards evening my acquaintance, accompanied by another man, came. I was a good deal the subject of their conversation; but it passed on to other matters, among which I remember the word Thug to have been first used. I understood too from their discourse, that there were many on the road between where we were and Indore, and that they were cautioning my father against them. The men said that they were soldiers, who had been sent out on some business from Indore; and as there were a good many of their men with them, they offered to make part of our escort. My friend was very kind to me, allowed me to play with his weapons, and promised me a ride before him on his horse the next day. I was delighted at the prospect, and with him for his kind and winning manner; but I did not like the appearance of the other, who was an ill-looking fellow—I shall have to tell you much more of him hereafter.

We started the next morning: our two acquaintances and their men joined us at a mangrove outside the village, where they had been encamped, and we proceeded on our journey. In this manner we travelled for two days, and my friend performed his promise of taking me up before him on his horse; he would even dismount, and lead him, allowing me to remain on the saddle; and as the animal was a quiet one, I used to enjoy my ride till the sun became hot, when I was put into the doolie with my mother. On the third day I remember my friend saying to my father, as they rode side by side—

'Yoosuf Khan, why should you take those poor lads of yours on to Indore with you? Why not send them back from the stage we are now approaching? I and my men are ample protection to you; and as you will belong to the same service as myself, there can be no harm in your trusting yourself and family to my protection for the rest of the journey; besides, the dangerous part of the road, the jungle in which he have been for the last two days, is passed, and the country before us is open. The only fear of Thugs and thieves existed in them, and they are now far behind.'

'It is well said,' replied my father; 'I dare say the lads will be thankful to me for sparing them a part of the long march back, and they have already accompanied us some fifty or sixty coss[1].'

On our arrival at the stage, my father told the lads they might return, at which they were highly pleased; and on their departure about noon, I gave many kind messages to my old companions and playfellows. I remember too giving an old battered rupee to be delivered to my little sister, and saying she was to hang it with the other charms and coins about her neck, to remind her of me. I found it again, Sahib; but, ah, under what circumstances!

At this period of his narrative, Ameer Ali seemed to shudder; a strong spasm shot through his frame, and it was some time before he spoke; at last he resumed.

Tell a servant to bring me some water, Sahib—I am thirsty with having spoken too much.

No, said I, you are not thirsty, but you shall have the water.

It was brought, but he scarcely tasted it—the shudder again passed through him. He got up and walked across the room, his irons clanking as he moved. It was horrible to see the workings of his face. At last he said, Sahib, this is weakness. I could not conceal it; I little thought I should have been thus moved at so early a period of my story; but recollections crowded me so fast, that I felt confused, and very sick. It is over now—I will proceed.

Do so, said I.

The juwans had been gone some hours, and it was now evening. My friend came to our abode, and told my father that the next two were short stages, and if he liked they might be made in one, as it would shorten the distance to Indore; but that we should be obliged to start very early, long before daylight, and that the bearers who carried the doolie could easily be persuaded to make the march by promise of a sheep, which the Patel of the village he proposed going to would supply free of cost, as he was a friend of his. My father seemed to be rather indignant at the idea of his taking a sheep for nothing, and said that he had plenty of money, not only to pay for a sheep, but to give them a present if they carried us quickly.

'Well,' said my friend, 'so much the better for we Sipahis have rarely much about us but our arms.'

'True,' returned my father; 'but you know that I have sold all my property at my village, and have brought the money to aid me in our service. Indeed, it is a good round sum.'

And my father chuckled at the idea.

'What! have you a thousand rupees?' I asked, my ideas of wealth going no further.

[1] Coss, about two miles.

'And what if it should be more?' said he, and the matter dropped; but even now I think I can remember that my friend exchanged significant glances with his companion.

It was then arranged that we should start with the rising of the moon about the middle of the night.

We were roused from our sleep at the hour proposed; and after the men had had a pipe all round, we set off. I was in the doolie with my mother. The moon had risen; but, as well as I can remember, there was but little light, and a slight rain falling, which obliged us to travel very slow. After we had proceeded a few coss, the bearers of the doolie put it down, saying that they could not get on in the dark and the mud, and proposed to wait till daylight. My father had a violent altercation with them: and as I was now wide awake, and it had ceased to rain, I begged to be taken out of the doolie, and allowed to ride with my friend. He did not assent as readily as usual; yet he took me up when the bearers had been scolded into going on. I observed to him that some of the soldiers, as I thought them, were absent. My remark attracted my father's notice to the circumstance, and he asked our companion were they were. He replied carelessly, that they were gone on in advance, as we had travelled as yet so slowly, and that we should soon overtake them.

We proceeded. We came at last to the deep bed of a river, on the sides of which there was some thick jungle, when my friend dismounted, as he said to drink water, and told me the horse would carry me over safely. I guided him on as well as I could; but before I had got well across the stream, I heard a cry, and the noise as if of a sudden scuffle. It alarmed me; and in looking back to see from whence it proceeded, I lost my balance on the horse, and fell heavily on the stones in the bed of the river, which cut my forehead severely. I bear the mark now.

I lay for a short time, and raising myself up, saw all the men, who I thought were far on before us, engaged in plundering the doolie. I now began to scream with all my might. One of them ran up to me, and I saw it was the ill-looking man I have before mentioned. 'Ah! we have forgotten you, you little devil,' cried he: and throwing a handkerchief round my neck, he nearly choked me. Another man came up hastily—it was my friend. 'He must not be touched,' he cried angrily to the other, and seized his hands; they had a violent quarrel, and drew their swords. I can remember no more; for I was so much frightened that I lost all consciousness, and, as I suppose, fainted.

I was recovered by some water being forced into my mouth; and the first objects which met my eyes were the bodies of my father and mother, with those of Chumpa and the palankeen-bearers, all lying confusedly on the ground. I cannot remember what my feelings were, but they must have been horrible. I only recollect throwing myself on my dead mother, whose face appeared dreadfully distorted, and again relapsing into insensibility. Even after the lapse of thirty-five years, the hideous appearance of my mother's face, and particularly of her eyes, comes to my recollection; but I need not describe it, Sahib; she had been strangled! She, my father, and the whole party had come to a miserable and untimely end. I heard a narrative of the particulars of the event, many years afterwards, from an old Thug; and I will relate them in their proper place.

When I recovered my consciousness, I found myself once more before my friend who had saved my life. He supported and almost carried me in his arms, and I perceived that we were no longer on the road. We were rapidly traversing the jungle, which extended as far as I could see in every direction; but the pain of my neck was so great, that I could scarcely hold up my head. My eyes seemed to be distended and bursting, and were also very painful. With my consciousness, the remembrance of the whole scene came to my recollection, and again I fell into insensibility. I recovered and relapsed in this manner several times during this journey; but it was only momentary, only sufficient to allow me to observe that we still held on at a rapid pace, as the men on foot were between running and walking. At last we stopped, and it was now broad daylight; indeed, the sun had risen. I was taken off the horse by one of the men, and laid under a tree on a cloth spread on the ground, and after some time my friend came to me. Desolate as I was, I could not help feeling that he must have had some concern in the death of my parents; and in my childish anger I bitterly reproached him, and bade him kill me. He tried to console me; but the more he endeavoured, the more I persisted that he should put me to death. I was in dreadful pain; my neck and eyes ached insufferably. I heaped all the abuse I could think of upon him, and the noise I made attracted the notice of the ill-looking man, whose name was Ganesha.

'What is that brat saying? Are you too turned woman,' cried he fiercely, addressing the other, whose name was Ismail, 'that you do not put the cloth about his neck, and quiet him at once? Let me do it, if you are afraid.'

And he approached me. I was reckless, and poured forth a torrent of vile abuse, and spat at him. He untied his waistband, and was about to put an end to me, when Ismail again interfered, and saved me; they had another violent quarrel, but he succeeded in carrying me off to some little distance, to another tree, where some of the band were preparing to cook their victuals; and setting me down among them, bidding them take care of me, he went away. The men tried to make me speak, but I was sullen, and would not; the pain of my neck and eyes seemed to increase, and I began to cry bitterly. I lay in this manner for some hours I suppose; and at last, completely tired out, fell asleep. I woke towards evening; and when Ismail saw me sit up, he came to me, soothed and caressed me, saying that I should henceforth be his child; and that it was not he, but others, who had murdered my parents. I remember begging him to do something for my neck, which was swollen and still very painful. He examined it, and seemed to be struck with the narrow escape I had had of my life.

He rubbed my neck with oil, and afterwards put upon it a warm plaster of leaves, which relieved it greatly, and I felt easier for its application. He remained with me; and some of the other men, sitting down by us, began to sing and play to amuse me. I was given some milk and rice to eat in the evening; but before it was time to sleep, Ismail brought me some sherbet of sugar and water, which he said would make me sleep. I suppose there was opium in it, for I remember nothing till the next morning, when I found myself in his arms on horseback, and knew that we were again travelling.

I pass over the journey, as I remember nothing of it, except that Ganesha was no longer with us, which I was very glad of; for I hated him, and could not bear his presence. Even in after years, Sahib, though we have been engaged together in Thuggee, I always bore a deep-rooted aversion to him, which never changed to the last.

Ismail and seven men were all that remained of the band; and we proceeded, by long and fatiguing marches, to a village in which he said he resided, and where I was to be given up to the care of his wife. We arrived at last, and I was introduced to a good-looking young woman as the child of a relation, whom he had long ago adopted as a son, and had now brought home to her: in fine, I was formally adopted by them as their own, and my sufferings were speedily forgotten.

CHAPTER II

I MUST have been at this time about five years old. It will strike you perhaps as strange, Sahib, that I should remember so many particulars of the event I have described; but when I was imprisoned some years ago at Delhi, I used to endeavour in my solitude to recollect and arrange the past adventures of my life; one circumstance led me to the remembrance of another; for in solitude, if the mind seeks the occupation, it readily takes up the clue to past events, however distant, and thought brings them one by one before the imagination, as vividly fresh as the occurrences of yesterday; and from an old Thug's adventures, which I heard during that imprisonment, I found my memory to serve me well. I was in possession of the whole of the facts, as I have related them to you, and I have only perhaps supplied the minor points from my own mind. I particularly recollect the scene with Ganesha, which he has since related to me, and told me, that such was his rage at the abuse I poured on him, that, had it not been for the dread of Ismail's vengeance, and of his power, he would have sacrificed me in his fury.

But to return to my story, if you are not tired of it.

No indeed, said I; I am becoming more and more interested in it.

Well, resumed Ameer Ali, I was kindly nursed and tended by Ismail and his wife. The curiosity of the villagers was a good deal excited by my appearance, and I have since suspected Ismail thought I might one day reveal what I knew of my origin; and for this reason I was never allowed out of his or his wife's sight. I must then however have speedily forgotten all about it, or at least have retained so confused and indistinct a recollection of the circumstances, that, had I endeavoured to relate them to any one, I could not have made them intelligible, and should have been disregarded.

Ismail, in his village, carried on the trade of a cloth merchant, at least when he was at home. He daily sat in his shop, with different kinds of cloths before him for sale; but it was very plain, even to me, to see that he was restless and uneasy. He would very often be absent for days together, without his family knowing where he had gone; and he would suddenly return with large quantities of cloth and other goods, which were always exposed for sale. I continued to be the object of his greatest care, and I reciprocated his affection, for indeed I was more kindly treated by him than I ever had been by my father, who was a proud and ill-tempered man. My new mother, too, never gave me reason to be displeased with her; for having no child of her own, I was her pet, and she lavished on me all the kindness in her power. I was always well-dressed, and had every indulgence that a child could wish for.

I was about nine years old, I think, when my kind protectress died of a fever while Ismail was on one of his excursions, and I was taken by a neighbour to his house, until he returned. I shall never forget his despair when he found his home desolate. Young as I was, I could do but little to console him; but he used to go and deck her tomb with flowers every Friday, and bitter were his lamentations over her grave.

Poor Miriam!—for that was her name—it was well for you that you died; had you lived, what would now have been your condition! As the wife of a noted Thug, your reputation would have been blasted, and you would have become an outcast.

Sahib! she never knew what Ismail was. He was to her a man in prosperous circumstances. She had everything she could desire, and not a want remained unsatisfied; and so deeply and well laid were his plans, that she would never have known, till the day of his capture, that she was the wife of a professed murderer.

I pass over the next four or five years of my life, as I can remember no incident in them worth relating. Ismail, soon after the death of his wife, removed from the village where he had hitherto resided, and took up his abode in the town of Murnae, which was then in Sindia's possession, and I was put to school with an old man, who taught me to read and write Persian.

As I grew older, I observed that Ismail used very frequently to have a number of men at his house by night, and I was naturally curious to know who they were, and why they assembled. One evening that I knew they were expected, I feigned to lie down and go to sleep as usual; but when they had all come, I got up cautiously, and hid myself behind a purdah or screen at the further end of the room where they sat. After they had eaten what was prepared for them, they all drew together, and began conversing in a language I only partially understood; and I thought this strange, as I knew Hindustani and the common dialect myself, having picked up the latter by associating with the boys of the town. By and by, Ismail went to a closet very near where I lay, and his movement alarmed me greatly, as I was fearful of being discovered; he took from it a box, which he placed in the circle, and opened it. Rich as I had always thought him, I had no idea of the wealth it contained; there were quantities of gold and silver ornaments of all kinds, with strings of pearls and other valuables; they seemed all parcelled out into lots, as equally as possible, and to each man he gave one, reserving a considerable share for himself.

At last they began to speak in Hindustani. One of them, an elderly man with a venerable beard, said to Ismail—

'What do you intend doing with Ameer? He is almost a young man; and if he is to be one of us, it is high time he should be taught what to do. It is very dangerous to have him about the house; he might discover something, and be off before you knew anything of the matter.'

'Oh, I have no fear of him,' said Ismail; 'he is too fond of me; besides, he has no other protector in the world but myself. He was the son of———'

And here the conversation was carried on by Ismail again in the language I did not understand.

'It does not matter,' said another man, whose name was Hussein, and whom I knew very well, as he was employed by Ismail, to all appearance, as an agent for selling his cloth; 'the lad is a smart active fellow, and a great deal too knowing for you to let him go about everywhere with so little restraint; he will find out all one of these days, if he is not fairly brought among us. Besides, he is old enough to be of use in many ways, and he ought to be instructed in our profession, if he is ever to learn; depend upon it, the sooner he eats the goor, the more relish he will have for it. I brought up a lad myself; and when once he got his hand in, he was a perfect tiger at the work, and became so expert, that our oldest hands could hardly compete with him.'

'Well,' said Ismail, 'I believe you are right, and I foretell great things from this boy. He is brave and stout beyond his years, and there are but few who can excel him in his qusrut[1], which I have taught him ever since he was a child; but he is of so kind and gentle a disposition, that I do not know how to break the matter to him. I almost fear he will never consent.'

'Pooh!' said a third man, whom I had never seen before; 'these very kind-hearted boys are the best we could have; they are the more easily led and won over, and one has more dependence upon them. Put the matter in the proper light; talk to him of the glory of the business, and of our surety of Heaven. Describe to him all about the houris which our blessed Prophet (may his name be honoured!) has promised us, and tell him too of the heaven of Indur, all of which we know we are sure of; the one by our faith as Moslems, and the other by our profession. He will soon be won over, I am certain.'

'I think,' said Ismail, 'you have hit on the right way; the lad goes to the old foolish mullah of the Mosque whenever he can get a moment's leisure, who has so filled his head with stories about Paradise, which he reads to him out of the blessed Koran, that he is at times half beside himself, and this is the only point

[1] Gymnastic exercises.

on which he is assailable. I will talk him over, and have no doubt he will soon belong to us.'

'The sooner the better,' said Hussein, laughing; 'I like to see the first attempt of a beginner: he always looks so confoundedly innocent when the cloth is put into his hand, and he is told—'

'Silence!' cried the old man: 'suppose he was now to hear you, (and you were going on with a relation of the whole matter) he might take a different view of the subject, and be off, as I said before.'

'No, there is no fear of that,' said Ismail: 'but are you not tired with your march? remember, we have far to travel tomorrow, and by Allah! it is for some good too.'

'Ay!' said all, getting up; 'let us go to sleep; it is too hot to rest here; we shall be cooler in the open air;' and they left the room.

You may believe, Sahib, that my curiosity was at the highest pitch: who was Ismail? who were the rest? what was it I was to know, or to be taught? my mind was in a whirl. I could not sleep that night; I never closed my eyes; I seemed to be in a fever, so intense was my curiosity, and, I may say, my desire to know everything, and to become a partner with Ismail in whatever he was. Hitherto I had been looked upon, treated as a child; now that was to be cast aside. I was, like a snake, to throw off my old skin, and to appear in a new and brighter form. Who could my parents be? I had gathered from the conversation, that Ismail was not my father, and I taxed my memory to recollect such portions of my previous existence as might throw some light on the subject; but all was dark within me. I could remember nothing but poor Miriam, my mother as I used to call her; beyond this, though hard did I endeavour, I could recollect nothing. It was only in after times, as I have told you, and during a long imprisonment of twelve years, that my memory aided me.

The old mullah of the Mosque had hitherto appeared in my eyes the most learned of men; he had stored my mind with passages from the Koran, which had made me an enthusiast. When he spoke to me of the glories of Heaven, of the thousands of houris who would be at the command of every true believer, described their beautiful forms, their eyes like sapphires, their teeth of pearls, their lips like rubies, and their breath like the perfume of musk—the palaces of jewels, and the fountain of immortality and never-ending youth—I believed that I was destined to enjoy all. They had inflamed my imagination; and as I used to repeat them to Ismail, he too appeared as delighted as I was, and used to regret that he had never studied the blessed book, that he might enjoy its beautiful descriptions: yet the mullah was called a fool by Hussein, and I understand from him that theirs was a higher calling, their rewards more splendid than even those of the Moslem! What could they be! I burned to know; and resolved, that if Ismail did not break the matter to me, I would, of my own accord, lead him to the subject.

I said, I think, that my eyes never closed that night; when I rose in the morning I found that Ismail and the others were gone. He did not return for some days. This was nothing uncommon, certainly; but his proceedings had become mysterious to me for a long time before, and I could not help connecting his frequent and long absences with his true profession, whatever that might be. He could not be *only* a cloth merchant: there was nothing in that plodding business to hold out to him or to me the splendid hopes that Hussein and the rest evidently entertained, and with which I had no doubt he was familiar. It must be something beyond this, which I could not compass; and so see whether I could get any clue to it, I betook myself to the old mullah.

Azeezoola, for that was his name, received me with his usual kindness, but remarked that I must be ill, as my face, he said, was full of anxiety, and as though I was suffering from fever. I said I had had ague, but that I was better, and it would soon pass from me. I took my usual lessons in the forms, positions, and words of a Mohammedan's daily prayers; and when these were ended, I begged him to open the Koran, and explain again to me my favourite passages. The old man put on his spectacles, and rocking himself to and fro, read to me passage after passage of the book in Arabic, explaining the meaning to me as he read. It was the same I had heard often before; and when he had finished, I asked him whether there were not other portions of the book which he had concealed from me.

'No, my son,' said he; 'I have concealed from you nothing. My knowledge of this blessed book is indeed very limited; but oh! that you could have seen and heard the commentaries which my revered preceptor—peace be to his memory!—had written upon it. In them, so deep was his knowledge, that every sentence of some chapters, in which the true meaning is properly hidden from the uninitiated, formed a separate treatise; nay, in some passages every word, and indeed every letter, was commented upon. But he is gone, and is now enjoying the delights of the paradise I have revealed to you. All I can do is to read to you, and I will do it again and again, till you have by heart the parts which most interest you, and which are the cream of the book.'

'But,' said I, 'have you never heard of anything beyond what you have told me, in all your long experience? You are surely concealing something from me, which you fear to tell me on account of my youth.'

'No, indeed,' said the old man; 'it is true that some professors of our religion, sufis and others, whose creeds are accursed, have from time to time promulgated heterodox doctrines, which are plausible enough, and entrap the unwary; but they lead to ultimate perdition, and I think you are now too well grounded in your belief to be led away by them, young as you are.'

'Thanks to your kindness, I am,' said I, 'and it was only to try whether I had more to learn, that I have now questioned you as I have;' for I saw he either could not, or would not, reveal to me more. 'But tell me, father, what profession ought I to adopt to carry your wise instructions into the best effect?'

'Become a mullah,' said he; 'you will have to undergo much painful study, but in the course of time this obstacle will be overcome; and depend upon it, there is no station or profession so acceptable to God as that of one of his ministers. I will instruct you in the rudiments of Arabic, and your father when he sees your mind bent upon it will not oppose you; nay, he will send you to Delhi to complete the education I shall have begun.'

'Well, I will think of it,' said I. But it was very far from my intention to become a mullah. I could not disguise from myself that Azeezoola was miserably poor, and was dependent upon contributions he with difficulty collected for his maintenance. Besides Ismail was not a mullah, nor Hussein, nor any of their set; and I must become one of them, be they what they might, before my mind could be at rest. I went no more to him. I had got from him his little store of knowledge, and if once I had broken the subject of my future life to him, I should only be subjected to continual arguments in support of his views of what would tend to my benefit; and as I did not like them, I thought it better to stay away.

Would to God I had become a mullah! Anything would be preferable to my state at present, which must now for ever remain as it is. It is my fate however, and I ought not to murmur at the decrees of Providence. If it had not been written, would my father have been murdered? If it had not been written, should I have ever become a Thug? Assuredly not. Who can oppose Fate? who can avert its decrees? Yet would you not, Sahib, release me, and provide for me, if after many years you found me faithful?

Never, said I; you Thugs are too dangerous ever to be let loose again upon the world; your fingers would itch to strangle the first man you met, and before long we would hear of Ameer Ali Jemadar, with a gang of forty or fifty fellows, who would give us infinite trouble to catch. Would it not be so?

I believe you are right, said Ameer Ali laughing: in spite of my remorse at times, the opportunities would be too tempting for me to let them pass. And you know I have eaten the Goor, and cannot change. I am better as I am, for if you caught me again you would hang me.

I have not the least doubt we should, Ameer Ali: but go on with your story; you will forget what your train of thought was, if you digress in this manner. He resumed.

Nearly a month elapsed, and after this weary time to me, Ismail returned, accompanied by Hussein. My father, for so I shall call him, remarked a change in my appearance, which I accounted for as I had done to the mullah, and he seemed satisfied. But was I? O no! I was consumed by my burning curiosity to know all that was hidden from me. I could not sleep at nights, and became sullen, and oppressed with thoughts which led me to no conclusions. At one time I had formed the determination to leave my father, and seek my fortune: and had actually packed up a few of my clothes, and a little money I had, and resolved to leave the town in the night, little caring where my fate should lead me; but when the time came, the sense of my desolation so pressed upon me, that I abandoned the idea, and remained. I trusted to time for clearing up the mystery that hung over me, but at the same time determined that I would be more watchful over my father and his companions than I had ever been before. And many were the resolutions I made to speak to him on the subject nearest my heart; yet even when opportunities occurred, I could not bring myself to the task. It was not that I was timid—naturally I was brave—it was a mysterious consciousness that I should hear something (whenever I should hear it) that was strange, nay fearful, that deterred me; but why this feeling should have so possessed me I cannot now tell, yet so it was.

One evening Ismail sent for me to his sleeping-room. I had been rarely admitted to it, and my heart beat fearfully, with a presentiment that I was upon the crisis of my fate. Ismail too seemed to me to be disturbed; he bade me sit down, and we sat silently for some time gazing on one another; there was only a small oil light burning in a recess of the wall, which made the apartment very gloomy, and this trifling circumstance contributed still more to increase the morbid feeling within me. I believe I almost gasped for breath; I could bear it no longer. I arose, threw myself at his feet, and burst into a passionate fit of weeping.

'Why, Ameer, my child, my son,' said he kindly and caressingly, 'what is this? What has troubled you? Has some fair one bewitched you? Have you got into any difficulty while I have been away? Tell me, my boy; you know you have no one in the world so fond of you as your father, and, alas! you have now no mother.'

When my feelings gave me power of utterance, fearfully I repeated to him what I had heard from him and the rest, on the memorable night I have before related. When I had finished, I rose up, and with a throbbing heart said, 'I have erred, my father; my curiosity, a boy's curiosity, overcame me, but since then my feelings have changed; why I know not; I am no longer a boy, for I feel that I can do anything, and only implore you to put me to the proof;' and I folded my hands on my breast, and stood silent.

He was evidently much moved; dusk as it was, I could see his face working with emotions, and under expressions new to me.

At last he broke the silence, which had become to me insupportable. 'My son,' he said, 'you know more than I had ever intended you should. I have now no alternative but to make you such as I am myself, and my knowledge of your character leads me to anticipate much from you.'

'Trust me, only trust me!' I passionately exclaimed; 'you shall never have cause to regret it!'

'I believe you,' said he; 'and now attend well to what I shall say, for upon it your future existence depends. There can be no hesitation, no falling back on the world, when once you know all. You will have to undergo a trial which will stretch your courage to its utmost: will you go through with it? Dare you to brave it?'

'I dare,' cried I, for I was reckless.

He seemed to be absorbed in thought for a few moments, and then said,

'Not tonight, but I swear to you that in three days at the furthest I will conceal nothing from you.'

I was disappointed, yet full of hope, and he dismissed me to my repose.

Ismail performed his promise; but I can hardly describe to you, Sahib, the effect it then had on my mind: shall I endeavour to relate what his tale was? I only hesitate, as it began by his giving me a sketch of his life, which I fear would lead me from my own story—yet it would interest you greatly.

I doubt not that it would, Ameer Ali, said I; and when you have finished your own adventures you can return to it.

You are right, Sahib, I will omit it all except his concluding words, which, with his tale of wrong, endured and revenged, made me hate the world, and cleave to Thuggee as the only profession and brotherhood in which I could hope to find good faith existing. They were these, and they have ever been indelibly impressed on my memory.

'Thus far, my son, have I related some events of my life for your instruction, and I have little more to add. I need hardly now mention that I am a Thug, a member of that glorious profession which has been transmitted from the remotest periods, to the few selected by Allah for his unerring purposes. In it the Hindu and the Moslem both unite as brothers: among them bad faith is never known: a sure proof, that our calling is blessed and sanctioned by the divine authority. For where on this earth, my son, will you find true faith to exist, except among us? I see none in all my dealings with the world; in it each man is incessantly striving to outwit and deceive his neighbour: and I turn from its heartlessness to our truth, which is refreshing to my soul to contemplate. From the lowest to the highest among us, all are animated with the same zeal; go where we will we find the same brotherhood; and though differing perhaps, in many parts, in customs and points of practice, yet their hearts are the same, and all pursue the great aim and end of Thuggee with the same spirit. Go where we will, we find homes open to us, and a welcome greeting among tribes even of whose language we of Hindustan are ignorant; yet their signs of recognition are the same as ours, and you need but to be thrown among them as I have been, to experience the truth of my assertions. Could this be without the aid of Allah? So clashing are human interests, and so depraved is the social state of our country, that I own no such feeling could exist without the divine will. Some repugnance you will feel at the practice of the profession at first but it is soon overcome, for the rewards held out are too glorious to allow us to dwell for a moment on the means we use to attain them. Besides, it is Fate—the decree of the blessed Allah!—and who can withstand it? If he leads us into the undertaking, he gives us firm and brave hearts, a determination which no opposition can overcome, and a perseverance which never yet failed to accomplish its object. Such, my son, is what I would make you; you will enter on your calling at once in a high grade, under my auspices, a grade which others spend years of exertion to attain; you will never know want, for all my wealth shall be shared with you. Be firm, be courageous, be subtle, be faithful; more you need not. These are the highest qualifications of a Thug, and those which ensure honour and respect among our fraternity, and lead to certain success and high rank. As for me, I look but to see you at the head of a band of your own, to retire, and in quiet pass the remainder of the years allotted to me, content with hearing the praises which will be bestowed upon Ameer Ali, the daring and enterprising son of Ismail!—till then I shall be your guardian and instructor!'

CHAPTER III

'My father,' said I, 'you need say no more, I am yours; do as you will with me; long ere I heard this story from you, I had overheard a conversation between Hussein, yourself, and some others, regarding me, which has caused me great unhappiness; for I feared I was not thought worthy of your confidence, and it weighed heavily upon my mind. That was in fact the cause of the sorrow and heaviness you have remarked, and I longed for an opportunity to throw open my heart to you, and to implore of you to receive me among you. I am no longer a child, and your history has opened to me new feelings which are at present too vague for me to describe; but I long to win fame as you have done, and to become a member of the profession in which you describe true faith and brotherhood alone to exist. As yet I have seen nothing of the false world, and assuredly what you have said makes me still less inclined to follow any calling which would lead me to connection with it. Heartless and depraved I have heard it to be from others beside yourself, and I feel as though I were chosen by Allah to win renown; it can only be gained by treading in your footsteps, and behold me ready to follow you whithersoever you will lead. I have no friend but yourself, no acquaintance even have I ever formed among the youths of the village; for when I saw them following what their fathers had done, and what appeared to me low and pitiful pursuits, my spirit rose against them, and I have cast them off. My only friend is the old mullah, who would fain persuade me to become one like himself, and spend my days reading the Koran; but there is nothing stirring in his profession, though it is a holy one, and it consequently holds out no inducements to me, or any hope of gratifying the thirst for active employment which is consuming me. I have wished to become a soldier, and to enter one of the bands in the service of Sindia to fight against the unbelieving Feringhees [Europeans]; but this too has passed away, and now I desire nothing but to become a Thug, and follow you, my father, through the world. I will not disappoint you; my thirst for fame is too ardent, for anything but death to quench it.'

'May Allah keep it far from you,' said Ismail with feeling: 'you are the only solace to a life which has now no enjoyment but what is produced by the development of your thoughts and actions. I know, my son, you will not disappoint me. You see the state of prosperity I am blessed with, but you little know the power I have; my authority is owned by every Thug in this part of Hindustan, and a week's notice would see a band of a thousand men ready to obey any order I should give them. This will be proved to you in a few days, at the festival of the Dussehra; we shall all assemble, at least as many as will be requisite for the opening operations of the year, which will be undertaken on a scale of unusual greatness, for we have determined to take advantage of the confusion at present produced by the wars of Holkar and Sindia and the Feringhees; we anticipate much work and a stirring season, and the men are impatient for employment, after a long period of inactivity. I will take you to Sheopur, which we have decided on as our place of meeting, as the Zemindar is friendly to us and assists us in many ways. I will introduce you to my associates, and you will be initiated as a Thug in the usual manner.'

Thus, Sahib, our conversation ended: the night had passed in its relation, and I went to rest a different being from what I had been for many days before. I rose, and found all my former energy and spirit had returned to me; and whereas a few days before I went about like a love-sick maiden, I now held up my head, threw out my chest, and felt a man. It was true I was still a boy. I was only eighteen years old, but I did not suffer my thoughts to dwell upon this; a few years, thought I, and Inshallah! I shall be somebody. To prove to you, Sahib, the excitement that possessed me. I shall relate to you the following circumstance. I might have joined in the action before, but never should have dreamed of doing the deed of daring I then did, in the presence too of men who were soldiers by profession, but who hung back at the moment of danger.

It happened, a day or two after the conversation with my father which I have related, that a tigress with a cub came into a small tract of jungle which lay near our village: the first day she was seen she killed a shepherd, the second day another man who had gone to look for his body, and the third she grievously wounded the Patel of the village, a man who was held in universal estimation, and he died during the night. A general meeting of the villagers was held at the place set apart for deliberations, and it was determined that all the active men should proceed in a body and attack the beast in her lair. The next morning we all assembled before daybreak. There was one man, a huge large-whiskered and bearded Pathan, who volunteered to be our leader; he was literally hardly able to move for the weapons he had about him. Two swords were in his belt, which also contained an assortment of daggers of various sizes and shapes: a long straight two-edged sword hung over his left shoulder, the point of which nearly touched the ground; he had also a shield across his back, and in his right hand a matchlock with the match lighted. He addressed my father as we came up.

'Salaam aleikum! Ismail Sahib,' said he; 'is a quiet person like you coming out with us, and the Sahib-zadah too?'

'Yes, Khan,' replied my father, 'it is incumbent on all good men to do their utmost in a case of need like this; who knows, if the brute is not killed, but that some one else may become food for it?'

'Inshallah!' said the Khan, twisting up his mustachios, and surveying himself, 'we have determined that the brute dies today. Many a tiger has fallen from a shot from my good gun, and what is this brute that it should escape? May its sister be defiled! The only fear is, that it will not stand to allow us to prove that we are men, and not dogs before it.'

'As to that,' said my father, 'we must take our chance; but say, Khan, how will you move with all those weapons about you? why, you could not run away were she to rush out.'

'Run away!' cried the Khan; 'are our beards to be defiled by a brute? what are you thinking of this morning to suppose that Dildar Khan ever turned from anything in his life? Only let it come out, I say, and you will see of what use the weapons will be! Trust to me single-handed to finish it: first I shall shoot it with my matchlock; it will be wounded; then I shall advance on it thus,' said he, drawing the long sword and flourishing it, at the same time twirling round and round, and leaping in every possible direction.

'There!' said he, quite out of breath, 'there would not that have finished it? Why I am a perfect Rustam in matters of this kind, and killing a tiger is only child's play to Dildar Khan! why I could eat one, tail and all. But come along, and when the play begins, let no one come in Dildar Khan's way,' said he to the assembled group; 'for, Inshallah! I mean to show you poor ignorant people how a tiger can be killed by a single man.'

'I know the Khan to be as arrant a coward as ever breathed,' said my father to me; 'but come, let us see what he will do, for I confess I am anxious to behold him capering before the tigress.'

'By Allah!' said I, 'if he does perform such antics, the brute will dine on him to a certainty.'

'That is no concern of ours,' said my father; 'it is a matter of destiny; but I would venture a great deal, he never goes within an arrow's flight of her.'

We all set out, headed by Dildar Khan, who still flourished his long sword, holding his matchlock in his left hand, now and then smoothing up his mustachios, which grew, or had been trained to stick upwards from his lips, and reached nearly to his eyes. We soon came to the jungle, and on entering it I thought the Khan showed signs of fear.

'The beast can be but a panther after all,' said he, 'and it is hardly worth the while for Dildar Khan to put himself to trouble. See, boys,' continued he to some of us, 'I will wait here; if it should really turn out to be a tiger you can let me know and I will come and kill it.'

Against this, however, we protested, and declared that all would go wrong without him; and after some demur he again proceeded.

'I told you,' said my father, 'how it would be; but let us see how he will end the affair.'

We went on, till some bones and torn clothes, and the head of one of the unfortunate men who had been killed, lying near a bush, proved very plainly that the animal was not far off, and at these the Khan showed fresh signs of fear.

A moment afterwards, the tigress and a half-grown cub rushed past us with their tails in the air, and he rushed forward, but not in the direction the tigress had gone.

'That is not the way,' cried some, and at last he turned.

'This is child's play,' said my father; 'come, if we are to do anything, we had better set about it in good earnest.'

And we went on in the direction the beast had taken.

It led to an open glade, at one side of which there was a large rock, with some very thick bushes about it.

'She is there, depend upon it,' said an old hunter; 'I never saw a more likely place in life.'

We were all about thirty steps from the rock and bushes, and Dildar Khan did not at all relish his proximity to them.

'I beg to represent,' said he in a low voice to us all, 'that having killed so many of these brutes, I know best how to manage them; and as I am the best armed of the party, I shall take up my position near yonder bush, by which runs the pathway; she will take to it when she is driven out, and then you will see the reception she will meet with from Dildar Khan. Inshallah! I shall present the point of my sword to her, and she will run on it, then I shall finish her with one blow of my tegha[1].'

We all looked in the direction he pointed, and sure enough there was a bush, about two hundred paces off, on the pathway to the village.

'Not that one surely,' said my father; 'why, man, you will never see the beast from thence.'

'Trust me,' said the Khan, and off he went.

'I told you how it would be,' continued my father; 'directly he sees the animal, he will be off down the road as fast as he can. But come,' said he to the men, 'since the Khan thinks he will be of more use down yonder, I will lead you on, and we will see whether this eater of men cannot be got out.'

We were immediately divided into three parties, one to go either side of the bushes, the other by a circuit to get behind the rock and if possible upon it, in order to shoot her from above if she was to be seen; if not, at any rate to dislodge her by throwing stones. The arrangements were quickly completed, and though we

[1] A short, crooked, heavy sword.

were all within only a few yards of the bushes, there was no sign of the tigress. She expressed no displeasure at our near approach or preparations, as she had been disturbed before, and of course could not easily be driven out of her place of refuge. I was with one of the parties on the side, and had no arms but a sword and a light shield; indeed I had gone more as a spectator than aught else. We waited a few minutes, and one of the party who had been sent round appeared on the top of the rock; he was soon followed by three others.

'Are you all ready?' cried one of them: 'I shall heave down this stone.'

'Bismillah! away with it!' cried my father.

Three of them applied their strength to it, and at last it rolled over the face of the rock, and thundering down split into a thousand fragments. There was a moment of intense anxiety and suspense, but no tigress followed.

'Try whether you cannot see her,' cried my father; 'if you do, fire: we are all prepared.'

The men looked down in every direction, but said nothing. At last one of them was observed to be pointing to a particular spot, as though he showed the others something.

'By Allah!' said my father, 'he sees her; look out; she will rush forth before you are thinking of her.'

Every man blew his match, and planted his feet firmly. At last one of the men on the rock raised his matchlock and fired; it was answered by a tremendous roar which rent the skies, and out rushed the cub, apparently badly wounded, for before he had come a few yards he lay down and roared horribly; he was fully half-grown, and made a dreadful noise. One of the men of our party fired at him, and he did not move after the shot struck him.

'Now we shall have tough work,' said my father; 'she will be savage and infuriated beyond description: it is hardly safe to be here; but mind your aim, my lads, and she will never reach us; I never yet missed mine, but the shot may not be fatal; so look out for yourselves.'

Again my father called to the men on the rock to heave over another fragment. There was one very large one just on the brink. After a good many pushes it gave way, and as the former had done, shivered into atoms with a great noise. It was successful, the tigress rushed out towards our side, and stood for a moment. I had never seen a tiger before, and could not help admiring her noble appearance. There she stood, her tail erect, the end of it only waving from side to side, glaring on us with her fearfully bright eyes, apparently irresolute as to what she would do, and not noticing the body of the cub, which was close to her. We were all as silent as death, each man with his matchlock to his shoulder. My father fired, and then the others; I could see the whole distinctly, for I had no gun. She staggered when my father fired, he had evidently hit her; but the rest had missed, and she charged with another tremendous roar, right at our party; but the shout we set up, and the waving of our weapons turned her, and she set off at a slow canter towards the bush where Dildar Khan had stationed himself.

'Ya Allah!' cried my father, 'coward as he is, he will be killed —she will spare nothing now! what can be done?'

By this time the other party caught a glimpse of her, and every matchlock was discharged; she must have been hit again, for she stopped, turned round, growled, and showed her teeth, but again sprang forward. I imagine Dildar Khan had no idea that she was approaching him, as he had hid himself behind the bush and could have seen nothing of what had passed. 'He may escape,' said my father; 'it is possible, yet scarcely; what can be done?' No one made a reply, but an instant afterwards I had drawn my sword, and set off at full speed after the enraged brute.

'Ameer Ali, my son! come back, come back instantly! Ya Allah, he too will perish!' cried my father in an agony of apprehension.

But I heeded not, and who of that company had my fleet foot? Yet some of them followed me. As I ran, I saw the tigress was weak, and was badly wounded, but still she ran fast. I saw her approach the bush, and the miserable man Dildar Khan rush from behind it, and stand in her very path, with his arms stretched out, apparently paralysed with fear. Another instant she had crouched as she ran, and sprang upon him; he was under her, and she fiercely tearing his body. It did not stop me; I heard the cries of those behind me to turn off, but I did not. I do not think I gave the danger a thought; if I did, the excitement overpowered it. Another bound had brought me close to the brute, whose head was down, gnawing the body beneath her. I made but one stroke at her, which, praise be to Allah! was successful; the blade buried itself deep in the back of her neck, and she seemed to me to drop dead; I bounded off to one side, and watched for a moment. She was indeed dead, and lay, her limbs only quivering, upon the body of the man beneath her. Unfortunate coward! wounded as she was, she would not have turned after him, had he even had the presence of mind to avoid her; but he had thought to fly, and the sight of the animal had paralyzed his faculties. Though all passed in a moment, methinks now, Sahib, I see him, his eyes starting from his head, and his arms raised and expanded, as though wooing the animal's fatal embrace. Coward! had he remained behind the bush, he was safe, and might have shot her as she passed; but there he lay, a fearful spectacle, his face all bitten and lacerated, and the blood pouring from wounds in his stomach! He was quite dead. My father came up immediately; he embraced me, and burst into tears.

'How could you risk your life, my boy?' said he; 'how could

you be so rashly venturous of your life for so poor a wretch as he?' pointing to the body; 'did I not tell you he was a coward? Yet I am proud of you now, my son, and you have shamed us all. See!' continued he to the whole assembly, 'our faces are blackened this day by a boy; who among you could have planted so well-aimed and deep a cut? See! the blade has buried itself, and is half through the bone. Mashallah he is a brave boy!' and again my father hugged me to his breast.

'I beg to represent,' said old Benee Singh, my instructor in my athletic exercises, 'that some of the praise is due to me for my good teaching. I always told you, Ismail Sahib, that the Sahib-zada would be worthy of his father; may his riches increase, and may he live a thousand years! Yes, sir,' said he to me, 'often have I taught you that cut; you see you were running along, and cut over your left hand; it is few that can do that with any certainty, but you have caught the knack, and you want but a little practice to become as good a swordsman as myself. Perhaps too,' continued he to me, laughing, 'the heart of your teacher may be made glad today; under such an auspicious commencement, the Sahib-zada will remember the old Rajput.'

'That reminds me,' said my father, 'that I owe you a present; come to me this afternoon. Inshallah! we know how to be grateful for kindness, and it shall have its reward.' And he received when he came a handsome gift.

I must say, however, that under his tuition I had become highly expert at all manly exercises; I could use a gun, throw a spear, wrestle, knew the exact use of every description of sword, straight or crooked, single or double-edged, long or short, and in all these exercises there was not a lad of the village, and I may say of the country round, who could in any way compete with me.

That night my father said to me, 'Ameer, my son, tomorrow you accompany me to Sheopur. I need not tell you how this exploit will raise you in the eyes of your future companions. Already have I despatched intelligence of our proposed departure tomorrow, and some account of today's affair, enough only to make them curious to see the hero of it; and I have mentioned no particulars, which will make them the more anxious to hear them from me. You have hitherto been looked on with some suspicion by many members of my band; and were it not for my rank of Jemadar I should have been obliged to explain my intentions in regard to you long ago to them. I look therefore upon this event as particularly fortunate; as knowing you are to be publicly brought amongst them, they will receive you with greater warmth and respect, as having given so undeniable a proof of your bravery, in the presence too of old soldiers, who have most of them seen many a tough fight.'

'It was the will of Allah,' said I; 'else what power had a boy like me to do such a thing?'

'You are now no child,' replied my father; 'you have this day, or I mistake you much, thrown off every lingering feeling of boyhood; the change has been sudden, but it has been complete, and it will last, or I am deceived.'

'You are not,' I replied, 'I am not what I was; today's is the first blood I have seen spilled; I feel that it will not be the last.'

CHAPTER IV

THE day after my adventure with the tigress, I left our village with my father. We travelled on horseback, and on the fourth morning afterwards reached Sheopur, the town from which the grand expedition was to set out. It was here, too, that I was to be admitted into the band of Thugs, and I looked forward to my inauguration with much impatience, and perhaps some dread, for I knew not what ceremonies I had to go through. We put up in the house of Moedeen, where several other Thug leaders were also; and after refreshing ourselves, my father bade me accompany him to the council which was to determine on the future operations. I was presented to the members, ten in number, who were the jemadars of the different bands. I could see, from the respect and consideration with which my father was treated, that he was looked upon as the chief of the whole; I was gratified by the reception I met with; and my conduct in the affair with the tigress, the whole circumstances of which were related by my father, raised me at once to a high station in their respect.

As it still wanted two days to the festival of the Dussehra, my inauguration was postponed to that day; for it is esteemed a particularly fortunate one by the Thugs, and indeed by all classes. On it, you are already aware, that all great undertakings are commenced by armies, and, in like manner, by us Thugs; for the breaking up of the rains gives us a hope that the adventure will not be impeded by them; and the continuance of fine weather which follows it, allows the band to travel in comfort, and with better hope of booty from the chance of falling in with travellers, who also take advantage of the break in the weather to commence long journeys. Above all, it is a day peculiarly sacred to Bhowani, our patroness and goddess. Still, being a Mussulman, I could not then see why such respect was paid to the festival of the Dussehra, or indeed why it was kept at all; and I applied to my father for a solution of my doubts on the subject.

'It is necessary to your fully understanding this,' said he, 'that I should give you an outline of our belief in the divine origin of our profession, which is intimately connected with the faith of the Hindus, and by whom we Mussulmans have been instructed in the art of Thuggee.'

'This is wonderful,' said I; 'how do you reconcile any connexion between the faith of unbelievers and that of the blessed Prophet?'

'I cannot pretend to solve the difficulty,' said my father; 'but as their religion is far more ancient than ours, and no doubt had a divine origin, there are many points in it which one of the true faith may follow without offence, so that he does not join them in all their forms and professions. Indeed this is impossible, as no one can become a Hindu; but, as I told you before, Thuggee is one of the means by which Allah works out his own ends; and as the profession of it has been handed down to us from ages, and as it becomes the fate of those who are called to it to follow it, there is no possibility of avoiding the profession, though one desired it; and as a direct consequence, no sin in associating with Hindus in the practice of it, from whom it has had its origin. Do you understand me?'

'Perfectly' said I; 'it was not to question its propriety that I asked the question, but only to know how it was, that Hindu festivals were acknowledged and kept by us Musulmans.'

'The Dussehra is the only one,' said my father, 'which is observed; and the reason of this is, that it is the fittest time of the year to commence our enterprises, and has been invariably kept sacred by all Hindu Thugs. But I must tell you of the origin of Thuggee, that you may judge for yourself how ancient it is, and how well the instructions given by divine command have been followed up. In the beginning of the world, according to the Hindus, there existed a creating and a destroying power, both emanations from the Supreme Being. These were, as a matter of consequence, at constant enmity with each other, and still continue to be so. The creative power however peopled the earth so fast, that the destroyer could not keep pace with him, nor was he allowed to do so; but was given permission to resort to every means he could devise to effect his objects. Among others, his consort Devi, Bhowani, or Kali, for she is known under these and many other names, constructed an image, into which, on this occasion, she was empowered to infuse the breath of life. No sooner was this effected, than she assembled a number of her votaries, whom she named Thugs. She instructed them in the art of Thuggee, and, to prove its efficacy, with her own hands destroyed before them the image she had made, in the manner which we now practise. She endowed the Thugs with superior intelligence and cunning, in order that they might decoy human beings to destruction, and sent them abroad into the world, giving them, as the reward of their exertions, the plunder they might obtain from those they put to death; and bidding them be under no concern for the disposal of the bodies, as she would herself convey them from the earth. Ages passed on in this manner, and she protected her votaries from human laws, and they were everywhere found to be faithful: but corruptions crept in among them, with the increased depravity of the world; and at last, a gang more bold and curious than the rest, after destroying a traveller, determined, instead of following the old custom of leaving the body unnoticed, to watch and see how it was disposed of. They hid themselves, as they thought, secure from observation in the bushes by the side of the road, and waited the arrival of the goddess. But what mortal can escape the eye of divinity? She quickly espied them, and called them before her. Terror-stricken by her splendid and terrific appearance, and in the utmost dread of her vengeance, they attempted to fly; but she arrested their steps, and in an awful manner upbraided them for their want of faith.

'"You have seen me," said she, "and looked upon a power which no mortal has ever yet beheld without instant destruction; but this I spare you; henceforward, however, I shall no longer protect you as I have done. The bodies of those whom you destroy will no longer be removed by me, and you must take your own measures for their concealment. It will not always be effectual, and will often lead to your detection by earthly powers, and in this will consist your punishment. Your intelligence and cunning still remain to you. I will in future assist you by omens for your guidance; but this my decree will be your curse to the latest period of the world."

'So saying she disappeared, and left them to the consequences of their own folly and presumption; but her protection has never been withdrawn. It is true, the remains of those who fall by our hands are sometimes discovered, and instances have been known of that discovery having led to the apprehension of Thugs, at least so I have heard; but during my lifetime I have never known of one, and it is my firm belief that such instances have been permitted on purpose to punish those who have in some way offended our protectress, by neglecting her sacrifices and omens. You therefore see how necessary it is to follow the rules which have guided our fraternity for ages, and which cannot be changed without incurring the displeasure of the divine power; nor is there anything in our creed to forbid it. We follow the blessed precepts of our Prophet; we say our Namaz five times a day; we observe all the rules of our faith; we worship no idols; and if what we have done for ages, ever since the invasion by our forefathers of India, was displeasing to the apostle, surely we should have had, long ere this, some manifestation of his displeasure. Our plans would have been frustrated, our exertions rendered of no avail we should have dragged on a miserable existence, and long ere this should have abandoned Thuggee and our connexion with its Hindu professors.'

'I am convinced,' said I; 'for your relation is wonderful. Truly have you said that we are under the especial protection of Providence; and it would be sinful to question the propriety of any usages which have been transmitted from a period so remote, and followed without deviation. I will allow that I had thought this open connexion with Kafirs as offensive, because I was led to believe them sunk into the lowest depths of depravity and bad faith, from the representations of the old Mullah who was my instructor; but he must have been ignorant, or a bigoted old fool.'

'I will say nothing more than this,' replied my father, 'that you will be thrown much into the society of Hindus, all of good caste, and you will find them as faithful and as worthy of your friendship as any Mussulman; such, at least, has been my experience of them.'

On the day of the Dussehra the ceremony of my inauguration as a Thug commenced. I was bathed and dressed in new clothes which had never been bleached, and led by the hand by my father, who officiated as the Guru or spiritual director, and to whom seemed to be confided the entire direction of the ceremonies. I was brought into a room, where the leaders of the band I had before seen were assembled, sitting on a clean white cloth, which was spread in the centre of the apartment. My father then, advancing towards them, asked them whether they were content to receive me as a Thug and a brother, to which they all answered, 'We are.'

I was then conducted into the open air, accompanied by the whole number, when my father, raising his hands and eyes to the sky, cried in a loud voice, 'O Bhowani! mother of the world! whose votaries we are receive this thy servant—vouchsafe to him thy protection—to us; an omen which may assure us of thy consent!'

We waited for some time; and at last, from a tree over our heads, the loud twittering of the small tree-owl was heard.

'Jai Bhowani! Victory to Bhowani!' cried the whole of the leaders; and my father embraced me, saying—

'Be of good cheer, my son; the omen is most favourable. We could hardly have expected such an one: thy acceptation is complete.'

I was then reconducted to the apartment, and a pickaxe, that holy symbol of our profession, was placed in my right hand, upon a white handkerchief. I was desired to raise it as high as my breast; and an oath, a fearful oath, was then dictated to me, which I repeated, raising my left hand into the air, and invoking the goddess to whose service I was devoting myself. The same oath was repeated by me on the blessed Koran, after which a small piece of consecrated goor, or coarse sugar, was given me to eat, and my inauguration was complete. My father received the congratulations of the assembly on the fortunate issue of the ceremony, and he then addressed me as follows.

'My son, thou hast taken upon thee the profession which is of all the most ancient and acceptable to the divinity. Thou hast sworn to be faithful, brave, and secret; to pursue to destruction every human being whom chance, or thy ingenuity, may throw into thy power, with the exception of those who are forbidden by the laws of our profession, which are now to thee sacred. These are particular sects, over whom our power does not extend, and whose sacrifice is not acceptable to our divine patroness; they are Dhobis, Bhats, Sikhs, Nanukshahis, Mudaree Fakirs, dancing-men, musicians, Bhungis, Tailis, Lohars, Burraes[1], and maimed or leprous persons. With these exceptions, the whole human race is open to thy destruction, and thou must omit no possible means (but at all times dependent upon the omens by which we are guided) to compass their destruction. I have now finished: thou are become a Thug; and what remains of thy profession will be shown to thee by our guru, who will, under the necessary ceremonies, instruct thee in its details.'

'It is enough,' said I; 'I am yours to death; and I only pray that an opportunity may soon be afforded me to prove to you my devotion.'

Thus I became a Thug: had I commenced my career under other and ordinary circumstances—I mean, had I not been introduced to my profession by one so powerful and well esteemed as my father then was—I must have entered the lowest grade of all; and, had I proved myself to be active, intelligent, and brave, I might have risen in time to the highest. But this was spared me; and though too young myself to become a leader, I was in a rank above the rest, and was considered to be, and looked up to as, the person who was hereafter to fill my father's place whenever it should suit him to retire from active employment.

The business which the Thug leaders had assembled to deliberate upon, was a plan of my father's, for a large body under himself and two other leaders (one of whom was Hussein), to take the high road to the Dukhun; to advance together as far as Nagpur, from whence my father was to proceed to Hyderabad; and the others separating, one to go to Aurangabad, thence through Khandesh, by Burhanpur, to Indore, and back to Sheopur; the other also to Aurangabad, but from thence to Poona; afterwards, if possible, as far as Surat, and from thence homewards; but if the season should be too far advanced, they were to get to Burhanpur and home in the best way they could; finally, we were all to meet at Sheopur by the commencement of the next rainy season.

No opposition was made to this; on the contrary, it was highly approved of, as under the personal direction of Ismail, it could not fail of success, and as an expedition had not been made to the Dukhun for many years before. The other gangs were to proceed in various directions about Hindustan as far as Benares, and round through the Saugor and Nerbudda country—their proceedings to be guided by circumstances, which could not now be forseen.

Thus planned, but a few days elapsed before we set off on our journey: with us there were sixty men, with Hussein forty-five,

[1] Dhobis, washermen; Bhats, bards; Sikhs, a tribe of Hindus; Nanukshahis, a class of religious mendicants; Mudaree Fakirs, ditto; Bhungis, sweepers; Tailis, oilmen; Lohars, blacksmiths; Burraes, carpenters.

and with the other jemadar, whose name was Ghous Khan, thirty; making in all one hundred and thirty-five.

Before we commenced our journey, however, it was necessary to consult the omens; and as the ceremonies are somewhat curious, I shall relate them to you—observing, that no expedition, whether of a large or small body, can be undertaken without them.

The morning we were to separate on our different destinations, everything having been duly prepared, we repaired to a spot which had been chosen on the road, a short distance from the village, and the whole band was in attendance. Bhudrinath, a man of much intelligence and respectability, and who was learned in the conducting of ceremonies, bore the sacred pickaxe, which had been previously duly consecrated, and was immediately attended by my father and three other jemadars. My father, as the leader of the whole, carried a lotah[1] filled with water, suspended by a string which he held in his mouth, down his right side. Had that lotah fallen what a dire omen would it have been to him! Nothing could have averted his death in that year, or at furthest in the year following.

We moved slowly till we reached the spot fixed on, and there my father stood. Turning his face to the south, the direction we were to take, he placed his left hand on his breast, reverently lifted his eyes to heaven, and pronounced in a loud voice the following invocation to Bhowani:

'Mother of the universe! protectress and patroness of our order if this expedition be pleasing to thee, vouchsafe us thy help, and give us an omen of thine approbation!'

He was silent, and every mouth repeated the prayer aloud.

Now every one looked impatient for the omens: the band scarcely breathed, so intensely anxious was the suspense. Long we waited, perhaps half an hour: no one spoke; and the reverent silence of the assembled numbers had something exceedingly impressive in it. At last the pilhao, or omen on the left hand, was vouchsafed: a jackass brayed, and was almost instantly answered by one on the right, which was the thibao. What could have been more complete! such an omen had not been known for years, and promised that utmost success and a splendid booty. Loud and fervent were the cries of praise to Bhowani; and each, turning to his companion, congratulated him on the happy prospect.

Seven long hours my father sat on that spot, during which time all was prepared for the journey. At its expiration he arose, and we took the nearest road to Guneshpur.

At the stage where we stopped for the evening, the thibao and pilhao were heard by Bhudrinath, who carried the nisham, the pickaxe, or as it was now called, having been consecrated, *khussee;*

[1] A small brass or copper drinking-vessel.

and these renewed favourable omens produced an increased confidence in the expedition and its leaders. At the first streamlet we passed the next morning the band all sat down, and some goor and dal[1], which had been brought with us, was shared to all. Proceeding, favourable omens were again seen, and all declared that we should speedily gain a rich booty.

To me this was all strange and unaccountable; but the implicit faith which every one seemed to place in the omens, and the regularity with which the ceremonies were conducted, impressed me with a strong idea of their necessity; though, to my shame I say it, as I acquired confidence in myself, I scorned them as foolish! until misfortune, no doubt sent by Bhowani, brought me to my senses, and made me penitent.

In a few days we arrived at Guneshpur, and as yet we had no adventure. On reaching the town, the Sothas or inveiglers, whose duty it is to entice travellers into the power of the Thugs, were sent into the town, while we remained under a mangrove on the outside. They were absent most part of the day; and when they returned they were eagerly questioned for intelligence. The men who had been sent on this duty were two Hindus, one by name of Bhudrinath, whom I have mentioned before, a Brahmin, and the other a man of inferior caste, by name Gopal; but both were persons of the most bland and persuasive manners, and I was told that they rarely failed in their object. I was, among the rest, highly curious to hear their adventures in the town, and joined my father on his taking his place in the assembly.

Bhudrinath told us, that he had gone through the whole bazaar without success, when he was attracted to a bunnia's[2] shop by a respectable old man, who was in high dispute with the bunnia. He went up to him, and the old gentleman, who was in a violent passion at some attempted exaction on the part of the merchant, immediately accosted him, and begged him to be witness to the transaction, expressing at the same time his intention of having the man brought before the Kotwal for his dishonesty.

'The bunnia was very insolent and abusive,' Bhudrinath went on to say; 'and after some altercation, I contrived to settle the matter by dint of threats and persuasions. The old man seemed highly pleased with me; and it naturally led, after we left the shop together, to a conversation about whither I was going, and who I was. I took advantage of this, to convince him that the town was no safe residence for a traveller, even for a night, and discovered that he was a Persian mutsuddee, or writer in the service of the Rajah of Nagpur, whither he was travelling with his son.

'I of course alarmed him as much as I could with accounts of the thieves and Thugs on the road, and represented ourselves to be a company of travellers proceeding also to Nagpur, on our way

[1] Boiled peas.

[2] A huxter.

to the Dukhum, and associated together for mutual protection; and that we always rested outside the villages, as being the safest places when our number was so large. He seemed so struck with the proposal I made to him to come out and join us, that I lost no time in pressing him to leave the town, and I have succeeded. I have left Gopal, who joined us, to show him the way out, and assist him in packing up his things, and I have no doubt they will be here before sunset.'

'Barik Allah!' exclaimed my father; 'your face is bright in our eyes, Bhudrinath; and I have no doubt, lads,' said he to the knot of listeners, 'that the old Khayet[1] has abundance of money and jewels, and his plunder will help to see us on to Nagpur; so if he does not come to us of his own free will, we must even waylay him, and that too in the next march. A short time will decide this; and if he fails us, some of you lughas[2] must be off to prepare the bhil or place of burial.'

But we were saved the trouble; for the Khayet came into our camp, as he had said, by sunset, and was met at the confines of it by my father, and the two other jemadars. The respectability of his appearance, struck me forcibly; he was evidently a man of polished manners, and had seen courts and good society. After arranging his travelling cart to sleep in, by placing some tent walls around it for protection to his women, he and his son, an intelligent handsome-looking youth, came to the spot where my father and the other leaders had spread their carpets; and many of the band being assembled, there ensued a general conversation.

Who could have told, Sahib, the intentions of those by whom he was surrounded! To me it was wonderful. I knew he was to die that night, for that had been determined when he arrived in our camp, and while he was arranging his sleeping-place. I knew too that a spot had been fixed on for his grave, and that of those with him; for I had accompanied my father to it, and saw that it was begun; and yet there sat my father, and Hussein, Ghous Khan, and many others. The pipe and the story passed round, and the old man was delighted at the company he had fallen into.

'I thank you,' said he to Bhudrinath, 'that you brought me out of that unsainted village; truly here is some enjoyment in the society of gentlemen, who have seen the world: there I should have been in perpetual dread of robbers, and should not have slept a wink all night, while here I need not even to be watchful, since I am assured by the Khan Sahib,' pointing to my father, 'that I shall be well taken care of.'

'Ay!' growled out in a whisper an old Thug who sat behind me, 'he will be well taken care of sure enough, I will see to that.'

'How?' said I.

[1] Khayet, a caste of Hindus, usually clerks.

[2] Lughas, those of the band whose office it is to dig the grave and bury the dead.

'He gave the sign, by which I knew him to be one of the bhuttotes or stranglers who had been selected.

'I have an old grudge against him,' he continued, 'and the time is come when I can repay it.'

'Tell me how it happened,' said I in a low tone, for the man's face wore a savage expression as he said it.

'Not now,' said he, 'how can I? I will tell you tomorrow night when we meet in the mujlis[1]: the man is Brij Lall, as great a rascal as ever lived, one who has committed more murders and more villanies in his life than any of us Thugs. But his cup is full, his breath is already in his mouth; one squeeze from me, and it will go forth never to return.'

'And the boy,' said I, 'that fair, fine boy—surely he will be spared.'

'To tell all he saw, I suppose!' said the man; 'to deliver us up at the first place we come to! No, no, Mea, we know better, and so will you one of these days.'

And he went round and seated himself just behind the old man, who turned about as though he were intruded upon.

'Sit still, sit still,' said my father; 'it is only a companion: in an open camp like this every one is privileged to hear the conversation of the evening mujlis, and we usually find some one among us who can enliven the evening with a tale, until it is time to rest for the night.'

So the old Thug sat still: I could see him playing with his fatal weapon, the handkerchief, now pulling it through one hand and now through the other; and I gazed on the group till my brain reeled again with excitement, with intense agony I might call it with more truth. There sat the old man: beside him his noble-looking boy: behind them their destroyers, only awaiting the signal; and the old man looked so unconscious of danger, was so entirely put off his guard and led into conversation by the mild, bland manners of my father, that what could he have suspected? That he was in the hands of those from whom he was to meet his death? Ah, no! And as I gazed and gazed, how I longed to scream out to him to fly! Had I not known that my own death would have followed instantaneously, I had done it. Yet it would have been of no use. I turned away my eyes from them; but they returned to the same place involuntarily. Every movement of the men behind seemed the prelude to the fatal ending. At last I could bear the intensity of my feelings no longer: I got up, and was hurrying away, when my father followed me.

'Where are you going?' said he; 'I insist on your staying here; this is your initiation; you must see it, and go through with the whole.'

'I shall return directly,' said I: 'I go but a pace or two; I am sick.'

[1] Assembly.

'Faint-hearted!' said he in a low tone: 'see you do not stay long, this farce must soon end.'

A turn or two apart from the assembly restored me again, and I returned and took up my former place, exactly opposite the old man and his son. Ya Allah! Sahib, even now I think they are *there* (and the Thug pointed with his finger) father and son; and the son's large eyes are looking into mine, as my gaze is riveted on them.

Ameer Ali looked indeed as though he saw them, and stared wildly, but passing his hands across his eyes, he resumed.

Taajoob! said he, wonderful! I could have sworn they both looked at me; but I am growing old and foolish. Well, Sahib, as I said, I gazed and gazed at them, so that I wonder even now they saw nothing extraordinary in it. But no: the old man continued a relation of some treaties the Nagpur Rajah was forming with the English, and was blaming them for entering into any league with them against his brethren, when my father called out 'Tumbako lao (bring tobacco)!' It was the signal! quicker than thought the Thug had thrown his handkerchief round the neck of the old man, another one his round that of his son, and in an instant they were on their backs struggling in the agonies of death. Not a sound escaped them but an indistinct gurgling in their throats; and as the bhuttoes quitted their fatal hold, after a few moments, others, who had been waiting for the purpose, took up the bodies and bore them away to the already prepared grave.

'Now for the rest,' cried my father in a low tone: 'some of you rush on the servants; see that no noise is made; the bullock-driver and others can be dealt with easily.'

Some of the men ran to the place the Khayet had chosen, and surrounded the unsuspecting cart-driver and other servants, who were cooking under a tree. I saw and heard a scuffle, but they also were all dead ere they could cry out.

'Come!' said my father and Hussein, taking me by the arms and hurrying me along, 'Come and see how they are disposed of.'

I went, or was rather dragged along to one side of our encampment, where there was a ravine some feet deep, in the bottom of which a hole had been dug, and by the side of which eight bodies were lying—the father and son, his two wives, the bullock-driver, two male servants, and an old woman; also a servant, who was in the inclosure with the women. The bodies were nearly naked, and presented a ghastly spectacle, as they lay in a confused heap, but just visible from the brink of the ravine.

'Are they all here?' asked my father.

'Yes, Khodawund,' said one of the lughaos, whom I knew.

'Then in with them!' cried my father; and they were quickly

deposited in their last resting-place, the head of one over the feet of another, so that they might lie close.

'We had better open them,' said the lughao, 'for the ground is loose and they will swell.'

So gashes were made in their abdomens, and the earth quickly filled in on them; it was stamped down, the top smoothed, and in a few moments no one could have discovered that eight human beings had been secreted beneath the spot. We turned away from it, and every one betook himself to repose.

Sahib, can I describe to you how I passed that night! Do what I would, the father and son appeared before me; the old man's voice rung in my ears, and the son's large eyes seemed to be fixed on mine. I felt as though a thousand shiatans sat on my breast, and sleep would not come to my eyes. It appeared so cold-blooded, so unprovoked a deed, that I could not reconcile myself in any way to have become even a silent spectator of it it. Yet my father had joined in it, my father whom I loved intensely, and Hussein too. But all would not do; I could not tranquillize myself. I crept from beneath our little tent, and sat down in the open air. The moon shone brightly as ever, as now and then she emerged from beneath a passing cloud, and there was a cool breeze which fanned my thoughts were with the old man and his son, and the event to travel along in the heavens till she became overcast: and a few heavy drops of rain, as if she wept over the deed she had witnessed, drove me again under the tent. I crept close to my father, who was sound asleep, and embracing him with my arms, sleep came to my eyelids, and I woke not till the usual hour of prayer arrived, when I was roused by my father to join in the morning supplication.

We spread our carpets, and I repeated the form with him; but my thoughts were with the old man and his son, and the event of the preceding night.

Immediatley after it was over, our horses were saddled, and we set out on what proved to be a long march; for it was necessary to get as far as possible from Guneshpur, that no suspicion might attach to us.

In due time we arrived at the stage, and a man was sent into the town to purchase one rupee and a quarter's worth of goor or coarse sugar: what this was intended for I could not imagine, but it was soon made known to me when I asked my father.

'This,' said he, 'is the sacrifice of the Tupounee, in which we all join after any adventure similar to what you saw last night; it is a rite of the utmost solemnity, and must never be neglected.'

The man returned with the sugar, and a place having been chosen, Bhudrinath, the bearer of the khussee, was seated on a blanket spread for him, his face towards the west. All the best men and noted bhuttotoes seated themselves on each side of him, looking in the same direction as he did. My father then made a small hole in the ground near the blanket, upon which was placed the sacred pickaxe and the pile of sugar, and a piece of silver as an offering. A little of the sugar was then put into the hole by my father: he raised his clasped hands to heaven, and in a supplicatory manner cried aloud—

'Powerful and mighty goddess! who hast for ages vouchsafed they protection unto they votaries, and who particularly to Joora Naig and Khudeek Bunwaree gavest one lac and sixty thousand rupees in their need, we beseech thee in like manner to aid us, and fulfil our desires.'

This prayer was devoutly repeated by all around, and my father taking water in his hand sprinkled it upon the pickaxe and into the hole; he then took pieces of the sugar and presented them to each of the Thugs in succession, who ate it in silence: they then drank some water, and the pile of sugar was distributed among the rest of the assembled band, who likewise ate their portions in silent reverence; all except myself, for not having as yet strangled a man, I was not eligible to partake of it with the rest. However, my father had reserved a portion of his own for me, which he made me eat. After I had swallowed it he said—

'You have eaten the goor, and are now a Thug in your heart; were you to desire to forsake us you could not, such is the power it has, when consecrated as you have seen it, over the hearts of men. Were any one to find a portion and eat it, whatever might be his rank or condition in life, he would assuredly become a Thug; he could not avoid it, the power it would exercise over him would be irresistible.'

'This is wonderful indeed,' said I; 'have such things been known?'

'I could relate hundreds of instances had I time,' he replied; 'but ask Hussein, or any one, they will all tell you the same.'

In the evening, when all were assembled as usual, my father took me to task about my faint-heartedness, as he termed it.

'This will never do, my son,' said he; 'you, who ran in upon the tiger so nobly, ought not to shrink from such child's play as this; you must be a man, and behave better, and remember you have eaten the goor.'

'For shame, brother!' said Hussein; 'do not speak so to the Sahib-zada; remember you were no better yourself at first; do you not recollect the business at ——, and what difficulty I had to persuade Ganesha that you were in reality good stuff? Let the Sahib-zada but see one or two more of these affairs, and he will be quite a different person, he will become a tiger at the work. I do not fear, my son,' said he, turning to me and slapping me on the back; 'worse men than you have begun better, and ended in being chicken-hearted fellows, only fit to dig graves and be scouts. Old Hussein never yet was mistaken in any one, and you, Inshallah! will surpass your father. Only let him,' continued he.

again addressing my father, 'let him see one or two more affairs, and then try his hand himself: you will then see whether I am wrong or not.'

'It is well,' exclaimed my father; 'believe me, my son, I meant not to upbraid you, but I was fearful the feeling you displayed might grow upon you: be kind as you will to those around you, affectionate to your connexions, pity the poor, give alms to the needy; but remember that you are a Thug, and have sworn relentless destruction to all those whom Allah may throw in your way.'

'I am rebuked,' said I, 'and your words have sunk into my heart: never more shall you have to say of me that I flinched from my duty. Whenever you think fit I am ready to take the handkerchief.'

From that day I put myself under the tuition of the guru, or teacher of the band—an old Thug who was worn out with age, but had been considered to be one of the most dexterous bhuttotes, or stranglers, who had lived within the memory of any of the men of our company. He was a Hindu, a Rajput; and though his frame was dry and shrivelled, yet from his height, breadth of shoulders, and sinews, which were developed the more by the absence of flesh to cover them, it was easy to see that he had been a man of immense strength and power; and, added to this, if his great dexterity in using the handkerchief was considered, the stories of his superior prowess might easily be credited. I had hitherto not associated much with him, and beyond a courteous demeanour to each other, we had been but little acquainted; so I begged my father to take me to him, deliver me over to his care, and request of him to initiate me thoroughly in the practice of a bhuttote.

He was delighted at this spontaneous offer on my part, readily acceded to my wishes, and at once put me under the care of Hussein, and Roop Singh, the old Thug I have mentioned, who belonged to Hussein's party.

'For a few days,' said my father, 'I will not see you; you shall remain with them; and when you return to me, let me welcome you as ready and willing to take a part in the next affair we may be engaged in.'

The day after we began in earnest. Roop Singh repeated incantations over me. I ate no meat, indeed tasted nothing but milk for four days. Numerous sacrifices were made to the sacred pickaxe; every omen was observed, and as I sat under the trees after our daily march, scarcely a bird alighted on them but there was some conclusion drawn from it; and the appearances of different animals and birds as we commenced our march in the mornings were particularly observed and noted. I was naturally very inquisitive as to the meaning of all that was done to me and for me, but the old guru would not enlighten me.

'My son,' said he, 'when I was your age, these ceremonies were performed over me, to make me fearless and stony-hearted, active and cunning, so as to ensnare all who came within my reach, and to avoid my enemies; to make me fortunate, and to cause me to win fame. In all these I have never failed. Two others upon whom I have performed them are rising fast to be jemadars, such is their address and courage; and you too will be the same; therefore ask no questions. Content yourself with knowing that everything is going on properly and to my complete satisfaction, for I have not observed one unfavourable omen.'

On the fifth morning the handkerchief was put into my hand; and after having been bathed, anointed with sweet-smelling oils, and marked on the forehead with vermilion, as a votary of Bhowani, I was declared a bhuttote.

'One thing I forgot,' said the old man, laughing, as he gave me the cloth, 'and that was the principal perhaps. I have not shown you how to use it, and I have a peculiar knack of my own which is easily communicated. You will soon learn it.'

He took the cloth, tied a large knot at one end, with a piece of silver inserted in it; this he held in his left hand, the plain end being in his right, and about as much space between them as would nearly compass a man's neck: the closed hands had the palms uppermost.

'Now,' said he, 'mark this; and when you throw the cloth from behind, and have got it tight, suddenly turn your knuckles into the neck, giving a sharp wrench to either side that may be most convenient. If done in a masterly manner, instant death ensues.'

I took the cloth, and held it as he directed, but it did not please him.

'Give it me back, that I may show you more exactly on your own neck,' said he.

'Indeed, no,' cried I, laughing; 'you might think I was a traveller, and have me down in an instant, without intending it; but I perfectly understand the method.'

'Then try it on *me*, Ameer Ali; I shall see by the position of your hands whether you know anything about it.'

I obeyed him; the old man shook his head and laughed.

'That will never do; you could not kill a child in that way,' he said: 'when you feel my hands round your neck you will understand.'

So I submitted with as good a grace as I could, though I did not at all like the idea. My blood ran cold through me as I felt his chill, clammy hands about my neck. But he did not hurt me, and I saw where my error had been. I tried it on him as he had shown me several times, and was declared at last to be perfect.

'Now you only want practice, Ameer Ali,' said he.

'Inshallah! Roop Singh,' I replied, 'we shall have plenty of it. One beginning, and I fear not for the rest. Like a tiger, which, once having tasted human blood, will if possible take no other, and runs every risk to get it, so I feel it will be with me.' And it was so. Sahib! I knew myself—I had spoken truly.

CHAPTER V

NOTHING of any moment occurred during the rest of our march to Nagpur, if I except the deaths of a few solitary travellers, by the hands of a small portion of the band who had been sent to another road, that ran parallel to the one on which we marched; and as I know no particulars of them worth mentioning, I shall at once lead you, Sahib, to our encampment at Nagpur.

Outside the city is a large tank, on the margin of which the majority of the band encamped. My father and a few others put up in the town, for the purpose of converting the booty already obtained into money. It was not a difficult task, for as the property which had belonged to Brij Lall was easily saleable, we soon found purchasers among the numerous goldsmiths and sahoukars of the city.

In one of his dealings with a sahoukar, my father casually stated, that he was proceeding to Hyderabad with some men he had brought from his village, and for whom he was in hope of procuring employment under, as he said, his brother, who was in the service of the then reigning prince Sikundur Jah. The sahoukar at once proposed to accompany us, and to give my father and his men a handsome remuneration if he would protect him on the road; as he had, he said, been for some time on the look-out for an opportunity to put himself under the escort of a respectable man who might be travelling there with a number of followers.

At that time, Sahib, in consequence of the unsettled state of the country, and the many rumours there were of wars, any man of respectability, who was idle in his village, and could persuade a few companions to accompany him as their leader, was sure of employment as a soldier, if he presented himself at any of the courts of Hindustan or the Dukhun. Sindia, Holkar, the Peshwah, every prince in fact had a large army, which was tolerably paid; and it was better to serve with them, than to pursue any other occupation. We had met several bands of such men on our road down to Nagpur, so that our company presented no extraordinary or suspicious appearance, especially under my father, who looked like a soldier, was always well armed and dressed, rode a fine horse, and on occasions of residing in, or even passing through, a city, was always attended by a number of the Thugs as his escort; and his appearance was certainly what he represented himself to be to the sahoukar.

My father readily agreed to the sahoukar's terms, and bound

himself down in a day or two afterwards to be at his disposal, and to afford him protection as far as Hyderabad. At a secret conference they had that day, the sahoukar, as my father told me, informed him that he was going to take down a good deal of treasure, some valuable jewels and some merchandize, by which he hoped to get a handsome profit at Hyderabad. Nay, he even went so far as to show him what he was going to take with him; and you cannot imagine, Sahib, the joy that was diffused in our camp at the certainty of so rich a booty.

In order to give our band as much of the appearance of soldiers as possible, my father purchased for those who had none, matchlocks, swords, and shields, and distributed them: and, in truth, when all the men were drawn up to be examined, they were a fine-looking set of fellows; for as this expedition had been considered one of extreme adventure, none but the youngest and most able-bodied had been selected for it. They were all informed of the agreement which had been made with the sahoukar, cautioned to put on as military and swaggering an air as possible, and, in short, to behave as soldiers would, during the part of the journey they would have to appear as his escort.

This was in the evening, and during the night the camp was a scene of jollity; the booty in view, nay almost within their grasp, was sufficient to cheer them. A set of dancing girls was invited from the city, and in listening to their songs the best part of the night was passed.

We expected the sahoukar anxiously all the day, and just at nightfall he came to our camp in a small travelling cart, with one or two servants and two or three small ponies, on which a tent and his baggage were laden, and ten bullocks with their drivers. Altogether, there were eight men, including himself.

We saw but little of him during our march to Amraoti; my father and Hussein used sometimes to sit with him in his tent during the evening, and I was also introduced to him. He was a large, unwieldy man, and I began to think whether he would not be a good subject for my first trial. I mentioned my thoughts to my father, and he was much pleased with me.

'I had intended to have appointed you to be his bhuttote,' said he; 'he is too fat to make any resistance, and he will be the easier work for you, who have not as yet tried what you can do.'

So from that time I looked upon him as my first victim.

I daily went to my instructor to gain fresh insight into my profession, and practised the handling of the cloth in every way he pointed out to me. He one day proposed to inveigle a lonely traveller into our camp, in order that I might try my hand upon him first; but I objected to this, as I felt confident in my own powers, and was determined, as I had selected the sahoukar, that he should be the first man.

I pass over our journey, as nothing worth mentioning occurred on the road. We arrived at the town, and took up our quarters in the bazaar. I was much struck with its apparent opulence and prosperity; but it was not to be wondered at, as it was the place where all the merchandize and manufactures of Hindustan were brought to be distributed over the Dukhun, and where all the spices, drugs, and other articles of trade arrived from the south, to be sent to different parts of Hindustan.

The town seemed to be full of sahoukars' houses and large shops; and in the bazaars were displayed every article that I had ever heard of, besides many others from the Europeans at Bombay which I had never seen before; and I wandered about every day in company with my father, admiring and wondering at all I saw.

The sahoukar's business detained him some days at this place, at the end of which we again set forward, with an addition to his people of three men, who drove a few bullocks heavily laden with cloths, which we heard were of the most costly description, being those of Benares, which are justly celebrated for their richness and beauty. Nor did this addition at all disconcert our plans, for in consequence of the sahoukar having accompanied us, Hussein's party still remained; and indeed, if it had not, there were plenty of my father's to have secured the whole without trouble.

From Amraoti to Mungloor is three stages, 'and there,' said my father, 'I shall decide on the place for the ending of this matter. If I remember right, there are some low hills and ravines not far beyond it, which will give us excellent opportunities for concealing the bodies. And do you, Hussein, inquire, who among your men know the ground, for it will be necessary to send some one who does with the lughas.'

Inquiries were accordingly made when we reached our first stage, a village named Baum, and it was discovered that three men were intimately acquainted with the whole of the road, and had been on the point of coming forward to recommend that one spot in particular should not be neglected. They were closely questioned by my father and Hussein, and they gave a very clear description of a place which seemed to be so well fitted for the purpose, that it was at once determined on, and the men promised an extra reward if they would exert themselves.

I now felt that my time had come; that in a very few hours I might take my place with the rest, having established my right to be their equal.

Perhaps it was weakness, Sahib, but from that time I avoided the sight of the sahoukar as much as possible. I saw him once or twice on the road; but an involuntary shudder crept through me, and, like a fool, I almost wished I were back again at our village. But it was too late to retract; I had a character to gain, and the esteem of him who best loved me, my father, to secure. To turn back was impossible, and to evince the smallest cowardice was to degrade myself irretrievably. I had therefore no resource but to do my best; and, in truth, when the sahoukar was not before me, I felt no reluctance to perform my part, but, on the contrary, the same desire I had before experienced to distinguish myself.

We reached Mungloor. It is a large town, full of Mahomedans, and celebrated for the shrine of Meer Hyat Kalundur, a saint of great antiquity. His tomb is held in particular veneration, and it was judged highly expedient that we should offer up our prayers for the success of our enterprise. Accordingly, my father, myself, Hussein, and some other Mahomedans went to the tomb, and having observed all the ceremonies required and directed by the attendant mullahs, we were sitting in conversation with two of them, when we discovered, by a casual sign made by my father to Hussein, which was recognised by them, that they were Thugs! Most extraordinary, thought I; here are sacred ministers of our faith Thugs as well as ourselves. But after some conversation with them, I could see that my father esteemed them lightly.

'These fellows can hardly be Thugs,' said my father to Hussein, as we descended the steps of the shrine into the outer court, where many of the men had put up for the day, 'and we had better caution the people against getting acquainted with them. I do not think they will notice us further as it is, but they might do so did they know whom we have with us.'

'You are right,' said Hussein; 'it might perhaps be better were the men told not to disclose the matter.'

They were accordingly cautioned: and it turned out that we had done right, as we heard afterwards that the mullahs were most inquisitive, and could not understand how it was that we had come so far and were going so much further without an object; and I have no doubt, had we not acted as we did, and disclosed our intentions to, or asked for assistance from them, that they would have either betrayed us to the village authorities, or insisted on such a share of the spoil, which we dare not have refused, as would have materially lessened ours.

After prayers we returned to the place where we had put up, and found a man belonging to the sahoukar waiting for us. He said his master would stay that evening where he was, with a friend, instead of coming outside the village to our encampment, but that my father was to leave some men with him as a guard: and that he would set out early in the night, as he was determined to go on to Bassim, a town some distance off, where he had another friend, whom he wished to visit; that as it was so long a march we must start early, so as to allow time for a halt for refreshment at a village half way.

My father did not like the idea of sending the men into the village, lest they should be recognised as Thugs by any of the Thug villagers; yet he could not but acquiesce, and some were sent as soon as night closed in, that there might be hardly a chance of their being known. In the meantime every preparation was made by the party of grave-diggers who were to precede us, and at nightfall they also left the ground, fourteen in number, with the two who knew the spot in company with them. They were confident as to the precise place they should fix on, and described the hills as little more than low mounds, caused by some high land breaking into ravines; that, if they remembered right, the road was very stony, and crossed by several small streams, whose banks were lined by thick brushwood; and that in any one of these, in which there might be no water, the bhil, or grave, should be prepared. They were also desired to place men in advance to give information, that we might all take our places, and fall on, when the signal was given.

It was now generally known to all that I was to have the sahoukar to myself, and many thronged about me to see how I looked forward to my first trial; every one cheered me, and I must own this gave me great confidence. As the time approached, my soul burned for the work like that of a young and brave soldier to see the first flash of his bright sword in anger. My father enjoyed my demeanor in silent satisfaction; he spoke not, but there was exultation in his eye as he looked fondly upon me, and I felt that I should not disappoint him.

The whole band seemed to be impressed particularly with the importance of the present matter, for they collected into groups, and though each man knew exactly what he had to do, and what was appointed for his comrade, yet they seemed to be discussing the whole, till one by one they separated, and each stretched himself out to gain the little rest he could, before the time arrived which would call him into active, nay deadly strife—my father and Hussein too, all except myself. I was sitting outside our slight tent, when Roop Singh came to me.

'Baba!' said he as he sat down, 'how feel you? is your heart firm and your blood cool?'

'Both,' said I: 'nothing can change my heart; and feel my hand, is my blood hot?'

'No,' said the old man, taking it in his; 'it is not, nor does it tremble; this is as it should be. I have seen many prepare for their first trial, but never one so coolly and calmly as you do; but this is all in consequence of the blessed Muntrus which have been read over you, and the ceremonies you went through.'

'Perhaps so,' said I; 'but I think I should have been much the same without them.'

'Now, may Bhowani forgive you, proud boy,' he replied; 'you know not their efficacy; was there ever a prouder being than I was—a Rajput by birth, and one of the purest tribes? Had I not slain wild beasts, or helped to slay them from my childhood? But when a man was shown me, and the handkerchief alone put into my hands to destroy him with, indeed I trembled; nor was it for a long time that I could be brought to attempt it. But,' continued

Roop Singh, 'you have one more ceremony to go through, which on no account must be neglected; go, call your father, Hussein, and Bhudrinath, that they may be present.'

We were all soon assembled, and the guru led the way into an adjoining field. He stopped, and turning to the direction in which we were to proceed, raised his hands in a supplicatory manner, and cried, 'O Kali! Maha Kali! if the traveller now with us should die by the hand of this they new votary, vouchsafe us the thibao!'

All of us stood silently; and wonderful to relate, even at that late hour an ass brayed on the right hand. The guru was overjoyed.

'There!' cried he to the others, 'was there ever so complete an acceptation of a votary? The omen almost followed the prayer.'

'Shukur Allah!' exclaimed my father, 'it is now complete; he will go forth and conquer. There only remains for you to tie the knot.'

'That I will do when we return,' said the guru; and when we reached our encampment, he took my handkerchief, and untying the knot which had been previously made, he retied it, placing a piece of silver in it. Presenting it to me, he said—

'Receive this now sacred weapon; put your trust in it; in the holy name of Kali, I bid it do your will!'

I received it in my right hand, and carefully tucked it into my waistband, that I might not lose it, and that it might be ready for action when required.

We remained in conversation for some time, and then threw ourselves on our carpets to snatch a short rest, till one of our men from the village came and told us that the sahoukar was preparing to move, and had sent him on to warn us.

The band were quickly roused and our beasts laden, and we drew up by the side of the road to await his arrival. He was not long in coming, and we all moved on together.

The night was beautiful, the road excellent, and we pushed on in high spirits. The booty we were to possess, the tact with which the whole matter had been managed from the first, would mark it as an enterprise of a superior description, one that any one of us would be proud to mention, and which would cause a considerable sensation, not only in the country, but among the numerous bands of Thugs of Hindustan, more especially those we were to rejoin at the conclusion of our season.

We had proceeded about two coss, when there was a murmur among the men who led, and one of the scouts was an instant afterwards seen making his way to where we were. My father recognised him as one of those he had sent on.

'Bhilla manjeh?' (have you cleared the hole?) he eagerly inquired.

'Manjeh!' said the man; 'it is cleared, and it is all ready. See you yon low hills? A streamlet, as I told you, runs from them; and it is rare bhil that we have made, Jemadar Sahib. You will say we have done well.'

'And how far may it be?' demanded my father.

'About half a coss,' said the man: 'a short distance from hence the road becomes stony, and continues so till you are above the pass—take advantage of it;' and he fell in among the others.

The men were silently warned to be at their posts, and each man, or two men, as it was necessary, placed himself close to the one to whom he had been assigned. By designed obstructions in front, the bullocks belonging to the sahoukar, with their attendants, were brought immediately about the cart in which he rode, and the whole being gathered into one place were the easier to be secured. The preparations again roused me, and I grasped the handkerchief firmly, thinking every moment that the signal was about to be made; but we still crept on at a slow pace, for the road was narrow and lined by thorny bushes; and the men in front proceeding as slowly as possible, we were kept exactly in our proper place, and expected every moment to reach the spot.

As we approached the small hills, the jungle became pretty thick, and appeared doubly so by the moonlight, and we passed many places where I thought the deed might have been done with advantage. But I was wrong, for the lughas had selected an admirable one.

A man came from the front, whispered a few words to my father, and again went on: this increased my anxiety. We crossed a small hollow, ascended a bank, and below us I saw what I was sure was the place. The banks of the rivulet were high and steep, covered with thick underwood matted by trailing creepers. A few higher trees nearly met over its bed, in which could be just discerned a small thread of water, looking like a silver snake as the moon's rays fell on it through the dark foliage. A hundred thieves might lie there, thought I; and who could ever know the fate of a traveller who might so easily be surprised in such a spot?

I was roused from my train of thought by my father, as he called out 'Hooshiaree!' (caution). This was the preparatory signal. He went to the side of the cart, and represented to the sahoukar that we had reached the stream, and that the bank was so steep, and the bed so stony, that he must get out and walk over to the other side, if no further. This was quite sufficient: the man got out, and after seeing the cart safely down the steep bank was preparing to follow himself.

The whole scene is now before me. The bullocks and their drivers, with the Thugs, were all in a confused group in the bed of the little stream, the men shouting and urging on their beasts: but it was easy to see that every man had a Thug close to him awaiting the signal. They were only a few feet below us, and the stream was so narrow that it was with some difficulty all could stand in its bed, especially when the cart reached the bottom.

Above stood my father, Hussein, and myself—the sahoukar, one of his servants, and several other Thugs.

I was eagerly awaiting the signal; I tightly grasped the fatal handkerchief, and my first victim was within a foot of me! I went behind him as being preferable to one side, and observed one of the other Thugs do the same to a servant. The sahoukar moved a step or two towards the road—I instinctively followed him—I scarcely felt that I stirred, so intensely was I observing him. 'Jai Kali!' shouted my father: it was the signal, and I obeyed it!

As quick as thought the cloth was round his neck—I seemed endued with superhuman strength—I wretched his neck round—he struggled convulsively for an instant, and fell. I did not quit my hold, I knelt down on him, and strained the cloth till my hand ached: but he moved not—he was dead! I quitted my hold. and started to my feet: I was mad with excitement!—my blood boiled, and I felt as though I could have strangled a hundred others, so easy, so simple had the reality been. One turn of my wrists had placed me on an equality with those who had followed the profession for years—I had taken the first place in the enterprise, for I had killed the principal victim! I should receive the praise of the whole band, many of whom I was confident had looked on me as only a child.

I was roused from my reverie by my father.

'You have done well,' he said in a low and kind voice; 'you will receive the reward of this soon; now follow me, we will go to the grave. Ere this the bodies have been collected, and I myself must see that they are properly disposed of. There will be a noise about this business, and it will need great exertion for us to get out of the road we are now travelling.'

I followed him. We descended into the bed of the stream, and were led to the grave by one of the men; others bearing the body of the Sahoukar followed. We passed up the bed of the stream for a short distance; and near the mouth of a small nullah, the bed of which was dry, a number of the men were standing.

'The grave?' asked my father.

'It is up there,' said one; 'you will have to creep, and the thorns are very bad.'

'It matters not,' he replied; and we entered the place.

The banks of the rivulet were perhaps two or three yards high, and the bed so narrow that but two persons could advance abreast. The creepers and trees were matted overhead, and the sides so thick that it was impossible that ony one could have got down from above. The tangled character of the spot increased as we proceeded, until it became necessary to free our clothes from the thorns which caught us at every step. In a few moments we heard the sound of voices, and after creeping almost on all fours through a hole which had apparently been forced through the underwood, we came upon the grave.

There was only one; it occupied almost the entire breadth of the stream; it was very deep, and the earth, or rather sand, had been thrown out on each end. The lughas were sitting there, sharpening stakes cut from the jungle; but they could scarcely be seen from the darkness of the place, which the thick wood above only partially allowed the moonbeams to penetrate. They were conversing in a low tone in the slang of the band, which I had not learned: my father spoke to them, or rather to their leader.

'You have had your wits about you,' he said, 'and we will think well of you when we make the distribution: this is a grave that even a jackel could not discover. Again I say, Peer Khan, you have done this properly, and it is well I have seen it, that I may speak of you as you deserve; but you must be quick—the night advances.'

'It is finished, Khodawund,' replied the man; 'we do but wait for another body which they say is coming, and the filling-up will be done immediately.'

As he spoke, the body of the sahoukar was brought up by three men, who railed at it for its weight.

'It is their wont,' he said; 'do not speak to them; only watch what they do; for you must see all, that you may be fully acquainted with your duties.'

I was silent. The corpse was dragged to the brink and thrown in, as also that of the servant who had been killed close to the sahoukar: incisions were made in their abdomens, and sharpened stakes driven through them.

'Were it not for the precaution you see,' said my father, 'the ground might swell, and the jackels would drag out the bodies; in this way however it is impossible.'

When all was finished, quantities of stones which had been collected were thrown upon the bodies, afterwards thorns, and the whole was covered up with sand, which was carefully smoothed.

'I think this will do, Jemadar Sahib,' said Peter Khan; 'we may now leave the place. It is not likely that any one will come here to look for the Sethji or his people, and the Sahib-zada has seen how cleverly we have done our work.'

'Enough,' said I; 'I shall know how to act as a lugha myself, should I ever need it.'

My father beckoned me to follow him. I stayed to see some dry sand thrown over the place, and proceeded with others. The hole in the underwood made by us was closed up with great care; and a branch of a bush being broken off, and trailed after him by the hindmost man, obliterated every footmark in the dry sand of the nullah.

CHAPTER VI

The rest of the band, with the cart and laden bullocks, had proceeded some way before we overtook them. We passed through a thin jungle for some distance, emerging from which we found ourselves on a wild, bare plain, here and there studded with straggling brushwood. We all collected together, and lighting fires, the hookahs passed round, and each one related his achievement, and gloried in the prospect of a speedy division of the booty we had acquired.

To arrange our future proceedings was by no means an easy matter, as it was necessary to get past Bassim, where the sahoukar had friends, and his cart and bullocks might possibly be recognised in the town. My father's advice was to travel till daylight, and then to withdraw to one side of the road as far from observation as possible; to remain there as long as we could, and then to push on beyond Bassim. At this halt too there was to be a grand division of the spoil, as least of as much of it as could be divided; and Hussein's party was to seperate from us and pursue their road in the best way they could, in the direction which had been pointed out to them. Accordingly we again started, and after passing some villages halted about sunrise at some distance from the road, near a grove of trees, in which there was a well of water. Before the men betook themselves to cooking their meal after the march, they were all assembled; and the quantity of goor having been brought, the ceremony of the Tupounee was performed as I have before described. I was now entitled to a seat on the blanket with the other bhuttotes: I was their equal. The ceremony ended, I untied the knot of my handkerchief, as directed by my father, and taking out the piece of silver, presented it with some rupees to my guru, touching his feet at the same time in reverence. This was the last of my ceremonies of initiation. I was a bhuttote, had fairly killed my man, and held myself to be the equal of any of my associates.

After this my father and Hussein brought forth all the plunder of our late enterprise. It was magnificent: there was a good quantity of gold and silver in money; but the principal valuables were the jewels which the sahoukar was taking to Hyderabad for sale, and the cloths and brocades on the bullocks: they were of the richest description.

The distribution of these was a matter of great difficulty, and it was impossible to satisfy everyone; besides, the pearls and diamonds would have lost a great deal of their value by being divided among the men. So it was agreed to share the ready money, cooking-utensils, and other effects of the sahoukar, also the least valuable cloths, into two equal portions as nearly as possible, in proportion to the number of men in each band; that my father was to have charge of the jewels, which he was to sell at Hyderabad to the best advantage, as also of the most valuable cloths; and that the proceeds of these were not to be divided until we again reached our place of rendezvous.

The division of the ready money, upwards of three thousand five hundred rupees, gave to each man a considerable sum, enough at any rate to support him for some time, the more especially as the share of the former booty was not nearly expended; for every man lived as frugally as possible, and all seemed intent upon vying with each other as to who should have the largest share at the general division. Nay, many even denied themselves the meanest luxuries, and it was not uncommon to see a man eating his cakes without ghee, or anything but pure water.

Bhudrinath however, one of the most skilful of the band, was a complete exception to what I have said. He was a short, stout, active fellow, a man who aspired to be a jemadar, and with some reason. I have mentioned him before as the bearer of the sacred pickaxe. He was one of the most experienced among us, and had conducted small expeditions, in which he had acquitted himself much to the satisfaction of those who had entrusted him with them.

Our encampment broke up towards evening. Friends were seen embracing each other, and wishing mutual success; at length they all departed: we watched them over the brow of an eminence not far off, and then started ourselves.

Leaving the beaten road to Bassim, we struck off into one to the left, and, as it promised to lead to some large town, we followed it, as well to avoid discovery as to court new adventures. By the light of a bright moon we travelled most of the night, passing through a dreary country, in many parts covered with jungle, and never entering a village save to ask the road, or get fire to light our hookahs. Indeed we were often repulsed in this. There appeared to be a general dread of robbers, and the walls and gates were usually manned by armed men, on the intimation of our approach being given by the dogs as we passed: but no questions were asked us, as to who we were or where we were going, although perhaps our numbers might have excited suspicion.

In this manner, and without knowing where the road we had taken would lead us, we travelled for some days; and as we had purposely avoided the principal roads, is was not to be expected that we should meet with anything in the way of adventure, or with any travellers whom we could entice into our society. At last we came upon a broader road than that on which we had been travelling; and as we had left any danger from our late deed far behind us, we determined to follow it, in the hope that it would lead us towards Hyderabad, or some large village in its direction, from whence we could get upon a well-travelled road and carry on our vocation. As it was, we had gained a respectable booty even for a whole season; but scarcely two months had passed, and we could not afford to go on so far as Hyderabad in inactivity.

The road led us on for some hours, till large mangroves, with here and there the white top of a Hindu temple peeping over them, gave us intimation that we were approaching a place of consequence. It turned out to be the town of Oomerkhér, a wealthy place, surrounded with most luxuriant cultivation of wheat and other descriptions of grain.

'It will be our own fault,' said my father, 'if we find not some game here. Having encamped on the other side of the town, the sothas must carefully pass through the bazaars, and this evening may bring us booty enough to recompense us for staying here.'

The duty of a sotha was one which I had also to learn: men were even more proud of excelling in it, than in that of a bhuttote, for it required the greatest tact and powers of dissimulation, ability to support characters and disguises, a smooth tongue, and polite demeanour. Bhudrinath was one who united all in an eminent degree; he was a short, stout, active man, as I have mentioned, but extremely handsome, and with a most winning manner. It was his constant boast that he never marked out a victim whom he did not strangle with his own hands.

We passed through the town, describing ourselves as merchants from Hindustan; and as the bales of cloth when stopped by the collector of tolls were readily shown by my father, and the duty demanded on them cheerfully paid, our assertion was credited, we were civilly treated by the authorities, and shown an excellent piece of ground for our encampment.

'Now dress yourself in your best clothes,' said Bhudrinath, 'and come with me into the town. Remember, your father is a merchant, you are a jemadar commanding his escort, I am a brulaadmi (respectable person) belonging to you; we will take with us Peer Khan, who although a lugha is an excellent sotha, and a respectable fellow when he is dressed and armed; and it is hard if we do not pick up somebody.'

Our meal was soon cooked and eaten, and after carefully attiring ourselves we set off into the town to seek for adventures. It astonished me to see the indifference with which the practised hands proceeded, considering the object they had in view; for to me there was as much excitement in this, as in what I had already learned and practised. I confess our appearance was remarkable. I was very noticeable from my dress and arms, which were of the richest description, consistent with the appearance I had assumed. My face was then much fairer than it is now, Sahib, with a mustachio already well formed, and my figure, though perhaps somewhat slender, gave promise of future strength and power. Contrasted with my companions, I felt I was superior to them in appearance; and a little pardonable vanity gave me an air and swagger which were not unfitting the military profession I had set up.

We entered the town and betook ourselves to the Chowree[1], where the Kotwal[2] and some respectable persons were sittting, surrounded by a few armed men as is usual. As we passed by them we were invited to enter, and received with great politeness. I was placed in the seat of honour by Bhudrinath, who took his station at some distance. A desultory conversation began. My father's name was asked, where he was going, and what he had brought for trade; who we were, and in the short the general object of our journey, by, as they told us, an unfrequented road, at least from Hindustan. The tone in which this question was asked seemed to me so significant, that I thought for an instant we were suspected, and I was endeavouring to frame a reply when Bhudrinath stopped me.

'I represent,' said he, addressing the man who had asked the question, 'that we were set astray at that abode of unsainted people Nagpur. Either with a view to deceive us, or (Allah knows it may be so, I have heard of such things,) perhaps of robbing us, persons from whom we asked information, told us the best and most frequented road was by this place; and truly the town you have the fortune to dwell in is a place of great beauty and fertility, and is evidently in the hands of a most wise governor, and one who protects his people. How, Jemadar Sahib, have I not said truly?'

'Indeed,' said I, 'you have; and the kindness we have as yet met with shows that the servants of the governor are worthy of their master. Truly it is not to be wondered at if the town is prosperous and beautiful in such hands; and such is the mellifluous speech of the Kotwal, that we are impressed with the greatest opinion of the discernment of the exalted person who has selected him.'

'May your condescension never diminish,' said the Kotwal; 'your slave is not worthy of these encomiums; he is less than the least. If my lord could but see the dispenser of benefits under whose beams he lives, he would indeed say that the court of

1 The place for deliberation and assembly in a village usually a room with an open front.

2 The chief police officer, and superintendent of bazaars.

Hyderabad is worthy of being compared with any in Hindustan, as having formed such a pattern of excellence.'

'Well,' said I, 'we shall only be too glad to lay our nuzzurs[1] at the feet of this patron of yours, and no doubt we shall see in him a pattern of noblemen, as specimen of what we may expect to see at the capital of the Dukhun. When may we hope to be admitted to the presence?'

'In the evening, after prayers,' said our acquaintance; 'it is then that justice is dispensed to these poor unbelieving cultivators, and the durbar is enlivened by the presence and heavenly music of a set of dancing-women, whom my lord has brought with him from the city.

'We will come,' said I; 'and I pray you to give your lord notice that we have accepted your invitation to visit him; nay that we are desirous of paying our respects to him.'

As I finished speaking, an elderly man of decent appearance had entered the Chowree; he was a Hindu, and looked like a merchant. He demanded, in rather a peremptory tone, a place to rest in, declaring that if he did not get it immediately he would go and complain to the ruler of the town.

The spirit of the old Kotwal seemed to be roused by the man's behaviour, and he declared in round terms that he would not give a foot of ground, or an empty shop, without he was civilly asked.

'Look you, gentlemen,' said he to us; 'I ask you to decide between us; I swear by the Prophet, I care no more than a snap of my fingers for him; I have seen twenty thousand better; and if he goes to complain, why let him go; he will be driven from the presence with stripes. People like him come in hundreds every day, and who can trouble themselves in looking after them?'

'You and your master may be the portion of the devil,' said the old merchant; 'ever since I have entered the territories of the Nizam I have been treated in this manner. But it is only what I have heard before; not a night have I passed without an alarm of thieves; and God knows, if I had any protection, I would rather lie outside your wretched walls than in the zenana of your Aumil himself. Your bunnias are rascals: I am refused grain at nearly double the price I paid yesterday: I am refused shelter at night. In God's name, what am I to do? Gentlemen,' cried he to us, 'what am I to do?'

Bhudrinath answered, as I was going to speak, and to my astonishment angrily.

'What would you have, O discontented man? I suppose some place has been offered to you, and you have thought it not good enough; or are you drunk with opium? or has hunger after your journey spoilt your temper? Go, betake yourself to the bazaar; be thankful that you can get any place; and, if no one will

[1] Nuzzur, a propitiatory gift of ceremony.

shelter you, lie in the street; bethink yourself that many a better man has done so before you.'

The man stood aghast: he looked first at us, then at the Kotwal and his men, while expressions of delight at his discomfiture ran through the Kotwal's party: 'Well said!' 'Proper fellows!' 'He ought to be turned out of the village,' etc. At last, without saying a word, he threw down his turban and ran out, bellowing as loud as he could.

We all burst into a hearty fit of laughter. 'That is a queer fellow,' said I to the Kotwal; 'I doubt not you have often such to plague you; but send for him back, we will make him ashamed of himself, and I will beg you to give him a place to stay in.'

'As you will,' replied he; 'but for your intercession I should not have troubled myself about him. Many such have it to deal with. One day a fellow comes swearing he is cheated by everyone, another that he can get nothing to eat, when perhaps both are too stingy to buy; another, that he has no shelter, when he will not pay the trifle demanded by the bunnea for the use of his shop. A fourth must have every delicacy to be found in a city, and he is furious because he cannot get them; when, if they were all before him, he could not afford to buy one. In short, sirs, there is no end to the fancies, foolishnesses, and I may say tyranny, of travellers, and who think me, I suppose, to possess superhuman power, and to have Djins (genii) at my command, to bring them whatever their foolish ideas may desire.'

'You have indeed no easy situation, and to please every one is impossible,' said I; 'but here comes the merchant;' and he entered.

'Take up your turban, good fellow,' said the Kotwal, 'and do not be angry; you are no child to be quarrelling with decent people; have you never travelled before, that you should be angry and throw dust on our beards in this manner? In God's name, take up your turban; and do some one of you go and see that the good man gets a place for himself.'

The man looked irresolute for an instant, then took up the turban, and walked sulkily out, accompanied by the person desired to attend him. Bhudrinath gave me a sign, and we took our leave. We had scarcely got out, when he said, 'That man is ours, now see how I will manage him. I dare say he has but few persons with him, and he will be easily disposed of.'

We kept our eye on him and his attendant, and watched him take possession of a shed of wretched appearance, with many symptoms of dissatisfaction. We loitered purposely, till we saw that he was alone, and then went up to him.

'Ram! Ram! Sethi,' said Bhudrinath, addressing him; 'what a place is this they have put you into after all, not fit for hogs to lie in! That rascally Kotwal, for all his smooth tongue, is an arrant knave I warrant; and I have heard,' continued he, lowering his voice, 'that he has in his employ a number of thieves, whose business it is to cut away travellers' saddle-bags from under their heads at night, and when the poor man goes to complain in the morning he is beaten out of the village. Did you not hear so, Jemadar Sahib?'

'Yes, indeed,' said I; 'don't you remember the man who met us at the village some coss from this, and warned us of the thieves of Oomerkhér, and said he had been robbed of everything he possessed, and then driven out with scarcely a rag to cover him? It was then that I determined to encamp outside, where we might have our own sentinels, and where, if we are robbed, it would be our own fault.'

'Allah help me! I am a lost man!' cried the merchant: 'I know not what to do;' and he beat his head with his clenched hand. In those bags is all I am worth in the world; I fled from Surat to save myself from the oppression, and it appears that the further I fly the worse usage I meet. It was only two nights ago—after watching till my eyes nearly started from my head from want of sleep, and not being able to sit longer, I lay down and my eyes closed—that an attempt was made to cut my bags from under me; and as I woke, the thieves snatched away two of my cooking utensils and the cloth I had about me. What could I do? Had I run after them, some fellow would have been off with my bags; so I sat still, and screamed for help. The villagers were soon assembled about me, and when I told them what had happened, a villain, who called himself the Patel, abused me for defaming his village; and I was actually thrust without the gates, and left to pursue my way in the dark, in momentary dread that I should be pursued, and perhaps robbed and murdered. Oh, my unhappy fate!' cried he; 'what will it not lead me to! Fool that I was to leave my own country, to become the sport of unblessed brutes, such as I have met in this wild country.'

'Well,' said Bhudrinath in a compassionate tone, 'you have been used very ill, and you ought to go and complain to the Hakim here; report says he is a just man, although those under him may be thieves and rascals.'

'No, no, no!' cried the man; 'go and complain! and be fleeced of my last rupee! The great man would require a nuzzur, and every dependant would ask for one; did I dare to refuse, my situation would be worse than it is now. No, no! I have not been robbed as yet, and please God, if I could only get out of this town, I would attach myself to some party of respectable persons going the same road.'

Bhudrinath turned to me, and took me a few paces aside. 'The bait has taken,' said he; 'our net is now round him; you must draw it tightly.'

'How?'

'By inviting him to our encampment; I will propose it.'

Bhudrinath again addressed him, while I turned away. 'Sethji,' said he, 'you are a man in misfortune, and if we don't help you out of this place you will assuredly be robbed of everything you possess. You must come and put up in our encampment; that is to say, if the Jemadar Sahib will permit it: but the truth is, we are very careful, and allow no one to approach it, as we are escorting a merchant from Benare to Hyderabad, who has a large amount of goods with him.'

'For God's sake! for the sake of your father and mother!' cried the poor wretch, 'for the sake of your children, intercede for me! do not suffer me to be robbed and murdered here. Ali! Jemadar Sahib,' said he to me, catching me by my dress, 'you are my father and my mother; a word from you, and I am safe, and my poor merchandise will reach its destination. Allah knows, if anything happens to me on the road, my house will be made desolate, my employers will seize my wife and children. Jemadar, you can protect me from this; you can save my life from these fears, which make me most wretched, and are consuming my soul!'

'Thooh! good man,' cried I, spitting on the ground, 'do not be so abject. Inshallah! I am able by God's favour to afford protection to one who is a prince among merchants, and you are too poor to think of. In His name follow us, and we will take care of you; we are going to Hyderabad ourselves, and you can remain among the servants; do you, Peer Khan, bring this man out to us.'

Peer Khan remained, and we returned to our camp. On the way we determined that he should die before evening, or when it should become dusk, and we would then go into the town and visit the evening durbar of the Hakim.

In a short time we beheld the merchant and Peer Khan, with another man, driving two ponies apparently heavily laden towards our camp.

'Come, this is more than I hoped for,' said my father, 'there are two of them; and two ponies well laden must afford something worth taking: we cannot expect this to be as profitable work as the last, but much may come out of it.'

The men approached, and the merchant was presented to my father.

'To your kindness,' he said to me, 'I owe all I possess, and if these poor bags might be allowed to remain along with the rest of the merchandize you are protecting, it would increase the favour and they would be safe.'

'Surely,' I replied, 'you can unload your beasts; and there is the pile of goods, you can put your bags on the top of it.'

It was curious to see the behaviour of the men of the band; they appeared to have an instinctive knowledge of the purpose for which the men had been brought into the encampment. They did not evince the smallest savageness of demeanour, as perhaps might have been expected; on the contrary, every one was most civil and attentive to the strangers; one offered to rub down the ponies, another to make a place for cooking, a third to bring grass from the town, or anything they might require for their meal. In a short time we observed the appearance of care and anxiety on the face of the merchant give place to a cheerful expression, and long before evening for the men were among a knot of the Thugs, listening to their stories, and themselves relating their adventures. Little did they think what preparations were making, and that in a few short hours they would cease to be counted with the living!

CHAPTER VII

MEANWHILE a consultation was held as usual at my father's tent, and the different parts were assigned to us. The office of bhut-tote fell to me, and the merchant was delivered to my hands. I now experienced none of the hesitation which had formerly troubled my mind; I only longed for objects to exercise myself on, to perfect my hand in the peculiar knack it required. I had before me the example of those I most looked up to, and to equal or excel them was my sole ambition. I was determined to excel, and the excitement of the whole system proved a powerful stimulus. In this matter too I had acted a prominent part as a Sotha; and I began to pride myself on my ingenuity in seconding, as I had done, one so completely an adept as Bhudrinath.

We agreed to put the men to death immediately after evening prayer.

We had in our camp a boy about twelve years old, the son of one of the Thugs, who sang very beautifully, and his father used to accompany him on the saringee[1]. It was our custom of an evening after prayers to send for the youth and be entertained by his songs; and he sang so well, that he often collected a considerable sum from among us. On this occasion he was called, and when he had begun, a message was sent to the merchant to come and partake of our entertainment. He came, and his servant also; the latter was a fine stout man, whiskered and mustachio'd, and from the dialect he spoke I concluded him to be a Rajput of Meywar, whose inhabitants were a noble race and brave to a degree. I eyed him, as he sat down in his place, with a half-formed determination to change the merchant for him. Bhudrinath had been allotted to him; and as I reflected on my own powers and his, I felt assured that if he was thought equal to it, I was superior to him, though I might not be considered so. Another thought, and my determination was made; I proposed the exchange to Bhudrinath.

'As you please,' said he in a whisper, 'but yonder is a tough fellow; these Meywaree Rajputs are active as panthers, and to tell you the truth I did not half like the idea of being allotted to him; but there is no help for it, and if I were to fail there are twenty others who would finish him. But do you think yourself equal to him?'

[1] Native violin.

'Yes, I do not fear him; I have besides, a reputation to win, and do not care running a little risk.'

'As you will,' he replied; 'but you must mention it to your father.'

I did so. The merchant was too much absorbed in the boy's song to attend to us, and the servant was in extasies, as it was one of his own country.

'Are you able to do it? Do not try else,' said my father; 'the man is armed, and has a dagger at his girdle; a sword I do not fear, but daggers are awkward things, and you might be wounded.'

'And suppose I was,' I replied, 'do you think the fear of that deters me? No, no! I have taken this on myself, and I will, with your permission, go through with it.'

'As you like, my son, I will not oppose you; you have a name to gain, and you do well to run some risk: I will observe you narrowly, and be ready to succour you should you require it.'

The usual phrase, 'Pān lao!' (bring pān,) was to be the signal; and as we changed places, myself and Bhudrinath, I fancied the servant eyed us with some suspicion; I thought I saw him loosen the dagger in his girdle; perhaps it was fancy, and yet he must have thought there was danger. He stood up and looked round at us: and as I contemplated his brawny form, naked from the waist, his chest covered with hair, and his muscular arms, I thought for an instant I had overrated my strength; but to recede would have been cowardly. The only plan was to attack him standing. I moved towards him, and cast a keen look on my father, by which I intended that he should give the signal as soon as I had gained my place, the man had just turned round to look at me and get out of my way, and I was just telling him not to move, as I was passing on, when the signal was given.

Was it that I was a moment late, or that he had caught a glimpse of the fate of his master, or that in reality he suspected all was not right, that he was in danger? I know not; but as I threw the cloth around his neck, he drew his dagger: to have loosed my hold would have been followed by instant death, he would have plunged it into me; and he struggled so much, that, it spite of my great strength, he almost succeeded in getting his other hand between his neck and the cloth. All this happened in less time than I take to say it. My danger was imminent, but, as fortune would have it, a Thug attempted to seize the hand which held the dagger; this diverted his attention from me for an instant: although half choked, he made an immense effort, which nearly shook me off, and reached the unfortunate man—he plunged the weapon into his heart!

The man uttered a loud groan and fell, and the blood spouted forth over us both; but the action had given me a fresh hold, I was able to use my knuckles, and who could live under the strength I put forth? The Rajput's dying struggles were tremendous, but I would not quit my hold: my father rushed to me:

'Where is the cord?' he cried; 'he will not die in this manner; where is the cord? pass it about his neck, and let two of you pull.

'No, no! I exclaimed, 'he is nearly finished; let me alone, this work is my own, no one shall interfere.' Fortunately, having thrown the man on his face, I was able to kneel on his back, and he was soon past the ability to use his dagger. At last there was one convulsion stronger than the previous ones, and he lay still—he was also dead—my second victim!

I arose, breathless and exhausted; and as I looked on the prostrate corpse before me, I felt indeed that there had been danger —that I had escaped from a deadly struggle, and that my art had triumphed over strength. Almost beside the body lay that of the man who had aided me, who had received a desperate wound. All had been so occupied with me, that they had overlooked the poor sufferer; he was lying with his face to the ground groaning.

'For God's sake,' said I, 'turn him round, the wound is in his stomach: can nothing be done for him?'

Some of the men accordingly turned him, but it was plain to see that there was no hope of life; the blood spurted in a stream both from the wound and from his mouth: he made several attempts to speak, but in vain; he died almost instantly. While I was engaged in the struggle, I several times fancied that the Rajput's dagger had reached me, as I endeavoured to avoid it by screwing my body as far away from him as possible; but the excitement was too great for me to feel the wound, if there was any. Yet now, on putting my hand to my side, I found, by the blood on my garment, that I was wounded; the blood too was observed by my father.

'Protection of Allah! he is wounded!' he cried. 'My son, my son, did I not warn thee? did I not bid thee beware of that Rajput? Thou wast no match for him, my son; and now thou art wounded, and what can be done?' and my father sat down, fairly overpowered with his emotions.

I felt that the wounds were but scratches, and hastened to open my vest. 'There,' said I, showing the wounds, 'I said he would do me no harm; and what are these? a thorn from a hedge would have caused a deeper and more painful one.'

'Shookur Khoda!' exclaimed my father; 'you are not hurt after all;' and the old man's eyes fairly ran over with tears as he looked at the wounds, 'but I had feared the worst after that horrid sight. Ai, Mahomed! thou was a faithful servant.'

The bodies of the merchant and the Rajput were instantly stripped, and removed to the grave which had long before been prepared for them; it was made inside a small tent, where my father, myself, and some others slept, and where it was secure from observation. I never was more struck with the despatch and ingenuity of the lughas than on this occasion. I had but delayed to have my slight wounds dressed, and to bathe and cleanse myself from the blood I was covered with, when I went to see the grave, thinking to find it still open. I was perfectly astonished—there was no sign of the earth having been disturbed; the place where the hole had been dug had been carefully beaten down and plastered over with mud; and, but that it was wet, no one could have told that it had been touched by the hand of man. My father's sleeping carpet and mine were then laid over the place.

'Now,' said I to Bhudrinath, 'let us put on our best clothes and visit the Hakim. Will you come too, my father?'

'No, Béta (no, my son,) I have enough to do to keep all quiet here: some one must remain; and you and Bhudrinath have deserved your amusement, so go and take it. And here,' cried he to some of the Thugs, 'take your shields and swords, and accompany my son; and see that you look like soldiers, and not like Thugs, for the night.'

Six or eight were soon ready, dressed in clean clothes and armed and by this time, the moon haven risen, and it being the hour appointed by the Kotwal for the evening durbar, we set off to the town.

Truly, dressed as we were in the handsomest clothes we could select, we looked not only soldiers but handsome fellows. Each of us had given a knowing cock to his turban; and mine, of the richest gold tissue, passing several times under my chin, set off my face, by giving me a particularly martial appearance. My arms were of the richest description; a sword with a hilt inlaid with gold, its scabbard covered with crimson velvet, with a ferrule to it of silver, of an open pattern, which covered nearly half of it. In my girdle, which was a Cashmere shawl, were a peshkubs or knife, with an agate handle, inlaid also with gold, and a small jumbea or Arab dagger, also highly ornamented with gold and silver. I carried, too, a shield of rhinoceros' hide, the manufacture of Sylhet, and painted and gilt in the beautiful manner of Hindustan, the bosses being of silver, richly chased and ornamented. My dress was of the finest muslin, which showed my shape through it to the greatest advantage; and rich cloth-of-gold trowsers completed a dress at once elegant, and calculated not only to impress an observer with my correct taste, but to convince him that I was a person, if not of rank, of respectability.

Bhudrinath's and Peer Khan's appearance was something less showy than mine; but they looked good and true men, and fair seconds to one of my pretensions.

So we set off to the town, and passing the gate went to the Kotwal's Chowree, where we hoped to meet with him, or with some one who would direct us to the durbar. At is happened, the

Kotwal was there; and relinquishing his employment of caring for travellers, he accompanied to introduce us.

We walked through some of the streets, picking our way through tethered cattle and all the abominations of a Mahratta town, and at last reached a respectable-looking gateway, around which a number of soldiers were standing and lounging. Our friend the Kotwal passed us through them; and after traversing two open courts, we reached the place where the entertainment and assembly was going on. A fine-looking old man questioned us as to who we were, to which the Kotwal replied for us, that we were respectable persons desirous of paying our respects to the Nawab Sahib; to which I added, that, having heard much of his great name and hospitality, we considered that it would be unpolite to pass through his town without paying our compliments to him, and becoming acquainted with so estimable a person.

'You are welcome,' said the old man; 'there is nothing pleases the Nawab Sahib so much as to see strangers, wherever they may come from; and, Inshallah! you will have no cause to regret having taken this trouble.'

'On the contrary,' I replied, 'we cannot think it trouble, but an honour seldom allowed to such poor persons as we are. But pray lead us to the presence.'

We ascended a few steps into the hall, where sat the Nawab, surrounded by a number of persons. Before him was a group of dancing-women, displaying their charms, and entrancing their hearers with songs of Persia and Hindustan. Our conductor bade us wait for a moment; and going up to the Nawab, said a few words to him, intimating our arrival.

'Khamoosh!' (silence!) cried the Nawab, and it was repeated by a dozen voices; 'let the strangers be admitted.'

We were ushered on, leaving our shoes at the edge of the pure white cloth which was spread over the part of the room which led to the Nawab's musnud. On seeing us he made a polite salutation; and I stepped forward, and enveloping the hilt of my sword in an embroidered scarf I had thrown loosely about my shoulders, I presented it as a nuzzur.

'Kubool hooa,' said the old gentleman, placing his hands upon it; 'it is accepted; sit down near us. Inshallah! we are much pleased with your appearance, and bid you heartily welcome to this our poor durbar.'

To be polite I resisted this civility, protesting that I was far too humble an individual to allow myself so much honour; but he was not to be denied, and accordingly I seated myself in the most respectful attitude, with my heels under me; and placing my sword and shield before me in the best manner to display their beauty, I turned to the Nawab, who seemed to be contemplating my appearance.

'Mashallah!' said he to me, 'thou art a brave-looking young fellow: now tell me who thou art, and who these respectable persons are that accompany thee.'

'I beg to represent in your service,' I replied, 'that I am nothing but a poor soldier, a Syud by birth; I have a few men with me, for whom and myself I am going to Hyderabad to seek service. I am come from Hindustan: my father, who is at our camp, is a merchant going to the city with merchandize. These persons,' I continued, pointing to Bhudrinath and Peer Khan, 'are two of my associates; and being superior to the rest, I have ventured to bring them to present their nuzzurs to the presence.'

'By all means, Meer Sahib; we delight to see good and stout-looking fellows. Any one such is a pearl in the eye of an old soldier like myself. Let them be brought forward,' said he to an attendant; and both advancing made the requisite salutations, and presented the hilts of their swords as I had done.

The ceremonies of introduction being concluded, the musicians and dancing-women were desired to recommence, and I had a moment's leisure to survey the apartment and the scene before me.

The apartment opened, through three large wooden arches, into the courtyard which we had crossed; and between them were hung large purdahs or curtains of English scarlet cloth, which could be let down as occasion required. The room was lofty, and behind where we sat the walls were ornamented with stucco-work in rich designs. Above, on one side, was a small gallery thickly screened, from whence the inmates of the zenana could observe all that was passing below without being seen. Before us the dancing girls were moving with their peculiar floating motion, and singing, while they expressed the amorous words of their song by their gestures. Another set were sitting down by their side, waiting for their turn to be called, and both were splendidly dressed and covered with jewels.

Nawab Hussein Yar Jung Bahadur, a fine-looking wiry old soldier, polite and courtly in his manner, was a good specimen of the noblemen of the Dukhun; though perhaps not so effiminately polished as those of Delhi, yet he was one whose appearance commanded respect; and his bright keen eye, and the seam of a wound on his right cheek, showed that he had seen battle-fields and was familiar with war. His dress was of plain Dacca muslin; but a string of large pearls round his neck, which he used as a rosary, and the beautiful sword lying before him on the carpet, would prove to the most casual observer that he was a man of rank and consequence.

He observed me looking round, and addressed me thus:

'We are in a poor place here, young man; but what can be done? The duty of the government must be performed, and we cannot carry our house about with us. However, we have made the place as decent as it could be, considering we are in the jungle; and, by the favour of the Prophet, we have brought bright eyes and sweet voices with us, and we do not lack amusement. Say, what thinkest thou of our selection? Yonder is Zora, sitting down, second to few in Hyderabad for beauty of person and sweetness of voice: the other, now singing, is one we picked up on the way hither; but Inshallah! in a short time she will be fit company for the other, and we shall take her down to the city with us, to astonish our acquaintances.'

The dancing-girl Zora, hearing her name mentioned, turned round and looked towards me. I was instantly dazzled by her beauty. She was not so fair as some of her profession I had before seen; but if she was not so fair, her features were small and regular; and her large antelope-like eyes, when turned full on me, seemed to pierce me through.

'Now you must see my pride, Zora, dance,' said the Nawab. 'Inshallah! your heart must be hard if she does not make it ache, as she has done that of many a one.'

The group who had hitherto been singing were desired to be seated, and Zora prepared to stand up. The bells for her ankles were brought, and she tied them on. The musicians to accompany her tuned their instruments, and after a short prelude she stood up. If I had been struck with her appearance sitting, how much more splendid was it now! She was not tall, but exquisitely formed, as far as could be judged from her peculiar dress, which was so loose from under her arms as completely to hide her form to her ankles; but it was of the richest description.

It was made of a dark lilac-coloured gauze, in bands alternately with gold tissue; the bottom trimmed with gold tissue very broad, as far as her knees, upon which there was rich embroidery in gold thread and seed pearls. Around her she had thrown with extreme grace a scarf of the lightest muslin and silver, of the same colour as her dress; so thin was it, that as she moved it seemed almost to float away from her in the air caused by her motion. The colour of the scarf round her head, in contrast with her complexion, made it appear much fairer than it really was, and her large soft eyes still more brilliant and swimming.

The musicians began their usual prelude, and with it one of Zora's companions, a pretty girl, the slow movements of the dance. After a few turns she resumed her place, and Zora herself, like the full moon emerging from a cloud, sailed towards us with a slow and graceful motion. How shall I describe to you, Sahib, her exquisite movements! Every turn displayed her form to greater advantage, and I gazed till my soul was fairly entranced. But how much more was I affected when she began to sing! Having performed the dance, both the slow and quick, she ceased; and after a prelude by one of the musicians behind her, she broke out into an impassioned ghuzul.

It was one I was very fond of myself. I listened till I could have fallen at her feet and worshipped her as a peri from heaven. My soul was so intoxicated with the blessed sounds I heard, that I was insensible to all around me.

She at length ceased; and the Nawab, who had been observing me attentively, asked me what I thought of the songstress and her dancing.

'Most wonderful is it,' I replied; 'my liver has become water before her fascinations. It is fortunate for me that I am not to live within their influence, or I were lost for ever. I could forego fame and my profession to lie at her feet and dream away my existence.'

'You talk like a foolish boy,' said the Nawab, 'and must not give way to such fancies; many a man has been ruined for ever by them. Persons like her are greedy and insatiable of money, as we are told of the sea, which swallows up everything that is cast into it, without showing a sign on its surface beyond that of the transient ripple.'

'Cannot they love?' I asked; 'are they so utterly mercenary?'

The night was far advanced; and requesting leave to depart, I rose to be gone. I was passing the tuwaifs (dancing-girls), when an old woman pulled me by the sleeve, and said hurriedly, 'If you seek an opportunity, there is another who desires one: be secret, you shall hear more from me.' My blood boiled; I slipped a piece of money into her hand, and departed.

CHAPTER VIII

I SAID my blood boiled: could it be that one so lovely, one who had kept company with the nobles and men of wealth of Hyderabad, had seen aught to admire in me, who was unused to courtly scenes, and was even yet a boy, deficient in manner and address? Could it be that from my dress and appearance she thought me rich, one who would squander my substance upon her? These thoughts were passing through my mind, and we had nearly reached our encampment without my having interchanged a word with my companions. The silence was broken by Bhudrinath.

'How is this, Meer Sahib?' said he; 'what has tied your tongue? Have you nothing to talk about after our night's entertainment, no remarks to make on the beautiful kunchinee? By Allah! though it is a Mahomedan oath, I would almost be content to give up the heaven of Indra, and turn Mussulman, were I sure of being attended in the paradise of Mahomed by a set of houris just such as she. And to think of her belonging to that old wretch the Nawab, and to be buried in this hole of a Mahratta village, when she might have half the nobles of Hyderabad at her feet were she there! By Allah! I say again, it were worth the while to try and entice her away from the old sensualist, and it would be something to talk about, not to mention her company on the road, and the rare addition she would make to our evening amusements.'

'Why,' I replied carelessly, 'the girl is, as you say, of surpassing beauty, and no doubt feels herself uncomfortable in this abode of swine; yet to get her away would be no easy task, and what should we do with her when we got her?'

'I shall try and see if her coming with us is any such marvellous difficulty,' he rejoined; 'and you know if afterwards there is any pursuit, she and the rest of her people are easily provided for.'

'Now you speak like a cold-blooded Thug,' I retorted, (for deny it as much as I would to myself, I could not but feel that the dancing-girl had more than interested me) 'and I would sooner quit you all, and get back to Hindustan the best way I could, than that a hair of her head should be injured.'

'I did but jest, Meer Sahib; you know I am not one who wars with women, except when they come before me in the fair and lawful exercise of my vocation.'

'I am not angry,' said I, 'though I certainly felt my blood rise when you alluded to her. We will consider about the rest in the morning, and if we can but persuade my father that the girl comes of her own accord, I do not anticipate any objection.'

'Did she say aught to you?' he eagerly inquired.

'No,' said I; 'how could she in that crowd? but you know I understand Persian, thanks to the old mullah my teacher, and you do not; and from the words of the last plaintive song she sang, and her mode of expressing them, I have a shrewd guess that she is tired of confinement, and of her mate. You know the old proverb, "Kubootur bu kubootur, bāz bu bāz"—pigeons mate with pigeons, and hawks with hawks.'

'Well,' said Bhudrinath, 'according to that she is more likely to look to you than to me; and you know I am a Brahmin; therefore I leave her and the matter to your management: I am ready to assist when I can be of use. Inshallah! as you people say, we shall make a corner-stone of the old fellow's beard and laugh him to scorn.'

'Ameen!' said I, 'we will try at all events, and you shall hear from me in the course of tomorrow more upon this subject.' We then separated for the night; and I was glad Peer Khan and the rest of the men had been so far behind us, as not to have been able to overhear any part of our conversation. I confess that, as I lay down to sleep, I earnestly desired the success of our scheme, though as yet it could hardly be called one; and though I had in some degree struggled with it, I had not been proof against the fascination of the dancing-girl; nor indeed was it to be wondered at after the words of the old woman.

Soon after the morning prayer, the leaders of the band were assembled to see the opening of the bags of him who had died the evening before. My father presided in the assembly, and one by one they were brought from the pile of merchandize. We had indeed got a prize; and it was not to be wondered at that the care of them had cost the man they belonged to so much anxiety. In each of them, among a quantity of old clothes, rags, and old copper vessels, were concealed small boxes filled with precious stones, pearls, small diamonds, rubies, and emeralds; and in two of the boxes were sets of ornaments made up, and set with jewels; and two in particular, a bazu-bund, or ornament for the arm, and a sir-pésh, or ornament for the turban, were particularly splendid.

My father, who had a good deal of experience in these matters, pronounced the whole to be worth at least fifteen thousand rupees, and offered the band the alternative of distributing the whole in as equal portions as he could, or of waiting till our arrival at Hyderabad, where they could easily be sold for ready money. The latter, after some deliberation, was determined on, as had been the case with the former booty.

I proposed, as I knew that we might perhaps run short of money on the road, especially if we met with no more rich travelers, to offer one of the two ornaments for sale to the Nawab, and, as I had made his acquaintance, to take it to him myself. The proposal was agreed to, and I was not without hope that by some lucky chance I might fall in with the old woman who had spoken to me the night before, and might be able to arrange a meeting with her, which should guide us in our future plans; so accordingly about noon I called Bhudrinath to accompany me, and we proceeded to the palace, as it was called by the villagers.

By the way we met with our friend the Kotwal; but I cut him short with 'Another time, Kotwal'—for it seemed as though we were to have a long story—'another time, my friend, we will pay you a visit; but at present the matter we have in hand is urgent, and it being past noon we are afraid of being denied admittance and so you must excuse us.'

'Of course,' said he, 'I will not detain you, and I shall not fail to present myself at your camp this evening to receive your further commands.'

'That means,' said Bhudrinath as we moved on, 'that he expects a present. These worthies have been my study for many years.'

'Ay,' said I, 'we must pay him well, and he will be the first to cry up our praises should anything happen; but do you anticipate anything?'

'Not I,' said he; 'I wish we could always do our work as securely, and get as well paid for it; but here we are at the Nawab's gate.'

An attendant at our request took in our names to the Nawab, and after a short delay we were again ushered into his presence, and received with the same civility as we had been the night before. After some desultory conversation, I opened the object of our visit.

'Khodawund,' said I, 'my father pleads an attack of fever and cold for not attending to present his nuzzur at your feet, and he trusts you will pardon his seeming neglect. In his behalf I have brought a rare piece of jewellery for your inspection, which he hopes may please you; and by its purchase you will not only materially assist him, but it will become the property of one worthy to possess and wear it.'

Thus saying I produced the ornament for the turban, and laid it before him. He was evidently much struck with its beauty and the fine water of the precious stones, and after turning it in every position he could to catch the exact light for it, laid it down with a kind of sigh.

'It is indeed beautiful, and worthy of the turban of Bundugan Ali himself; but,' said he, 'I am too poor to buy it; its value must be very great.'

'No doubt,' said I, 'my grandfather must have paid handsomely for it; but times have altered and we have been glad to sell our family property for whatever it would fetch. In this instance, far be it from your slave's intention to put a price upon an ornament without peer in its fashion; yet methinks it would so well become the forehead of my lord that he ought not to let slip such an oportunity of possessing it, to be enabled to show it one day at the court of his prince.'

'Thou sayest truly; and if I may, I will but show it in the Mahal, and see how the persons of my household like it Inshallah! they will approve of it, and then we will see if we can come to terms about it.'

'Certainly,' said I; the time has been when it would have been nothing for our house to have presented a tray of such to one of my lord's power and rank; but we are reduced, as I said, and are no longer fit possessors of what we dare not wear.'

The Nawab took the jewel and went into his zenama: he was absent a long time, but we could see by his face on his return that it had been approved of.

'They have looked at it in a thousand ways, and have discovered that there is good fortune to come with it: not that I need any; but you know what a parcel of old women are,' said he. 'And now I will ask what may be the price: you know we nobles of Hyderabad are not overburthened with money, and you must be moderate in your demand.'

'Why,' said I, 'I am flattered by the opinion of those who have seen it, and can only say, that my grandfather may his memory live for ever!) paid so large a sum for the jewel that I am afraid to mention it. My lord must observe particularly its exquisite water. He, I say, collected the stones one by one during a long period of his life, and they cost him alone six thousand rupees; the gold around them is somewhat more; but my father will esteem himself fortunate if five thousand rupees be given for it.'

'It is too much,' said the Nawab with a sigh: 'where have I five thousand rupees to lay out in such a bauble as this? My friends, I have been gratified by the sight of it, but to purchase it is out of the question; the money I have not. Yet stay; allow me to have it valued by a jeweller, and we may perhaps come to terms.'

'By all means,' said I; 'I have told my lord no lie in stating the price of it: but let the jeweller see it; he may fix a smaller sum; and such is our urgent necessity for a little ready money that perhaps we may be induced to take something less.'

The jeweller was accordingly sent for, and arrived after a short time. He was shown the jewel; and from the expression of admiration on his countenance, I could see we had not overvalued it. He took it to the light, and putting on his spectacles examined it in every possible way. At last he returned, and taking the spectacles from his nose, asked the price we had fixed on it. I told him.

'At the time this was made up,' said he, 'no doubt it was worth the sum you mention, for the stones are of rare water; nevertheless, we all know that men cannot afford to expend money as they used to do, and, all things considered, perhaps at present four thousand rupees would not be too much, and indeed a fair price.'

'It is too little; we must be content to sell other articles to supply our necessities: so Nawab Sahib,' said I, 'with our profound thanks for your condescension, we ask leave for our departure;' and I took up the jewel and arose.

'Stay,' said he; 'I offer you three hundred rupees more: four thousand three hundred, surely that is sufficient.'

'Make it five hundred,' I replied, 'and it is yours.' After much haggling on both sides, the price was fixed at four thousand four hundred and fifty. Of this, two thousand five hundred were paid by the Nawab's treasurer in money, and for the rest, at my request, a bill was made out by a sahoukar of the village on Hyderabad. And after again offering our thanks to the Nawab, we took leave of him for ever.

'Not a bad morning's work,' said I to my companion as we walked homewards, attended by some of the Nawab's soldiers, escorting the men who carried the bags of money: 'the sight of the coin will gladden my poor old father's heart; and it will be something to divide among the men, who are really in want of money, and will keep them comfortably till we reach the city, even though we should fall in with no more rich prizes.'

'Indeed, you may congratulate yourself on your address and good manners; for without them you could not have carried the matter off in the way you have done,' said he. 'Now if I, though I am a far older Thug, had tried it, I should have most likely failed for want of a plausible story. The old fellow swallowed the account of your grandfather, as if it had been as true as that we are now here. By Krishna thou art a rare boy!'

'These matters sharpen one's intellect; and though I could not deceive an unfortunate traveller as you can, you see I am of some use at a pinch, Bhudrinath.'

'All will come in time,' said he; 'I do not despair of you after this: and if you accompany me in my work, you will soon excel me I think.'

'We shall see,' I returned; 'but our errand is not complete; w have not met the old woman.'

'Ha! so that plan is still in your head,' cried he; 'I warrant it you dreamed of the kunchinee last night, and your young heart is all on fire.'

'No,' said I laughing, 'not quite that; but I have some hope, and I shall return to the Kotwal's chowree after a little time, and perhaps the old creature may be in the bazaar, and may see me.'

'Shall I accompany you?' asked he.

'No,' said I; 'I think it would mar the business: I will go alone;

the presence of another besides myself might prevent her, if I meet her, from being communicative.'

'As you will,' said he; 'as you are determined to carry the matter to the utmost, you have a better chance of success than I have; and besides you are a principal, while I could only be an agent.'

Thus conversing, we arrived at the tents; and dismissing the soldiers, and money-carriers with a handsome present, I had the bags moved into my father's tent, who was asleep; I ranged them before him, and awakening him, pointed to them.

He rubbed his eyes, grumbling at being aroused from his slumber; but they were quickly fascinated by the sight of the bags, and I could not help laughing heartily at his astonishment as he took them up one by one, guessing at their contents.

'What, my son! Ameer Ali, where hast thou got all this? there must be five hundred rupees in each of them! One, two, three, four, five,' said he, counting them; 'two thousand five hundred! impossible! My son, what has thou been doing? My brain is in astonishment. Where didst thou get it?'

'There is just what you say, father,' said I; 'each contains five hundred, or nearly. It is the price of the jewel you gave me to sell, which it seems was worth more than we thought for. I asked at a venture five thousand rupees, and have brought you four thousand four hundred and fifty, which was as much as I could get: here are hoondees[1] for two thousand, and the rest is in the bags.'

'As much as you could get, boy!' cried my father; 'why thou hast done wonders. Mashallah! we are rich indeed; this is more than I ever expected:' and, his eyes fairly running over with tears, he embraced me warmly.

'Now,' said I, 'as I have done good service, I have in return a favour to beg, which I hope my father will grant; and it is a matter I dared not settle without his sanction.'

'Say on,' said my father; 'I can deny thee nothing.'

'Why,' continued I, 'there is a tuwaif of surpassing beauty, who sings like a bulbul, and who is anxious to accompany us to Hyderabad. I dared not allow it without speaking to you.'

The old man's visage clouded. 'A tuwaif!' said he; 'and dost thou not remember, my son, all the cautions I have given thee against persons of her condition, and hast thou so soon forgotten them as to get into their company on the first occasion which presented itself?'

'I represent,' said I, 'that neither have I forgotten them, nor have I gone into her company. I saw her at the Nawab's durbar last night, but did not even speak to her.'

'Then how knowest thou that she desires to go from hence?'

[1] A bill of exchange.

'I have heard it,' said I, 'from one who is attached to her, an old woman, who, I doubt not, will be here before the evening.'

My father shook his head. 'I do not disbelieve thee, my son,' said he; 'but I mistrust thy young heart and hot temper: it is a danger too great to be encountered; for once with us, and she would get thee into her toils, and then father, duty, and profession will be alike forgotten, and I should lose thee, my son, which would kill me.'

'Do not think so I pray, my father,' said I; 'there is not the danger you anticipate; she would follow us, and we should see but little of her, except we desired her presence to sing to us on the dreary evenings of our journey. And grant me this request, I pray you; 'tis the only one I have ever asked, and perhaps I deserve something for what I have done hitherto.'

'Thou dost indeed,' he replied; 'anything else would have been gladly granted without a demur on my part: however, I have confidence in thee, my son, and therefore have it as thou wilt, I will not gainsay thee in the matter.'

So far therefore there was no objection: yet my young heart smote me as I thought on the concealment I had made of her being in the pay and service of the Nawab, and that her connexion with him might bring us all into trouble; however, thought I, women have sharp wits; and if she truly desires to get away from him, she will take her own measures.

As soon as I could, therefore, I set off to the bazaar; and after loitering along the row of shops, and purchasing articles that were really required by us, I ascended the steps which led to the chowree, and was soon in conversation with the Kotwal, who entertained me with the gossip of the town, and did not fail to endeavour to impress me with a high sense of his power and influence. More than once I was on the point of confiding to him my plan, and offering him a bribe to assist me; but I checked myself, on the consideration that he might take my money and afterwards play me false. As it happened, however, I was not long in suspense, for I saw the old woman in the bazaar beneath me, making the best of her way in the direction of the gate of the town by which I had entered; so I took my leave of the worthy Kotwal, begging him to come to the camp in the evening for a reward for his civility and exertions.

I had, however, lost sight of the old woman before I got fairly down into the street; and following the direction she had taken, overtook her just beyond the gate.

'Mother,' said I, 'am I he whom you seek?'

'Ai mere jān! (ah, my soul!) have I at last found thee, my prince? Surely I have not ceased in my endeavours since last night to meet thee; I saw thee enter the palace, but my old limbs would not carry me quick enough to overtake thee.' And she threw her hands over my head, and cracked every joint of her fingers by pressing them against her temples.

'Are we secure against observation here?' she continued; 'for I have much to say to thee, and that quickly.'

'Not here,' I replied; 'I will go on to our tents yonder, and you can follow me; I will wait for you near them.'

The old woman hobbled up to me as I stood under a mango tree, secure from observation. Quite out of breath, she sat down: when she had recovered herself, she untied a corner of the cloth about her person and presented me with a small ring.

'This,' said she, 'is from her you know of: and for the love of Allah, my soul! do you exert yourself for her: she is dying in this place, and is subject to all the torments the caprice of that unblest Nawab can think of. She is one day in favour and loaded with kindnesses, another, in a fit of jealousy or rage, he deprives her of every comfort, shuts her up in a lonely room, and will not even allow me to go to her. You, my son, are young and brave; you will not suffer her to continue in this state, she who is the pearl of Hyderabad, who has found favour in the sight of princes and nobles. For the sake of Allah, exert yourself, and she is free, and will accompany you to the end of the world. She has seen you, and your beauty has entered into her soul and is consuming her liver; and between this and her former miseries, she is today in a state of madness, so that even I cannot pacify her.'

'I am ready, mother,' said I: ''tis true I have never been blessed with hearing a word from her, save in her songs; but I can understand them; and there was one she sang which has been ringing in my ears ever since I heard it. Say, had it any reference to me and herself?'

'You have guessed well,' she replied; 'I told her to sing it, in the chance of its being understood, and blessed be Allah it was not in vain: but the time is passing fast, my son, and what can be done?'

'Nay,' said I, 'that I wish to hear from yourself, for I know not how to proceed; neither do I know this town, nor the house where she lives, so what can I advise? I am helpless in this matter, yet willing to the utmost.'

'Listen then,' said the old woman; 'I will describe the place, and you must come after me and see it from the outside, that you may know it in the night. The place she is now in, and where she will most likely sleep tonight, is a small tiled house, at the corner of the wall of the zenana toward the street. There are two windows, some distance from the ground, yet not so high but that she might get out, if any one helped her on the outside. There is no other way of her escaping; for it would be impossible for her to get through the zenana, and afterwards through the open courts, which are full of soldiers. Say, will you dare the adventure; or be a coward, a namurd, who would not risk a drop of blood for a woman, and one so fair as she is?'

'I am no coward, I believe,' said I, 'though I have no deeds of arms to boast of. I accept the risk, and I pray Allah to defend us! Are there soldiers near the place?'

'No,' said she, 'not one; the only danger is at the village gate, which is always guarded: How will you pass this?'

'If that is all,' said I, 'trust to me; and Inshallah! we will laugh at the Nawab's beard in the morning. But tell me, how do you intend to contrive to accompany us?'

'Ah, I have arranged that already. I am allowed free egress at any hour of the night, upon the various pretences or necessities of my mistress; and I can get out at midnight and meet you anywhere you may determine.'

'This is good,' said I; 'now come and show me the place.'

She guided me through the gate we had just passed, and turning down a narrow alley desired me to mark the various windings as we went along which I did. We at last reached a street between two high walls, one of which was the Nawab's zenana; and passing on, we arrived at length under a small tiled house, which answered the description she had given of it.

'This is the place,' she said; 'and that is the window from whence she must descend. It is not very high, as you see, and there will not be much difficulty in her getting out.'

'I see none,' I replied, 'if she has only a stout heart. Tell her to tie her sheets together and drop them over; we will be below, and take care she reaches the ground easily.'

'I will,' said she; 'and now away! we may be seen, and if so, Allah be our help!'

'She sees us!' cried I; 'for there is a hand stretched forth from the window.'

'It is she!' said the old woman; 'and oh! what joy it must be to her to know that there are persons anxious and willing to serve her! Now, my poor bird, thou shalt no longer have a cage, though it be a gilded one. But away, my soul, away! do not loiter here; a smile from her were dearly purchased now, and tonight you will have thousands, ay with her blessings too.'

'I go,' said I; 'but fail not, nurse; for your life see that all is right; you must meet us at the corner we last passed.'

The old woman nodded her assent, and I withdrew as quickly as possible from the spot, though I would have given worlds for one glance, for one approving smile, from the object of my love. As soon as I reached the tents, I summoned Bhudrinath, told him of my success, and unfolded to him the plan as it stood at present. He was rejoiced, and saw nothing objectionable in it.

'I have one thing however,' said he, 'to represent, which you may do or not, as you please.'

'What is it? say on.'

'Why,' he replied, 'although it will be, as you say, an easy enough matter to get out of the town, I by no means think it so easy to get in.'

'By Allah! you say truly,' said I; 'what advice can you give to aid my plan?'

'You see,' rejoined he, 'that the gates are guarded; I tried myself to get in last night, before midnight, as I had an affair of my own to look after, and the fair one expected me; but the sons of dogs at the gates (may their sisters be defiled!) swore I was a thief, and after interchanging abuse for a long time they finally shut the wicket in my face, and I was forced to return in the worst of all possible humours. So my advice is, that we go in before nightfall, and take up our quarters in the shop of a bhutteara[1] with whom I have scraped an acquaintance; the fellow will not suspect anything if we leave his place in the night, as I hinted my bad fortune of last night to him today, and he was the one to propose my coming to his place in the evening, to go wherever I pleased afterwards.'

'Your plan is a good one,' said I, 'and I thank you for your bad luck last night; but for it, we might have gone and knocked our heads against the gate to no purpose.'

After evening prayer Bhudrinath and myself went into the town; and it was well we did so, for the men at the gate knew him perfectly, and good-naturedly joked him about his bad success the night before.

'Thou art beforehand with us tonight, my friend,' said one fellow; 'and thou art wise, for hadst thou come later we should have shut the door in thy face as before.'

'You might have been more civil,' said Bhudrinath laughing. 'I suppose, though you would not let me in, you will let me out in case I should bring any one with me?'

'Why, that is not against orders exactly, but you would have to pay toll; so, if you have not brought money with you, you had better stay where you are.'

'I may find some probably,' said Bhudrinath to the speaker, enough at any rate to fill your hookahs for some days, if there is occasion.'

'Agreed,' said all the fellows; 'a bargain, by Allah! a few rupees, and you may take any one you please, the Nawab's harem too to boot, though there is not much in it by all accounts.'

'Who is your wughyra, your officer?' said I; and one of the men stepped out. 'I am he, may it please your nobility, and I can wink at an honest fellow's doings as well as another.'

'Provided you are paid for it,' said I.

'Of course,' said he laughing; 'we are lucky when chance throws gentlemen like you in our way.'

[1] A cook who dresses food for travellers.

'Here then,' said I, 'are five rupees, to entertain yourselves with; and see that you don't get drunk, or the blame will fall on us.'

'May your condescension increase!' cried the whole; 'we are your worship's devoted servants.'

'Now how do you mean to get out?' asked Bhudrinath as we passed on.

'Not this way,' said I, 'if I can help it, for there will be a disturbance about the matter; and if we go out here it will give a clue to our discovery. We will try the other gate first.'

'I would lay a wager they are all drunk in an hour,' said he, 'and we may then open the gate for ourselves; but here is the bhutteara's shop, and those kabobs smell very savoury; I sometimes wish I was not a Brahmin, that I might eat them as you do.'

'Ah,' said I, 'it is well for you to say that; but perhaps they may have proved too tempting at some time or other.'

'By Krishna! I swear you wrong me,' cried he; 'Brahmin I am, and will be; you know my creed tells me that I have been successively transformed through every grade of suffering humanity, and now that I have reached the top, I am not such a fool as to descend to the bottom and undergo the whole pain over again for the sake of a few kabobs.'

'You are right,' said I; 'nevertheless I will try them; I could not eat when I wished at my tent, but their smell has raised my appetite wonderfully.' And in a short time my fingers were pretty deep in a smoking dish of kicheree and kabobs, as hot as pepper could make them.

'Friend Bhutteara,' said I when I had done, 'surely the Shaitan himself must visit your shop now and then, for no other could eat these scraps of meat, except he had a mouth of brass.'

'I beg pardon,' said the fellow, 'but I was away on business and I suspect my daughter must, as you say, have put too much pepper in them; but I can make my lord a cup of sherbet, a poor imitation of what true believers will drink in Paradise, and it will cool his mouth.'

'And a hookah, if you please,' said I, 'then I shall feel more comfortable.'

CHAPTER IX

I HEARD the bhutteara bustling about in the interior of his house for a while, and was gratified to see that he so evidently exerted himself to please me. In a short time more the sherbet was prepared, and its grateful coolness, with the rosewater which had been mingled with it, allayed the irritation of my mouth, and enabled me to enjoy a hookah, which, if served in a less costly apparatus than that the Nawab had offered me, was as good in flavour: its pleasing fumes composed me, and quieted the feverish excitement I had hitherto been in.

'You appear comfortable,' said Bhudrinath.

'I am so,' I replied; 'and I doubt not you envy me, in spite of your Brahminical belief.'

'Perhaps I do,' said he; 'yet having never tasted the luxuries of meat and other things you set such value upon, I cannot estimate them sufficiently, and I care not about them: nay more, the very idea of meat, the sight of it in its raw state, the blood, the garbage accompanying it, are loathsome to me; and I very much question, were I to become a Mahomedan, whether I could ever bring myself to it. Pah! the idea is horrible.'

I could not help laughing heartily at his disgust, and he was not angry. 'But,' said I, 'how are we to wake at the proper time? an hour too soon or too late, and our enterprise is ruined.'

'I was thinking of the same thing,' he replied and turning to the bhutteara, he asked him how late he remained up: 'For,' he continued, 'my friend and I have a small matter on our hands about midnight. Can we trust to you to awaken us?'

'Certainly,' said the man; 'I never shut up my shop till after midnight, for sometimes travellers drop in, and, poor hungry souls, the first place they seek is the bhutteara's shop, and were there not something hot for them woe be to me!'

'Here is a trifle over and above the price of the kabobs,' said I, throwing him a few rupees, 'to keep you awake.'

He picked up the money with many salaams and good wishes, and my hookah being smoked out, and feeling drowsy, I laid myself down and slept, but not long. As is often the case, excitement overpowered sleep, and I awoke in alarm lest I had overslept the time; I had not however done so. Looking round me, I saw the bhutteara busily employed in cooking cakes, while his little daughter was turning some kabobs on the fire; he observed me, and said, 'You are soon awake, Sahib, it wants a good hour yet of your time; you had better go to sleep again; you see I have work in hand which will keep me up beyond that time, for some travellers have arrived, and it is as much as I can do to satisfy their hungry stomachs.'

'I cannot sleep again,' said I; 'I am refreshed, and another hookah or two will keep me awake till it is time to go.'

'I understand you,' said he: 'you young men are hot-blooded, and are always seeking adventures; but it is only as it ought to be: I would not give a cowrie for a young fellow who had not the spirit you appear to possess.'

'May you prosper,' said I; 'but let me have another hookah, for truly the first has left a grateful flavour in my mouth.'

He disappeared into the interior of his house for a short time and returned with it.

'Now,' said he, 'if the first pleased you, you cannot but be gratified with this; it is prepared from a choice receipt, and it is only persons of rank and taste like yourself to whom I ever give it: it would be lost on the multitude.'

It was, as he said, delicious; and my pipe had been refilled several times to my great satisfaction, when he told me the time I desired was come.

'Yonder star,' said he, 'rises over the houses a short time before midnight, so rouse your companion; you will be expected.'

I did so; Bhudrinath was soon awake, and ready to accompany me. We took leave of our host, and directed our way through the now deserted streets to the place of assignation.

'We are wonderfully like two thieves,' said he to me; 'what if the village watch should catch us? we should look very foolish.'

'I see no danger of it,' said I: but hardly were the words out of my mouth, when we saw the patrol coming down the street before us. There was an open gate close to us, and stepping inside we hid ourselves behind the large doors. We had however been observed, and as the men passed, one said he was sure he had seen two men lurking there.

'Nonsense,' said another fellow, 'you are always seeing men in the dark. Come along! it is just midnight, and I am sleepy; we will go a little further and then beat the duphra[1]; if there are any theives about they will run away.'

A loud yawn was a pretty good proof of the truth of his assertion, and they passed on. Just as we emerged from our hiding-place, the duphra and horns were sounded, and answered from the other sides of the town; and then all was again as still as death, save when a village dog howled his wild cry to the moon.

'There is now no danger,' said I; 'come on, we are near the place.'

A few paces further brought us to the corner where the old woman said she would await our coming, and there to our great joy we found her.

[1] A large tambourine.

'My blessings on ye that ye are come,' said she; 'I thought the night would never wear away, and I have been waiting here for some hours.'

'Is all prepared?' said I: 'is she ready?'

'Ay, that she is; I warrant the hours have gone as slowly with her as with me; and listen,' said the old woman, 'she has hit upon a rare device, which will mislead suspicion:' and she laughed heartily.

'For the love of Allah be quiet!' said I; 'were we heard as seen we are undone.'

'For that matter there is not much to apprehend, for this house on one side is deserted, and inside the wall, on the other, is nothing but the Nawab's garden, where no one stays at night.'

'Tell me then what her plan is; can we assist it?'

'Oh no,' said the woman; 'it is of her own invention, and a rare one too. I had just come to her, when she sent me out to get a bladder-full of blood. I could not make out what she wanted it for, but I went and bought it, though I had to get a kid killed on the pretence that the meat was suddenly required. Well, no sooner had I returned, than she poured some of it on her bed, crumpled and daubed the sheets, tore off pieces of her dress and scattered them about the room, also some of the beautiful hair from her head, which she also threw about, and in short made the place look as if she had been wounded, and there had been a scuffle to get her out. Ah, it was a rare device! and the best of it is, that a Nawab, who lives at a distance, and who has been trying to get this one to give her up, (and there has been much quarrelling between them on the subject,) will be suspected, and it will never be thought that she has run off on her own accord.'

'T'is wonderful,' said I; 'and, proverbial as is woman's wit, yet, by Allah! this is an instance which ought to be written in a book; but we are delaying here to no purpose.'

'Come then,' said the old woman; 'it is but a few steps further.'

We stationed ourselves under the window, in which there was a strong light burning; and the old woman giving a sharp but low cough, a figure was seen at the casement; it opened; it was she!

'Is he here?' said a low, sweet voice, which thrilled through me.

'Yes, lady, the humblest of your slaves is here, and prays you to be quick, for the sake of Allah; there is no time to lose.'

'I will be with you instantly,' replied she.

'Do so,' said I; 'but be quick, or we are lost.'

She withdrew from the window, and a few instants after re-appeared and let down a box and bundle. I unfastened them, and she drew up the sheet.

'Now,' said she, 'I come; but what is to be done with the sheet? I must fasten it inside ere I descend.'

'Leave that to me,' said I, 'only come down.'

A few instants more were occupied in fastening the cloth, and she then stepped out on the ledge. My heart beat audibly lest she should fall and hurt herself, and we should be observed; but I and Bhudrinath placed ourselves underneath, to catch her if she fell. It was however unnecessary, for she was on the ground in an instant, and I had pressed her to my heart!

'The rest must not be left undone,' said I; and ascending by the sheet, I entered the window. The room was a small one, and, by the hasty glance I threw around it, it appeared indeed as though there had been a scene of violence and bloodshed. Clothes were strewn about, the floor and bed were stained with blood, and pieces of torn apparel, lying here and there, gave to the whole the appearance of what was intended. I did not stay a moment, but unfastening the sheet, threw it down, and getting outside the window dropped to the ground. The shock hurt me considerably, but is was not the time for complaint. We held a hurried consultation as to which gate we should go out by, Bhudrinath again preferring the one by which we entered. This, however was overruled by all of us, and guided by the old woman we took our way to the other. We met not a soul in the lonely streets, and, by the blessing of Allah, on reaching the gate we found the wicket open, and the man who should have guarded it fast asleep, with his shield under his head and his sword by his side. Stealthily and slowly we passed by him, lest our footfall should awake him; and gaining the outside, we hurried along under the shadow of the walls until we gained the plain on which was our encampment.

When fairly within our guards, who were stationed round the spot, the fair being, who had hitherto clung to me, suddenly sunk down. To fetch water for her was the work of the moment, and after forcing some into her mouth she recovered.

'I was overcome with joy,' said she, throwing herself at my feet; 'and, indeed, if you knew the anxious suspense I have been in ever since last afternoon, you would believe me. At one time I was overjoyed at the prospect of deliverance from my hateful servitude, and again, as the night wore on, and I tried to count the hours, I sometimes thought that the time had passed, and that my preparations had been but a mockery. And now to find myself free and with you, ah! my lord, it is too much joy—my heart is like to burst.'

I raised her up and caressed her, and seating her under a tree, put my arm around her, and we sat in the lovely moonlight in silence; she could not speak, and I would not break the current of her thoughts, whatever they might be.

How long we sat there I cannot tell; we were interrupted by the old woman. 'This is no time for dalliance,' said she; 'my lady requires rest; and methinks, sir, were you to find means of getting us on before morning breaks, we should elude pursuit, and you could follow us.'

'You say truly,' said I, 'and it shall be cared for.'

Fortunately the cart of the sahoukar had not been sold, and though it was still laden with his effects, there was plenty of room in it for the two females.

I went to Bhudrinath, whom I found fast asleep after his night's work; when he was fully awakened, he seemed to comprehend that his services were again required.

'What, more work!' said he. 'Well, Meer Sahib, I am ready; what is it?'

'It is too bad for me to rouse you so soon,' said I, 'and to require you to go on with this matter; for Allah, who sees my heart, alone knows how grateful it is to you for your assistance this night.'

'Do not say so, my young friend,' cried he laughing; 'I would do anything for a little fun and excitement.'

'Why,' I rejoined, 'you must know the old woman has advised instant flight from hence; so you and some of the men must be ready to be off before daylight; and as I have prepared the old sahoukar's cart for her, you will be easily able to get eight or ten coss from hence tomorrow, and the same next day, when you must halt till we come up. Remember you are a Mussulman for the time, and she must be protected and screened as though she were the wife of one.'

'I understand,' said he, 'and I will do my trust faithfully.'

'I believe you,' I replied, 'and now for the road—which to take I am undecided. I have heard that two branch off from this to Hyderabad.'

'Stay,' said Bhudrinath; 'I think Peer Khan knows both. I will go and bring him; you know he is one of my set.'

He went, and returned with the man.

'I have explained all to him,' said he, 'and now hear what he has to say.'

'I beg you to represent,' said Peer Khan, 'that I know both roads, but not perfectly; still I should think what the Meer Sahib counsels the best, for the other is a sad lonely road, and few travellers go by it: as to the chance of being pursued, we must trust to our good Taqdir (destiny), which has brought us thus far without an accident, and Inshailah! will carry us on.'

'Well, Peer Khan,' said I, 'you must be the guide; you are the only person who knows anything about the road, and I can only say that if you are steady and faithful I will make you a handsome present when I overtake you at Nirmul.'

'May your condescension increase, Meer Sahib,' said he; 'but putting the enam out of the question, you know very well that there is not a man among us who would not give his blood tomorrow, or at any time he might be called upon, for you, but come, Bhudrinath, as we are to start soon, I had better get the men together, and be ready.'

I returned to the tent, where I found Zora and the old woman sitting covered up in their sheets, and warming themselves over a fire they had lighted. In a few words I told them of the necessity of flight, and added, 'Alas! I do not accompany you now; we have had a consultation on the subject, and have determined that for the sake of mutual safety, we must for the present separate. Allah, who sees my heart, knows that it will burn with anxiety and care while I am absent from you; for know, lady, that from the time I first beheld you in the durbar, my soul hath been consumed by your beauty, and as then I was plunged into despair at the thought that you never could be mine, so now is the excess of grief that I must part with you.'

She was silent for some time; but at last throwing back her veil, and again displaying her beautiful face to me, she put her hand into mine. 'I trust you,' said she; 'I have no fear now except for you; I will go without a murmur, for I see how necessary it is for us to separate; yet assure me, my beloved, that you will not be long away, and I am content.'

'I repeat,' said I, 'only two days at the furthest; we shall follow you tomorrow evening, or the next morning; and once that we are in motion I will push on till I overtake you, when we will wait for my father and the rest.'

'By what road do we travel?' asked the old woman.

'By Nirmul,' said I; 'it is out of the way, and we have therefore chosen it; it is not probable that the Nawab's people, if he sends any out, will take that direction.'

'You are right,' she replied; 'they will not. But I would give much to see him tomorrow, when the flight of this pretty bird is known.'

'What shall we care,' said I, 'except to laugh at his old beard? I will go into the town as soon as the alarm has spread, and you shall have all the news when we meet again.'

'Now bid me start,' said Bhudrinath, who then entered the tent, 'and I am off. For the present I am Jumal Khan, by which name inquire for me on the road.'

'May Allah protect you all! You have a precious charge, my friend,' said I, 'and would that I could even now take your place.'

The women were soon ready, and I saw them comfortably settled in their vehicle.

'Now I am off,' cried Bhudrinath: 'drive on the cart; and do some of you fellows keep about it, as though it were a decent man's zenana.'

'Allah Hafiz!' said I, 'and may the Prophet guide you safely!' They went on; I stood watching them until a turn in the road hid them from my sight, and I betook myself to my tent, where throwing myself down, sleep soon came over me.

I was awakened by my father, who came into the tent where I was lying; he seemed angry with me for having been out all night, as he said, on some unprofitable if not unworthy business; 'but,' said he, 'it is time for the morning prayer, and after that I will hear what you have been about.' I accompanied him to the skirts of our camp, where, spreading our carpets, we watched for the blush of dawn to go through the usual forms; when they were over, he seated himself and desired to hear what I had done: I fear me no good,' said he, 'but tell me.'

So I recounted the events of the night, and was prepared for a severe lecture, and a great deal of advice and reproof. I was for once agreeably disappointed; instead of being angry, he laughed heartily at the whole affair, and applauded our arrangements in having sent Zora out of the way.

The sun was barely risen, when there arose a noise from the town, and it was plain enough to us that the discovery had taken place. The whole place was in a ferment; people hurried out of the gates and collected into groups, and by the pointing to our camp, and their gesticulations, we were obviously the suspected persons; and, as we had anticipated, about twenty horse and some foot-soldiers issued from the gate nearest to us, and came directly towards us. They surrounded our little camp, and one or two who appeared the leaders of the party rode up, and in an authoritative manner demanded to see our leader.

I had previously arranged with my father that he was to continue to support his character as a merchant, and to put me forward as the jemadar of the party; and as he knew that I had appeared in the character at the Nawab's durbar, and supported it well, he had readily acceded to my request.

'You see the leader,' said I, 'in my poor person; and what may be the demands of the Nawab Sahib so early? is there any thing his poor servant can do to prove how much he is impressed with the kind treatment he has received?'

'You must be content to be our prisoner,' said the man haughtily, 'until your camp is searched; a strange event has happened, and you are suspected.'

'Of what?' said I, appearing thunderstruck; 'of what can I be suspected? But the camp is before you sirs; by all means search it. Perhaps,' said I bitterly, 'your town has been robbed, and it is not wonderful that persons of respectability should be suspected in this unmannerly country.'

'Peace!' cried the man, 'we must do our duty; and I for one, for the sake of appearances, should be glad to find that you had not requited the Nawab's hospitality with treachery.'

'I am dumb,' said I, 'notwithstanding that I am in utter astonishment at your words; but by all means search the place, and afterwards perhaps you will in kindness unravel this mystery to me.'

He rode with me to my tent, and dismounting entered it with me, followed by two or three of his men. There was nothing in it but the carpet and mattress on which I had slept, a few cooking utensils, and some of the bales of plunder piled up at the further end.

'She is not here,' said Azim Khan, the leader of the Nawab's party, 'let us go to the other tent.'

I accompanied them, and making a salaam to my father, told him that the Nawab's people wished to search his tent, as they had done mine, and added, 'Do not oppose them, lest the Nawab should in truth see reason to suspect us.'

'Certainly not,' said my father; 'here is the tent, and I am the Nawab's slave; it is not likely that an old man like me should have women concealed here.'

So his tent was searched as mine had been, and afterwards the temporary screens of the men; but nothing was found, and the party were evidently disappointed.

'We are on the wrong track, and I told you so,' said Azim Khan to the leader; 'depend upon it, as I told the Nawab, it is that rascal Sheffi Khan's work: we all know him to be in the employ of the Hakim of Nursi, who wanted to get the girl, and we had better be after him than wasting our time here.'

'A girl!' cried I; 'truly this is most wonderful; for the sake of Allah satisfy my curiosity; what is all this about? By your head,' said I to the leader, 'but that it seems a serious matter, I feel much tempted to laugh at the idea of my poor camp being searched for a girl—some slave, I presume, who has run away or been carried off by her lover; say, Sahib, what has happened?'

'Why, it is no laughing matter to us, whatever it may be to you,' said the leader; 'send your men out of hearing, and you shall have the whole story.'

'Away with you!' cried I to our men, who had crowded round; 'this is no tale for your ears.'

'The affair is this,' said the man: 'until last night, there was in the zenana of the Nawab a dancing-girl of surpassing beauty and accomplishments; but early this morning her apartment was found empty, marks of violence everywhere about it, blood on the sheets of her bed, and some of her hair and portions of her clothes strewn about the room. There was no alarm in the night, the gates of the town were closed and guarded as usual, and it seems some work of the Shaitan that this should have taken place, and that we should have had dirt thrown on our beards without knowing by whom. There is the Nawab raving and swearing like a madman, his zenana is all in confusion; and, what is worst of all, he threatens to discharge every one of us, without we either bring back the girl or get him intelligence of her within three days.'

'Protection of Allah!' cried both I and my father, 'this is most extraordinary. And have you no suspicion who has insulted you in this manner?'

'Why,' said the man, 'you were the first suspected, as being strangers and a large party, and we were desired to search your camp: but here we find nothing but bales of goods: and indeed you are not likely persons to have carried her off, for I question whether you ever saw her.'

'I dare say,' said I, 'she was one of the women who were in the durbar the other night, when I paid a visit to the Nawab.'

'Very likely,' he returned; 'were those you saw good-looking?'

'They were both so,' said I: 'one was tall and fair, the other was shorter and not so fair, but very handsome.'

'That was the girl,' said the man; 'I have seen her myself once or twice, when I could get inside of a night. But I am wasting my time here, and must return; you may depend upon my fully exonerating you from any suspicion in the matter.'

'Your favourable opinion,' said I, 'will no doubt have its due weight: and I pray you to carry our condolence to the Nawab, and say that if we have permission we will wait on him to express it.'

'I will deliver your message,' said he; 'but I think you will not be admitted, as really he is in great grief, more on account of the insult, perhaps, than the loss of the girl. I take my leave.'

He saluted us and rode off; and not long after a servant of the Nawab came, with a civil message and some fruit, to say that his master regretted he could not see us, and was sorry that he had been under the necessity of searching our camp. We dismissed him with a present, and reiterated our condolences, which he promised to deliver. 'And now,' said I to my father, 'this is no place for us longer; we must be off. What say you to a march in the afternoon?'

'It is good,' said he; 'we will go: tell the men to be prepared.'

CHAPTER X

We were on our way towards Nirmul in the afternoon, and as we had heard no more of the Nawab and his distress, we were relieved from our anxiety; but I was in great dread the whole time we remained at the town after the Nawab's people had left us, lest some chance should open to them a clue to detect us. The bhutteara might possibly reveal what he knew of our proceedings; for although he knew not our object, still our remaining with him for so short a time, (as he must have formed a notion that we were after some woman) coupled with the disappearance of Zora, might have led him to suppose, and very naturally so, that we had carried her off. Fortunately however no ill effects did ensue, and on the third day after leaving Oomerkhér we reached Nirmul.

As I entered the town I saw Bhudrinath in a shop, sitting with his back to the street, in conversation with a decent-looking man, a Mussulman by his appearance. He did not observe me, but on my calling out his assumed name he hastily rose, and assisting me to dismount embraced me cordially.

'Is she safe?' I asked in a low tone, so as not to be overheard by his acquaintance.

'She is,' he replied; 'you have nothing to fear; and she is all impatience to behold you again.'

Sahib, I did not lose an instant in again beholding my beloved, and pressing her once more to my heart. She was more lovely than ever; and after some fond chidings for my delay, and a relation of all the anxiety she had suffered in my absence, and the fatigues of her journey, we gave ourselves up to that voluptuous feeling of joy and security, which those only know who have loved and been separated from each other under circumstances of doubt or danger. After passing some time with her I rejoined Bhudrinath.

'Who was the man you were conversing with when I came up?' I asked.

'Why,' said he, 'from what I have picked up as yet, I suspect he has urgent reasons for getting away from hence as fast as he can; in other words, he has been helping himself to more than he ought in some revenue affair, and his safety depends upon flight. I told him I expected you and your party, and that he would have a good opportunity of getting away if he chose to mix with us. You see,' added Bhudrinath, 'that when once I have fixed my eye upon any one, it is against my principles to let him escape me;

now, as this is the case, we must have that man—first, because of my principles, as I said, and secondly because of the money which most assuredly he has in his possession: do you comprehend?'

'Perfectly,' said I laughing; 'your argument is an admirable one; therefore I will second your endeavours with all my heart. How shall we proceed?'

'Why,' said Bhudrinath, 'that is a somewhat difficult matter to determine, for I do not know where the fellow lives; but he promised to be with me soon, and I dare say he will not be long away.'

'We must spread the carpet of patience,' said I, 'and sit on it, I suppose, till he makes his appearance; meanwhile I see no reason why I should not eat.'

Well, Sahib, I went inside the purda, where my well-dressed meal awaited me, and Zora and I had our fingers very soon buried in a smoking dish of kicheree and a very good curry. While I was thus employed, I heard the usual salutation pass between Bhudrinath and his acquaintance, and when I had satisfied the cravings within me, which had been grievous to bear, I joined them.

'This is my brother, of whom I have spoken to you,' said Bhudrinath, presenting me to him; 'he has now, as you see, overtaken me, and we shall journey on together. All his men are encamped outside the town, but as he is more comfortable with me, you see him here.'

We exchanged salutations, and, by way of drawing him to the subject, I asked Bhudrinath when we should start.

'I cannot delay,' said I; 'that detention at Nursi was most inconvenient, and but for that we should have been far on the road by this time.'

The man stared at me, and at last said to Bhudrinath, 'Surely you must be joking when you say this gentleman is your brother; why, you are much older, and your features do not resemble in the least.'

'We are not real brothers,' he replied, 'but cousins; you know that cousins usually call themselves brothers.'

'But how comes it,' said he, 'that he is the jemadar of your men, and not you, who are the eldest?'

'Why, it is a long story, and would not interest you,' said Bhudrinath; 'suffice it to say, that he is the son of the elder branch, who married long after my father, having lost his first wife; so, by the consent of the family and my own, he was declared leader, though he must confess I am his adviser.'

I pretended to be ashamed of my dignity, and allowed, though I was nominally superior, yet that I could not get on at all without my *cousin*.'

'Well,' said the man, 'you have curious customs in your country, but in every one they differ. Here your relative situations would be reversed; and so I suppose I must treat with you, Jemadar Sahib; I dare say your cousin has told you all about me.'

'He has,' said I, 'at least as much as you have told him; but we are both present, and what you say to one equally concerns the other; so I pray you speak on without reservation.'

'I will not then recur to the past,' said the man; 'suffice it to say, that I have every reason to wish to get out of this place, as far as Hyderabad; there I shall be secure from my enemies. I therefore propose to accompany you, if you will guarantee me protection and concealment on the road.'

'We are ready to do that,' said I; 'but you will allow we shall run some risk; for, besides protection and concealment upon the road, we must defend you if necessary; and all this requires some recompense.'

'True, and I am in no condition to drive a bargain, therefore you must name your own terms.'

'You are liberal, I see,' I rejoined, 'and you shall find us to be so also. Perhaps one hundred and fifty rupees will not be thought by you exorbitant?'

'It is not; half I will pay you now, and the other half when we arrive.'

'Agreed,' said I, 'it is satisfactory; and now say how you intend to travel. If I have permission, I would advise a mode which would be certain to escape detection.'

'What is it?' cried he eagerly.

'That you should hire or buy a cart, and travel in it, at any rate for a few marches; my brother has his zenana with him, and you could not be discovered; no one would dare to search a cart which held females.'

'By Allah it is a rare plan!' said the man; 'I wonder it never entered into my head. Yet cart I have none; and how to get one without giving a clue to my flight—'

'Do not distress yourself about it,' said Bhudrinath; 'furnish us with the money—about one hundred rupees will be enough—and I will go and purchase one, and account to you for whatever may be over.'

'And my camels, and horses, and servants,' said the man, 'what can be done with them?'

'How many of them are there?' I asked.

'There are two camels and two horses; and I have three or four servants, whom I wish to accompany me.'

'Then send them all to our camp at night,' said I; 'they will not be seen, and if necessary they can be sent on a march.'

'You are ready-witted people,' cried he, 'and what has cost me days and nights of anxiety, you have settled satisfactorily in a few moments. Now I clearly see there is no time to be lost; and I go to bring the money, and give directions to my people.'

So he left us.

'Well done,' cried Bhudrinath to me, 'you fairly took the words out of my mouth, and I think the fish has taken the bait.'

'I think so too,' said I; 'the fellow may be a very sharp revenue-collector, but he is no match for you and me; and you see he is a greater man than we thought for, as he speaks of his horses, camels, and servants: no doubt we shall have a good round sum from him.'

I hurried to my father, leaving Bhudrinath to manage everything his own way if I should not return in time to meet the man we expected.

He was surprised to see me, and exclaimed, 'I did not think you would have left your adored so soon; to what am I indebted for this early visit?'

'Nay,' said I, 'father, do not mention her; it sounds like banter, and I have other work in hand just now than attending even to Zora.'

'Ay, indeed! and now tell me, my son, what thou hast in view.'

'Why,' said I, 'Bhudrinath and I have secured a man in the town, who promises to be almost as good a prize as either we have had before; and when you see two horses, some camels, and servants come into your camp this evening, do you allow them to remain, and start them off as early as may be tomorrow morning towards Hyderabad.'

'I will do as you wish,' said my father; 'but tell me, Ameer Ali, what is this you are about? Are you sure there is no risk, no danger?'

'As far as I can see there is not; but hear what has been done already, and then judge whether the matter ought to be persevered in or not. If you do not like it we will drop it at once.' So I told him all.

'You are both of you doing your work well, and I approve of it greatly,' said the old man; 'I will on my part receive the camels, &c., and will send on a party of gravediggers this very night. We will set off tomorrow night or early the next morning.'

Bhudrinath was absent when I reached the house in the town and I had to wait a long time for his return, which was not till near evening; however, I had the society I best loved, and the hours fled quickly. I was nevertheless overjoyed to see him return with a cart and two fine bullocks. He had purchased the whole from a set of dancing-girls, and the cart was fitted with curtains, in the manner of those used to carry women.

When it was brought up to the house he dismissed the driver with a small present.

'There,' said Bhudrinath, 'is ninety-five rupees' worth, and the concern is cheap enough; our only care is now for the person who is to ride in it.'

'Where is he?' said I; 'are you sure of him?'

'As sure,' said Bhudrinath, 'as I ever was of any one; he is now gone to take leave of the Hakim of the place, and will pretend he has done all his business. He has sent his camels and people to the camp, and strict orders to obey whoever there may be there in authority, and I myself directed them to go to your father and receive instructions from him. The man himself will be here at nightfall.'

'Inshallah!' cried I, 'truly may we say we are fortunate; nothing has gone wrong.'

Just as we had completed our preparations our friend came, and by this time it had become quite dark, so that he joined us unobserved; and as we had sent word to him that the cart had been purchased, he brought with him what we supposed to be his valuables; one of his servants carried the bundle, which appeared carefully tied up in waxed cloths, and his hookah, and his bedding.

'Are you sure you have omitted nothing?' he asked.

'Certain,' said I; 'everything is ready. I have been to the gate, and have told the guard that we have a long march before us and will pass out a little after midnight with two carts and our people.'

'Well,' said he, 'then here is your money'; and he counted out seventy-five rupees to me.

'Now we have nothing to desire,' said I, 'but to be informed of your name, which hitherto you have not told us.'

'Call me Kumal Khan for the present,' he replied; 'you shall know my real name at Hyderabad.'

'As you will,' said I; 'doubtless you have good reasons for not discovering yourself to us. Meanwhile, as you say, Kumal Khan will do as well as any other name: therefore, Khan Sahib, I think the sooner we take some rest, the more we shall be refreshed for our journey tomorrow.'

'I can lie down anywhere,' said he; 'I dare say I shall sleep moreover, which my care and anxiety have prevented my doing for some nights past.'

He spread his carpet and covered himself up. Bhudrinath followed his example, and in a short time they were both asleep, as their deep breathing testified.

Strange destiny, I thought; there lies the man who has but a few hours to live, side by side in peaceful slumber with one who will be actively employed in his destruction. A few hours and their situations will be changed, oh, how changed! one to lie senseless in the earth, the other to live and breathe, and to tax his wits to gain fresh victims. 'Ya, Allah!' I exclaimed involuntarily, 'thy purposes are inscrutable!'

We were roused at the time appointed by the men, and our preparations for departure quickly completed. I saw Zora safely deposited in her cart, as also her old attendant, next Kumal Khan in his; and putting myself at the head of the party, we were soon beyond the gates of the town and at the encampment. Here I sent on Zora's cart, and desired one of the men to come back and give us due notice should he meet the Tillaees, or scouts, on the road. I then sought out my father, and inquired whether he had allotted bhuttotes and shumsheas (persons to hold the hands) to the servants and grooms.

'I have settled everything,' he replied, 'and given every man his instructions: there will be no difficulty if all is ready before us. But are you sure that Kumal Khan, as you call him, is not armed?'

'He has a sword,' said I, 'but what of that? Bhudrinath and I will easily manage him, and he will not be on his guard.'

'Then keep well behind,' said my father; 'if there is any scuffle he will not hear it, and I will send a man back to you when we meet the first of the scouts. You can then do as you please; either bring him on, or deal with him there, as you like.'

'Very good,' said I; 'we will be guided by circumstances.'

I saw with secret exultation how beautifully everything had been arranged, as our men and our acquaintance's servants passed me. To every one of them was attached one of the most expert bhuttotes, with two others to assist if necessary: yet they disposed themselves so carelessly that suspicion was out of the question. Each one as he passed threw a look of intelligence towards me, as much as to say, 'here is work we delight in;' and I felt truly excited as the whole band was before me, their arms glancing brightly in the moonbeams.

This, thought I, is the joy my father told me of; and what could raise such feelings within me in the common plodding pursuits of life? When these fellows are but my own, then shall the name of Ameer Ali be dreaded and feared; men shall wonder at it: many a timid woman's heart shall beat as she listens to stories of me, and allows her fancy to picture to her him of whom she hears such deeds of daring bravery. 'Yes,' cried I aloud, for I could not control myself, 'the time will come, ay, and soon: the present is poor work to what I have thought of, and will put into execution!'

The voice of Bhudrinath recalled my ideas. 'In the name of Narayun and all the gods,' said he, 'what are you talking about? Come, we wait for you.'

I urged my horse down the bank, and was with him in an instant. Kumal Khan put his head out of the curtains, and asked if we had assembled our men.

'Yes,' said I, 'they are all before us, except my cousin, myself, and a few of our attendants, who will stay round you.'

'That is right,' said he; 'I shall sleep, if this vile jolting will let me. Oh that I were on my horse, instead of being cooped up in this cart!'

'Patience,' said Bhudrinath; 'I dare say you will soon be out of it again.'

'That I shall, my friend,' said he, 'when I dare show myself;' and so saying he shut the curtains.

Bhudrinath and I rode on some time in silence: at last we reached a rising ground, which apparently led down to the bed of a river, for I thought I saw the water glistening in the moon's rays. The jungle was thicker than before, and I involuntarily turned to Bhudrinath.

'Surely this is the spot,' cried I; 'we must wait for the cart;' for we had preceded it a long way.

'We had better do so,' he replied; 'it will soon be up.'

We had just heard the rumbling sound of the wheels, when the man I had sent on with it came up to us.

'What news?' I asked; 'is all prepared?'

'By this time it is,' said the man; 'when I met the first scout I returned to tell you: they have fixed on a beautiful spot, and I doubt not that the band are waiting for you, having done their share of the night's adventure.'

'Well,' said I, 'we don't want you here, so go on again.' But he begged hard to remain, and I allowed him.

As Kumal Khan passed us, Bhudrinath gave the driver the signal; he nodded his head in compliance: and telling the men who were to hold our horses to be near and in readiness, we got behind the cart, and followed it down the descent. About half-way down, the bank of the road sloped into it, and rose into a small eminence. I marked the place, and saw that the driver had done the same: the cart gradually diverged from the track; one wheel went up the bank; it leaned fearfully over, and at last came down with a terrible crash.

We were off our horses in an instant, and ran up: Kumal Khan was groaning beneath it.

We lifted it up and got him out; but he was either so frightened or hurt he could not speak. At last he recovered; and the first words he uttered were a volley of abuse at the driver.

'Look!' cried he; 'a smooth road, not a stone or a peeble, and yet that son of a base mother must needs drive up yonder bank, and has nearly killed me.'

'He shall be well punished for his carelessness,' said I; 'but are you hurt, Khan?'

'My right arm is very painful,' said he holding it; 'and I wish to Allah I had a horse to ride, instead of going further in that concern.'

'It cannot now be helped,' said Bhudrinath; 'and it is well none of your bones were broken. We will keep nearer you in future, and see that the fellow drives more carefully.'

The cart had been by this time set fairly in the road again, and Kumal Khan's mattress and pillow arranged. As he turned away from us, and laid hold of one of the posts of the curtains, and had his foot on the wheel to get in, I threw the handkerchief round his neck.

'What—what is this?' was all that escaped him; the rest was an indistinct gurgling in his throat for an instant. The wrench I gave to his neck must have extinguished life, for he relaxed his hold of the post, and fell to the ground without sense or motion.

'Neatly and cleverly done!' cried Bhudrinath; 'I could not have managed it better myself; you see he does not stir—he is dead enough. Now Meer Sahib, believe that a man can be killed before he touches the ground.'

'I must see you do it,' said I; 'this fellow held on by the cart for some moments. But come,' I added to the men, 'lift the body into the cart, we have no time to lose.' They bundled it in, and we set off as rapidly as the bullocks could trot.

'What if he should revive with this jolting?' said I to Bhudrinath.

'Never fear,' he replied; 'if he does, he will only have to be killed over again; but depend upon it he is dead enough; no man ever survived the wrench you gave him—his neck is broken. The old guru has taught you well, I see plainly.'

'I own I feel, more confidence every time I do it,' said I; 'and I should not care if even now I had one or two more fellows to try my hand upon.'

'Nay,' said Bhudrinath laughing, 'rest you content with what we have done. See, we are at the bhil, and yonder is the whole band collected.'

We rode up to the spot, and the first inquiry was from my father: 'Have you brought him?'

'Yes,' said I; 'the earth that held him is in the cart.'

'Did he do it?' he eagerly asked of Bhudrinath, and pointed to me.

'Ay, did he,' he replied, 'and most properly too: he had him all to himself; I did not interfere.'

'Alhumd-ul-illa!' cried my father; 'he is a worthy son. Come,' continued he to all the men, 'do not loiter here, but make the best of your way to the river-side; we will follow, and I dare say overtake you.'

Seeing there was no more to be done, I pushed on to the river, the Godavery, and finding that all had been ferried over, I urged on my horse to overtake Zora's cart; for I knew not what she would think of my absence, nor how I could well account to her for it satisfactorily; but I trusted to chance to frame some excuse. I passed the men, who were straggling along in parties of ten or twelve; but still I did not see the cart, though I had desired those who were in charge of it not to drive fast. I became anxious, and urged my horse into a gallop.

Well it was that I did so, for when I had proceeded some distance I heard a confused clamour before me. Could she have been attacked by thieves? was my instant thought. It was probable; for the road was narrow and the jungle thick on both sides, and seeing the few men with the cart, thieves might have surprised them. I drew my sword, to be prepared, as the noise and screams seemed to increase, and in a few moments more arrived at the spot. There indeed was a scene of violence! the moon was still shining brightly, and I could see all before me.

The cart was surrounded by the five or six men I had sent on with it, and who were defending their charge bravely: two of the robbers, as I supposed, were stretched on the ground; the rest were aiming cuts at my men, which they parried; but just as I got up, one of my men fell, and the rest looked exhausted. I suspect neither party observed my arrival, so intent were they on their own proceedings, and I could see that my cry of 'Bismillah!' accompanied by a cut which struck down one of the robbers, was as startling to them as unexpected; while my faithful men, who now saw me plainly, set up a shout, and attacked their opposers with renewed spirit.

The scuffle lasted only a few moments longer: throwing myself from my horse, I drew my pistol from my girdle, and discharged it at a thief who was coming up to me with his sword uplifted: the ball passed through his body, and he fell. On this the rest of the band turned and fled. We pursued them for a short distance, and secured a youth who was one of them; the rest got clear off.

CHAPTER XI

WHEN we returned to the cart, my first business was to soothe my poor Zora, whose screams, added to those of the old attendant, and the oaths, execrations, and shouts of the contending parties, had made a din which defies description. I found her terribly alarmed of course, but the rascals had not been suffered to approach her; and when she was assured by me that I should not again quit her side, she was calm, and gave me a history of the attack; which was, that as they were going along, the thieves began to pelt them with stones from the bushes on the sides of the road; and at last, perhaps not thinking them armed, rushed from their concealment, and the fight began.

The wounded thief was unable to walk, so he was put into the cart with the dead body; the boy's arms were tied behind his back, and a cord passed round his neck which I tied to my own saddle. Leaving twenty men to guard the wounded, we then quickly proceeded.

We arrived at a large village before the sun rose; but the villagers were up, and the herds of cattle were pouring out of the gates on their way to the pastures. We desired the men to take up the encampment under some tamarind trees, and my father, myself, and Bhudrinath went to the gates, and desired to see the Patel or whoever might be the chief authority.

After waiting a long time we were told that the Aumil expected us, and were ushered into his house, where he sat in a verandah, apparently used by him generally to transact business in. He was a Hindu, a Khayet by caste, and, as those persons usually are, was polite and courteous in his manners. My father was spokesman on this occasion, and after introducing himself as a merchant, and us as leaders of the men who escorted him—the old Oomerkhér story—he told him of the attack which had been made on us, of which however he seemed for a time to be perfectly incredulous.

'Impossible!' said he; 'there has not been a highway robbery, or an attempt at one, for years, ever since some notorious thieves were caught and beheaded here: you must be under some mistake.'

'You have not mentioned our wounded men, and that several of the thieves have been killed by us,' said I to my father: 'perhaps this worthy gentleman will believe us when he sees them, or finds the bodies of the rascals; and again, you forget that two of them are in our custody.'

'Indeed!' cried the Aumil, 'that alters the case; but the truth of the matter is, that so many travellers beg for escorts from village to village, and set forth their having been threatened between here and Nirmul, that I am become difficult to satisfy, or to be persuaded that any danger has existed.'

'We require no escort,' said my father; 'we are strong enough to take care of ourselves, having, as you have heard, beaten off these thieves; all we want is a few men to bring up our wounded, and justice done on the rascals we have caught.'

'It would be well for us,' said Mohun Lall, 'if all travellers were to defend themselves like you; we should have but few thieves in the country, for they would find theirs a losing trade. But I think you said you had one of them unhurt; where is he? we may perhaps get something out of him.'

I sent for the lad, and he was questioned for some time about the gang, and where it was probable they had gone; but he would not answer a word, and the man who was interpreting for us gave up questioning him in despair.

'He will not say a word in this manner,' said Bhudrinath; 'give him the lash. I dare say that will make him speak.'

'True,' said Mohun Lall; 'I was going to send for a korla[1];' and he called to one of his men to bring one.

The thief shuddered as he saw it, and was again asked if he would confess; but he remained silent.

'Throw him down,' cried Mohun Lall, 'and cut the skin from his back.'

In an instant he was thrown with his face to the ground, and the lash, wielded by a stout fellow, brought blood at almost every stroke: but in vain: he would not speak a word— not even a cry for mercy.

'This is of no use either,' said one of the men who held him; get a bag full of ashes. I'll warrant he speaks fast enough when that is put over his face.'

A leather bag, such as is used to give grain to horses, was filled with burning-hot ashes, and brought. It was tied over his mouth, and at the same time he received some hard thumps on his back to force him to breathe. This apparently had the desired effect; for after a short time, during which the torture must have been great, he muttered something and the bag was withdrawn.

'You think to make me confess,' said the rascal as soon as he could speak, 'but it is in vain. I know well where my people are gone, and I curse the authors of their discomforture;' and he poured a torrent of abuse on me. 'Yes,' continued he, pointing to me, 'it was you who struck down my father, and as he is dead

[1] A whip.

I want no more than to die also; you may hang me as soon as you please.'

'Ha!' said Mohun Lall, 'I had forgotten him; let him be brought.'

I had left the fellow badly wounded, but did not think there was any danger of his life. When he arrived, however, carried on a bed, it was evident he was dying; he scarcely breathed, and the rattle was in his throat: we did not therefore trouble ourselves further about him, but endeavoured to make the son confess; the whip and hot ashes were both resorted to again without effect, and all our endeavours only produced fresh execretions and abuse.

'There is no bearing this any longer,' cried Mohun Lall; 'the fellow must be hung. I know these rascals, and were we to keep him for a year we should never get a word of intelligence out of him, so there is no use in delay.'

'As you will,' said my father; 'perhaps he will confess when the rope is round his neck.'

'We shall see,' replied Mohun Lall; 'but I do not think it. Send for the Mangs.'

These wretches, everywhere the vilest of mankind, were soon present, and the thief was made over to them.

'You see,' said Mohun Lall to him, 'you have no chance of escape; will you now confess and take service with me? I will protect you.'

The fellow hesitated, looked at his father, and appeared irresolute; but a second glance at his expiring parent again rallied him.

'Not for all the wealth you could give me,' cried he, drawing himself up and looking at us proudly. 'Had *he* been alive, and in your power, I might have taken your service; but you could not protect me now, and I would rather die by the hands of your people than by those of my associates, from whom I could not escape.'

'Away with him!' cried Mohun Lall to the Mangs; 'see that you do your work properly.'

'And our mamool (customary present), Maharaj, you must not forget that.'

'No, no,' cried he; 'but away with ye; I am polluted by your presence; go to the Kotwal after you have done, and he will have received orders to give you a sheep and as much liquor as will make you all drunk.'

The fellows made many most profound salaams, and went off with their wretched companion.'

'Where will they hang him?' said I; 'I should like to see him again, and try if I can't persuade him to live to become a decent fellow.'

'Somewhere beyond the gate,' said Mohun Lall: 'I do not know the place myself, but my people will show you. You will do little good however I am afraid; and after all, why should you trouble yourself about him?'

'It is no trouble,' I replied, 'I have simply a curiosity upon the subject, and will see the last of him.'

'I will accompany you,' said Bhudrinath; and we took our leave and followed the executioners.

About an arrow's flight from the gate were two scraggy, gnarled, and almost leafless neem-trees, beneath which stood the group we sought, and round them all the urchins and idle men of the village. We hastened up to them, and found that everything was prepared: a rope with a noose in it hung over a branch, and one of the Mangs was coolly sharpening a knife upon an old stone idol which lay beneath the tree—for what purpose I could not make out; however my business was not with them, but with the wretch who was so near his death. He had seen us approach, and I thought was urging the Mangs to dispatch him before we came up; but they did not do so, as they imagined we brought some other orders to them. I addressed the robber: 'Will you not live?' said I: 'so young as you are, have you no love of life? I now again promise you protection if you will confess, as you have been asked to do before.'

'Let the cords be somewhat loosened which bind my arms,' said the robber, 'and I will speak to you; at present I am in too much pain to talk.'

'Loosen them,' said I to the Mangs; 'and one of you hold the rope in case he attempts to escape.'

The robber smiled faintly at what I said, and continued. 'You have taken an interest in me, and although I owe my present condition to you, yet sooner or later I should have come to the same end, or fallen by some shot or sword-cut; therefore I forgive you my death. But again I repeat I have no wish to live; nor, miserable as I am, can you suppose I would purchase my life by an act of treachery to my companions. Had my father lived, and remained in Mohun Lall's power, I would have promised anything; but he is dead; my uncle too fell by the hands of one of your men in the attack on your cart; and whom have I left in this world to care for that I should live? One day has seen the end of my family; and it was our fate. Yet bear to Mohun Lall my hate, and the curses of a dying man. It is he who has killed me, and for this he will have to pay a fearful retribution. And now,' said he turning to the Mangs, 'do your horrible office; I have no more to say.'

I was going to speak again, but Bhudrinath stopped me.

'What is the use?' said he; 'the fellow is obstinate, and, depend upon it, if he were spared, it would only be to lead good men into danger, if not into destruction: let him die, he deserves it.'

The Mangs looked to me for orders, and I told them to proceed: it was clearly of no use to delay. The robber was again tightly pinioned and thrown on the ground, and the Mang who held the knife he had been sharpening, dexterously cut both sinews of his legs close above the heel; he was then raised up, the noose put round his neck, and in another instant he was pulled up to the branch and struggling in his death agony.

'Pah!' said Bhudrinath, turning away, 'it makes me sick; what a contrast this is to our work, where he who is to die scarcely knows that the handkerchief is about his neck before he is a dead man!'

'You say truly,' said I; 'we have the advantage; but these Mangs are miserable, outcast wretches. What else could you expect from them? Now let us go to the camp; my father will be there, and we will see what this Kumal Khan had with him.'

When we arrived, we found that all his baggage had been examined. There were two boxes, the contents of which we looked to see with some impatience. One was nearly filled with papers relating to his business as a revenue-collector, and these were burned as fast as they could be looked over by me. In the bottom, however, was a bag filled with gold, which Bhudrinath held up in triumph.

'This is something better than musty paper,' said he, putting it on one side; 'now for the other box.'

It was broken open, and proved a rich prize indeed. After the clothes with which the top was covered had been removed, a number of bars of silver met our expecting eyes.

The box was not, however, emptied, and under another layer of clothes were ten bars of gold of the same size as the silver ones.

'Here is the cream of the matter,' cried Bhudrinath as he took up the first; 'Allah knows how much there is! but it is clear the man was worth killing; and finely indeed must he have plundered the unfortunate cultivators.'

The bars of gold and silver were made over to my father, to be placed among the other plunder we had got; and all that now remained to be seen were the clothes he had worn and his waist-bag. There was not, however, much in it.

'Stay,' said Bhudrinath, 'here is another bundle, which was in the humeanah.'

I took it from him, and unrolled fold after fold of clean paper. 'Why, there is nothing here,' said I; 'I suppose he kept this to write on.'

'Go on to the end, nevertheless,' said my father; 'let us see all.'

After removing three more folds I came to another small packet, which was tied up with thread. 'Here is something at last,' said I, breaking it open: 'bills of exchange, in the name of the blessed Prophet! and, I doubt not, of value too. Have we any one who can make them out?'

'I cannot read the writing,' said Bhudrinath, 'but I can make out the figures if they are not written in Persian.'

'Ah, no,' said I, 'they are Nagri or Gujeratti; so try your skill.'

'This,' said Bhudrinath, after examining one, 'is for two thousand rupees: see, these are the figures.'

'I dare say you are right,' said I, handing the rest to him; 'what are these for?'

'Here is a second for four hundred.'

'Not much,' said my father; 'but go on.'

'The third is for—let me see again,' said Bhudrinath: 'ah, I am right, it is for two thousand two hundred; and the last is for two hundred and forty.'

'That is, let me see,' said I, 'four thousand eight hundred and forty. Well, we have got a good prize.'

'Yes!' cried my father, 'we should be well off if they were worth anything to us; but they are no better than the waste paper we have burned.'

'How?' said I; 'we should get the money if we presented them, surely.'

'You do not reflect,' said my father, 'that if we did so, it would lead to our detection in this matter: so destroy them.'

'Indeed,' said I, 'I will not, but will keep them for stolen money; and I dare say were we to affect to be this Kumal Khan's agents, we might get the amount.'

'As you will,' said my father; 'but remember you take no steps about them without consulting me.'

So I kept them, and had afterwards reason to be glad that I had done so.

The next morning we rose before day: the omens were consulted, and proved favourable, and all prepared for prosecuting our march. We were soon ready, and I stationed myself near Zora's cart, which was in front.

On the fifth morning after this we were to reach Hyderabad: it was estimated as seven coss distant, so we did not start so soon as usual; we wished to reach it when the day was well advanced, in order to attract as little attention as possible, for our numbers were considerable. We therefore divided into three parties, one under my father, one under myself, and the other under Surfuraz Khan, a friend of my father whom we had met on the road, and who with his men had been admitted into our company; and we agreed to meet again in the karwan, which was the usual resort of all travellers, and where we were told we should find accommodation in the serais which were used by them. Mine was the first division to move, and my father said he should remain with the baggage, and bring it leisurely along, as he should have to pay the usual duties upon the property we had secured, at the various toll-houses.

Accordingly at full daylight we set out. It was a lovely morning, cold, yet not so cold as in our own country, where the frost is often seen on the ground, and the grass feels crisp under the foot of the traveller until the sun rises; still a good shawl was a welcome addition to my usual clothing.

We passed the village of Ulwal, its white pagoda peeping from among groves of tamarind and mango trees, and its large tank now glistening in the rays of the sun; and pursuing our way, we saw, on passing a ridge of rocks, the camp of the army at the far-famed Hussain Sagor, or, as it is more often called, Secunderabad. The tents of the English force glittered in the bright sun, and behind them lay a vast sheet of blue water.

We had heard much of this lake from many persons on our journey, and as we passed it a strong breeze had arisen, and the surface was curled into a thousand waves, whose white crests as they broke sparkled like diamonds, and threw their spray into our faces as they dashed against the stonework of the embankment. We stood a long time gazing upon the beautiful prospect, so new to us all, and wondering whether the sea, of which we had heard so much, could be anything like what was before us. I have since then, Sahib, twice seen the sea; I need not attempt to describe it, for you have sailed over it; but when I saw it first, methought I could have fallen down and worshipped it, it appeared so illimitable, its edge touching as it were the heavens, and spread out into an expanse which the utmost stretch of my imagination could not compass—a fit type, I thought, of the God of all people, whom every one thinks on; while the hoarse roar of the waves as they rolled on, mountain after mountain, and broke in angry fury against the shore, seemed to be a voice of Omnipotence which could not fail to awaken emotions of awe and dread in the most callous and unobservant!

As yet we had seen nothing of the city; but there was a ridge not far off, and as we ascended it I could no longer control my impatience. I spurred my horse, and before I reached the top shut my eyes, that whatever was before me might burst upon my view at once.

My horse slackened his pace when he reached the top, and allowing him to go on a few steps I opened my eyes, and glorious indeed was the prospect before me.

Beneath lay Hyderabad, the object of many a conjecture, of many an ardent desire to reach it—the first city of the Dukhun, justly celebrated throughout the countries I had passed. I had imagined it, like every other I had seen, to be in the midst of a plain, and that all that would be visible of it would be here and there a minaret rising out of large groves of trees: but Hyderabad presented a different aspect.

I stood on the crest of a gentle slope, which to my right hand was broken at some distance by rude, rocky hills, and to the left appeared gradually to descend into a plain, which stretched away almost uninterruptedly to the horizon. Before me, on the gentle rise of the valley, and beyond where I supposed the river to be, lay the city, its white terraced houses gleaming brightly in the sunlight from amidst what seemed to me at the distance almost a forest of trees. The Char Minar and Mecca Musjid rose proudly from the masses of buildings by which they were surrounded; and here and there a white dome, with its bright gilt spire, marked the tomb of some favourite or holy saint, while smaller mosques, I might say in hundreds, were known by their slender white minarets.

Beyond the city rose another connected chain of rocky hills, which ran along until they met those on the right hand, and shut in the valley on that side. The city seemed to be of immense extent; but I thought from the number of trees that it was composed principally of gardens and inclosures, and was much surprised afterwards, when I entered it, to find its streets so filled with houses, and the whole so thickly peopled.

It was altogether a most lovely scene: the freshness of the morning, the pureness of the air, and the glittering effect of the city and its buildings caused an impression which can never be effaced from my memory. I have seen it since, and though it is ever truly beautiful, it never struck me as it did that day. But I was then young, full of spirits, and flushed with the consciousness of my own powers, just developing, and assuring me that they would lead me to eminence.

One by one, as the Thugs came up, each ejaculated his praise of the beautiful scene, and all declared that the capital was worthy of the encomiums they had heard lavished on it. Inquiring the nearest road to the karwan, we descended the slope, and threading our way through numberless suburbs we reached the place, and were at the end of our journey. We were grateful for it, and for the protection and success we had met with. We took up our abode for the present in a sarai which surrounded a large and richly ornamented mosque; and for our greater convenience I went in search of an untenanted house, and after some difficulty succeeded in hiring a small place, the property of a merchant who resided next door. It contained only three rooms, and the verandah, which was the shop; but it was enough for my father and myself, and there was a small room with a strong door, in which we stowed away all our plunder.

Zora was overjoyed at reaching the place of her birth, and what was in reality her home, and could talk of nothing but the delight of meeting with her relatives and friends, and the surprise her arrival would excite in them all, as she said they had considered her lost to them ever since the Nawab had carried her off. The almost certainty of her being separated from me as soon as she was again in their power never occurred to her, and I determined that before she visited them I would lay all my fears before her, convinced that her affection for me would be the best guide for her conduct.

Our landlord the merchant was very civil and attentive to our wants, though his civility evidently proceeded in a great measure from curiosity as to who we were and what was our object. I stated to him in a few words our old story—of my father being a merchant, and myself a soldier of fortune who had accompanied him in search of employment. He was now curious to know of what my father's stock in trade consisted; but we were resolutely silent upon the subject, although he offered his agency to dispose of our goods.

'For,' said my father to me afterwards, 'our goods I know are valuable, and I know not their worth; nor have we as yet opened the bales; we will do so tomorrow morning, and assort them: we will then go into the city to the shops of the sahoukars, and inquire for articles similar to them, find out their prices, and by this means be enabled to value our own. Were we to offer them in ignorance of their market prices, we might be suspected; and though we may not get what they are intrinsically worth, we shall no doubt be able to sell the whole for a handsome sum.'

I agreed with him perfectly, and the next morning we set to work to open the bales.

Their contents were indeed costly—brocades, cloth of gold, fine muslin scarfs, also woven with gold and silver patterns, plain muslins, and a few shawls, besides fine cloths of different kinds for wearing-apparel, and sarees with silk and tissue borders, the latter from the looms of Nagpur. These and the jewels in our possession, when laid out and assorted, made a display on which we feasted our eyes for some time, wondering at their magnificence; and after I had made an inventory of the whole, my father and myself, attired in handsome clothes and mounted on the best of our horses, attended by a few of the men, took our way into the city.

Crossing over an old but massive bridge, below which ran the river, now a shallow stream, we entered by the gate at the head of it, and inquiring our way went direct to the chowke, or market-place, where we trusted we should find goods exposed for sale similar to our own. The streets were narrow and dirty, and the interior of the city certainly did not answer the expectations we had formed from its outside and distant appearance; still there were evident tokens of its wealth in the numbers of elephants, on the backs of which, in canopied umbaras, sat noblemen or gentlemen, attended by their armed retainers. Crowds of well-dressed persons paraded the streets, and as the festival of the Moharram had just commenced, cries of 'Hassan! Hussein! Doola! Deen! Deen!' and a thousand others familiar to us resounded on every side.

We made our way as well as we could through the throng, and our attendants were often obliged to clear us a passage, which exposed them to the jeers and abuse of the multitude, as they were recognised as strangers from their dress and language. Once or twice I observed a hand laid on a sword by some respectable person who had been jostled or pushed by our men, and heard a deep threat muttered; but we managed to get along, and at length came to a broader street, where the crowd was less dense; and here that noble building, the Char Minar, burst at once upon our view.

'How grand!' I exclaimed, stopping my horse and looking up to the huge minarets, which seemed to pierce the clouds; 'to see this alone is worth a journey from Delhi.'

The minarets formed the four corners of the building, and from them sprang immense arches which supported a roof, upon the top of which a small mosque was built. It did not look capable of supporting the immense weight of the whole, and yet it had stood for centuries, and the fabric was unimpaired.

It is the hour of prayer,' said my father, interrupting my gaze: 'and hark! the Muezzin calls from the Mecca mosque; thither we will now proceed, and afterwards transact our business.'

I followed him, and passing by the Char Minar, we turned up a street to our right, and stopped our horses at the gate of the mosque.

A feeling of awe mingled with admiration came over me as we entered the court-yard and advanced along a raised causeway to the foot of a flight of steps which led up to the interior. On either side of us were the graves of princes and nobles, many of them of elegant forms and richly carved; but the building itself engrossed my entire admiration. Five lofty and wide arches opened to view the interior of the edifice, where an equal number appeared in depth; and where the arches met, the eye was perplexed by the innumerable points and ornaments, which, running into each other, completed a roof of exquisite design and workmanship. To add to its beauty, the whole was of stone, carefully smoothed; whereas the Char Minar and the other buildings I had as yet seen were of stucco.

But I had little time to observe more; the sonorous and melancholy call of the Muezzin had ended, and the few attendants for the afternoon prayer had spread their carpets and commenced their devotions. We joined them, and kneeling on our outspread waistbands, went through the usual forms, while the low murmur of the prayers of all ascended to the fretted roof and added to the solemnity of the scene.

To the majority of those present there was perhaps nothing new or uncommon; but I, who had escaped the dangers of our journey and those attendant on our profession, felt that it went to my heart; and murderer as I was, though not as yet callous, I was softened, and my tears flowed fast as I repeated the words of prayer, and the impressive language of the blessed Koran in which they were couched.

The ceremony concluded, we rose; and though I was well disposed to linger in the sacred edifice and observe more of its beauties, my father hurried me away, and we returned to the Char Minar.

'Here,' said my father, 'those useful rogues the dullals[1] are to be met with. They will try to cheat us, no doubt, as it is their trade; but as we are not purchasers, we may avail ourselves of their aid to find out the houses of the merchants who deal in our articles, and it may be that the fellow we fix on will be intelligent and assist us to dispose of our property.'

We stopped on reaching the building, the lower part of which was sadly disfigured by numbers of wretched huts and stalls, where venders of vegetables and sweetmeats sat, and served out their goods to the passers-by. My father, calling to a decent-looking young Hindu, of intelligent countenance, asked him where he could meet with a dullal, as he was a stranger in the city, and wished to see some clothes and other goods, which he did not know where to find.

'I am one at your service, noble sir,' he replied; 'and I know well the richest warehouses, and can lead you to any you wish; and,' added he, 'there is not a sahoukar or dealer in the city who will not readily give your poor servant, Mohun Das, a character for sobriety and trustworthiness.'

'You had better not say much of your good qualities till they have been proved,' said my father; 'your tribe has not the best reputation on these points.'

'Ah,' said the man, 'my lord is well aware that (alas that I should say it!) the majority of our tribe are a sad set; nevertheless, his slave will not be found to be like them; for having begun by being honest, he has not found it worth his while to be otherwise.'

'That is as much as to say you would be dishonest if it suited your interests,' said I: 'but come, the day wears fast, and we are anxious to be out of this crowd before dark.'

The fellow gave me a knowing look, accompanied by a shrug of his shoulders, which could not be mistaken: what I had said had proved to him that we were on our guard.

'What description of goods may you be in search of?' said he; 'any may be procured, from the shawls of Cashmere and brocades of Benares to the meanest article.'

'Benares fabrics are what we require,' said I; 'a few handsome rumals and doputtas, and a turban or two, to adorn ourselves for the minister's durbar.'

'You shall see them,' said the dullal, girding his shawl about his waist. 'Now follow me, and keep a good eye on me, lest you lose me in the crowd.' And so saying, he descended the steps of the building, and led us along some of the principal streets, till

[1] Brokers.

he dived into an obscure alley, and stopped at the door of a house which certainly promised nothing from its exterior.

'A very unsatisfactory search we should have had,' said I to my father, 'had we endeavoured to find out a merchant ourselves. It is well we took this fellow with us.'

'These merchants, I have heard, usually choose these secluded places on account of their security,' replied my father. 'It would not do in a lawless place like this to expose goods for sale as they do in other cities. But they are well known, and easily found out by strangers if they apply to the dullals as we have done.'

We were ushered into the interior of the house, and were received by a large fat man, the very counterpart of the sahoukar I had killed. I started involuntarily at the resemblance; but soon recovering myself, and assured by his civility, I seated myself, as did also my father, and we quickly entered on the object of our visit.

One by one bales were opened and their contents spread before us. The sahoukar's stock seemed to be interminable and of great value. We selected several articles, and inquiring the prices of those which we inspected, of which I made memorandums, we desired them to be kept for us, saying that we would call the next day with money to pay for them. The sahoukar pressed us to take them with us, and the dullal offered his security for us; but for obvious reasons we declined, and took our leave of the merchant.

The dullal accompanied us as far as the Char Minar, where my father, slipping a piece of money into his hands for his trouble, told him we now knew our way home, and bid him come early in the morning to the karwan and inquire for the house of Rugonath das Sahoukar, where he would get tidings of us.

'So far I am satisfied,' said my father; 'our goods, as you will have observed; are equal in quality to those we saw, and by the prices affixed to them we have a good earnest of a large sum of money, if we can only dispose of them, a matter I apprehend of no difficulty if properly managed.'

The next morning came the dullal.

'Canst thou be secret?' asked my father at once, and throwing him a couple of rupees. The fellow started and trembled.

'If such is my lord's will,' said he, his teeth almost chattering with fear, 'I can; but I am a poor man, a very inoffensive man. I am my lord's slave, and rub my nose on his feet,' cried he at last, fairly throwing himself on the ground and rubbing his forehead against the ground, as he saw my father's brow contracting, and his face assuming an expression of anger at the evident suspicion which the man had of us.

'Why,' cried my father, as the fellow lay on the floor whimpering, 'what is this? what chicken-hearted son of a vile woman art thou? In the name of Allah get up! Because a man who, Inshallah! is somebody, asks thee whether thou canst be secret, must thou of necessity think thou are going to have thy throat cut?'

'Do not talk of it,' cried the wretch, shutting his eyes and shuddering. 'I am a poor man and a miserable Hindu; what would my lord get by cutting my throat?'

'Nay,' said my father, 'this is beyond bearing; the fellow has not the soul of a flea. Kick him out into the street, and beat him on the mouth with a slipper: there are plenty of dullals to be found beside him.'

'Pardon, noble sir!' cried the fellow—the mention of his trade leading him to suppose that he was required in the way of his calling—'pardon my foolishness. My lord's threatening aspect turned my liver into water; but now that he smiles again, I am assured that no harm is meant.'

'Harm! surely not to such a wretch as thou,' said my father; 'but since thou art inclined to listen to reason, sit down, and hear what we have to say to thee.'

'I can be secret,' cried the dullal; 'let my lord speak.'

'It will fare badly with thee if thou art not,' said my father, again looking grimly at him: 'but listen. I am a merchant; I have never been at this city before; but hearing at Delhi that an investment of valuable goods, such as we saw yesterday, was likely to sell well here, I have brought one down with me. I knew not the selling prices here, and therefore engaged thee to show me some goods, that I might be able to regulate the sale of my own. Now, canst thou manage it for me?'

'Surely, surely,' said the fellow in delight, 'nothing is more easy. My lord will not of course forget my perquisites on the sale?'

'Thou shalt have five rupees in every hundred's worth disposed of,' said my father: 'will this content thee?'

'It is a princely offer, and worthy of my lord's generosity,' said the dullal. 'Might I be permitted to see the goods?'

'It is necessary that you should see them, and here they are,' rejoined my father; and he opened the door of the room where they were, and one by one displayed the contents of the bales.

'This is indeed a rich stock,' said the dullal: 'you may be able to sell most of the cloths, but I question whether the whole, unless you intend to remain here some time.'

'That depends upon circumstances over which I have no control,' said my father; 'if I cannot sell them all here, I shall take what remains to Poona.'

'Well,' said the man, 'if I am permitted, I will make memorandums of all that there is here, and in the course of tomorrow will let you know what can be done. I cannot do so earlier, for I shall have to visit all the dealers.'

'Do what you think best,' said my father, 'and here are ten

rupees for your expenses. Now begone, and let me see you again at this time tomorrow.'

The fellow made many salaams and took his leave.

'Did you ever see so pitiful a wretch?' said my father. 'For two cowries I would have strangled him on the spot, to put an end to so disgraceful a coward.'

'Let him pass,' said I; 'he is but a Hindu, and not worth thinking of. But you are not going to let him off with all the money you have promised him?'

'Of course not,' replied my father; 'you understand I suppose what is to be done?'

'Perfectly,' said I; 'leave him to me.'

I went to Zora, my own gentle Zora. She had been speaking much of visiting her kindred, and though I had put her off as well as I could since we arrived, I saw with concern that I had no longer any pretext for detaining her. I could have fled with her—I think I could. Such was the intensity of my love for her, that, had I had the courage to speak of flight and she had agreed to accompany me, I verily believe I should have forsaken father, associates and profession, and committeed myself to the world.

And if I had, said the Thug, musing, should I have been worse off than I am now? Should I ever have worn these disgraceful fetters? Have ever doomed myself to perpetual imprisonment and a state of existence which I would to heaven were ended, and should be ended, but that I have (and I curse myself for it,) a mean, base, ay, cowardly lingering for life! Sahib, I tell you it would have been well for me had I then fled—fled from guilt and crime, into which I daily plunged deeper. With my soldierlike figure, my address, my skill in the use of arms, I might have gained honourable service; I might have led armies, or have met a soldier's death on some battle-field! But it was not so written; it was not my fate, and I am what I am—a curse to myself, and to all with whom I have ever been connected.

Zora! she thought not of my anxiety; all she hoped for, cared for now, was to see her mother and her sister. She assailed me with importunities that I would send her, and assured me that she would not be long absent, but go to them she must—they would so rejoice to see her again, and would welcome me as her deliverer. After seeing them she would return to me, and we should never again be parted.

'Alas!' I said, 'my Zora, you know not what you ask. Do you think that those charms are of no value to your mother and sister? You have owned to me that you are far more beautiful and attractive than any of those you are connected with. In your absence they will have sunk into obscurity, and they will hail your return as the earnest of more wealth and more distinction.'

'Nay, these are cruel words, my beloved,' she replied; 'you well know that I have never deceived you, and that as true as that I breathe my soul is yours for ever. So let me go, I pray you, and in a few hours I shall be again with you, and pressed to your honoured breast.'

'Be it so,' said I sadly; for though I hardly dared think it, I felt as if this was our parting for ever. 'Go then; and if you return not, I will come to you by the evening.'

A covered zenana cart was easily hired, and the driver seeming perfectly to understand where she wished to go, she stepped joyfully into it, attended by her old servant, and, with two of my men to attend her, she left me.

They soon returned, but they knew nothing, save that there was great joy in the house when her relatives saw her. Towards evening I could no longer control my impatience, and taking one of them with me, I mounted my horse and rode to her house.

It was situated nearly opposite a fountain, which is in the centre of the street below the Char Minar, and I had passed it the day before. I was easily admitted; and oh! what joy was evinced when I entered the room, where Zora, her sister and mother were seated! 'He is come!' cried my poor girl, and she rushed into my arms. She strained me to her breast for an instant, and then holding me from her, 'Look, mother!' she cried; 'look on him; is he not as I said? Is he not as beautiful and brave?'

The old lady approached me, and passing her hands over my face cracked her knuckles and every joint of her fingers by pressing the backs of her hands against her temples, while the tears ran down her cheeks: this she did as often as there was a joint to crack; and then she caught me in her arms and hugged me, crying at the same time like a child.

The sister received me, I thought, rather coldly. Had I been less handsome, perhaps, she would have been more cordial; she did not seem to like Zora's having so handsome a lover.

'May the blessing of the Prophet and the twelve Imams be on you and your posterity!' cried the old lady when she had recovered her breath to speak. 'May the gracious Allah keep you in his protection, and may the lady Muriam and the holy Moula-ali bless you! You have made a desolate house full again, and have changed our weeping to joy. What can I say more? Who could have thought it was our Zora when a cart stopped at the door? Zenatbee was just saying that it was that vile wretch Sukeena, come to pretend condolence, while in reality she rejoiced at our misfortune, which left her without a rival; and I was saying—no matter what I was saying—when we heard a faint cry, as if of astonishment, and a bustle, and we did not know what to think; when in rushed our lost Zora, our pearl, our diamond; and then I thought my old heart would break with joy, for my liver seemed to be melted; and I have done nothing since, Meer Sahib, but sit opposite to her, and stroke her face with my hands, and gaze into her eyes, to assure myself that I am not mistaken. Inshallah! to-morrow I will send five rupees to every shrine in the city, and distribute sweetmeats to fifty beggars in the name of the Imam Zamin; besides, I will have a tazea made, and will no longer wear these mourning garments. Ah! Meer Sahib, if you knew how I have sat day after day, and wept till I am reduced to a mere shadow of what I was! and all my friends tried to console me, but in vain, I would not be comforted.' And her tears flowed afresh at the recollection.

What the old lady was before her grief commenced, I cannot pretend to say; but in her present plight she appeared the fattest woman I had ever looked upon. She could now talk; she rolled from side to side when she stirred, and lifted her feet as an elephant would do among a dense crowd of people. It was painful to see her in her tight trowsers; at every movement she made, especially when she sat down, they appeared about to split, and let out a mass of flesh which was in rebellion against its confinement. She ought to have worn a petticoat; but no, the old lady had her vanity, and still prided herself on the beauty of her limbs, which I heard afterwards had really been strikingly symmetrical in her youth.

We sat conversing and relating our adventures, until the evening fell, and I spread my carpet for prayer.

'Ah, he is a good Syud,' said the old woman; 'I like to see the young fond of their devotions; but it is ever thus with the noble race from Hindustan.'

I was preparing to take my departure, when they one and all cried out against it. 'What! leave our house before you have broken bread and drunk water with us?' It was not to be thought of—I must stay: dinner was prepared; they were just on the point of sending for me when I came, and above all it was the ninth day of the Moharram, and I must stay were it but to see the procession of the Nal Sahib. That sacred relic, one of the shoes of the horse the blessed prophet rode when he fled to Medina, would be carried in grand procession, and I should never have a chance of seeing the like again. These reasons, and many imploring looks from Zora, made me speedily determine; so sending away my horse and the man, with a message to my father to say I should not return, I gave myself up to a night of enjoyment, such as I little expected when I parted with Zora in the morning.

The dinner was excellent, and the old lady's cooking unexceptionable. There were all sorts of curries, with but a mouthful in each litle cup, but still sufficient of each to leave an exquisite flavour in the mouth, only to be replaced by another surpassing it—pilaus of various kinds, and sweetmeats—and, to crown all, some delicious wine of the infidels called the Francees, which the old lady pronounced not to be wine, but sherbet, and allowed to the Huzoor himself, the great Sikundur Jah. It certainly was very delicious, and elevated the spirits. At the end, after taking a whiff or two, she carefully wiped the mouth-piece, and presented me with her own hookah, the fragrance of which was beyond that of ambergris or musk. I was in paradise—I was intensely happy!

'You have heard me sing,' said Zora to me, 'when I was in captivity, and after the fatigues of travel in our little tent, where there was no scope for my voice: now my heart is glad and bounding, and you shall hear me again—may the Prophet pardon me for singing during the Moharray! and you shall say which you like best; my sister shall accompany me till I am tired, and I will then accompany her.'

A saringhee was brought; Zenat tuned it, and taking the bow played a short prelude. It was one to the most entrancing sounds I had ever heard. Zora surpassed all her former attempts, it was ravishing to listen to her; and her sister, who was a perfect mistress of the instrument (a strange thing for a woman) gave it its full force of melody and expression. You know, Sahib, how nearly it accords to the human voice; and now, as accompaniment and song rose and fell together, it appeared as though two of the richest, fullest voices were pouring forth strains such as angels might have come down from the skies to hear.

But at last the noise of drums and shouting outside became so great, that both gave up in despair.

'A plague on them all!' said she; 'and I in such voice that I could have sung to you all night! And have I sung well?'

'Ay, have you,' said I; 'but methinks the first song you ever sung to me, at the palace in Oomerkhér, will dwell longer on my memory than any I have heard since.'

'Ya Allah!' exclaimed Zenat, who had moved to the window; 'was there ever a sight so magnificent! Come and see; 'tis passing fast, and will be soon out of sight.'

CHAPTER XII

ZENAT's exclamation drew us to the window. 'Quick!' she said; 'look out, or you will lose the sight; they are even now passing the Char Minar.'

We did look out, and the sight was indeed magnificent. A crowd of some hundreds of people were escorting a Punjah, that holy symbol of our faith; most of them were armed, and their naked weapons gleamed brightly in the light of numberless torches which were elevated on lofty bamboos; others bore aftab-geers, made of silver and gold tinsel, with deep fringes of the same, which glittered and sparkled as they were waved to and fro by the movements of those who carried them. But the object the most striking of all was the Char Minar itself, as the procession passed under it; the light of the torches illuminated it from top to bottom, and my gaze was riveted, as though it had suddenly and startingly sprung into existence.

The procession passed on, and all once more relapsed into gloom; the Char Minar was no longer visible to the eye, dazzled as it had been by the lights; but as it became more accustomed to the darkness, the building gradually revealed itself, dim and shadowy, its huge white surface looking like a spectre, or I could fancy like one of the mysterious inhabitants of the air whom, we are told, Suleeman-ibn-Daood and other sages had under their command, and were thus enabled to describe. Again, as we gazed, another procession would pass, and a sudden flash as of lightning would cause the same effect; interior and exterior of the edifice were as bright, far brighter they seemed, than at noonday.

I was enraptured. Zenat had left us to ourselves, and we sat, my arm around my beloved, while she nestled close to me, and we murmured to each other those vows of love which hearts like ours could alone frame and give utternace to.

Long did we sit thus—Sahib, I know not how long—the hours fled like moments.

'Look!' cried Zora, 'look at that mighty gathering in the street below us; they are now lighting the torches, and the procession on the Nāl Sahib will presently come forth.'

I had not observed it, though I had heard the hum of voices; the gloom of the street had hitherto prevented my distinguishing anything; but as torch after torch was lighted and raised aloft on immense poles, the sea of human heads revealed itself. There were thousands. The street was so packed from side to side, that to move was impossible; the mass was closely wedged together, and we waited impatiently for the time when it should be put in motion, to make the tour of the city.

One by one the processions we had seen pass before us ranged themselves in front, and as they joined together, who can describe the splendour of the effect of the thousands of torches, the thousands of aftab-geers, of flags and pennons of all descriptions, the hundreds of elephants, gaily caparisoned, bearing on their backs their noble owners, clad in the richest apparel, attended by their armed retainers and spearmen, some stationary, others moving to and fro, amidst the vast mass of human beings!

One elephant in particular I remarked—a noble animal, bearing a large silver umbara, in which sat four boys, doubtless the sons of some noblemen from the number of attendants that surrounded them. The animal was evidently much excited, whether by the noise, the lights, and the crowd, or whether he was *must*, I cannot say, but the mahout seemed to have great difficulty in keeping him quiet, and often dug his ankoos into the brute's head with great force, which made him lift his trunk in the air and bellow with pain. I saw the mahout was enraged, and, from the gestures of some of the persons near, could guess that they were advising him to be gentle; but the animal became more restive, and I feared there would be some accident, as the mahout only punished him the more severely. At last, by some unlucky chance, the blazing part of a torch fell from the pole upon which it was raised on the elephant's back; he screamed out with the sudden pain, and raising his trunk rushed into the crowd.

Ya Alla what a sight it was! Hundreds, as they vainly endeavoured to get out of the way, only wedged themselves closer together, shrieks and screams rent the air; but the most fearful sight was, when the maddened beast, unable to make his way through the press, seized on an unfortunate wretch by the waist with his trunk, and whirling him high in the air dashed him against the ground, and then kneeling down crushed him to a mummy with his tusks. Involuntarily I turned away my head; the sight was sickening, and it was just under me.

When I looked again, the brute, apparently satisfied, was standing quietly, and immediately afterwards was driven away; the body of the unfortunate man was carried off and deposited in a neighbouring shop; and all again became quiet.

All at once the multitude broke out into deafening shouts of 'Hassan! Hussein! Deen! Deen!' the hoarse roar of which was mingled with the beating of immense nagaras[1]. The sound was deafening, yet most impressive. The multitude became agitated; every face was at once turned towards the portal from which the sacred relic was about to issue, and it came forth in another

[1] Large drums.

instant amidst the sudden blaze of a thousand blue lights. I turned my eye to the Char Minar. If it had looked brilliant by the torch-light, how much more so did it now. The pale sulphureous glare caused its white surface to glitter like silver; high in the air the white minarets gleamed with intense brightness; and, as it stood out against the deep blue of the sky, it seemed to be a sudden creation of the genii—so grand, so unearthly—while the numberless torches, overpowered by the superior brightness of the fireworks, gave a dim and lurid light through their smoke, which, as there was not a breath of wind, hung over them.

All at once a numberless flight of rockets from the top of the Char Minar sprung hissing into the sky, and at an immense height, far above the tops of the minarets, burst almost simultaneously, and descended in a shower of brilliant blue balls. There was a breathless silence for a moment, as every eye was upturned to watch their descent, for the effect was overpowering. But again the shouts arose, the multitude swayed to and fro like the waves of a troubled sea; every one turned towards the Char Minar, and in a few instants the living mass was in motion.

It moved slowly at first, but the pressure from behind was so great that those in front were obliged to run; gradually, however, the mighty tide flowed along at a more measured pace, and it seemed endless. Host after host poured through the narrow street; men of all countries, most of them bearing naked weapons which flashed in the torch-light, were ranged in ranks, shouting the cries of the faith; others in the garb of fakirs chaunted wild hymns of the death of the blessed martyrs; others again in fantastic dresses formed themselves into groups, and, as they ran rather than walked along, performed strange and uncouth antics; some were painted from head to foot with different colours; others had hung bells to the ankles, shoulders and elbows, which jingled as they walked or danced; here and there would be seen a man painted like a tiger, a rope passed round his waist, which was held by three or four others, while the tiger made desperate leaps and charges into the crowd, which were received with shouts of merriment.

Some again were dressed in sheepskins, to imitate bears; others were monkeys, with enormous tails, and they grinned and mowed at the crowd which surrounded them. Now, some nobleman would scatter from his elephant showers of pice or cowries among the crowd below him; and it was fearful, though amusing, to watch the eager scramble and the desperate exertions of those undermost to extricate themselves—not unattended by severe bruises and hurts. Bodies of Arabs, singing their wild war-songs, firing their matchlocks in the air, and flourishing their naked swords and jumbeas, joined the throng, and immediately preceded the holy relic, which at last came up.

It was carried on a cushion of cloth of gold, covered by a small canopy of silver tissue; the canopy and its deep silver fringes glittering in the blaze of innumerable torches. Mullahs dressed in long robes walked slowly before, singing the Moonakib and the Murceas[1]. Men waved enormous chourees of the feathers of peacocks' tails, incense burned on the platform of the canopy, and sent up its fragrant cloud of smoke, and handfuls of the sweet ubeer were showered upon the cushion by all who could by any means or exertions get near enough to reach it.

Gradually and slowly the whole passed by: who can describe its magnificence? Such a scene must be seen to be felt! I say *felt*, Sahib, for who could see a mighty multitude like that, collected for a holy purpose with one heart, one soul, without emotion? Hours we sat there gazing on the specatacle; we scarcely spoke, so absorbed were we by the interest of the scene below us. At length however the whole had passed, and the street was left to loneliness and darkness: the few forms which flitted along here and there, looked more like the restless spirits of a burial-ground than human beings—and the silence was only now and then broken by a solitary fakir, his bells tinkling as he hurried along to join the great procession, the roar of which was heard far and faintly in the distance.

Just as we were about to retire, a number of men formed themselves into a circle around the pit in which were a few lighted embers; but some bundles of grass were thrown on them, the light blazed up, and drawing their swords they danced round and round the fire, waving their weapons, while all shouted aloud in hoarse voices the names of the blessed martyrs. The blazing fire in the centre lighted up their wild forms and gestures as they danced, tossing their arms wildly into the air. Now they stood still, and swayed to and fro, while the fire died away and they were scarcely perceptible. Again more fuel was thrown on, the red blaze sprung up far above their heads, and their wild round was renewed with fresh spirit.

The night was now far spent, and the chill breeze which arose warned us to retire. Indeed Zenat and her mother had done so long before, and we were left to ourselves.

Sahib! that was the last night I passed with my beloved, and the whole of our intercourse remains on my memory like the impression of a pleasing dream, on which I delight often to dwell, to conjure up the scenes and conversations of years past and gone —years of wild adventure, of trial, of sorrow, and of crime.

I can picture to myself my Zora as I parted from her on the following morning; I can again hear her protestations of unalterable love, her entreaties that I would soon return to her; and above all I remember her surpassing loveliness, and the look of anguish I might call it with which she followed me as I left her,

[1] Hymns peculiar to the Moharram.

after one long passionate embrace. These impressions, I say, still linger on a mind which has been rendered callous by crime, by an habitual system of deception, and by my rude intercourse with the world—my deadliest enemy; and they are refreshing and soothing, because I have no wrong toward her to charge myself with. I rescued her; she loved me, and I loved her too; we wanted nought but a longer intercourse to have strengthened that affection, which would have lasted till death. But why should I talk thus? Why should I, a convicted felon and murderer, linger on the description of such scenes and thoughts? Sahib, I have done with them; I will tell you of sterner things—of the further adventures of my life.

I returned to my father: he was not angry at my absence, and I found Mohun Das, the dullal, closeted with him, and also another sahoukar-looking person. Mohun Das had been eminently successful: the sahoukar I saw was the assistant in a wealthy house who had need of all our goods, and he was come to see them before the bargain was finally closed. They were displayed to him, both goods and jewels; he approved of all, said he would return shortly with an offer for them, and having made a list of the whole he departed.

'Now,' said Mohun Das, 'about the price; what do you ask?'

'You know better than I do,' said my father, 'therefore do you speak, and remember, the more they sell for the more you get.'

'I have not forgotten your munificence,' said the dullal; 'and I say at once the cloths are worth sixteen, and the jewels ten thousand rupees; but you must ask thirty thousand—you will get twenty-five I dare say.'

'It is too little,' said my father; 'they cost me nearly that sum: and how am I to pay my guards if I get no profit? I shall ask thirty-five for the whole.'

'Well,' said the dullal, 'if you do, so much the better for me; but mark what I say, you will get no more than my valuation; however, if you will trust me and leave it to my judgement, I will get a fair price.'

'I will; but recollect, twenty-five thousand is the least.'

'Certainly, said the dullal; 'I go to do your bidding.'

'Go,' said my father; 'Allah Hafiz! be sure you return quickly.'

It was noon before he returned, but it was with a joyful face when he did come.

After many profound salaams, he exclaimed, to my father, 'You have indeed been fortunate; your good destiny has gained you a good bargain. I have got thirty thousand six hundred rupees for the whole; we had a long fight about it and wasted much breath; but, blessed be Narayun! your slave has been successful: see, here is the sahoukar's acknowledgement.'

My father took it and pretended to read; I was near laughing at his gravity, as he took the paper and pored over the crabbed

Hindi characters, of which he did not understand one—nor indeed any other, for he could neither read nor write.

'Yes,' said he gravely, 'it is satisfactory; now how am I to be paid?'

'The sahoukar will arrange that with you in any way you please,' said the dullal: 'ready money or bills are equally at your service; but as all transactions are generally at six months' credit, the interest for that time at the usual rate will be deducted.'

'And if I take bills, I suppose the interest will be allowed till I reach Benares, or whatever place I may take them upon.'

'Certainly.'

'Good,' continued my father; 'do you attend here with the sahoukar, and we will settle all about it, and he can take away the merchandise whenever he pleases.' So the dullal departed.

It was now about the time when the tazeas[1] were to be brought to the edge of the river to be thrown into the water, and as the Karwan was not far from the spot, I proposed to my father to send for our horses and ride thither to see the sight.

He agreed, the horses were quickly brought, and we rode to the bridge over which the road passes into the city. Taking our stand upon it, we beheld beneath us the various and motley groups in the bed of the river; there were thousands assembled; the banks of the river and the bed were full—so full, it seemed as if you might have walked upon the heads of the multitude. The aftabgeers and the tinsel of the various tazeas glittered in the afternoon sun—the endless variety of colours of the dresses had a cheerful and gay effect—and, though it was nothing to the grand appearance of the procession at night, still it was worth looking at. The tazeas were brought one by one by the various tribes or neighbourhoods to which they belonged, and thrown into the pools in the bed of the river, for deep water there was none; but there was sufficient for the purpose, and as each glittering fabric was cast in, it was assailed by hundreds of little ragged urchins, who quickly tore the whole to pieces for the sake of the ornaments; and there was many a warm contest and scramble over these remains, which excited the laughter of the bystanders.

One by one the various groups returned towards their homes, looking wearied and exhausted; for the excitement which had kept them up for so many days and nights was gone. In many a shady corner might be seen, lying fast asleep, an exhausted wretch—his finery still hanging about him—his last cowrie perhaps expended in a copious dose of bhang, which, having done part of its work in exciting him almost to madness during the preceding night, had left him with a racking brain, and had finally sent him into oblivion of his fatigue and hunger.

[1] The model-tombs of the martyrs Hassan and Hussein, borne in procession in the Moharram.

The Moharram was ended: we stayed on the bridge till the time for evening prayer, when, repairing to an adjacent mosque, we offered up our devotions with the others of the faithful who were there assembled. This done, I told my father I should again visit Zora, and most likely remain at her house all night: he bid me be sure to return early in the morning, on account of our business; and having promised this, I departed.

I rode slowly through the now silent and almost deserted streets: the few persons whom I met were hurrying along to their homes, and had no common feeling or interest with each other as before. I passed along the now well-known track, and was soon at the house which held all that was most dear to me on earth. I sent up my name and dismounted; I expected the usual summons, and that I should see that countenance I longed to behold welcoming me from the window. I waited longer than I could assign a cause for in my own mind; at last my attendant returned, and as he quitted the threshold the door was rudely shut after him, while at the same time the casements of the windows were both shut. What was I to think of this? Alas! my forebodings were but too just. My attendant broke in upon my thoughts by addressing me.

'Her mother, whom I have seen,' said he, 'bade me give you her salaam, and tell you that her daughter is particularly engaged and cannot receive you. I ventured to remonstrate, but the old woman became angry, and told me that she had behaved civilly to you, and that you could not expect more; and further, she said, "Tell him from me, that he had better act the part of a wise man, and forget Zora, for never again shall he see her; it will be in vain that he searches for her, for she will be beyond his reach; and I would rather that she died, than become the associate and partner of an adventurer like him, who, for all I know, might inveigle her from home, and, when he was tired of her, leave her in some jungle to starve. Go and tell him this, and say that if he is a wise man he will forget her".'

'And was this all?' exclaimed I in a fury; 'was this all the hag said? I will see whether I cannot affect an entrance;' and I rushed at the door with all my might. In vain I pushed and battered it with the hilt of my sword, it was too securely fastened within to give way. I called out Zora's name—I raved—I threatened as loud as I could to destroy myself at the door, and that my blood would be upon the head of that cruel old woman. It was all in vain, not a bolt stirred, not a shutter moved, and I sat down in very despair. A few persons had collected, observing my wild demeanour; and as I looked up from my knees, where my face had been hidden, one of them said, 'Poor youth! It is a pity his love has been unkind and will not admit him.'

'Pooh!' said another, 'he is drunk with bhang; Allah knows whether we are safe so near him! he has arms in his hands; we ought to get out of his way, your drunken persons are ticklish people to deal with, let alone their being a scandal to the faith.'

I was ashamed; shame for once conquered anger. I walked towards my horse, and mounting him rode slowly from the place. How desolate everything appeared! The night before, I had reached the summit of happiness. I cast one look to the window where I had sat in sweet converse with her whom I was destined no more to behold; I thought on her words, and the glittering scene was again before me. Now all was dark and silent, and accorded well with my feelings. I rode home in this mood, and throwing myself down on my carpet, gave myself up to the bitterness of my feelings and unavailing regret. A thousand schemes I revolved in my mind for the recovery of Zora during that night, for I slept not. One by one I dismissed them as cheating me with vain hopes, only to be succeeded by others equally vague and unsatisfactory. I rose in the morning feverish and unrefreshed, having determined on nothing. There was only one hope, that of the old woman the nurse; if I could but speak with her, I thought I should be able to effect something, and as soon as I could summon one of the men who had attended Zora, I sent him for information.

CHAPTER XIII

I HAD not seen Bhudrinath now for some days, and fearing he might think me neglectful, I went to the sarai in which he and the men had put up.

'Ah!' cried he when he saw me approach, 'so we are at last permitted to see the light of your countenance; what, in the name of Bhowani, have you been about? I have sought you in vain for the last three days.'

'Tell me,' said I, 'what have you been doing, and you shall know my adventures afterwards.'

'Well then,' said he, 'in the first place, I have made a series of poojahs and sacrifices at the different temples around this most Mahomedan of cities; secondly, I have seen and mixed in the Moharram; and lastly, I have assisted to kill seven persons.'

'Killed seven persons!' I exclaimed in wonder, 'how in the name of the Prophet, did you manage that?'

'Nothing more easy, my gay young jemadar,' he replied: 'do you not know that this is the Karwan, where travellers daily arrive in numbers, and from which others are as frequently departing? Nothing is easier than to beguile them to accompany us a short distance, pretending that we are going the same road: why a Thug might live here for ever, and get a decent living. The people (my blessings on them!) are most unsuspicious; and thanks to Hunooman and his legions, there is no want of rocks and wild roads about the city, which give capital opportunities for destroying them.'

'Ajaib!' I exclaimed, 'this is very wonderful; and who were they?'

'Not in the least extraordinary,' said Bhudrinath coolly, 'if you think on it;—but to answer your question. The first was a bunnia who was going to Beeder; we took him to Golconda, and buried him among the tombs, and we got seventy rupees and some pieces of gold from him. The second were two men and their wives, who said they were going to Koorungul: where that is Bhugwan knows! but it is somewhere in a southerly direction. We killed them about three coss from the city, among some rocks, and left them there.'

'That was wrong,' said I, 'you should have buried them.'

'Not at all wrong, my friend; who will take the trouble of inquiring after them? Besides, we had not time, for the day had fully dawned, and we feared interruption from travellers; we got above two hundred rupees, and two ponies, which I have sold for thirty rupees.'

'Well,' said I, 'these make five; and the other two—'

'They lie there,' said Bhudrinath, pointing to where a horse was picketed; 'they were poor devils, and not worth the trouble of taking out; we only got forty-two rupees from both.'

'Dangeruos work,' said I; 'you might have been seen.'

'Oh! no fear of an old hand like me; every one was off to the city to gape at the show, and we were left alone. I was deliberating whether we should not accompany them on the road we came in by, and by which they were going; but Surfuraz Khan cut short my doubts and uncertainties by strangling one fellow on the spot, and I followed his example with the other; the bodies were concealed till night, and then buried.'

'But is there no fear of the grave bursting?' I asked.

He laughed. 'Fear! oh no, they lie deep enough; and you know our old tricks.'

'Well,' said I, 'it is most satisfactory, and I have missed all this, have been a fool, and have lost my mistress into the bargain.'

Bhudrinath laughed immoderately; but seeing the gravity of my face, he said.

'Never mind, Meer Sahib, care not for my merriment; but truly thy face wore so lack-a-daisical an expression, that for my life I could not have refrained. Cheer up, man, there is plenty of work in store for you; women will be faithless, and young and hot-brained fellows will grieve for them; but take a friend's advice, make your profession your mistress, and she at least will never disappoint you.'

'Your advice is good,' said I; 'nevertheless the mistress I have lost is, as you know, worthy of regret, and I shall miss her for many a day. But tell me, what have you now in hand—anything in which I may have a share?'

'Why no,' he replied, 'nothing; but if you are so inclined, we will take a ramble this evening through the bazaars, we may perhaps pick up somebody.'

'Of course I will be with you, for in truth my hand will get out practice if I neglect work. But have you seen my father?'

'I have not,' said Bhudrinath; 'I hear he is very much engaged about the property, and do not like to disturb him.'

'You are right, he is,' said I; 'but he will finish all today, and get the money. I suppose after that we shall not stay long here, and for my part I care not how soon we set off; I am anxious for new scenes and adventures, and we are not likely to do much here. Is not Surfuraz Khan here?'

'No; he is gone with a party of seven travellers towards Puttun-cherroo, and has taken ten or fifteen of the best of the men with him; he will not be back probably before night, if then.'

'Who were the travellers?'

'Bunnias, I heard,' said Bhudrinath carelessly; 'I did not see them myself, and Surfuraz Khan was in too great a hurry to give me any information.'

'Out upon me!' I exclaimed, vexed at my idleness; 'here have I been amusing myself while all this has been going on: for the sake of the Prophet, let us do something soon, that I may settle scores with my conscience, for I have hardly assurance enough to look you in the face after my behaviour.'

'Well,' said he, 'come this evening; if we can't decoy any one, we will kill somebody for amusement and practice.'

'I agree,' said I; 'for by Allah! I must do something. I am as melancholy as a camel, and my blood, which boiled enough yesterday, seems now scarcely to run through me;—it is not to be borne.'

I found when I reached home that the dullal had arrived, and with him the sahoukar's clerk, and some porters to carry the goods, as well as fellows with matchlocks and lighted matches, and others with swords and shields to escort them. I stared at them.

'One would think you were going to battle, Séthji,' said I, 'with all those fierce fellows; I am half afraid of them.'

The fellows laughed; and the clerk replied,

'They are necessary, and we always have them. If our goods were stolen, nay carried off before our eyes, should we get any redress? no indeed: we therefore protect our property the best way we can.'

'Now,' said my father, 'take your goods and be off with them; they are no longer mine, and I fear to allow them to remain under my roof.'

'Surely,' said the clerk, 'they will be out of your way directly; and now let us speak about your money, or will you take some merchandise as part of it?'

'Not a bit, not a bit,' replied my father; 'I want all my money in rupees—no, stay, not all in rupees; give me five thousand in silver and the rest in gold, it will be easier carried.'

'I suppose you mean five thousand rupees, and the rest in gold bars; well you must purchase gold according to weight, and the best is twenty rupees a tola—but you had better take bills, and the exchange is favourable.'

'No, no; no bills,' said my father, 'but the gold; if I remember rightly, the price of gold was high when I left Delhi, and was likely to remain so; and I have plenty of persons for my guard if robbers should attack me.'

'You forget me,' cried the dullal, 'and my per-centage.'

'Make yourself easy,' said I; 'it will be paid out of the five thousand rupees; it will be about fifteen hundred I think.'

'What did you say? Fifteen hundred! to whom?' asked the clerk.

'To this dullal,' said I; 'I suspect the rascal is cheating us.'

'Cheating! surely he is; why Mohun Das, good man, what have you been about? Are you mad, to ask so much?'

'Ah, it was my lord's offer and promise,' said he, 'and surely I shall now get it; pray what business is it of yours?'

'What ought he to have?' asked my father.

'One per cent is ample,' replied the other; 'and you might have saved this too if you had only applied yourself to the different sahoukars.'

'We were strangers,' said I, 'and knew not their places of residence; so we were obliged to have recourse to this rascal, who offered his services.'

'What! did you not take me from the Char Minar? Did you not promise me five per cent, and bind me to secrecy about the sale of your goods?' cried the dullal.

'Listen to him,' said my father; 'he raves. Now, Meer Sahib, did not this bhurwa come begging and beseeching for employment, and when I said I would try him, and asked his terms, he said he was miserably poor, and would take whatever was given him; was it not so? And now, Punah-i-Khoda! We are to be bearded in this manner, defrauded of fifteen hundred rupees, where we have not as many cowries to give, and made to eat dirt into the bargain. Beat him on the mouth with a shoe! Spit on him! May he be defiled so that Ganges' water would not purify him; may his mother, sisters, and all his female relatives be'—

'Nay, my good friend,' said the Sahoukar's clerk, 'be not thus rash and hot-headed, nor waste your breath upon so mean a wretch; since you have employed him something must be given, it is the custom, and next time you will know better; say, may I pay him the one per cent, which will be three hundred and six rupees?'

'Three hundred and six rupees! Allah, Allah! where am I to get the half?' cried my father: 'for the love of the Prophet, get me off what you can; I swear by your head and eyes that I am a poor man, and only an agent; is it not so, Meer Sahib? am I not miserably poor?'

'You certainly cannot afford to pay so much money as one per cent on this large sum,' I replied; 'nevertheless, as such appears to be the custom, you had better give something, say one hundred and fifty rupees.'

'Certainly,' said my father; 'I am ready; I will not refuse any thing in reason; but so large a sum—I was quite astounded at the impertinence of the demand, and lost my temper like a fool.'

Mohun Das stood all this time with his eyes and mouth wide open, looking from one to the other, every word that was uttered increasing his astonishment and disappointment.

'Do you pretend to say,' screamed he at last, 'do you pretend to say that I am not to get my money, my fifteen hundred rupees, for which I have toiled night and day? And do you pretend to say

I came to you first? did you not take me with you from the Char Minar?'

'Nay, here is the Char Minar again! for the sake of Allah,' said I to the clerk, 'if you really know this fellow advise him to be quiet; what have I, who am a soldier, to do with this filthy traffic; he may provoke a patient man once too often, and people with weapons in their hands are not safe persons to play jokes with;' and I twisted up my mustachios.

I have told you, Sahib, what a coward the fellow was: he fell instantly on the ground and rubbed his forehead against the floor.

'Pardon! pardon!' he cried, 'most brave sirs! anything, whatever you choose to give me, even ten rupeees, will be thankfully received, but do not kill me, do not put me to death—see, I fall at your feet, I rub my nose in the dust.'

'You fool,' cried the celrk, holding his sides with laughter, for he was a fat man; 'you fool; ah, Mohun Das, that I should have seen this! In the name of Narayun, who will do you any harm? Are you a child—you, with those mustachios? Shame on you, man! Dullal as you are, be something less of a coward; get up, ask for your money boldly, ask for whatever these gentlemen please to give you, though indeed you deserve nothing for your impertinent attempt at deception.'

He got up and stood on his left leg, with the sole of the right foot against the calf, his hands joined, his turban all awry, and the expression of his face most ludicrously miserable.

'Ten rupees, my lord,' he faltered out; 'your slave will take ten rupees.'

We all once more burst into a peal of laughter; the gomashta's sides appeared to ache, and the tears ran down his cheeks.

'Ai Bhugwan! Ai Narayun!' cried he, catching his breath; 'that I should have seen this! Ai Sitaram! but it is most amusing. Ten rupees! why, man,' said he to the miserable dullal, 'you just now wanted fifteen hundred!'

'Nay,' said my father, 'let him have his due; you said one hundred and fifty—that he shall have; do you, Meer Sahib, go with this worthy sahoukar to his kothee, and bring the money; I dare say he will give you a guard back, and you can hire a porter for the gold and silver.'

'Certainly, you shall have the men,' said the gomashta: 'and now come along; I shall have to collect the gold. and it may be late before it can be weighed and delivered to you, and the rupees passed by a suraff.'

As we went on, the dullal said to me, 'You will pay me at the kothee, will you not?'

'We will see,' said I; 'the money is none of mine, and I will ask advice on the subject.'

'Not your money! whose then?'

'Why his who has employed you, and from whom you are to get

one hundred and fifty rupees,' I said: 'are you a fool? Why do you ask?'

'Ah nothing, only I was thinking'—

'Thinking of what?' I asked; 'somewhat rascality I doubt not.'

'Ah,' said he, 'now you speak as you did at the Char Minar.'

'By Allah!' said I, stopping and looking at him, 'if ever you mention that word again'—

'Never, never!' cried the wretch trembling; 'do not beat me: remember it is the open street, and there will be a disturbance; the words escaped me unawares, just as I was thinking—'

'That is twice you have said that, and by Allah! I think you have some meaning in it; what *would* you be at?'

'Nothing, nothing,' said he; 'only I was thinking—'

'Well!'

'I was only thinking that you are an adventurer, who has accompanied that rich merchant from Hindustan.'

'Well, and what of that? You knew that before.'

'You are not rich?'

'No indeed,' said I, 'I am not.'

'Then,' said the wretch, 'why not both of us enrich ourselves?'

'How?' I asked.

'Refuse the guard, or take some men I will guide you to; they will do whatever you like for five rupees a-piece; we will fly with the money, and there is a place in the rocks close to this where I have plunder hidden—we will go thither and share it.'

'Where is the place you allude to—is it far?' I asked.

'No,' said he; 'will you come? I can show it you from a distance; we need not get up the rocks—there is danger of being seen in the daytime.'

I followed him for a little distance, and he pointed to a huge pile of rocks at the back of the Karwan and Begum Bazaar.

'There, do you see a white spot about half way up on a rock?'

'I do,' said I.

'That is the spot,' he replied; 'it is known out to myself and a few others; whatever I can pick up I put there.'

'What do you get?'

'Ah, little enough; sometimes a shawl, a brocade handkerchief, or some gold, anything in fact. But why do you ask? Will you do what I said and join us? There are sixteen of us; one is yonder disguised as a fakir, the rest are hard by and will accompany us.'

'Dog!' cried I, dashing him to the earth, 'dog! dost thou know to whom thou speakest? Here there is no one,' (for we had got to the back of the houses,) 'and it were an easy task to send thee to Jehanum; one blow of my sword, and that false tongue would cease to speak for ever:' and I half drew it. I knew the effect this would have: there was the same grovelling cowardice he had displayed before; he clung to my knees; I spurned him and spat on him. 'Reptile!' cried I at length, wearied by his abjectness, 'I would scorn to touch thee; a Syud of Hindustan is too proud to stoop to such game as thou art; lead me to the sahoukar, for by Allah I distrust thee.'

'Nay, in this matter I have been honest,' said the wretch; 'the money is sure.'

'It will be well for thee that it is,' said I, 'or I swear to be revenged; lead on, and beware how you go; if I see one attempt at escape I will cut you in two, were it in the middle of the bazaar.'

'Then follow me closely,' said he; and he gathered up his garments, which had become disordered, and we again entered the crowded bazaar.

We were soon at the sahoukar's, who awaited us: the money and gold were told out, and a receipt I had brought with me given, and accompanied by the guard of soldiers I took the pleasure to my father.

'Meer Sahib, kind Meer Sahib,' said the dullal, as we approached our dwelling, 'you will forget all that has passed; Bhugwan knows I was only jesting with you! I love to play such tricks—nay, I have always been of a jesting disposition;' and he laughed in his terror. 'You will not forget my little perquisite, my hundred and fifty rupees, I know you will not.'

'Peace!' cried I, 'if you wish to get a cowrie. Has it not been promised to thee on the word of two of the faithful? thou shalt get the uttermost farthing.'

I dismissed the sepoys with a small present when the money had been lodged in our strongroom, and as they went, the miserable dullal looked after them as though he thought with them had departed his last chance for existence. It certainly drew to a close.

'Give me my money and let me depart,' said he in a hollow voice.

'Wait,' said I, 'till it is counted out for you.'

'Ah, I had forgotten the dullalji,' cried my father; 'I will get out his due.'

CHAPTER XIV

My father counted out the money and handed it over to the dulal; his countenance brightened as he viewed it, and he made numberless salaams and protestations of thanks. 'Now you must write a receipt for the money,' said my father.

'Surely,' replied the fellow, taking a pen out of his turban, 'if my lord will give me paper and ink.'

'Here they are,' said I; 'write.'

He did so, gave me the paper, and tied the money up in a corner of his dhoti, which he tucked into his waistband. 'Have I permission to depart?' he asked; 'my lord knows the poor dullal, and that he has behaved honestly in this transaction. Whenever my lord returns to Hyderabad, he can always hear of Mohun Das, if he inquires at the Char Minar; and he will always be ready to exert himself in his patron's service.'

'Stay,' said I, 'I have somewhat to say to thee;' and I related to my father the whole of the conversation I have just described.

'Is it so? said he to the miserable being before him; 'is it so? Speak wretch! Let me hear the truth from thy own lips; wouldst thou have robbed me?'

But the creature he addressed was mute; he stood paralysed by fear and conscious guilt, his eyes starting from his head, his mouth open, and his blanched lips drawn tightly across his teeth.

'Thou hast deserved it,' continued my father; 'I read in that vile face of thine deeds of robbery, of murder, of knavery and villainy of every kind; thou must die!'

'Ah, no, no! Die? my lord is pleased to be facetious; what has his poor slave done?' and he grinned a ghastly smile.

'Thou wouldst have robbed me,' said my father, 'when I trusted thee with my whole substance; thou wouldst have left me to starve in a strange land without compunction; thou hast robbed others and cheated thousands: say, art thou fit to live, to prey longer upon the world thou hast already despoiled?'

He threw himself at my father's feet; he grasped his knees; he could scarcely speak, and was fearfully convulsed and agitated by extreme terror. 'I am all that you say,' he cried, 'thief, murderer, and villain; but oh! do not kill me. My lord's face is kind—I cannot die—and my lord has no sword, and how will he kill me?' He had only just perceived that we were both unarmed, and he made a sudden rush at the door. 'The Kotwal shall know of this,' he cried; 'people are not to be terrified with impunity.' The door was fastened; he gave several desperate pulls and pushes at it; but I was at his back, and the fatal handkerchief was over his head: he turned round and glared on me—the next instant he was dead at my feet.

'There!' cried my father exultingly, 'judgement has overtaken him, and the memory of his crimes will sleep with him for ever; we have done a good deed.'

'Yes,' said I, 'a good one indeed; he confessed himself to be a murderer, robber, and knave—what more need you? and so young too for this accumulation of crime!'

'Drag him in here,' said my father. 'I like not to look on him; and go for the Lughaees; he must be buried at night in the small yard of the house; I dare not have the body carried out in this crowded city.'

'It shall be done,' I replied; 'but think what an escape we have had; had you not told me to go with the wretch, we should have lost our money.'

'Yes, my son, and even had we got it, had you not suspected that five per cent was too much, I should certainly have paid the sum; but I saw your drift, and I think took up the clue admirably. We have cheated the knave both out of his money and his life.'

'True,' said I, 'it has been a good adventure, and amusing withal; besides it promises further advantage.'

'From the rock and the fakir?'

'Yes: there will be good booty.'

'Take care,' said my father; 'the band may be there, and they will give you a warm reception.'

'I will go and consult with Bhudrinath,' said I; 'the adventure will just suit him and Surfuraz Khan; we will do nothing rashly.'

Bhudrinath was at the serai waiting for me.

'So Meer Sahib,' said he, 'you are still in the humour for a frolic; how many lives will satisfy your worship tonight? There is no lack of men in this abode of villainy.'

'I am in the humour,' said I, 'but not for what I intended; I have better game in view.'

'Ha!' said he, 'so *you* have been acting Sotha; and pray what may this game be?'

'One that will require stout hearts, and maybe naked weapons,' I replied: 'are you willing to accompany me?'

'To death,' said Bhudrinath; 'but I cannot for my life see what you are driving at.'

'Listen,' I replied; and I related to him the whole history of the dullal.

'Cleverly done, very clevely indeed, my young jemadar,' said he, when my relation was ended; 'no one could have managed it better from first to last; the rascal deserved his fate; and now I suppose we must search out these hidden treasures in the rock.'

'Exactly,' said I; 'I would do so this very night if I knew how to go about it properly.'

'Let me see,' said Bhudrinath, musing; 'we shall not want many men, six or eight resolute fellows will be sufficient. You and I, Peer Khan, Motee-ram, and four others are ample; there is no use waiting for Surfuraz Khan, he will not now be back before the morning. But how to get intelligence of the place, and whether any of the rascals are there at night?'

'Can no one personate a fakir?' said I; 'a kulundur, anything will do. He might go up now, as the spot is close by, and bring us news in an hour or so.'

'I have it!' cried Bhudrinath. 'Here, some one call Shekji to me.'

Shekhji came. He was an old man, with a long beard; but he was an able fellow and a rare good hand with the handkerchief.

'Shekhji,' said Bhudrinath, 'sit down, I have something to say to you. You can personate a fakir, if necessary, can you not?'

'Certainly,' replied the old fellow, 'Musulman or Hindu, all kinds are familiar to me. I know all their forms of speech and have many of their dresses.'

'It is well,' said Bhudrinath; 'now listen. You must go and disguise yourself this instant; we have an enterprise in view;' and he related our proposed scheme and what had preceded it. 'And now,' continued Bhudrinath, 'you must be wary, and by dark you must return and tell us of the place, and if there are men there.'

'Is the fakir who lives there a Hindu or Musulman?'

'I saw the impression of spread hands in whitewash on the rock, so he must be a Musulman,' said I.

'Then I know how to act,' cried the Thug. 'Sahibs, I take my leave, and will not fail you. I shall be with you by the time I am required.'

'Will he manage it?' I asked Bhudrinath. 'Methinks it is a delicate business.'

'Never fear him,' said Bhudrinath; 'he is a most accomplished rogue and is a capital hand at disguise, especially as a fakir, and once got us considerable booty by enticing five Nanukshaee fakirs among us who had picked up a good deal of money and were going to build a well with it. Besides, he is as brave as a lion, and you have seen his other work.'

As we were talking Surfuraz Khan came in.

'Ours has been a good business,' he cried exultingly, 'and there is good spoil. We have killed all the men, and the plunder is coming in charge of our fellows.'

'That is so far good,' said I; 'but is there any ready money, or is it all goods?'

'Both, Meer Sahib, both; but methinks you need not be so ready to ask, when we have not seen your face ever since we have been in the city. We might all have been taken and safely lodged in

Puntoo Lall's huwélee for all you knew of the matter, I do not like such conduct.'

I was enraged at his speech, and was about making an angry reply when Bhudrinath interfered.

'Peace!' said he, 'no brawls: it is disgraceful and only fit for drunkards and smokers of ganja; listen to me. Surfuraz Khan, you are no boy, and ought not to let your anger have sway; listen, and hear what our young jemadar has been about, and I swear by Bhowani I think he will yet put us all to shame.'

He then related all I had told him, on hearing which Surfuraz Khan's angry feelings gave way in a moment; he rose and embraced me.

'I was wrong,' said he, 'and you must forgive me; and to prove that I am more than ever your friend, I beg you to allow me a place in this adventure, for, by Allah! it promises to be a strange one.'

'Willingly,' said I; 'we thought you would not arrive in time, but now you are come I would not on any account that you did not accompany us.'

'So you have strangled the fellows you took out,' said Bhudrinath. 'Had you any trouble?'

'None whatever,' replied the Khan. 'We took them out on the Masulipatam road, and found a spot on the other side of Suroonuggur; we threw the bodies into a well and returned by another road. Soobhan Allah! this is a rare place, and we might remain here for years and have some amusement every day. I think I shall stay here.'

'You may do as you please about that,' said I, 'when we have shared the spoil we have got. You will then be free, but I should be sorry to lose you.'

In such conversation we continued till it was dusk, and then assembling the men we intended to take, eight in all, and seeing that our arms were in good order, we waited in great anxiety for the return of our emissary.

At last he came.

'There is no time to be lost,' said he. I went up to the place and found the fakir. He is a fine sturdy young fellow, and at first warned me to descend; but when I told him I was hungry and weary, that I had just arrived from Hindustan, and did not know where to lay my head, and begged for a crust of bread and water in the name of the Twelve Imams, he was pacified, and admitted me into his cave, gave me some food and a hookah, and we sat carousing for some time. I pulled out my opium-box and took a very little; seeing it he begged for some, and has taken such a dose that he will not wake till morning. I left him fast asleep.'

'He shall never wake again,' said I: 'but did you observe the place? Where can the plunder be hidden?'

He lives in a cave, between two enormous rocks,' said Shekhji. 'It was nearly all in darkness, but I saw a corner at the back of it built up with mud and stones, which he said was his sleeping-place, and I suspect it is there that the plunder is concealed.'

'Come then,' said I: 'there is not a moment to be lost; if we delay we may chance to find the rest of the gang. This is just the hour at which they are all out in the bazaars, stealing what they can.'

We all sallied out, and conducted by our guide, crept stealthily along the foot of the rocks till we gained the narrow pathway by which we were to ascend.

We held a moment's conference in whispers, and bidding five of the men stay below until we should tell them to ascend, Bhudrinath, myself, and Surfuraz Khan crept up the narrow track to the mouth of the cave, whither the old Thug had preceded us.

'He still sleeps,' said he in a whisper; 'but tread softly, lest you wake him. He lies yonder, close by the lamp.'

'Mind, he is mine,' said I to Bhudrinath; 'do you and Surfuraz Khan hold him;' for as I looked on the powerful form before me, I felt this precaution to be necessary. But he slept; how was I to throw the rumal about his neck? Bhudrinath solved the difficulty; he gave the fakir a smart blow with the flat of his sheathed sword upon the stomach, and the fellow started up to a sitting posture.

'What is this? Thieves!' was all he could say; my handkerchief was ready, and now it never failed me—he was dead in an instant.

'Now trim the lamp,' said I to Bhudrinath. 'Call up three of the men, and let the others remain below to look out.'

Bhudrinath tore a piece of rag off the clothes of the dead fakir, which he twisted up into a thick wick and put into the oil vessel; its strong glare lighted up the interior of the cave, and we saw everything distinctly.

'Here is the wall which I spoke of,' said Shekhji, 'and we had better search behind it.'

We did so. There were piles of earthen jars in one corner, which we at first supposed to contain grain or flour, and indeed the first two uncovered had rice and dāl in them; the third felt heavy.

'This has something in it beyond rice,' said I; 'examine it closely.' The mouth was stuffed with rags, but when they were removed we beheld it filled with money—rupees and pice mixed together.

'This was not wise,' said Bhudrinath; 'the Shah Sahib ought not to have mixed his copper and silver, the silver will be tarnished; but we can clean it.'

The next pot was the same: the last was the best; it was full of gold and silver ornaments, rings anklets and armlets. We shuddered to see that many of them were stained with blood.

'The villains!' I exclaimed; 'that wretch then told the truth when he confessed himself to be a murderer; the city is well rid of him. But we must not stand talking. Do one of ye tie these things up and be ready for a start, while we look out for further spoil.'

But there was nothing else in this corner, no bales of cloth or other articles as we had exepected. We were looking about to find any other place of concealment, and had nearly given up our search when Surfuraz Khan, who had gone outside called to us.

'Come here,' he cried; 'there is a place here which looks suspicious.'

We ran to the spot, and found the hole he had discovered to be between two rocks; it was dark within, and a man could but just enter by crawling upon his hands and knees.

'Give me the light,' said I; 'I will enter it if the devil were inside.'

'Better the devil than any of this infernal gang,' said Bhudrinath to me as I entered.

I found no one, and the space within, which was so low that I could scarcely stand upright was filled with bundles.

'Neither the devil nor any of the gang are here,' cried I to those outside, 'so do some of you come in quickly and see what I have found.'

I set myself to work, as did also the others, to untie the different bundles, and we were all busily employed. I had just opened one which contained, as I thought, brass cooking-pots and water vessels, and was overjoyed to find some gold and others silver, when the alarm was given from outside. We all got out as quickly as we could and inquired the cause.

'There are two men,' said the scouts, 'whom we have watched come round the corner of the houses yonder and approach the bottom of the rocks; they do not walk fast, and appear to be carrying loads of something.'

'Only two,' said I, 'then they are easily managed. Put out the light and conceal yourselves at the entrance of the cave; we must fall upon them as they enter.'

We had just taken our posts behind a rock which was close to the mouth, our rumals ready, and two with their swords drawn, when one of the fellows called out, 'Ho! Sein! Sein! Come down and help us up. Here we are, laden like Pulla-walas, and thou hast not even a light to show us the way.'

'Not a word,' said I, 'as you value your lives. Let them come.'

'May his mother be defiled!' said the other fellow. 'The beast is drunk in his den and does not hear us. I will settle with him for this.'

I suppose he stumbled and fell, for there was another series of execrations at the fakir, the load, and the stones, but in a few moments more they both reached the platform and threw down their bundles, which clanked as they fell.

'Where is this drunken rascal?' said one, a tall fellow as big as the one we had killed. 'No light for us! and I warrant the brute has either smoked himself dead drunk or is away at the bhang-khana just when he is wanted.'

The other sat down, apparently fairly tired and out of breath.

'Go inside,' said he; 'you will find the lamp and cruse of oil behind the wall. I will not stir an inch.'

The first speaker entered, cursing and abusing the fakir. Surfuraz Khan and I rushed on him and dispatched him; but the other hearing the scuffle cried out and attempted to escape. He was not fated to do so however; his foot slipped, or he stumbled over one of the bundles he had brought, and fell, and before he could rise had received his death-wound by a cut in the neck from one of the men behind the rock, who darted out upon him.

'Enough of this work,' said I; 'we had better be off; first however let us pay one more visit to the hole and get what we can, and do one of you see what is in the bundles.'

We again entered the hole, and each taking a bundle we got out. Those the fellows had brought only contained cooking-pots and a few cloths, so we left them behind, and made the best of our way to the serai laden with our booty.

I have forgotten to tell you, Sahib, how many more proofs we discovered in that cave of the bloody trade of these villains. Many of the bundles were of wearing apparel, and most of them covered with blood; one that I opened was quite saturated, and as the still wet gore stuck to my fingers, I dropped it with mingled disgust and horror.

CHAPTER XV

WHEN we returned we had a good laugh over our success. The adventure was novel to us all, and we pictured to ourselves the mortification and chagrin of the robbers, when they should arrive, at finding their stronghold plundered of all its valuables, and their friends lying dead at the threshold, instead of being ready to receive them and recount their adventures of the evening.

As a better place of security, I took the jewels and silver vessels I had found to our house, and locked them up in the strong-room, to be disposed of afterwards as best they might be.

My father, I need not say, was overpowered with joy, and every new feat that I performed seemed to render me more dear to him. He caressed me as though I had still been a child.

'Wait till these actions are known in Hindustan, my son,' said he with enthusiasm; 'I am much mistaken indeed if they do not raise you to a rank which has been attained by few, that of Subadar.'

I did not reply to him, but I made an inward determination to venture everything to attain it. I was aware that nothing but a very successful expedition, coupled with large booty and a deed of some notoriety and daring could raise me to the rank my father had mentioned; but that it could be attained I had no doubt, since others had reached it before me—and why should not I, whose whole soul was bent upon winning fame through deeds which men should tremble to hear?

Two days after our adventure at the robbers' cave, the whole of the Karwan and adjacent neighbourhood were thrown into great excitement from the discovery of the dead bodies by their smell, and the number of vultures they attracted. Various were the conjectures as to the perpetrators of the violent deed, and many attributed it to the treachery of some of the band of robbers; however, all agreed that a great benefit had been done by unknown agents. Much of the stolen property was recovered; among it was some of great value which had been stolen from a sahoukar a short time before, and which in our hurry and confusion had escaped us; but, as it was, we had got a considerable booty. All the gold and silver was secretly melted into lumps by one of our men who understood how to do it, and it was valued by weight at upwards of seven thousand rupees.

On a general division of the proceeds of the booty being proposed, which amounted in a gross sum, by the sale of the camels, horses, bullocks, carts, and various valuables, to about fifty thousand rupees, all the Thugs agreed that it had better be reserved until the return of the expedition to our village; and meanwhile twenty rupees were disbursed to each inferior, and fifty to each jemadar, for their present wants. My father now talked of leaving the city; but I entreated a further stay of ten days, as, in concert with Bhudrinath and Surfuraz Khan, I had laid out a plan for dividing our gang into four portions, one to take post on each side of the city, and to exercise our vocation separately, the proceeds to be deposited as collected in one place, and to be divided when we could no longer carry on our work.

The plan was favourably received by him, and that day it was put into execution. We paid the trifling rent of our house, and on the pretence that we were about to leave the city and return to Hindustan, quitted the Karwan and took up our quarters on the other side, in a suburb which bordered upon the Meer Joomla tank. Bhudrinath and his party went into the Chuddar Ghat bazaar, near the magnificient mansion of the Resident, as, being a grand thoroughfare, it was frequented by numerous travellers, and from thence branched off many roads both to the north and east. Surfuraz Khan with eight men continued at the Karwan, as he was less known than we were. Another larger party took post on the western road from the city towards Shumshabad, under Peer Khan and Motee-ram, who were resolved by their exertions to merit the trust which had been confided to them.

Our plan succeeded wonderfully; not a day passed in which the destruction of several parties was not reported, and though the booty gained was inconsiderable, yet it was probably as much as we could expect, and it was all collected and deposited in our new abode, from whence my father disposed of such as met a ready sale.

I pass over my own share in these little affairs. I had thought, when I selected the quarter I did, that there would have been more work than turned out to be the case; I was disappointed in the small share which fell to my lot, in despite of my utmost exertions to the contrary, and entreated Bhudrinath or Surfuraz Khan to exchange places with me; they however would not; they had laid their own plans, and as I had myself selected my station I had no right to any other, nor ought I to have been dissatisfied.

It was very early in the morning of the eighth day after we had commenced operations, that Bhudrinath came to me in great alarm.

'We must fly,' said he, 'the city is no longer safe for us.'

'How?' I asked in astonishment; 'what has happened? Has aught been discovered, or have any of the band proved faithless and denounced us?'

'I will tell you,' replied Bhudrinath; 'it is a sad affair—some of our best men are taken and in confinement. You know

Surfuraz Khan to be daring, far beyond the bounds of discretion, and that for this reason few hitherto have liked to trust themselves to his guidance; and but for this fault he would ere now have been one of our leading jemadars, for he is a Thug by descent of many generations, and his family has always been powerful.'

'But the matter,' cried I impatiently; 'what in the name of Shaitan have we to do with his ancestors? By Allah! you are as bad as a—'

'Nay, I was not going to make a story about it,' said Bhudrinath mildly, for nothing could provoke him, 'so do not lose your temper; but listen. Surfuraz Khan then yesterday evening got hold of two sahoukars, who were on the eve of departure for Aurungabad; he persuaded them to put up in the sarai with him, and they were to start the next morning. They were supposed to be rich, as their effects in two panniers were brought into the sarai, and carefully watched by them. By some unlucky chance, just as the evening set in, they were visited by two or three other merchants whom they seemed to know, and who persuaded them to wait for another week, and to join them in their journey up the country. To the extreme mortification of Surfuraz Khan they agreed to the proposal; but as they said there would be danger in removing their bags from the sarai at night, they told their friends they would sleep there, and join them in the morning. Surfuraz Khan I hear made every exertion by persuasion to induce them to alter their determination, but in vain. So you know there remained but one alternative, which was to put them to death in the sarai, and to dispose of the bodies as well as they could; besides, the circumstance of the men being afraid to risk their bags by removal at night, looked as though they were of value. I must own, Meer Sahib, it was tempting; it would even have been so for you or me— much more for the Khan! Had he even waited till towards the morning, done the business and started leaving the bodies where they were, he could have got clean off with the booty, which was large, and he could have come round the back of the city and joined you or me; any one of us could have taken his post in the Karwan, and no one would have been at all suspicious. But no, he did not reflect; the men were killed almost immediately after their friends left, and their bags plundered: as it is, we have got some of the spoil in the shape of two strings of pearls, but the best are gone.'

'And how was the matter discovered? You have not said.'

'Why,' continued Bhudrinath, 'one of the sahoukars' friends shortly after returned with a message; Surfuraz Khan made some excuse that they had gone out, but would soon return. The fellow waited for a long time; but at last growing suspicious he went away, and returned with the others, who insisted upon a search for their friends. Surfuraz Khan had contrived to bury the bodies in the yard, but some articles were found on his person which the others positively swore to, as also the bags in which they had been; and the upshot of the whole was, that they were all marched off to the city by a guard which was summoned from somewhere or other for the purpose, except one of them, by name Himmat Khan, one of Surfuraz's own people, who happened to be absent.'

'It is a sad business truly,' said I, 'and I do not exactly see what is to be done to extricate them.'

'Nor I,' replied Bhudrinath; 'but this evil comes of not taking the omens, nor attending properly to them when they are taken.'

'Nonsense!' said I, 'you are always prating about these foolish omens, as if success lay more in them than in stout hearts and cunning plans. I believe them not.'

'You will rue it then one day or other,' said Bhudrinath; 'depend upon it you will rue it; I tell you I could mention a hundred instances of the disastrous effects of disregard of omens, and what I say will be readily confirmed by your father.'

'Pooh,' said I, 'he is as superstitious and absurd as yourself; why do you not make your lamentations on my want of faith to him, instead of troubling me with them?'

'I would,' he replied, 'but that he seems to have given over the charge of the whole expedition to you, and to have forgotten his station as the leader and conductor. Did any one ever hear of a whole band being separated, and each pursuing a separate course, without the omens being taken, or a solemn sacrifice offered to Bhowani?'

'I thought you had performed all the rites you seem to think so necessary,' said I sneeringly, 'and if you have not, to whom else have we to look but to you, who are the Nishan-burdur? By Allah and his Prophet! Bhudrinath, methinks you have deceived us all; and,' said I, my anger rising, 'I bid you beware how you speak of my father as you have done; remember that I am able and willing to avenge any word which may be spoken against him, and I will do it.'

'Young man,' said Bhudrinath gravely, 'you well know me to be one who never enters into idle brawls or quarrels, and these angry words of yours are wasted; keep them I pray you for those who will gratify you by taking offence at them—to me they are trifles. Your placing no dependence upon the omens, which have been considered by Thugs both of your faith and mine to be essential to our success, is only attributable to your inexperience; the necessary offerings have been neglected by us, and behold the punishment. Though at present it has fallen lightly upon us, there is no saying how soon the whole of us may be in danger; suppose any of those taken are put to the torture and denounce us, how should we escape?'

'Then what do you counsel?' said I.

'I would first propose an offering to Bhowani, and then such measures for the deliverance of those who have been seized as may be hereafter determined on by us all.'

'Perform the ceremonies by all means,' said I; 'you and my father know how to do so; my ignorance might mar your object, so I will keep away from you till they are over.'

'You are right, it might, and I am glad to hear you at length speak reasonably: where is your father?'

'You will find him asleep within,' said I, 'and you had better go to him.'

Sahib, the sacrifices were made, the omens watched, and declared to be favourable. What they were I know not; I cared so little about these ceremonies then, that I did not go near them, or even ask what had been done. It was only in after days that their value and importance were impressed upon me by a series of misfortunes, which were no doubt sent to check my presumption; since then my faith in them has been steadfast, as you will hereafter learn.

My father and Bhudrinath returned to me with joyful countenances. 'Bhowani is propitious,' said they, 'in spite of this little display of her anger: the truth is, we had in some manner neglected her, but she is now satisfied.'

'Since that is the case,' said I, 'we had better be stirring and doing something for the poor fellows; but what to do I know not. When did you say they were seized, Bhudrinath?'

'About the middle of the night.'

'Then they are now in confinement somewhere or other, and it will be impossible to effect their release by day: a bribe I dare not offer, for they say Hussein Ali Khan, the Kotwal, is an upright man. When is it likely they will be brought before him?'

'I know not,' said Bhudrinath, 'but it can easily be ascertained;' and he went into the street, and soon returned: 'I asked an old bunnia the question, or rather, at what time the Kotwal held his durbar, and he told me in the first and second watches of the night.'

'Then,' said I, 'they must be rescued by force, and I will do it.'

'Impossible!' cried both at once.

'But I tell you I will do it,' said I: 'where is Himmat Khan? With him and six of our best men I will do it, if they will stand by me. Do any of them know the Kotwal's house?'

They were summoned, but none knew it.

'Then,' said I, 'I will go even now and find it out, and will return when my plan is perfected.'

'And I will go and bring some of my men,' said Bhudrinath; 'I will be back by noon.'

'See that they bring their swords and shields, Bhudrinath; some of them may volunteer to accompany me.'

'I will do so for one, Meer Sahib; I have confidence in you in spite of your want of faith;' and he laughed.

'I understand you,' said I; 'you forgive me?'

'Certainly; did I ever quarrel with you?'

'No indeed, though you had cause; I was foolish.'

'Why, what is all this?' said my father; 'you have not surely been offended with each other?'

'It is nothing,' I replied, 'for you see the end of it; but I am losing time, I must depart.'

I went into the city, and easily got a person to show me the Kotwal's habitation. It was in a long, narrow street, which did not appear much of a thoroughfare. This exactly suited my purpose, for we could have done little in a crowded place. It seemed very practicable to surprise the men who should escort our friends, and I had no doubt, if suddenly attacked, they would scamper off, and leave their prisoners to their fate.

I returned and laid the result of my inquiries before my father. He was not averse to the undertaking, but was in much alarm at the prominent part I should have to play, and the chance of our being defeated.

'But,' said he, 'my son, these thoughts are the cowardly ones which affection often suggests, and Allah forbid they should have any effect with you; go, in the name of the Prophet, to whose protection I commend you.'

Towards evening therefore, myself Bhudrinath, and six others, two of whom were Rajpoots, who swore to die rather than come back unsuccessful, went into the city. We separated, but kept in view of each other, and they all followed me to the street in which the Kotwal resided. There we lounged about for some hours, and I grew very impatient. Would they ever come? Had they even before this been tried, condemned, and cast into prison? were questions I asked myself a thousand times. That the durbar was being held I knew, by the number of persons who went in and came out of the house, but still there was no sign of our brethren.

I was sitting listlessly in the shop of a tumbolee, almost the only one in the street, when Himmat Khan came up to me. I saw by his face that he had news, and descended from the chubootra upon which the man exposed his goods, and turned round a dark corner.

'They come,' said he, panting for breath from anxiety; 'I have been watching one end of the street and Khoseaal Singh the other: they are coming by my end, and will be now about half way up.'

'And by whom are they guarded?' I asked.

'Oh,' said he, 'a parcel of Line-walas, about twenty soldiers with old muskets; we could cut through a hundred of them.'

'Have they their bayonets fixed?' I inquired.

'They have; but what of that? they are cowardly rascals, and you will see will run away.'

'Then,' said I, 'run and tell Bhudrinath, who is yonder; tell him to walk down that side, I will go down this; when we are near them I will give the jhirnee.'

My four men had now joined me, as I told them to do if they saw me speak to any one: Bhudrinath was joined by his, and by Khoseal Singh, who had given up his watch at the other end and arrived at the critical moment. Our parties proceeded down the street exactly opposite to each other. I thought not of danger, though it was the first time I had ever drawn a sword in anger against a fellow-creature, and I was about to precipitate myself into what might be a sudden and desperate combat. Our shields apparently hung loosely and easily in our arms, but they were tightly grasped, and our swords were free in their scabbards. I saw the party approach; they marched carelessly, and had not the arms of my companions been tightly bound, and the whole tied together by a rope, which the leader of the party held in his hand, they might have easily escaped.

Our men joined together in the middle of the street and when we were close to the coming party, I cried in a loud tone, 'Bhai Pān lāo!' It was the signal—our swords flashed from their scabbards, and we threw ourselves on the sepoys. I cut right and left, and two men fell; the others were as successful: I rushed to the prisoners, and a few strokes of my sword and of those who were nearest cut their bonds and they were free. As Himmat Khan had said, the whole of the sepoys fled on the instant of the attack.

'Fly to the gates, my brothers, or they will be shut!' I cried; 'fly through these narrow dark streets; no one will know who you are, nor trouble themselves about you.'

We all dispersed in an instant. I cast a hurried look around me as I returned my bloody sword into its scabbard, and saw five poor wretches lying on the ground and groaning. It was enough: I too fled down the nearest street which offered, reached the gate I had entered by, and when I got on the embankment of the Meer Joomla tank, I plunged among the gardens and inclosure which are below it, and by the various lanes which led through them soon reached my father's house.

The attack on the escort of the prisoners, Sahib was so sudden and over so quickly, that I can give you but a faint idea how soon it was made and finished: it occupied less time than I have taken to tell it, and I have often wondered since that the noise and confusion, not only caused by us, but by a few passengers who witnessed the fray, did not alarm the whole street, and cause the inhabitants to rise on us.

By morning all our companions were present at the different places of rendezvous; but thinking we were no longer safe about the city, my father sent them all out of the way to the camp at Hassain Sagor, where he bid them wait, for we knew that it would never be searched for us.

Nothing now remained to detain us but to dispose of the plunder we had gained during the last ten days, and there was none of much value; a few strings of pearls, several shawls, and some unset precious stones were the best, and they were soon sold: the gold and silver as before had been melted down.

CHAPTER XVI

The day after the rescue of our brethren we held a consultation, at which the principal members of the band were present. I need not relate particulars; suffice it to say, that all agreed in thinking we had remained long enough consistently with our safety, and it was resolved to depart in the course of the next day, or at most the day after. One by one the parties, as they were then divided, were to take the nearest road towards Beeder, which led through Puttuncherroo; and the last-mentioned place was to be the rendezvous whence we should proceed in company.

'For the love of Allah! young man,' cried a low and sweet voice as I passed under the gateway of a respectable-looking house; 'for the love of Allah, enter and save my mistress!'

Fresh adventures, thought I as I looked at the speaker, a young girl, dressed like a slave. 'Who are you?'

'It matters not,' said the speaker; 'did you not pass this way yesterday afternoon, in company with two others?'

'I did, and what of that?'

'Everything; my mistress, who is more beautiful than the moon, saw you, and has gone mad about you.'

'I am sorry,' said I, 'but I do not see how I can help her.'

'But you must,' said the girl; 'you must, or she will die; follow me, and I will lead you to her.'

I hesitated, for I had heard strange stories of lairs spread for unwary persons—how they were enticed into houses for the gratification of wicked women, and then murdered. But the thought was only momentary. 'Courage! Ameer Ali,' said I to myself; 'trust to your good Nusseeb, and follow it up. Inshallah! there will be some fun.'

'Look you,' said I to the girl, 'you see I am well armed; I will follow you, but if violence is shown, those who oppose me will feel the edge of a sharp sword.'

'I swear by your head,' said the girl, 'there is no danger. My lord is gone into the country and has taken all the men with him; there is no one in the house beside myself but two slaves and three old women.'

'Then lead on,' said I; 'I follow you.'

She entered the gateway and conducted me through a court into an open room, where sat a girl richly dressed and of great beauty! but she covered herself immediately with her doputta, and cried when she saw me, 'Ya Allah! it is he, am I so fortunate?'

'Yes, lady,' said I, 'your slave is at your feet, and prays you to remove that veil which hides a houri of paradise from the gaze of a true believer.'

'Go,' said she faintly; 'now that you are here I dare not look on you; go in the name of Allah! what will you not have thought of me?'

'That your slave is the most favoured of his race,' said I; 'I beseech you to look on me, and then bid me depart if you will.'

'I cannot,' said the fair girl, 'I cannot, I dare not; ah, nurse, what have you made me do?'

The old woman made me a sign to take the veil from her face, and I did so gently; she faintly opposed me, but it was in vain; in an instant I had removed it, and a pair of the loveliest eyes I had ever seen, fixed their trembling gaze upon me—another, and I had clasped her to my heart.

'That is right,' said the old woman; 'I like to see some spirit in a lover; Mashallah! he is a noble youth;' and she came and cracked her fingers over my head.

'Now I will leave you,' said she; 'you have a great deal to say to each other, and the night is wearing fast.'

'No, no, no!' cried the girl, 'do not leave us; stay, good nurse, I dare not trust myself with him alone.'

'Nonsense,' cried the old woman, 'this is foolishness; do not mind her, noble sir;' and she left the room.

'Lady,' said I, 'fear not, your slave may be trusted;' and I removed from her, and sat down at the edge of the carpet.

'I know not what you will think of me, Sahib,' she said, 'and I am at a loss how to confess that I was enamoured of you as I saw you pass my house yesterday; but so it was; my liver turned to water as I looked on your beauty, and I pined for you till my attendants thought I should have died. They said they would watch for you, and Allah has heard my prayer and sent you.'

'He has sent a devoted slave,' said I; 'one whose soul burns with love, such as that of the bulbul to the rose: speak, and I will do your bidding.'

'Hear my history, and you will know then how I am to be pitied,' said the fair girl; 'and it is told in a few words. I was the daughter of humble parents, but I was as you see me—they say I am beautiful; they married me to my husband—so they said—but they sold me. Sahib, he is old, he is a tyrant, he has beaten me with his shoe, and I have sworn on his Koran that I will no longer remain under his roof. Yes, I have sworn it: I would have fled yesterday, but I saw you, and I prayed Allah to send you, and he has done so. Now think of me what you please, but save me!' And she arose, and throwing herself at my feet clasped my knees. 'You will not refuse me protection? If you do, and your heart is hard towards me, one thing alone remains—I have prepared a bitter draught, and tomorrow's sun will look upon my dead body.'

'Allah forbid! lady,' said I. 'He who has sent me to you has sent you a willing and a fearless slave: fly with me this instant, and I will lead you to a father who will welcome you, and a land far away where our flight will never be discovered.'

'Now—so soon?' she exclaimed.

'Ay, lady, now; leave your house this moment; I will protect you with my life.'

'I dare not, Sahib, I dare not; ah, what would become of us if we were discovered? You would escape, but I—you know a woman's fate if she is detected in intrigue.'

'Then what can be done?' said I. 'Alas! I am a stranger in the city, and know not what to advise.'

'I will call my nurse; let us leave all to her.—Kullo!'

The old woman entered. 'What are your commands?' said she.

'Listen,' said I; 'I love your fair charge with an intensity of passion; this is no place for us to give ourselves up to love, for there is danger, and we must fly: I am a stranger in the city, and am on the eve of departure for my home, which is in Hindustan, and whither I will convey her safely; she is willing to accompany me, and your aid and advice are all that is required.'

'To fly! to leave home and every one for Hindustan, and with one unknown! Azimabee, this is madness; how know you who he is, and where he will take you? I will not assist you. I was willing that you should have a lover, and helped you to get one; but this is madness—we shall be ruined.'

'Mother,' said I, 'I am no deceiver; I swear by your head and eyes I can be faithful; do but help two poor creatures whose affections are fixed upon each other, and we will invoke the blessings of the Prophet on your head to the latest day of our lives. I leave here tomorrow; my father is a merchant and accompanies me; he has ample wealth for us both, and I am his only child: we shall soon be beyond any chance of pursuit, and in our happiness will for ever bless you as the author of it. Ah, nurse, cannot you contrive something? Is there no spot on the road past Golconda which you could fix on for our meeting? I can reward you richly, and now promise you one hundred rupees, if you will do my bidding.'

Azima gathered courage at my words, and fell at the feet of the old woman.

'Kulloo!' she cried, 'have you not known me as a child? Have I not loved you from infancy? Alas! I have neither mother nor father now; and has *he* not beaten me with a shoe? Have I not sworn to quit this house? And did you not swear on my head you would aid me?'

'What can I do? What can I do?' cried the nurse; 'alas, I am helpless; what can an old woman like me do?'

'Anything, everything,' I exclaimed; 'woman's wit never yet failed at a pinch.'

'Did you not say you had made a vow to visit the Durgah of Hussein Shah Wullee?' cried Azima; 'and did you not say you would take me to present a nuzzur at the shrine of the holy saint, if I recovered from my last illness?'

'Thou hast hit it, my rose,' said the nurse; 'I had forgotten my vow. Sahib, can you meet us at the Durgah tomorrow at noon?'

'Assuredly,' said I, 'I will be present. Good nurse, do not fail us, and another fifty shall be added to the hundred I have already promised.'

'May your condescension and generosity increase!' cried she. Sahib, I have loved this fair girl from her infancy, and though it will go sorely against my heart, I will give her into your hands, rather than she should be further exposed to the indignities she has already undergone.'

'Thanks, thanks, good nurse, I believe you; but swear on her head that you will not break your faith.'

'I swear,' said the old woman, placing her hands on Azima's head, 'I swear she shall be thine.'

'Enough,' I cried, 'I am content; now, one embrace, and I leave you. I shall be missed by my father, and he will fear I am murdered in this wild city.'

We took a long, passionate embrace, and I tore myself from her.

'Tomorrow,' I cried, 'and at the Durgah we will met, never again to part. So cheer thee, my beloved, and rouse all your energies for what is before you. Tomorrow will be an eventful day to us both, and I pray the good Allah a prosperous one.'

'It will, it will,' cried the nurse; 'fear not for anything. Nurgiz is faithful, and shall accompany us; the rest are long ago asleep, and know not you are here. But now begone; further delay is dangerous, and Nurgiz will lead you to the street.'

She called, and the same slave who had ushered me in led the way to the door.

'By your soul, noble sir, by your father and mother, do not be unfaithful, or it will kill her.'

'I need not swear, pretty maiden,' said I; 'your mistress's beauty has melted my heart, and I am hers for ever.'

'Then may Allah protect you, stranger! That is your road, if you go by the one you came yesterday.'

I turned down the street and was soon at home. My father was asleep, and I lay down; but, Allah! Allah! how my heart beat and my head throbbed! A thousand times I wished I had carried off the beautiful Azima; a thousand times I cursed my own folly for having left her, when by a word from me she would have forsaken home and every tie and followed me; but it was too late. In the midst of conflicting thoughts and vain regrets I fell asleep; but I had disturbed dreams. I thought her dishonoured lord had surprised us as we tasted draughts of love, and a sword glittered over his head, with which he was about to revenge his disgrace.

Again I fancied one of the mullahs of the Durgah to be him, and just as she was about to depart with us, and was stepping into a cart, he rushed to her and seized her, and I vainly endeavoured to drag her from him. I woke in the excitement of the dream, and my father stood over me.

'What, in the name of the Prophet, is the matter with you, Ameer Ali, my son?' cried the old man. 'It is the hour of prayer, I came to awake you, and I find you tossing wildly in your sleep and calling on some one, though I could not distinguish the name; it sounded like a woman—Azima, I think. What have you been about? Had you any bunij last night?'

Bunij was the cant phrase for our victims, and I shuddered at the ideas it called up.

'No, no,' I said, 'nothing. Let me go and perform my ablutions; I will join you in the Namaz. It will compose my thoughts, and I will tell you.'

Our prayers finished, I related my adventures of the past night. He laughed heartily at my relation of the scene with Zora's mother, and declared I had served her rightly; but when I came to that with Azima, his countenance was changed and troubled; however he heard me to the end without interruption, and I augured favourably from it. I concluded all by throwing myself at his feet and imploring his sanction to our union.

'You have gone too far to retract, Ameer Ali,' said he. 'If you do not fulfil your promise to Azima she will drink the poison she has prepared; you will be one cause of her death, and it will lie heavy on your conscience; therefore on this account I give you my sanction. I am too old, a few years must see my end, and all I have long wished for is to marry you respectably and to see your children. I endeavoured to effect a marriage-contract in Hindustan before we left, but I was unable to do so. There is now no occasion for one; you have made your choice and must abide by it; Allah has sent you your bride and you must take her—take her with my blessing; and you say she is beautiful, in which you are fortunate. Money you will want, as you have promised some to her nurse; if she is faithful, give her from me an additional fifty rupees; and you had better take gold with you—it will be easier carried.'

'Spoken like my beloved and honoured father!' I exclaimed, 'and I am now happy. I ask your blessing, and leave you to carry our plans into execution. We shall meet again at Puttuncherroo in the evening.'

'Inshallah! we shall,' he replied. 'Be wary and careful. I apprehend no danger, but you had better take some men with you.'

'I will,' said I, as I rose to depart; 'I will take some of my own, whom I can trust;' and I left him.

My horse was soon ready and my men prepared; but some conveyance was necessary for Azima, and I ran to a house a short distance off where dwelt a man who had a cart for hire. I had been in previous treaty with him, to be ready in case I should get intelligence of Zora, and had engaged him to go as far as Beeder.

'Come,' said I, 'Fazil, I am ready, and the time is come.'

'And the lady?' said the fellow, grinning.

'Ah, she is ready too, only make haste, we have not a moment to lose.'

'Give me twenty rupees for my mother, and I will harness the bullocks and put in the cushions and pillows.'

'Here we are,' said I; 'now be quick—by your soul be quick!'

'I will be back instantly,' said he; and he disappeared inside his house, but returned almost immediately with the cushions and curtains of his cart.

'There,' said he, as he completed his preparations and jumped on the pole, where was his driving seat, 'you see I have not been long. Now whither shall I drive? to the city?'

'No,' said I; 'to Hussein Shah Wullee's Durgah. Do you precede, and we will follow you, for I know not the road.'

'I know it well,' said he; 'follow me closely.'

'Does it lead through the Begum Bazaar or the Karwan?' I asked.

'Through both, or either, just as you please.'

'And there is no other way?'

'There is, but it is somewhat longer. We must go by the English Residence and turn up towards the Gosha Mahal; the road will lead us far behind both the Karwan and Begum Bazaar.'

'That will do,' said I; 'I wish to avoid both.'

'Bismillah! then,' cried the driver, 'let us proceed;' and twisting the tails of his bullocks, a few gentle hints from his toes about their hindquarters set them off into a trot, which however they exchanged for a more sober pace before we had got far. I allowed him to proceed to some distance, and then put my small party in motion.

CHAPTER XVII

We soon passed the suburbs of the city, and held on our way towards the Durgah. I was not without hope that we might fall in with Azima on the road; but in this I was disappointed. As we passed over the brow of an eminence, the tombs of the kings of Golconda broke on our sight, occupying the whole of a rising ground in front. I had never before seen them, indeed I knew not of their existence, and they were the more striking on this account. I was astonished at their size and magnificence, even from that distance; but how much more so when we approached them nearer! We had plenty of time before us, and I proposed, if the Durgah should not be much further, to diverge from the road and examine them. I rode up to the driver of the cart, and asked him how far we were from the place of our destination.

'You cannot see the Durgah yet,' said the man, but it is just behind the tombs, on the border of a large tank; you cannot miss it; you will see its white dome and gilt spire above the tamarind trees which surround it.'

'Very good,' said I; 'do you go on thither, and if you are asked any questions, say that you belong to a party which is coming out from the city. We shall go to the tombs, and will join you shortly.'

The driver kept to the road, and we, diverging from it, directed our way to the mausoleums of the departed kings. As we approached them, their immense size, and the beautiful groups which they assumed as our point of view shifted, struck forcibly on the mind, while the desolation around them added to their solemn appearance.

The silence and desolation were oppressive, and we scarcely made a remark to each other, as we traversed one by one the interiors of the noble edifices—some of them dark and gloomy and filled with bats and wild pigeons, whose cooing re-echoed within the lofty domes—and others, whose wide arches admitted the light of the day, and we were more cheerful in appearance.

'Enough,' said I, after we had examined some of the largest; 'we do but loiter here while we may even now be expected. Yonder is the Durgah, and we had better go to it and be prepared; she cannot now be long absent.'

I saw as we approached the sacred edifice that our cart was ready; but there was no other, and my mind somewhat misgave me that Azima had been unable to keep her appointment; and I resolved within myself that, should she not arrive before noon, I would return to the city and seek my bride, for such I now considered her. I could not leave so lovely a creature to the rude treatment she would experience from him to whom she was united —one who was undeserving to possess a jewel such as she was: but it was still early, and perhaps some hours must elapse before she could reach the Durgah, which was farther from the city than I had anticipated.

I entered the holy precincts, and after offering up a gift upon the shrine of the saint, I put up a fervent prayer that the object we had come for should end successfully. This done, I sat down under the shade of the trees, and entered into conversation with one of the many mullahs who attended on the tomb, and who were constantly employed in reading the Koran over the grave of the saint. He asked me who I was: I told him I belonged to the city, and had brought my wife to perform a vow to the saint, on her recovering from a dangerous illness; 'but she is not yet come.' said I; 'I rode on with some of my attendants, and she will follow, and will soon be here.'

Hour after hour passed, and yet Azima did not come. Sahib, I was in torment of suspense and anxiety: could she have met with any misfortune? Could her lord have returned home unexpectedly? Could she have played me false? Ah, not the last! her grief, her misery, were too strong to be feigned, and what object could she have had in dissembling? Noon came, and the music of the Nobut began to play—still no signs of her. My patience was fairly exhausted, and I went to the place where my horse stood, mounted him, and bidding the men remain where they were, I rode on towards the city. I had scarcely got beyond the small village by which the Durgah was surrounded, when I saw three carts with curtains to them carefully closed approaching. My heart beat quickly with hope, and I determined to return; one of them surely is her, thought I, and I will await her coming in the Durgah.

'She comes!' cried I to Peer Khan, as he eagerly asked the cause of my quick return, 'she comes! Bid Fazil have his cart in readiness, and take it round to the gate which leads towards Puttuncherroo.'

I dismounted and stood at the gate.

The first cart arrived; it was filled with dancing-girls, who had a vow to sing at the shrine, one of them having lost her voice some time before, but had recovered it, as they supposed, at the intercession of the holy Wullee. They passed me, and I soon heard their voices singing one of their melodies inside the tomb.

The second arrived; three old women got out, bearing some trays of sweetmeats for the mullahs, the offering of some lady of rank, who was ill, and begged their prayers and intercession with the saint for her recovery.

'Mother,' said I to one of them, 'saw you aught of a cart with three females in it, my zenana in fact, on the road from the city?'

'Yes,' said the woman, 'they are close behind us; their vehicle broke down in a rivulet we had to pass, and is coming very slowly, but it will be here directly; and the ladies are safe, for I spoke to them and offered to bring them on; but the damage had been repaired somehow or other, and they declined my offer.'

'Alhumd-ul-illa!' I cried, 'they are safe then; I have been waiting here since morning and in anxiety enough about them.'

'No wonder,' said the old lady, 'for the khanum seemed to be pale and weakly-looking; but, Mashallah! she is beautiful, and my lord too is in every way worthy of her.'

'She has been ill,' said I carelessly, 'and her coming is in consequence of a vow she made.'

'May Allah give her a long life and many children! I feel an involuntary interest in a pair whom he hath joined together, in every way so fitted for each other; but I go, noble sir; my companions await my coming.'

She also passed on, and in a few moments more the cart I so longed to see turned the corner of some projecting houses, and advanced slowly towards the gate. How my heart throbbed! was it her, my life, my soul, or was I doomed to a third disappointment? It stopped, and I could have fallen down and worshipped the old nurse, who first emerged from the closely-curtained vehicle; I ran towards her, but was stopped by the driver.

'It is a zenana, noble sir,' he said, 'and courtesy requires you to go out of sight, lest their faces should be seen in descending.'

'Peace, fool! the women are my own.'

'That alters the case,' said the man; 'and my lord's displeasure must not fall on his slave for this delay; the axletree cracked in passing a rivulet, which is a circumstance no foresight could have prevented, seeing that it was newly fitted after the Moharram.'

'It matters not,' said I; 'but you may now leave us; I will return and pay your hire: there is an empty cart yonder which I will engage for them to return in.'

The fellow retired to a short distance, and my breath went and came as I put my head into the curtains and saw my beloved sitting unveiled, beautiful beyond description, and her fine features glowing with the excitement of her success.

'Shookur khoda!' she exclaimed, 'you are here, my own best and dearest; you have not been unfaithful to your poor slave.' I caught her in my arms, and imprinted numberless kisses on her lips.

'Toba! Toba! for shame!' cried the old nurse; 'cannot you refrain for a while? Assist her to dismount, and we will go into the Durgah.'

I did so; and closely enveloped in a boorka, and leaning on the old woman and Nurgiz, Azima followed me into the inclosure.

'Can you support the fatigue of further travel, Azima?' I asked.

'I am strong and can bear anything, so I am with thee and thou with me,' she replied. 'Dearest, I am now secure; but oh the suspense I have endured since I last saw you, and until I was fairly out of that vile city!'

'Tell me,' said I, 'how did you contrive to elude suspicion?'

'When you left us,' replied Azima, 'I thought my happiness had fled for ever; I would have given worlds to have called you back, and to have fled with you then. I had seen your noble face, I had heard your vows of love; Allah had sent me a lover such as my warmest fancy had painted to me, while I was daily suffering torments which the fond and loving only can feel, when their affection is returned by severe and bitter insult; and I thought I had lost him, that I had only gained a few moments of bliss, which would appear like one of those dreams that had often cheated my sleeping fancy, to leave me when I awoke to the bitter realities of my sad lot—and I was inconsolable; but my kind old nurse and Nurgiz soothed me. They told me they would die for me, and assured me you would be faithful; so I gathered courage, and Kulloo proposed that we should make immediate preparations for flight.'

She had just spoken, when Kulloo came to us. 'All is prepared,' said she; 'I have dismissed the other cart, and your new one is now ready;—do not delay.'

There was no occasion for her to hurry us, we were as well inclined to set off as she was, and we rose and followed her. The cart was ready—my men with it, and Nurgiz already inside. Azima got in, and her old nurse followed.

'You too?' cried I.

'Yes, Meer Sahib; my home is at Beedar, whither I will accompany you; the city is no longer safe for me: my life would be forfeited were I ever to enter it again, and fall in with that prince of devils, Nusrut Ali Khan, whose house now dishonoured, and whose beard we have spat upon.'

'Drive on,' I exclaimed to Fazil; 'go fast as you can; we must reach Puttuncherroo before night-fall.'

The road from the Durgah, after passing the tank upon which it was situated, led through a wild pass; piles of rocks frowned over us, and the road was at times so narrow that the cart could scarcely proceed. We reached Puttuncherroo late in the evening, and to my inexpressible joy found my father and the whole band safely arrived and comfortably encamped under a large banyan tree, by which was a fakir's tomb. One of our small tents had been pitched for Azima, and after seeing her settled for the night, I joined my father.

'You are a lucky fellow,' said he, when I had told him of all my success; 'I have been in anxious suspense about you, especially when the evening set in and you came not; but now there is no danger, we are once again in the country and the roads are our own. And now tell me what is your new bride like? Is she as handsome as Zora?'

'She is quite as handsome,' said I; 'the full moon is not more beautiful; she is tender in her love, and of an affectionate and kind disposition: you must see her tomorrow; she is now fatigued with travel.'

'And you must be fatigued also, my son, and hungry too. I have a rare pilau ready for you.'

It was brought; and after sending a portion to Azima, my fingers were very soon busied with the rest of the contents of the dish; and I enjoyed it, for I had tasted nothing but a few of the sweetmeats Azima had brought with her during the whole day.

CHAPTER XVIII

On the fourth morning we reached Beeder. If not so striking in its outward appearance as we approached it as Hyderabad, this city was nevertheless interesting. The summit of a long tableland broke into a gentle descent, and from it Beeder suddenly opened on our view. The walls of the town occupied the crest of a high ridge; and over them one tall minaret, and what appeared another rude unfinished one, of great height, towered proudly. On the right hand the large white domes of some tombs peeped out of a grove of mango trees, with which the hill was clothed from top to bottom; and there was a quiet solemnity about the approach to the now nearly deserted capital of the Dukhun, the favourite residence of the once proud and powerful Bhamunee kings, which accorded well with our feelings, and formed a powerful contrast to the busy city we had just left. Some of our men who had gone on in advance, had chosen a spot for our encampment near the gate of the city upon the road we were to take in the morning; but separating from my party, I rode through the town, which, though now mean in comparison to what it must have been, was more striking than I had expected to find it.

I joined the encampment on the other side, which now presented its usual bustling appearance: some were already cooking their morning meal by the edge of the well, others were bathing, and all talking and conversing in that joyous manner which showed their minds were free from care and full of happiness, at the prospect of a speedier return to their home than they had anticipated, and well laden with a rich booty.

'My father, this is a city full of true believers,' said I, as I joined him; 'mullahs there must be in plenty, and I pray you to send for one, that the nika may be performed, and that I may receive Azima at your hands as my wife.'

'I will not oppose it, my son; but the old Mullah, whoever he may be, will think it strange.'

'He may think what he pleases,' said I; 'but I can no longer live without her; therefore pray consider the point settled, and send for him at once.'

Accordingly Peer Khan was despatched for the holy person, who duly arrived: he was received with the greatest courtesy by my father, and the object for which he was required was explained to him. He expressed the utmost astonishment; it was a proceeding he had never heard of, for persons to celebrate a marriage on a journey, and was in every respect improper and indelicate.

When he had exhausted his protestations, my father replied to him.

'Look you, good Mullah,' said he, 'there is no one who pays more respect to the forms and usages of our holy faith than I do. Am I not a Syud of Hindustan? Do I not say the Namaz five times a day, fast in the Ramazan, and keep every festival enjoined by the law? And unwilling as I am to do anything which may be thought a breach of the rules of our faith, yet circumstances which I cannot explain render it imperative that this ceremony should be performed; and if you refuse, all I can say is, that there is no want of mullahs in Beeder, and if you do not perform it some less scrupulous person must, and earn the reward which I now offer to you;' and my father laid two ashrufees before him.

'That alters the case materially,' said the mullah, pocketing the money. 'Since the ceremony must be performed, in Allah's name let it take place; it was no doubt fated that it should be so, and you will therefore find no person in Beeder more willing to read the form of the nika than myself; let me I pray you return for my book,—I will be back instantly;' and he departed.

'There,' cried my father, 'I thought it would be so. No one can withstand the sight of gold: from the prince on the throne to the meanest peasant, it is the same; its influence is all-powerful. With it a man may purchase his neighbour's conscience, his neighbour's wife, or his daughter with it a man may bribe the venerable Cazee of Cazees, in any city he pleases, to declare him innocent, had he committed a hundred murders, forged documents, stolen his neighbour's goods, or been guilty of every villany under the sun; with it, a good man *may* be better—but that is rare—a bad man increases his own damnation: for it, any one will lie, cheat rob, murder, and degrade himself to the level of a beast; young women will dishonour their lords; old women will be bribed to assist them. A man who has hoards will practise every knavery to increase them, yet is never happy; those who have no money, hunger and thirst after it, and are also never happy. Give it to a child to play with, and by some mysterious instinct he clutches it to his bosom, and roars if it be taken from him. In short, its influence cannot be opposed; old and young, rich and poor—all are its slaves. Men's wisdom is nothing; men's eloquence is nothing; their character nothing; their rank nothing: but this vile metal, which has no voice, no intellect, no character, no rank—this rules our destinies on earth as surely and as potently as Allah himself does in heaven.'

'Allah ke Qoodrut!' said I with a sigh; 'your words are true, my fataher, now that one thinks on them; and we have had a precious specimen in the sudden change of opinion in the worthy mullah who asked no further questions when he saw your gold. But here comes the subject of our conversation, with his book under his arm; I will prepare Azima.'

I went to her. 'Dearest,' cried I, seating myself and passing my arm round her waist, 'Dearest, the time is come, when, with the blessing of Allah and my father's sanction, you will be mine for ever, and when the law shall bind us together, for death alone to separate us. A mullah has come; and with your permission, now, even now, the nika shall be performed; further delay is idle, and I am consumed with the burnings of my love.'

'So soon, Ameer Ali? Oh, not until we reach your home. What will your father think of my consenting to this wild union?'

'He sanctions it, beloved! 'twas he who sent for the mullah; 'twas he who persuaded him to perform the ceremony; and they but await my return to the tent to read the words which make you mine for ever.'

'Alas! I know not,' said the fair girl; 'I am another's wife—how can this be done?'

'Forget the hateful marriage,' I cried; 'Azima, these objections will kill me. Am I not your slave? are we not now on our way to a distant land, where he from whom you have fled will never again hear of you? Ah, do not continue to talk thus, for it seems like a bitter mockery that you should have fled with me, now to deny yourself to me.'

'No, no, no! do not say so, Ameer Ali; you saved me from insult, and from a miserable death to which I had doomed myself. I am your slave, not you mine; do as you choose with me; let it be even as you will. I will follow you till death.' And she hid her face in my bosom.

'Then,' cried I, 'beloved, the preparations are soon made. Call Kulloo, and let her know all.'

The old woman came, and was overjoyed to hear of my proposal.

'I had feared you would not have bound yourself by this tie, Meer Sahib,' said she, 'and my mind sorely troubled me on the subject; but now I am easy, and I will give my precious child to you with joy and confidence: may you be blessed in her, and see your children's children. Would that I could proceed with you! but I am old, and my bones and spirit would not rest easily in a strange land: your generosity and what I have scraped together is enough to make me comfortable for life, and when my hour comes I shall die content.'

'Then be quick,' said I; 'put up a screen and I will call the mullah; you can all three sit behind it while the ceremony is read.'

A cloth was stretched from one side of the tent to the other, and fastened to the ground: my father, myself, and the mullah sat on one side, the females on the other.

'All is ready, Mullah-ji,' said I; 'begin.'

He opened his book and read the usual service in Arabic. I did not understand a word of it, neither indeed did he; but it was sufficient that it had been read—the ceremony was complete, and Azima was mine for ever.

From Beeder, Sahib, we had no adventures worth relating till we reached Ellichpur, by which town we directed our route homewards; however, we did not travel by the same road as we had done in coming down; which would have led us by Mungrool and Amraoti, and we had good reasons for avoiding both places; the remembrance of the fate of the sahoukar would necessarily be fresh in the memory of the inhabitants of the latter place and our appearance was too remarkable to be easily forgotten. So we struck off from Nandair on the Godavery towards Burhanpur, and when we reached Akola in the berar valley, we turned again toward Ellichpur, and reached it in safety. You must not think, however, that during this long journey we were idle; on the contrary, we pursued our avocation with the same spirit and success with which we had commenced and continued our fortunate expedition; and no traveller, however humble, who joined our party, or was decoyed among us, escaped: and by this means, though our booty was not materially increased, yet we collected sufficient to support us, without taking aught from the general stock, which was to be divided when we reached our home.

At Ellichpur we encamped under some large tamarind trees, close to the Durgah of Rhyman Shah Doolah. It was a quiet lovely spot. Below the Durgah ran a small river, which had its rise in the neighbouring mountains; and over its stream the hallowed buildings of the saint, embowered in thick trees, seemed to be the abode of peace and repose. Thither Azima and myself, attended by some of our men, went, as soon, as we had rested ourselves a little and changed our road-soiled garments, to present our offerings at the shrine, and to offer up our thanksgivings for the continued care and protection of Allah.

This done, I sent her back to our camp, and entered into general conversation with the mullah, as was my wont, in order to gather information to guide us in our enterprises; and from so large a city as Ellichpur I had some hope that we should gain a valuable booty.

We conversed upon many topics of everyday occurrence; at last, one of the mullahs asked me where I had come from, and whither I was going. I said I was a horse-dealer, who had been down to Hyderabad with horses from Hindustan, and was now returning, having disposed of them. 'And the men who accompany you, who are they?' asked the mullah.

'My father, who is a merchant, is one,' said I; 'besides him there are the grooms and attendants who accompanied us, and several travellers who have joined us from time to time as we journeyed hither.'

'Then you are a kafila?' said the mullah.

'Exactly so,' said I; 'and feeling ourselves to be strong, we are determined to try the road to Jabalpur by Baitool, which, though unsafe for small bodies, presents no obstacle to our numerous party.'

'Certainly not,' he replied; 'and the road will save you a long distance which you would have had to travel had you gone round by Nagpur; and since you are bent on trying the jungle road, perhaps you would not have any objection to an increase to your party? and I think I could get you one.'

'Certainly not,' said I, 'if the travellers are respectable.'

'Highly so,' said the mullah; 'the person of whom I speak is a man of rank, no less than a Nawab, who is returning to his nephew, who rules over Bhopal.'

'Ah, I have heard of him I think,' said I; 'you do not mean the Nawab Subzee Khan, as he is called?'

'The very person, and a fine old soldier he is. It is a pity he is so addicted to the subzee or bhung, for which however he has gained a name which it is well known has struck terror into his enemies on the battle-field, and has fairly superseded any other he may have had.'

'It is a pity,' I said; 'for report speaks well of the noble Khan, and his deeds of arms are known to all who have sojourned in Hindustan: I shall be glad to accompany him, for 'tis said also that he is a rare companion.'

'You have heard rightly,' said the mullah. 'The Nawab will be here before sunset, as he always comes to converse with us and drink his bhung; if you will step over from your encampment when I send to you, I will introduce you to him.'

'Thanks, worthy mullah,' said I; 'you only need to summon me, and I will attend your call with pleasure.'

I left him soon after. Here was the commencement of an adventure which promised fairly to eclipse all our former ones; the rank of the Nawab, the number of followers he would necessarily have with him, and the noise there would be made about him when he was missed—all contributed to render this as pretty an adventure as a Thug seeking plunder and fame could desire.

I did not mention a word of my hopes to any one; I was determined to have this matter all to myself, both in plan and execution. If I succeeded, my fame and character were established for ever, and I could not fail with so many to back me. A momentary thought flashed across me—that the Nawab was a man of war, that he would be armed to the teeth; and who was I that I could oppose him? But I dismissed it in an instant as unworthy. My confidence in my own prowess, both as a Thug and with every weapon, whether on foot or on horseback, was unbounded; it had never as yet been checked, and I feared nothing living, I believe, in the form of man.

I waited very impatiently till towards evening, when, as I was sitting at the door of my tent, I saw a man on horseback, attended by a small retinue, among whom to my great astonishment was a young good-looking girl mounted on a spirited pony, coming down the road from the city. He passed near our camp, and crossing the river, ascended the opposite bank and entered the Durgah. Was this my new victim? I was not long in suspense; a message soon came from the mullah, requesting my company; and taking my sword and shield with me I followed the man who had come to call me.

CHAPTER XIX

SEATED with the old mullah I have before mentioned, the Nawab Subzee Khan Buhadur (for by that name alone I knew him) was quaffing his bitter and intoxicating draught. Around him stood some of his retainers, fierce-looking fellows, one or two of them with deep scars on their rough visages, which showed they had bravely followed their noble master through many a hard-fought field. Behind him sat the slave I have mentioned, a slender fair girl, who was busily prepared in making a fresh bowl of the infusion the Nawab was so fond of.

The mullah introduced me. 'This,' said he, 'my lord, is the young man I spoke of. I need repeat no praises of him, for no doubt your discerning eyes will at once observe that he is a person of respectability and good breeding, and a fit companion for one of my lord's exalted rank.'

I presented the hilt of my sword as a nuzzur, and after touching it with his hand, he bid me be seated near him on the carpet.

This I was too polite to do; so excusing myself on the ground of unworthiness of such honour, I seated myself on my heels on the edge of the carpet, and placed my sword and shield before me.

The sword immediately attracted his attention. 'That is a noble weapon, Meer Sahib,' said he; 'may I be allowed to look at it?'

'Certainly,' said I, presenting the hilt, 'the sword is at my lord's service.'

'Nay, Meer Sahib, I want it not; but I am curious in these matters, and have a choice collection, which I will one day show you.'

He drew it carefully from the scabbard, and as the brightly polished blade gleamed in the sunlight, he looked on it with a smile of delight, such as one would greet an intimate friend with after a long absence.

I must however describe him. In person he was tall and strongly made; his arms in particular, which were distinctly seen through his thin muslin dress, were remarkably muscular, and very long; his figure was slightly inclined to corpulency, perhaps the effect of age, which had also sprinkled his curling beard and mustachios with grey hairs; or it might be that these had been increased in number by the dangerous use of the drug he drank in such quantities. His face was strikingly handsome, and at once bespoke his high birth. A noble forehead, which was but little concealed by his turban, was covered with veins which rose above its surface, as though the proud blood which flowed in them almost scorned confinement. His eyes were large and piercing like an eagle's, and, but that they were swollen and reddened by habitual intemperance, would have been pronounced beautiful. He had a prominent thin nose, large nostrils, almost transparent, and a mouth small and curved like a bow, which, when the features were at rest, wore a habitual expression of scorn. His flowing and graceful beard and mustachios, which I have already mentioned, completed a countenance such as I had never seen the like of before, and have not met with since. The whole was inexpressibly striking, and in the meanest apparel the Nawab would at once have been pronounced by any one to be a man of high family and a gallant soldier.

A rosary of large pearls was about his neck, and with this exception he wore no ornaments. His dress was studiously plain, while it was neat in the extreme. I remarked two deep scars, one on the back of his head where it joined the neck, the other on his broad chest, and its deep seam was not concealed by the thin dress he wore. Such was Subzee Khan, who had won his renown in many a hard fight, and whom I was determined to destroy on the first opportunity.

He continued looking at the blade so earnestly and so long, that I began to think that it had possibly belonged to some victim of my father, who might have been known to the Nawab, and I was mentally framing a reply in case he should ask me where I got it, when he suddenly said, as he passed his finger along the edge, 'So, you too have seen battles, my friend; there are some slight dents in this good sword which have not escaped the touch of an old soldier. How did it come by them?'

'Oh, a trifling skirmish with robbers as I came down from Hindustan,' said I; and I related to him our affair with the thieves in the Nirmul road.

'It was well done,' said he, when I ended my account; 'but methinks you might have followed up your success and sliced some more of the rogues a little. This weapon would not have failed if your heart had not.'

'My heart never failed me yet, Nawab,' I replied; 'those who know me well, also know that I burn for an opportunity to prove that I am a man and no coward; but what could I do in that instance? there were but few of us, and the jungle was terribly thick —we could not have followed them in the dark.'

'You are right,' he replied; 'and what say you my young friend, to following the fortunes of Subzee Khan? He has at present naught to give thee; but, Inshallah! the time is fast approaching when men of tried valour may win something. My friend Dost Mahomed writes to me to come quickly, for he has need of leaders in his new enterprises; and methinks your figure and address would find favour with him. What say you? You are not fit to sell horses all the days of your life; and if you have turned any money in your present expedition, you cannot expend it in a manner more befitting your appearance than in getting a few men together, and offering your service. Dost Mahomed has need of such youths as you, and Inshallah! we will yet do something to win us fame.'

'May your favour increase, Bundé Nuwaz!' cried I; 'it is the very thing my soul longs for; with your introduction I cannot fail of obtaining service: and if once we have anything to do, you will find I shall not be backward.'

'Then you will accompany me?' said he; 'I am glad of it. You have some men with you I perceive, and some travellers; what say you to taking the direct road to Jabalpur? It is a rough one, but I am pressed for time; and that by Nagpur, though free from interruption or danger of robbers, is much longer.'

'I had determined on taking it, Nawab Sahib,' I replied, 'even before I saw you, for we are a strong party and well armed; but now I can have no hesitation. As for thieves or robbers, I have no dread of them, and my lord assuredly can have none?'

'None, since you have joined me,' he said; 'but with the few fellows I have, I confess I hardly liked to brave the jungle; for the bands who roam through it are strong and merciless, and it would be a sorry fate for Subzee Khan to fall in an unknown spot, after a life spent in battlefields.'

And yet you will do so, Nawab Sahib, said I internally; your death-blow will reach you in that jungle you dread, and no monument will mark the spot where the remains of Subzee Khan will lie.

'And when shall you be ready to move, Meer Sahib?' continued he; 'have you ought to delay you here?'

'Nothing,' I replied. 'I had purposed marching tomorrow morning, but if my lord wishes I can wait a few days.'

'Ah no—to-morrow morning I cannot move conveniently, but the day after I will join you here by daylight, and we will travel together.'

'Jo Hookum!' I replied; 'I shall be ready; and now have I permission to depart?'

'Certainly,' he said; 'I will no longer detain you. for I must be off myself. My friend Sulabut Khan has an entertainment of some kind to-night, and I have promised to attend it.'

I returned to my tent, and thought I longed to break the matter to my father, yet I refrained from doing so until the Nawab had fairly joined us, when I would introduce him properly.

As we were preparing to start the third morning before daylight, the Nawab rode into our camp and inquired for me.

I was speedily with him, and my father coming up to us, I introduced them to each other. After the usual compliments had passed, my father, unobserved by the Nawab, threw me a significant glance—I returned it, and he understood me: a look of triumph passed across his features, which gratified me, because to me alone was the band indebted for the adventure which was to follow.

Our party was soon in motion, and as the light increased with the dawning day, it revealed to me the person and dress of the Nawab, who now rode by my side. He was mounted on a splendid bay horse, which moved proudly and spiritedly beneath his noble master: the trappings of the animal were of crimson velvet, somewhat soiled, but still exceedingly handsome, for the saddle-cloth and headstall were embroidered with gold thread in a rich pattern.

But the rider chiefly attracted my observation: he wore a shirt of mail, composed of the finest steel links, exquisitely polished, over his ordinary clothes, at his waist it was confined by a handsome green shawl, which he had tied round him, and in which were stuck two or three daggers, mounted in gold and silver. His arms were cased in steel gauntlets, as far as the elbows, and greaves of steel protected his thighs. On his head was a bright steel cap, from the top of which a crimson steel tassal depended, and a shawl handkerchief was folded round it to protect his head from the heat of the sun. At his back hung a shield of rhinoceros hide, richly painted and gilt, a long sword hung at his side from an embroidered velvet belt which passed over his shoulder; and at his saddle-bow was fastened a small battle-axe, with a long and brightly polished steel handle.

Well did his appearance accord with his fame as a warrior. I had seen hundreds of soldiers at Hyderabad, but I had never yet looked on one so perfectly equipped as he who now rode beside me—nor one, could I but have attached myself to him, in whom I should have placed such confidence and followed readily into the deadliest strife. But what was the use of his weapons or his armour? They would not avail him—his hours were numbered, and his breath already in his nostrils.

'You observe me intently,' said he.

'I do,' I replied; 'for I have never yet seen so perfect a cavalier: horse, arms and accoutrements all agree in setting off their noble owner. Do you always travel thus?'

'Always, Meer Sahib; a soldier should never be out of his harness. The short time I have spent in idleness with that luxurious dog Sulabut Khan has softened my body, and even now I feel my armour chafe me. But the time comes when I shall need it, and I had as well accustom myself to it.'

We continued the whole of the march together, and he beguiled the way with relations of his adventures, battles and escapes. I was as much fascinated by them as by his powers of conversation, which were remarkable; and I often wished that I had met him as a friend, or enrolled myself under him, when I might have followed his banner and endeavoured to equal his deeds of valour.

But he was marked: in our emphatic language he was become a 'bunij,' and he was doomed to die by every rule and sacred obligation of our profession.

We reached our first stage without any adventure. Beyond it the villagers told us that the jungle grew thicker and thicker, that the road was very bad and stony, and above all that the Gonds were in arms, and plundered all whom they met with.

'Let them try us,' said the Nawab, as he listened to the relations, 'let them try us! Inshallah! they will do us no harm, and it may be some of them will get broken crowns for their pains.'

But the next morning we moved with more caution; our men were desired to keep well together, and I picked out a trusty few to surround the cart, which moved on with difficulty over the rough and stony roads; the Nawab and myself rode at the head of the party.

As we advanced, the road grew wilder and wilder; in many places it was narrowed almost to a foot-path, and the men were obliged to cut away the branches, which often nearly met across the road, so as to allow the cart to proceed. At other times it ran between high banks, which almost overhung us, and from which missiles might have ben showered on our heads, without a possibility of our being able to strike a blow in self-defence.

'That was an ugly place, Nawab Sahib,' said I, as we emerged from one of these narrow passes into a more open country, though still covered with jungle; 'had we been attacked there we should assuredly have fallen victims.'

'It was indeed,' said he; 'and I am thankful we have got out of it; if I remember aright it has a bad name. From hence however I think there are no more! the jungle becomes a forest, and there is not so much underwood. But look,' cried he, 'what is that? By Allah! the Gonds are upon us. Shumshere Alum!' cried he, in a voice which rang like the sound of a trumpet, 'Shumshere bu dust!' and his glittering blade flashed from the scabbard. Checking his horse, and at the same time touching its flanks with his heels, the animal made two or three bounds, after which the Nawab fixed himself firmly in his seat, pressed down his cap upon his head, and cried to me to be ready.

I was not behindhand; my sword was drawn and my shield disengaged, which I placed before me to guard me from the arrows. A few bounds of my horse, which was scarcely second to the Nawab's, brought me to his side, and we were followed by Bhudrinath and a few others mounted on ponies, and some men on foot with their matchlocks.

'Come on, ye sons of defiled mothers!' cried the Nawab; 'come on and prove yourselves true men; come on and try your cowardly arrows against stout hearts and ready weapons! Base-born kafirs are ye, and cowards; Inshallah! your sisters are vile, and asses have loved your mothers.'

I could not help laughing at the Nawab's gesticulations and abuse, as he poured it upon the Gonds and shook his sword at them. They would not move, and perched up as they were on the side of a hill, they prepared their bows to give us a volley—and down it came certainly; the arrows whistled past us, and one wounded the Nawab's horse slightly in the neck, at which the Gonds set up a shout of triumph.

'Ah, my poor Motee, thou art wounded,' cried he, drawing the arrow from the wound. 'Meer Sahib, those rogues will never come down; you had better give them a volley and disperse them.'

'Now, my sons,' cried I to my followers, 'whenever a fellow raises his body to fire, do you mark him.'

They did so. One Gond in particular, who was sitting on a rock drawing a large bow, which he placed against his feet, was a conspicuous object, and apparently careless of his safety. Surfuraz Khan aimed at him—fired—and in an instant he rolled over and over almost to our feet: the ball had hit him in the throat, and he was quite dead. The rest seeing his fate set up loud yells, and for a moment we thought they would have charged us: however another of their number fell badly wounded, and carrying him off they rapidly retreated to their mountain fastnesses. Pursuit would have been vain as it was impracticable.

We met with no further adventure during our march, and duly arrived at our stage by the usual hour.

'Ameer Ali,' said my father, coming to me shortly afterwards, 'is the Nawab to be ours or not? If you have invited him as a guest, say so; if not, you had better arrange something.'

'A guest!' cried I; 'oh no, he must be disposed of; there can be no difficulty where there are so many good places to destroy him.'

'Impossible!' said my father; 'on horseback it would be madness. He is a beautiful rider, and his horse is too spirited; the least confusion would make him bound, and who could hold him? We must devise some other plan.'

'Leave all to me,' said I; 'if there is no absolute necessity for selecting a place, I will watch my opportunity.'

CHAPTER XX

'I SUPPOSE you have long ere this guessed, my friends,' said I to Bhudrinath and Surfuraz Khan next day, 'why the Nawab is in our company?'

'We can have little doubt,' replied the former, 'since you have brought him so far: but tell us, what are your wishes; how is it to be managed? It will be impossible to attack him on the road; he would cut down some of us to a certainty, and I for one have no ambition to be made an end of just at present.'

'You are right,' said I; 'we must not risk anything; still I think my opportunity will not long be wanting.'

'How?' cried both at the same moment.

'Listen,' said I, 'and tell me whether my plan meets with your approval. 'During the march yesterday the Nawab was regretting that we did not fall in with a good stream of clear water, that he might take his usual sherbet: you know that the slave girl he has with him always prepares it. Now I am in hopes that we may meet one in to-morrow's march, and I will try all I can to persuade him to alight and refresh himself: while he is engaged in conversation with me, if we find him off his guard, we can fall on him.'

'Nothing is easier,' replied Surfaraz Khan; 'we cannot fail if he once sits down; his weapons will not then serve him.'

'I do not half like the job,' said Bhudrinath. 'Suppose he were to be on his guard, he would assuredly escape; and though both myself and the Khan here fear neither man nor devil, yet it is something out of the way to kill a Nawab; he is not a regular bunij, and I think ought to be allowed to pass free of harm.'

'Nonsense!' cried I. 'This from you, Bhudrinath? I am astonished. What, if he be a Nawab, is he not a man? and have I not fairly enticed him according to every rule of our vocation? It may be something new to kill a Nawab, but think, man, think on the glory of being able to say we had killed Subzee Khan, that valiant among the valiant: why, our fathers and grandfathers never did such an act before.'

In the evening the omens were duly taken, and proved to be favourable. We made all our arrangements that night, and next morning started on our journey in high spirits. The Nawab and I, as usual, rode together at the head of the party.

'This is an unblest country, Meer Sahib,' said he as we rode along. 'Didst you ever see so dreary a jungle, and not a drop of water to moisten the lips of a true believer from one end of the stage to the other? It is well the weather is cool, or we should be sorely tired in our long stages; and here have I, Subzee Khan, gone without my usual sherbet for three days on this very account. By Allah! I am now as thirsty as a crow in the hot weather, and my mouth opens in spite of me. Oh, that we could light on a river or a well in this parched desert! I would have a glorious draught.'

'Patience, Khodawund!' cried I, 'who knows but we may be near a stream? and then we will make a halt, and refresh ourselves: I am hungry myself, and should not care for an hour's delay to break my fast with some dates I have with me.'

'Ha, dates! I will have some too; my fellows may find something to eat in my wallets, and thou sayest truly, the cold wind of these mountains makes one hungry indeed.'

But coss after coss was left behind, and as yet no river appeared. I was beginning to think I had received false information, and was in no very good humour at my disappointment, when, to my joy, on passing over the brow of a hill, I saw the small river the villagers had spoken of below me.

'There,' said I, 'Khodawund! there at last is a river, and the sparkling of the water promises it to be good. Will you now halt for an hour? We can have a pipe all round, and your slave can prepare your sherbet.'

'Surely,' cried he; 'we may not meet with another and this is just the time when I like my sherbet best; send some one to the rear for my slave, and bid her come on quickly.'

I despatched a man for her, and reaching the stream, we chose a smooth grassy spot, and spreading the covers of our saddles, sat down.

One by one, as the men arrived, they also rested, or wading into the water refreshed themselves by washing their hands and faces in the pure stream, which glided sparkling over its pebbly bed; the beasts too were allowed to drink; and all the men sitting down in groups, the rude hookah passed round among them, while they cheerfully discussed the merits of the road they had passed, and what was likely to be before them. Casting a hasty glance around, I saw that all the men were at their posts, three Thugs to each of the Nawab's servants and retainers. They were therefore sure. Azima's cart was standing in the road, and in order to get her away I went to her.

'Beloved,' said I, 'we have halted here for a short time to allow of the people taking some refreshment, but you had better proceed; the road appears smooth, and we shall travel the faster to overtake you.'

'Certainly,' she replied; 'bid them drive on, for I long to be at the end of the journey. Poor Nurgiz and myself are well nigh jolted to death.'

'Ah, well,' I said, 'bear up against it for another stage or two. I promise you to get a doolie if I can, at the first large village or town we come to, and then you will be comfortable.'

'Now proceed, said I to the Thug who acted as driver (for I had purchased a cart on the road, soon after we left Beeder, and he had driven it ever since), 'proceed, but do not go too fast.'

She left me, and I returned to the Nawab. He was sitting in conversation with my father, and even now was evidently partially intoxicated with his detestable beverage.

'Ho! Meer Sahib,' cried he; 'what dost *thou* think? Here have I been endeavouring to persuade this worthy father of thine to take some of my sherbet. By Allah! 'tis a drink worthy of paradise, and yet he swears it is bitter and does not agree with his stomach. Wilt thou take a drink?' and he tendered me the cup. 'Drink, man! 'twill do thee good, and keep the cold wind out of thee; and as to the preparation, I'll warrant it good; for there breathes not in the ten kingdoms of Hind a slave so skilled in the art of preparing a subzee as Kureena yonder. Is it not so, girl?'

'My lord's favour is great toward his slave,' said the maiden; 'and if he is pleased, 'tis all she cares for.'

'Then bring another cup,' cried the Nawab; 'for what saith the song?' and he roared out the burden of one I had heard before—

"Peyala pea, to myn nē pea, phir kisee ko kya!"[1]

'and what is it to any one? All the world knows that Subzee Khan drinks bhung, and is not the worse soldier for it. Now with a few fair girls to sing a ghuzul or two to us, methinks a heaven might be made out of this wild spot.'

'It is a good thought, Nawab,' cried I, chiming in with his humour; 'we will get a set of tuwaifs from the next village we come to; I dare say they will accompany us for a march or two.'

'You say well, Meer Sahib; yours are good words, very good words; and Inshallah! we will have the women,' said the Nawab slowly and indistinctly, for he had now swallowed a large quantity of the infusion, which had affected his head. 'By Allah! they should dance too—like this—' continued he with energy, and he got up, and twirled himself round once or twice with his arms extended, throwing leering glances around upon us all.

It was irresistibly ludicrous to behold him. His splendid armour and dress but ill assorted with the mincing gait and absurd motions he was going through, and we all laughed heartily.

But the farce was proceeding too long, and we had sterner matter in hand than to waste our time and opportunity in such

[1] A cup (of wine) is drunk—then I have drunk it;
What is it to any one?

fooleries. So I begged him again to be seated, and motioned to Surfuraz Khan to be ready the instant he should see me go round to his back.

'Ho! Kureena,' cried he, when he had again seated himself, 'bring more subzee, my girl: by Allah! this thirst is unquenchable, and thou art excelling thyself today in preparing it. I must have more, or I shall never get to the end of this vile stage. I feel now as if I could sleep, and some more will revive me.'

'Fazil Khan, bring my hookah,' cried I as loud as I could. It was the signal we had agreed on.

'Ay,' cried the Nawab, 'I will beg a whiff or two, 'twill be agreeable with my sherbet.'

I had now moved round behind him; my rumal was in my hand, and I signalled to Surfuraz Khan to seize him.

'Look, Nawab!' cried he; and he laid hold on his right arm with a firm grasp.

'How dare you touch me, slave?' ejaculated Subzee Khan. 'How dare you touch a Nawab—?'

He did not finish the sentence. I had thrown the cloth about his neck, Surfuraz Khan still held his hand, and my father pulled at his legs with all his force. The Nawab snored several times like a man in a deep sleep, but my grip was firm and did not relax: a horse would have died under it. Suddenly, as he writhed under me, every muscle in his body quivered; he snored again still louder, and the now yielding form offered no resistance. I gazed upon his features, and saw that the breath of life had passed from the body it had but now animated. Subzee Khan was dead —I had destroyed the slayer of hundreds!

But no one had thought of his poor slave girl, who at some distance, and with her back turned to us, had been busily engaged in preparing another rich draught for her now unconscious master. She had not heard the noise of our scuffle, nor the deep groans which had escaped from some of the Nawab's people, and she approached the spot where Surfuraz Khan was now employed in stripping the armour and dress from the dead body.

Ya Allah! Sahib, what a piercing shriek escaped her, when she saw what had been done! I shall never forget it, nor her look of horror and misery as she rushed forward and threw herself on the body. Although master and slave, Sahib, they had loved.

Her lips were glued to those of the unconscious corpse, which had so often returned her warm caresses, and she murmured in her agony all the endearing terms by which she had used in their private hours to call him, and implored him to awake.

'He cannot be dead! he cannot be dead!' cried the fair girl—for she was beautiful to look on, Sahib, as she partly rose and brushed back her dishevelled hair from her eyes; 'and yet he moves not—he speaks not'—and she gazed on his features for a moment. 'Ah!' she screamed, 'look at his eyes—look at them—they will fall out of his head! and his countenance, 'tis not my own lord's—those are not the lips which have often spoken kind words to his poor Kureena! Oh, my heart, what a pain is there!'

'This will never do,' cried I; 'some of you put her out of her misery; for my part, I war not with women.'

'The girl is fair,' said Surfuraz Khan; 'I will give her a last chance for life.'

'Hark you!' cried he to her, 'this is no time for fooling;' and as he rudely shook her by the arm, she looked up in his face with a piteous expression, and pointed to the body by which she was kneeling and mourning as she rocked herself to and fro. 'Hear me,' cried the Khan, 'those who have done that work will end thy miserable life unless thou hearkenest to reason. I have no wife, no child: thou shalt be both to me, if thou wilt rise and follow me. Why waste further thought on the dead? And thou wast his slave too! Rise, I say again, and thy life is spared—thou shalt be free.'

'Who spoke to me?' said she, in tones scarcely audible. 'Ah, do not take me from him; my heart is broken! I am dying, and you would not part us?'

'Listen, fool!' exclaimed the Khan; 'before this assembly I promise thee life and a happy home, yet thou hearkenest not: tempt not thy fate; a word from me, and thou diest. Wilt thou then follow me? My horse is ready, we will leave the dead, and think no more on the fate of him who lies there.'

'Think no more on him! forget him—my own, my noble lover! Oh, no, no, no! Is he not dead? and I too am dying.'

'Again I warn thee, miserable girl,' cried Surfuraz Khan; 'urge me not to use force; I would that you followed me willingly—as yet I have not laid hands on thee.'

A low moan was her only reply, as she turned again to the dead, and caressed the distorted and now stiffening features.

'Away with the body!' cried I to some of the Lughaees, who were waiting to do their office; 'one would think ye were all a parcel of love-sick girls, like that mourning wretch there. Are we to stay loitering here because of her fooling? Away with it!'

My order was obeyed; four of them seized the body, and bore it off in spite of the now frantic exertions of the slave; they were of no avail; she was held by two men, her struggles to free herself gradually exhausted her.

'Now is your time,' cried I to Surfuraz Khan; 'lay hold of her in the name of the thousand Shaitans, since you must have her, and put her on your horse: you can hold her on, and it will be your own fault if you cannot keep her quiet.'

Surfuraz Khan raised her in his arms as if she had been a child; and though now restored to consciousness, as she by turns reviled us, denounced us as murderers, and implored us to kill her, he bore her off and placed her on his horse. But it was of no use; her screams were terrific, and her struggles to be free almost defied the efforts of Surfuraz Khan on one side and one of his men on the other to hold her on.

We proceeded about half a coss in this manner, when my father, who had hitherto been a silent spectator, rode up, as I was again vainly endeavouring to persuade the slave to be quiet and to bear with her fate.

'This is worse than folly,' cried he, 'it is madness; and you above all, Surfuraz Khan to be enamoured of a smooth-faced girl in such a hurry! What could we do were we to meet travellers? She would denounce us to them, and then a fine piece of business we should have made of it. Shame on you! Do you not know your duty better?'

'I'll have no more to say to the devil,' said the man on the left of the horse doggedly: 'you may even get her on the best way you can; what with her and the horse, a pretty time I am likely to have of it to the end of the journey;' and he quitted his hold.

'Ay,' said I, 'and think you that tongue of hers will be silent when we reach our stage? What will you do with her then?'

'Devil!' cried the Khan, striking her violently on the face with his sheathed sword, 'will you not sit quiet, and let me lead the horse?'

The violence with which he had struck caused the sword to cut through its wooden scabbard, and it had inflicted a severe wound on her face.

'There,' cried my father, 'you have spoilt her beauty at any rate by your violence; what do you now want with her?'

'She is quiet at all events,' said the Khan, and he led the horse a short distance.

But the blow had only partly stunned her, and she recovered to a fresh consciousness of her situation; the blood trickled down her face, and she wiped it away with her hand; she looked piteously at it for an instant, and the next dashed herself violently to the earth.

'One of you hold the animal,' cried the Khan, 'till I put her up again.' But she struggled more than ever, and rent the air with her screams; he drew his sword and raised it over her.

'Strike!' she cried, 'murderer and villain as you are, strike! and end the wretched life of the poor slave; you have already wounded me, and another blow will free me from my misery; I thought I could have died then, but death will not come to me. Will you not kill me?'—and she spat on him.

'This is not to be borne; fool that I was to take so much trouble to preserve a worthless life,' cried the Khan, sheathing his sword; 'thou shalt die, and that quickly.' He threw his rumal about her neck, and she writhed in her death agonies under his fatal grasp.

'There!' cried he, quitting his hold, 'I would it had been otherwise; but it was her fate, and I have accomplished it!' and he left the body and strode on in moody silence.

Some of the Lughaees coming up, the body was hastily interred among the bushes which skirted the road, and nothing now preventing us, we pursued our journey with all the speed we could. Thankful was I that I had sent on Azima in her cart; she was far beyond the scene of violence which had happened, and of which she must have guessed the cause had she been within hearing; but the driver of her cart had hurried on, and we had travelled some coss ere we overtook her. Strange, Sahib, that after that day Surfuraz Khan was no longer the light-hearted, merry being he had used to be. He was no novice at his work; hundreds of human beings, both male and female, had died under his hand; but from the hour he killed the slave he was an altered being: he used to sit in silent, moody abstraction, his eyes gazing on vacancy; and when we rallied him upon it, his only reply was a melancholy smile, as he shook his head, and declared that his spirit was gone: his eyes too would on these occasions sometimes fill with tears, and sighs enough to break his heart would escape from him.

He accompanied us to our home, got his share of the booty, which he immediately distributed among the poorer members of the band, and after bidding us a melancholy farewell, stripped himself of all his clothes, covered his body with ashes and went forth into the rude world, to bear its buffets and scorn, in the guise of a fakir.

I heard, years afterwards, that he returned to the spot where he had killed the girl, constructed a hut by the road-side, and ministered to the wants of travellers in that wild region, where his only companions must have been the bear, the tiger, and the wolf. I never saw him again after he parted from us, and many among us regretted his absence, and his daring skill and bravery, in the expeditions in which we afterwards engaged: his place was never filled among us.

I have no more adventures of this expedition to relate to you: we reached our home in due course without any accident or interruption; and who will not say that we enjoyed its quiet sweets, and appreciated them the more after our long absence, and the excitement and perils of our journey? I was completely happy, secure in the increasing love and affection of Azima, whose sweet disposition developed itself more and more every day. I was raised to a high rank among my associates, for what I had achieved was duly related to those who had stayed in our village, and to others who had been out on small expeditions about the country; and the immense booty we had acquired, and my father's well-known determination to retire from active life, pointed me out as a leader of great fortune, and one to whom many would be glad to entrust themselves in any subsequent expedition, as I appeared to be an especial favourite of our patroness.

The return of Hussein's party, about two months after we had arrived was an event of great rejoicing to us all when they reached our village. As we had agreed beforehand, at our separation, the whole of the proceeds of the expeditions of both parties were put into one, for general distribution, and on a day appointed it took place. Sahib, you will hardly believe it when I tell you that the whole amounted to very nearly a lakh of rupees.

It was carried by general acclamation that I should share as a jemadar, and according to the rules of our band I received one eighth of the whole. Bhudrinath and Surfuraz Khan received what I did, but the latter only of such portion as we had won since he joined us.

Upon the sum I had thus acquired I lived peacefully two years. I longed often to go out on small expeditions about the country, but my father would not hear of it.

'What is the use?' he would say. 'You have ample means of subsistence for two years to come; my wealth you know is also large, and until we find the supply running short, why should you risk life in an attempt to gain more riches, which you do not need?'

But my spirit sorely rebelled against leading such an inactive and inglorious life, and every deed I heard of only made me more impatient to cast off the sloth which I feared would gain hold on me, and to mingle once more in the exciting and daring exploits of my profession.

Still I was fond of my home. Azima had presented me with a lovely boy, who was the pride of my existence, and about the time I am speaking of I expected another addition to my family. I had already seen two seasons for departure pass, and a third was close at hand, but I suffered this also to elapse in inactivity, although I was repeatedly and strongly urged by Bhudrinath and others to try my fortune and head another band to penetrate into Bengal, where we were assured of ample employment and success.

But much as I wished to accompany them, my father still objected; something had impressed him with an idea that the expedition would be unfortunate; and so in truth it turned out. A large gang under several leaders set out from our village at the usual time; but the omens, although not absolutely bad, were not very encouraging, and this had a dire effect on the whole. They had not proceeded far when jealousies and quarrels sprung up among the several leaders; they separated from each other and pursued different ways. One by one they returned disappointed with their expedition having gained very little booty, scarcely sufficient to support them for the remainder of the year. But one party was never heard of more; it consisted of my poor friend Bhudrinath and six noble fellows he had taken with him. Years afterwards we heard his fate: he had gone down into Bengal, had visited Calcutta, and up to that period had been most successful; but there his men dissipated their gains in debauchery, and they set out on their return with barely sufficient to carry them a few marches.

They had nearly reached Benares, when absolute starvation staring them in the face, they attacked some travellers, and, as they thought, killed them. They neglected, however, to bury their victims, and one, who was not dead, revived: he gave information to the inhabitants of the nearest village. My poor friends were overtaken, seized, the property they had about them immediately recognised, and the evidence given by the survivor of the party they had attacked was convincing. What could oppose this? The law had its course, and they were tried and hanged.

Ameer Ali here stopped in his narrative, and promising to resume it in a few days, he requested permission to withdraw, and making his usual salaam departed.

A strange page in the book of human life is this! thought I, as he left the room. That man, the perpetrator of so many hundred murders, thinks on the past with satisfaction and pleasure; nay, he takes a pride in recalling the events of his life, almost every one of which is a murder, and glories in describing the minutest particulars of his victims, and the share he had in their destruction, with scarcely a symptom of remorse! Once or twice only has he winced while telling his fearful story; and what agitated him most at the commencement of his tale I have yet to hear.

With almost only that exception, his spirit has seemed to rise with the relation of the past; and his own native eloquence at times, when warmed with his tale and under the influence of his vivid imagination and faithful memory, has been worthy of a better pen and a more able translator than I am: but let this pass; I repeat, it is a strange and horrible page in the varied record of humanity. Murderers there have been in every country under heaven, from the time of Cain to the present—murderers from hate, from revenge, from jealousy, from fear, from the instigation of any and every evil passion of our nature; but a murder's life has even been depicted as one of constant misery—the worm that dieth not, the agony and reproach of a guilty conscience, gnawing at the heart, corroding and blasting every enjoyment of life, and either cousing its wretched victim to end his existence by suicide, to deliver himself up to justice, or to be worn down by mental suffering—a more dreadful fate perhaps than the others. Such are the descriptions we have heard and read of murderers, but these Thugs are unlike any others. No remorse seems to possess their souls. In the weariness of perpetual imprisonment one would think their imaginations and recollections of the past would be insupportable to them; but no—they eat, drink, and sleep like others, are solicitous about their dress, ever ready to talk over the past, and would, if released tomorrow again follow their dreadful profession with a fresh zest after their temporary preclusion from it. Strange too that Hindus and Moslem, of every sect and denomination, should join with one accord in the superstition from which this horrible trade has arisen. In the Hindu perhaps it is not to be wondered at, as the goddess who protects him is one whom all castes regard with reverence and hold in the utmost dread; but as for the Moslem, unless his conduct springs from that terrible doctrine of Fatalism, with which every true believer is thoroughly imbued from the first dawn of his reason, it is difficult to assign a reason for the horrible pursuit he has engaged in.

CHAPTER XXI

At the expiration of a week, Ameer Ali sent word to me that he was ready to resume his narrative, and I lost no time in requesting him to repair to my residence. He arrived, and making his usual graceful obeisance, I desired him to be seated.

The reader will perhaps like to know something of the appearance of the man with whom he and I have had these long conversations; and no longer to keep him in the dark on so important a subject, I will describe Ameer Ali to him. He is what would be called a short man, about five feet seven inches in height; his figure is now slender, which may be the effect of his long imprisonment—imprisonment it can hardly be called except that to one of his formerly free and unrestrained habits and pursuits, the smallest restraint must of course be irksome in the highest degree and painful to bear. His age may be about thirty-five or forty years, but it sits lightly on him for a native of India, and it has not in the least whitened a beard and mustachios on which he evidently expends great care and pains, and which are always trimmed and curled with the greatest neatness. His figure, as I have said, is slight, but it is in the highest degree compact, agile, and muscular, and his arms are remarkable for the latter quality combined with unusual length and sinewyness. His dress is always scrupulously neat and clean, and put on with more attention to effect than is usual to his brother approvers, his turban being always tied with a smart cock, and his waist tightly girded with an English shawl or a gaily dyed handkerchief, where one a shawl of Cashmere or a handkerchief of brocade was better suited to his pretentions. In complexion he is fair for a native; his face is even now strikingly handsome, and leads me to believe that the accounts of his youthful appearance have not been exaggerated. His forehead is high and broad; his eyes large, sparkling and very expressive, especially when his eloquence kindles and bursts forth in a torrent of figurative language, which it would be impossible to render into English, or, if it were rendered, would appear to the English reader, unused to such forms of speech, highly exaggerated and absurd. His cheeks are somewhat sunken, but his nose is aquiline and elegantly formed, his mouth small and beautifully chiselled, and his teeth are exquisitely white and even. His upper lip is graced with a pair of small mustachios, which would be the envy of many a gay lieutenant of hussars; while a beard close and wavy, from which a straggling hair is never suffered to escape, descends nearly to his breast, and hides a throat and neck which would be a study for a painter or a sculptur: to complete all, his chest is very broad and prominent, and well contrasts with the effect of his small waist.

His manner is graceful, bland, and polite—it is indeed more than gentlemanlike—it is courtly, and I have not seen it equalled even by the Mahomedan noblemen, with many of whom I have associated. Any of my readers who may have been in India, and become acquainted with its nobles and men of rank, will estimate at once how high is the meed of praise on this score which I give to Ameer Ali. His language is pure and fluent, perhaps a little affected from his knowledge of Persian, which, though slight, is sufficient to enable him to introduce words and expressions in that language, often when they are not needed, but still it is pure Urdu; he prides himself upon it, and holds in supreme contempt those who speak the corrupt patois of the Dukhun, or the still worse one of Hindustan. Altogether Ameer Ali is a character, and a man of immense importance in his own opinion and that of every one else; and the swagger which he has now adopted in his gait, but which is evidently foreign to him, does not sit amiss on his now reduced condition.

Reader, if you can embody these descriptions, you have Ameer Ali before you; and while you gaze on the picture in your imagination and look on the mild and expressive face you have fancied, you, as I was, would be the last person to think that he was a professed murderer, and one who in the course of his life has committed upwards of seven hundred murders. I mean by this, that he has been actively and personally engaged in the destruction of that number of human beings.

Now, Ameer Ali, said I, since I have finished describing your appearance, I hope you are ready to contribute more to the stock of adventures you have already related.

Your slave is ready, Sahib, he replied, and Inshallah Ta-allah! he will not disappoint you. But why has my lord described my poor appearance, which is now miserable enough? But might your slave ask what you have written—and the tone of his voice implied that he had concluded it could not be favourable.

Listen, said I, and I will read it to you. At every sentence the expression of his face brightened. When I had concluded, he said,

It is a faithful picture, such as I behold myself when I look in a glass. You have omitted nothing, even to the most trifling particulars; nay, I may even say, my lord has flattered me. And he arose and made a profound salaam.

No, said I, I have not flattered your external appearance, which is prepossessing; but of your heart I fear those who read it will judge for themselves, and their opinions will not be such as you could wish, but such as you deserve.

You think my heart bad then, Sahib?

Certainly I do.

But it is not so, he continued. Have I not ever been a kind husband and a faithful friend? Did I not love my children and wife while He who is above spared them to me? And do I not even now bitterly mourn their deaths? Where is the man existing who can say a word against Ameer Ali's honour, which ever has been and ever will remain pure and unsullied? Have I ever broken a social tie? Ever been unfaithful or unkind to a comrade? Ever failed in my duty or in my trust? Ever neglected a rite or ceremony of my religion? I tell you, Sahib, the man breathes not who can point his finger at me on any one of these points. And if you think on them, they are those which, if rigidly kept, gain for a man esteem and honour in the world.

But the seven hundred murders, Ameer Ali—what can you say to them? They make a fearful balance against you in the other scale.

Ah! those are a different matter, said the Thug laughing—quite a different matter. I can never persuade you that I was fully authorized to commit them, and only a humble instrument in the hands of Allah. Did *I* kill one of these persons? No! it was He. Had my rumal been a thousand times thrown about their necks and the strength of an elephant in my arms, could I have done aught—would they have died, without it was His will? I tell you, Sahib, they would not, they could not; but as I shall never be able to persuade you to think otherwise, and as it is not respectful in me to bandy words with my lord, I think it is time for me to recommence my tale, if he is ready to listen, for I have still much to relate. I have been so minute in the particulars of my first expedition, that perhaps I need not make the narrative of the other events of my life so prolix; indeed, were I to do so, you, Sahib, would be tired of writing and your countrymen of reading, for it would be an almost endless task to follow me in every expedition I undertook. I shall therefore, with your permission, confine myself to the narration of those which I think will most interest you, and which I remember to possess remarkable incidents.

Go on, said I; I listen.

Well then, said the Thug, Khodawund must remember that I told him I passed over three expeditions, and that I had partly determined to go on the third. It is of that expedition I would now speak, as it was marked by an extraordinary circumstance, which will show you at once that it is impossible for any one to avoid his fate if it be the will of Allah that he should die.

At the time I speak of I had been obliged to form another set of intimates in consequence of the loss of Bhudrinath and Surfuraz Khan, for both of whom I had the sincerest regard. Hussein, though I loved and revered him as my father's dearest friend, was now too old and grave to participate in all my thoughts and perhaps wild aspirations for distinction. So as Peer Khan and Moteeram, with whose names you are familiar, had now risen to my own rank, and proved themselves to be 'good men and true' in various expeditions, I took them into my confidence, and we planned an enterprise, of which I was to be the leader and they my subordinates. Fifty of the youngest, stoutest, and most active and enterprising of our acquaintances were fixed on as the band; and all having been previously warned, we met a few days before the Dussehra of the year 18— in a grove near our village, which was shady and well adapted for large assemblies, and was always used as a place of meeting and deliberations; it was considered a lucky spot, no unfortunate expedition ever having set out from it.

We were all assembled. It was a lovely morning, and the grass, as yet not even browned by the sun and drought, was as if a soft and beautiful carpet had been spread on purpose for us. The surrounding fields, many of them tilled by our own hands, waved in green luxuriance, and the wind as it passed over them in gentle gusts caused each stalk of tall jowaree to be agitated, while the sun shining brightly made the whole glitter so that it was almost painful to look on for a continuance. Birds sang in the lofty banyan trees which overshadowed us; hundreds of green parroquets sported and screamed in their branches, as they flew from bough to bough, some in apparent sport, others to feed on the now ripening berries of the trees; and the whole grove resounded with the cooing of innumerable turtle-doves, whose gentle and loving murmurs soothed the turbulence of the heart, and bade it be at peace and rest and as happy as they were.

My father and Hussein were present to guide us by their counsels and experience, and the matter in hand was commenced by a sacrifice and invocation to Bhowani; but as I have before described these ceremonies, it is needless to repeat them; suffice is to say that the omens were taken and were favourable in the highest degree; they assured us, and though I had little faith in them, notwithstanding all I had heard to convince me of their necessity, they inspirited the whole band, and I partook of the general hilarity consequent upon them.

My father opened the object of the meeting in a short address. He said he was old and no longer fitted for the fatigues and privations of a journey; he recapitulated all I had done on the former expedition, pointed out the various instances in which I had displayed activity, daring, and prudence beyond my years, and concluded by imploring the men to place implicit confidence in me, to obey me in all things as though himself were present, and above all not to give way to any disposition to quarrel among ich would infallibly lead to the same disastrous vertaken the expedition which had gone out the

They one and all rose after this address, and by mutual consent swore on the sacred pickaxe to obey me, the most impressive oath they could take, and any deviation from which they all firmly believed would draw down the vengeance of our Protectress upon them and lead to their destruction.

I will not occupy your time, Sahib, by a narration of what I myself said; suffice it to say, I proposed that the band should take the high road to the Dukhun, and penetrate as far as Jabalpur or Nagpur; from thence we would take a direction eastward or westward, as hope of booty offered, and so return to our home. Khandesh I mentioned, as being but little known to us Thugs, and where I thought it likely we might meet with good booty, as I had heard that the traders of Bombay were in the habit of sending large quantities of treasure to their correspondents in Malwa for the purchase of opium and other products of that district. I concluded by assuring them that I had a strong presentiment of great success, that I felt confidence in myself, and that if they would only follow me faithfully and truly, we might return in a few months as well laden with spoil as we had on the former occasion.

Again they rose and pledged their faith; and truly it was a solemn sight to see those determined men nerve themselves for an enterprise which might end happily, but which exposed them to fearful risk of detection, dishonour, and death.

CHAPTER XXII

Our meeting broke up, and I returned to prepare Azima for my departure. I had invented a tale to excuse my absence. I told her that the money which I had gained on my mercantile expedition to the Dukhun was now nearly expended; and although, in her society, and in the enjoyment of happines such as I had never hoped for, I had been hitherto been unwilling to leave my home, yet I could delay to do so no longer without absolute ruin staring us in the face. I added, that my father had placed a sum of money as my disposal for the purposes of trade; with which, if I met with the success I had reasonable ground to hope for, from the letters of my correspondents at Nagpur and other places, I could not fail of realizing a handsome profit—enough to allow us another continued enjoyment of peace and affluence.

Long and vainly she strove to overrule my determination, pointed out the dangers of the road, the risks to which I should be necessarily exposed, the pain my absence would cause her; but finding these were of no avail, as I told her my plans had been long laid, and that I was even now expected at Saugor, where my agents had collected the horses I was to take for sale, she implored me to take her and our children with me, adding that travelling was a matter of no difficulty to her, and that the children would enjoy the change of scene and the bustle and novelty of the camp.

But this also I overruled. It would have been impossible to take her, not to mention the expense of her travelling-carriage; and at last, after much pleading and objections of the description I have mentioned, she consented to remain; and placing her under my father's care on the morning we were to depart, I took an affectionate farewell of her.

Many were the charms and amulets she bound about my arms and hung round my neck, which she had purchased from various wandering fakirs and holy mullahs; and with streaming eyes she placed my hands upon the heads of my children and bade me bless them. I did so fervently and truly, for I loved them; Sahib, with a love as intense as were the other passions of my nature.

At last I left her. Leaving one's home is never agreeable, often painful; for the mind is oppressed with indistinct visions of distress to those one leaves behind, and is too prone to imagine sources from which it might spring, though in reality they exist not. It was thus with me; but the appearance of my gallant band, as they greeted my arrival among them with a hearty shout, soon dispelled my vague apprehensions, and my spirit rose when I found myself in the condition which had been the object of many a fervent aspiration. I was my own master, with men willing to obey me; and—Inshallah! I exclaimed to myself, now Ameer Ali's star is in the ascendant, and long will it gleam in brightness!

According to our rules, no one was to shave or eat *pān* until our first victim fell; and as this was a matter of inconvenience to many of the men, you may be sure we had our eyes in all directions, and our scouts well occupied in every village we passed through or halted at. But it was not till the fifth day that we met with any one who offered a secure and in every way eligible sacrifice; we had fallen in with bands of travellers, some going to, and others departing from, their homes, but they had invariably women in their company, and them I was determined to spare, as well for my wife's sake as from the injunctions of my father.

However, as I have said, on the fifth day, early in the morning, we came to a cross-road, and were glad to see a party of nine travellers, three upon ponies, having the appearance of respectable men, and the rest on foot, coming up the road a short distance from us. To our great joy they struck into the road we were about to take. We had halted in pretended indecision as to the road, and when they came up we asked it of them. They readily pointed to the one before us, and although expressing themselves astonished at our numbers, they agreed to accompany us to the village where we proposed to halt, and the road to which we had inquired of them. I soon entered into conversation with the most respectable of their party; and I replied, in answer to his inquiries, that we were soldiers proceeding, after our leave to Hindustan, to Nagpur, where we were in service. He told me in return, that he and his brother, one of the two others mounted, with a friend and some attendants, were on a travelling expedition; that they had come from Indore, and were going to Benares, as well for the purchase of cloths and brocades, as to visit that sacred place of Hindu pilgrimage.

Ho, ho! thought I, these are assuredly men of consequence going in disguise, and I have no doubt are well furnished with ready cash. No time must be lost, as they have come by a cross-road, and have not been seen in our company; there can consequently be no trace by which we could possibly be suspected on their disappearance; so the sooner they are dealt with the better. To this end I lagged behind a little, and imparted my determination to Peer Khan, who rode in the rear of all; by him it was told to another, and thus it circulated throughout the band before we had gone far. I was gratified and delighted to see how, as they became aware of what was to be done, each took his station, three Thugs to each traveller, and the rest disposed themselves around the whole, so as to prevent any possibility of escape.

I remembered the road well, for it was that which we had travelled before; and what Thug ever forgets a road? I knew also that, although the country around was open and bare, there was a river not far off, the sandy bed of which was full of the wild cypress, and the bodies could be easily disposed of in the brushwood.

When we arrived at the brink of the river, the man I had continued to converse with begged for a short halt.

'We have been travelling since midnight,' said he, 'and I for one am well tired, and should be glad of rest.'

I made no objection of course, for it was the very thing I wished; and dismounting, and leading my horse to the water, I allowed him to drink, and then joined the party, which had all collected, and were now seated; the travellers discussing a hasty meal they had brought with them, and the Thugs sitting or standing around them, but all in their proper places.

I was on the point of giving the *jhirnee*, and I saw the bhuttotes handling their rumals in a significant manner, when, thanks to my quick sense of hearing, I distinguished voices at a distance. It was well for us that I had not given the signal; we should have been busily engaged in stripping the bodies when the party I had heard would have come upon us. Of course they would have seen at a glance what we were about, and have taken the alarm. But our good destiny saved us. I hesitated, as I have said, and in a few minutes fourteen travellers made their appearance, and came directly up to where we were sitting. They were persons of all descriptions, who had associated for mutual protection, and I had half determined to destroy them also, when they relieved me greatly by taking their departure, wishing us success and a pleasant and safe journey.

On one pretence or another I delayed our associates until the other party had proceeded far beyond the risk of hearing any noise, should there be any; and now, seeing everything ripe for the purpose, I called out for some tobacco, the word we had agreed to use, as being least likely to attract attention or inspire suspicion. I had planted myself behind the man I had been speaking to, and as I spoke my handkerchief was thrown!—in an instant he lay a corpse at my feet. My work was done, and I looked around to see the fate of the rest; one poor wretch alone struggled, but his sufferings were quickly ended, and the party was no more.

'Quick, my lads!' cried I to the Lughaees, 'quick about your work!'

One of them grinned. 'Why?' said he; 'did you not observe Doolum and four others go away to yon brushwood when we reached this spot? Depend upon it they have the grave ready, or they have been idle dogs.'

And it was even so; the grave had been dug while the unsuspecting travellers sat and conversed with us.

We were so busily engaged in stripping the dead, that no one observed the approach of two travellers, who had come upon us unawares. Never shall I forget their horror when they saw our occupation; they were rooted to the spot from extreme terror; they spoke not, but their eyes glared wildy as they gazed, now at us and now at the dead.

'Miserable men,' said I, approaching them, 'prepare for death! you have been witnesses of our work, and we have no resource but your destruction for our own preservation.'

'Sahib,' said one of them, collecting his energies, 'we are men, and fear not to die, since our hour is come;' and he drew himself up proudly and gazed at me. He was a tall, powerful man, well armed, and I hesitated to attack him.

'I give you one alternative,' said I; 'become a Thug, and join our band—you shall be well cared for, and you will prosper.'

'Never!' he exclaimed; 'never shall it be said that Tilluk Singh, the descendant of a noble race of Rajputs, herded with murderers, and lived on their unblessed gains. No! if I am to die let it be now. Ye are many; but if one of you is a man, let him step forward, and here on this even sand I will strike one blow for my deliverance;' and he drew his sword, and stood on the defensive.

'I am that man,' cried I, though the band with one voice earnestly dissuaded me from the encounter, and declared that he was more than a match for me: 'I am that man: now take your last look on the heavens and the earth, for by Allah you never quit this spot!'

'Come on, boasting boy!' he exclaimed; 'give me but fair play, and bid none of your people interfere, and it may not be as you say.'

'Hear all of you,' cried I to them, 'meddle not in this matter—'tis mine and mine only. As for the other, deal with him as ye list;' and in an instant more he was numbered with the dead.

'These are your cowardly tricks,' cried the Rajput, now advancing on me, for he had stood contemplating the fate of his companion; 'my end may follow his, but I shall die the death of a soldier, and not that of a mangy dog as he has done.'

I have before told you, Sahib, that my skill in the use of every weapon was perfect, thanks to my good instructor; and I had never relaxed in those manly exercises which fit a man for active combat whenever he shall be called into it. My sword was the one Nawab Subzee Khan had so much admired, and I felt the confidence of a man when he has a trusty weapon in his hand and knows how to wield it.

I have said that the Rajput advanced on me; he had no shield, which gave me an immense advantage, but the odds were in his favour from his height and strength, yet these are a poor defence against skill and temper.

He assailed me with all his force and fury; blow after blow I caught on my sword and shield, with out striking one myself; he danced round me after the fashion of his people, and now on one leg now on the other, he made wild gyrations, and at intervals rushed upon me, and literally rained his blows at my person; but I stood fixed to the spot, for I knew how soon this mode of attack must exhaust him, and the loose sand of the river added to his fatigue.

At length he stood still and glared on me, panting for breath. 'Dog of a Kafir!' cried he, 'son of an unchaste mother, will nothing provoke thee to quit that spot?'

'Kafir!' I exclaimed, 'and son of a Kafir, thy base words have sealed thy fate;' and I rushed on him. He was unprepared for my attack, made a feeble and uncertain blow at me, which I caught on my shield, and the next instant my sword had buried itself deep in his neck. He fell, and the blood gushed from the wound.

'Shookur Khoda!' exclaimed Peer Khan, 'you have settled this business nobly; let me embrace thee;' and he folded me in his arms.

The Rajput was not dead; he had sufficient strength remaining to raise himself upon his arm, and he looked at me like a devil; he made many attempts to speak; his lips moved, but no sound followed as the blood prevented utterance.

'Some of you put him out of his pain,' said I; 'the man behaved well, and ought not to suffer.'

Peer Khan took my sword and passed it through his heart; he writhed for an instant, and the breath left his body.

'Away with him!' cried I, 'we have loitered too long already.'

The lugha took him by his legs and arms, to avoid his blood, and carried him away; others strewed a quantity of dry sand over the spot where he had fallen, and in a few minutes we were pursuing our way as if nothing had happened.

After this proof of my personal courage and skill, I may safely say I was almost adored by the whole band. They all assured me that a Thug having killed a traveller and a soldier in fair open combat was an unprecedented circumstance, and only required to be known to make me the envy of old and young, and I gloried in what I had done; their praise was sweet incense to my vanity.

The booty we got from the merchant and his brother was rich, and was of itself a fair amount of booty for any expedition. Some were even for turning back, but they were only two or three voices, and were easily overruled.

'It would be a shame,' I said, 'if while fortune favoured us we did not take advantage of our good luck.'

CHAPTER XXIII

We reached Jabalpur without another adventure of any kind, and rested there for two days. Peer Khan, Motee, and myself perambulated the bazaars during the whole time, but not a traveller could we meet with, nor could we learn that any were expected; it was therefore of no use to remain, and as we had still plenty of time before us, we could travel as leisurely as we pleased; so on the third morning we again proceeded.

The country between Jabalpur and Nagpur is a wild waste. Villages are not met with for miles and miles, the road is stony and uneven, and the jungle thick and dangerous for nearly the whole way. On this account the tract has always been a favourite resort of Thugs, and more affairs have come off in those few marches than perhaps in any other part of the country frequented by us. We were all regretting that we had not met with some bunij at Jabalpur, wherewith to beguile the weariness of the road, when at our second stage, soon after we had arrived, Motee, who had gone to look out for work for us, returned with the glad news that there was a palankeen at the door of a merchant's shop, surrounded by bearers and a few soldiers, which looked very much as if it belonged to a traveller.

'But he must be of rank,' said Motee, 'therefore I humbly suggest that you, Meer Sahib, should undertake to see who he is, and to secure him if possible.'

I followed his advice, and changing my travelling attire for a dress which would ensure my civil reception, I armed myself, and, attended by a Thug who carried my hookah, I sauntered into the village. I soon saw the palankeen and men about it, and in order to gain some intelligence to guide me, I went to a small tumbolee's shop directly opposite to it, and sitting down entered into conversation with the vendor of tobacco and pān.

'This is a wild country you live in, my friend,' said I.

'Yes it is indeed as you say,' he replied, 'and were it not for you travellers, a poor man would have little chance of filling his belly by selling pān and tobacco, but, as it is, my trade thrives well.'

'There do not seem to be many on the road,' said I; 'I have come from Jabalpur without meeting a soul.'

'Why the roads are hardly much frequented yet,' he rejoined, 'but in a month more there will be hundreds; and there,' he continued, pointing to the house over the way, 'there is almost the only one I have seen for some time.'

'Who is it?' I asked, 'and where has he come from? He was not with us.'

'I know not,' replied the tumbolee, 'nor do I care; whoever he is, he has bought a quantity of my stuff, and it was the first silver which crossed my hands this morning.'

I saw there was nothing to be got out of this man, so I went to a bunnia a little further off, and after a few preparatory and indifferent questions, asked him whether he knew aught of the traveller; but he knew nothing either, except that a slave-girl had bought some flour of him. 'They say,' said he, 'that it is a gentleman of rank who is travelling privately, and does not wish to be known; at any rate, Sahib, I know nothing about him; I suppose however he will come out in a short time.'

This is very strange, thought I; here is a gay palankeen, eight bearers and some soldiers with it, come into this wretched place, and yet no one's curiosity is aroused; who can it be? I will return to the tumbolee and sit awhile; I may see, though I cannot hear anything of this mysterious person.

I sat down at the shop, and calling to my attendant for my hookah remained there smoking, in the hope that some one might appear from behind the cloths which were stretched across the verandah: nor did I stay long in vain; I saw them gently move once or twice, and thought I could perceive the sparkle of a brilliant eye directed to me. I riveted my gaze on the envious purdah, and after a long interval it was quickly opened, and afforded me a transient momentary view of a face radiant with beauty; but it was instanly closed again, and I was left in vain conjecture as to the beautiful but mysterious person who had thus partially discovered herself to me. It would not have suited my purpose to have personally interrogated any of the bearers, who were lying and sitting about the palankeen, as it would have rendered them suspicious, and would have been impertinent; after all it was only a woman—what had I to do with women now? And had I not made an inward resolution never to seek them as bunij—nay, even to avoid parties in which there might be any?

So I arose and took my way to our camp, firmly resolving that I would pursue my march the next morning; for, thought I, she must be some lady of rank travelling to her lord, and Allah forbid that I should raise a hand against one so defenceless and unprotected; and I thought of my own lovely Azima, and shuddered at the idea of her ever being placed within reach of other members of my profession, who might not be as scrupulous as I was.

But, Sahib, the resolves of men—what are they?—passing thought, which fain would excite the mind to good, only to be driven away by the wild and overpowering influences of passion. Despite of my resolve, my mind was unquiet, and a thousand times fancy brought to my view the look she had cast on me, and whispered that it was one of love. I could not shake it off, and sought in the conversation of my associates wherewith to drive her from my thoughts; but it was in vain; that passionate glance was before me, and the beauteous eyes which threw it seemed to ask for another, a nearer and more loving.

In this state I passed the day, now determining that I would resist the temptation which was gnawing at my heart, and now almost on the point of once more proceeding to the village and seeking out the unknown object of my disquietude; and I was irresolute, when towards evening I saw a slave girl making towards the camp, and I went to meet her, but not with the intention of speaking to her should she prove to be only a village girl. We met and I passed her, but I saw instantly that she was in search of some one, for she turned round hesitatingly and spoke to me.

'Forgive my boldness, Sahib,' said she, 'but I am in search of some one, and your appearance tells me that it must be you.'

'Speak,' said I; 'if I can aid you in anything, command me.'

'I know not,' she replied, 'whether you are he or not; but tell me, did you sit at the tumbolee's shop this morning for some time, smoking a hookah?'

'I did, my pretty maiden,' said I; 'and what of that; there is nothing so unusual in it as to attract attention.'

'Ah, no!' said the girl archly; 'but one saw you who wishes to see you again, and if you will now follow me I will guide you.'

'And who may this person be?' I asked, 'and what can be his or her business with a traveller?'

'Your first question I may not answer,' said the girl; 'and as to the second I am ignorant; but, by your soul, follow me, for the matter is urgent, and I have most express commands to bring you if I possibly can.'

'I follow you,' said I, 'lead on.'

'Then keep behind me at some distance,' she said, 'and when you see me enter the house, step boldy in after me, as if you were the master.'

I followed her. But ah! Sahib, observe the power of destiny. I might have sat in my tent and denied myself to the girl, who, something told me, had come to seek me when I first saw her approach. I might, when I did advance to meet her, have passed on indifferently, and even when she spoke to me I might have denied that I was the person she was sent after, or I might have refused to accompany her; but destiny impelled me on, nay it led me by the nose after a slave-girl, to plunge into an adventure I fain would have avoided, and which my heart told me must end miserably. Sahib, there is no opposing Fate; by the meanest ends it works out the greatest deeds, and we are its slaves, body and soul, blindly to do as its will works! I say not Thugs only, but the whole human race. Is it not so?

It appears to me, Ameer Ali, said I, that poor Destiny has the blame whenever your own wicked hearts fix themselves on any object and you followed their suggestions.

Nay, I would have avoided this, cried the Thug, and have I not told you so? Allah knows I would not have entered into this matter; but what could I do? What were my weak resolves compared with His will? And yet you will not believe me. Sahib, I do not tell a lie.

I dare say not, said I; but the beautiful eyes were too much for you; so go on with your story.

The Thug laughed. They were indeed, said he, and accursed be the hour on which I saw them. But I will proceed.

The slave preceded me; at some distance I followed her through the village and its bazaars, and saw her enter the house before which I had sat in the morning. I too entered it, leaving my slippers at the door, and with the confident air of a man who goes into his own house. I had just passed the threshold when the slave stopped me.

'Wait a moment,' said she; 'I go to announce you;' and she pulled aside the temporary screen and went in.

In a few moments she returned and bade me follow her. I obeyed her, and in the next instant was in the presence of the unknown, who was hidden from my sight by an envious sheet, which covered the whole of her person, and her face was turned away from me towards the wall.

'Lady,' said I, 'your slave is come, and aught that he can do for one so lovely he will perform to the utmost of his power. Speak! your commands are on my head and eyes.'

'Byto,' she said in a low timid voice, 'I have somewhat to ask thee.'

I obeyed, and seated myself at a respectful distance from her on the carpet.

'You will think me bold and shameless, I fear, stranger,' said she, 'for thus admitting you to my presence, nay even to my chamber; but, alas! I am a widow, and need the protection you are able perhaps to afford me. Which way do you travel?'

'Towards Nagpur,' I replied; 'I purpose leaving this miserable place early tomorrow, and I have come from Jabalpur.'

'From whence I have also come,' she said, 'and I am going too to Nagpur. Ah, my destiny is good which has sent me one who will protect the lonely and friendless widow!'

'It is strange, lady,' said I, 'that we did not meet before, having come the same road.'

'No,' she replied, 'it is not, since I was behind you. I heard you were before me, and I travelled fast to overtake you. We have now met, and as I must proceed the remainder of my journey alone, I implore you to allow me for the stage to join your party, with which, as I hear it is a large one, I shall be safe, and free from anxiety.'

'Your wish is granted, lady,' I said; 'and any protection against the dangers of the way which your poor slave can afford shall be cheerfully given. I will send a man early to awaken you, and promise that I will not leave the village without you.'

She salaamed to me gracefully, and in doing so the sheet, as if by accident, partly fell from her face and disclosed again to my enraptured view the features I had beheld from a distance. Sahib, the shock was overpowering, and every nerve of my body tingled; only that a sense of decency restrained me, I had risen and thrown myself at her feet; but while a blush, as though of shame, mantled over her countenance, and she hastily withdrew the glance she had for an instant fixed on me, she replaced the sheet and again turned to the wall, bending her head towards the ground.

I thought it had been purely accidental, and the action at the time convinced me that she was really what she represented herself to be; and fearing that my longer presence would not be agreeable nor decent, I asked her if she had any further commands and for permission to depart.

'No,' said she, 'I have no further favour to beg, save to know the name of him to whom I am indebted for this act of kindness.'

'My name is Ameer Ali,' said I; 'a poor Syud of Hindustan.'

'Your fluent speech assured me you were of that noble race; I could not be mistaken—'tis seldom one hears it. Fazil! bring the pān and utr.'

She did so, and after taking the complimentary gift of dismissal, and anointing my breast and beard with the fragrant utr, I rose and made my obeisance. She saluted me in turn, and again bade me not forget my promise. I assured her that she might depend upon me, and departed.

She must be what she says, thought I; the very act of presenting pān and utr to me proves her rank; no common person, no courtesan would have thought of it. I shall only have to bear a little jeering from Motee and Peer Khan, which I will resist and laugh away; and this poor widow will reach Nagpur in safety, without knowing that she has been in the hands of murderers. But I said nothing that night to any of them. In reply to their numerous questions as to the fortune I had met with in the village, and whether I had discovered the unknown, I only laughed, and said I believed it was some dancing-girl, for I knew the mention of one would turn their minds from the thoughts of bunij, as it is forbidden to kill those persons by the laws of our profession; and with my suspicion they appeared satisfied.

Great, however, was their surprise when in the morning, after having delayed our departure longer than usual, I joined the party of the lady outside the village, and they understood that we were to travel in company.

I was overpowered by jokes and witticisms from Peer Khan and Motee, who declared I was a sly dog thus to secure the lady all to myself; and after protesting vehemently that I cared not about her, which only made them laugh the more, I became half angry.

'Look you, my friends,' said I, 'this is a matter which has been in a manner forced upon me. Who the lady is I know not. She has begged of me to allow her to accompany us, as she supposes us to be travellers, and I have permitted it; and whether she be old or young, ugly or beautiful, I am alike ignorant. We may hereafter find out her history, but, whoever she be, she has my promise of safe escort, and she is not bunij. You remember my resolution, and you will see I can keep it.'

'Nay,' said Motee, 'be not angry; if a friend is not privileged to crack a joke now and then, who, in Bhugwan's name, is? And as for us, we are your servants, and bound to obey you by our oath; so you may have as many women in your train as you please, and not one shall be bunij.'

So we pursued our road. Several times I could not resist riding up to the palankeen and making my noble horse curvet and prance beside it. The doors were at first closely shut, but one was gradually opened, and the same sparkling eyes threw me many a smiling and approving look, though the face was still hidden.

Alas! Sahib, those eyes did me great mischief—I could not withstand them.

About noon, when we had rested from our fatigue, and my men were dispersed in various directions, scarcely any of them remaining in the camp, the slave-girl again came for me, and I followed her to her mistress.

We sat a long time in silence, and the lady was muffled up as I had before seen her. Despite of all my conflicting feelings, I own, Sahib, that in her presence my home was forgotten, and my burning desire was fixed upon the veiled being before me, of whose countenance I was even still ignorant.

She spoke at last, but it was to the slave.

'Go,' said she, 'and wait without, far out of hearing; I have that to say to this gentleman which must not enter even your ears, my Fazil.'

She departed, and I was alone with the other, and again there was a long, and to me a painful silence.

'Meer Sahib,' she said at length, 'what will you think of me? What will you think of one who thus exposes herself to the gaze of a man and a stranger? But it matters not now; it has been done, and it is idle to think on the past. I am the widow of a Nawab, whose estate is near Agra; he died a short time ago at Nagpur, on his way from Hyderabad, whither he had gone to see his brother, and I was left friendless, but not destitute. He had abundance of wealth with him, and I was thus enabled to live at Nagpur, after sending news of his death to my estate, in comfort and affluence. The messengers I sent at length returned, and brought me the welcome news that there was no one to dispute my right to my husband's property; and that my own family, which is as noble and as powerful as his was, had taken possession of the estate and held it on my account; they wrote to me to return as quickly as I could, and among the respectable men of the land choose a new husband, by whom I might have children to inherit the estate. I immediately set off on my return—ah! Ameer Ali, how can I tell the rest! my tongue from shame cleaves to the roof of my mouth, and my lips refuse utterance to the words which are at my heart.'

'Speak, lady,' said I, 'by your soul, speak! I burn with impatience, and you have excited my curiosity now too powerfully for it to rest unsatisfied.'

'Then I must speak,' she said, 'though I die of shame in the effort. I heard at the last village that you had arrived; I say you, because my faithful slave, who finds out everything, came shortly after your arrival and told me that she had seen the most beautiful cavalier her thoughts had ever pictured to her. She recounted your noble air, the beauty of your person, the grace with which you managed your fiery steed, and above all the sweet and amiable expression of your countenance. The account inflamed me. I had married an old man, who was jealous of my person, and who never allowed me to see any one but my poor slave: but I had heard of manly beauty, and I longed for the time when his death should free me from this hated thraldom. Long I deliberated between the uncontrollable desire which possessed me and a sense of shame and womanly dignity; and perhaps the latter might have conquered, but you came and sat opposite to the hovel in which I was resting; my slave told me you were there, and I looked. Allah! Allah! once my eyes had fixed themselves on you, I could not withdraw them; and as the hole through which I gazed did not afford me a full view of your person, I partially opened the curtain and fastened my soul with your appearance. You went away, and I fell back on my carpet in despair. My slave at last restored me to consciousness, but I raved about you; and fearful that my senses would leave me, she went and brought you. When you entered, how I longed to throw myself at your feet! But shame prevailed, and, after a commonplace conversation, though my soul was on fire and my liver had turned into water, I suffered you to depart. I told my people that I must return to Nagpur, as I had forgotten to redeem some jewels I had left in pledge, which were valuable; and they believed me—Ameer Ali!' cried she, suddenly throwing off her veil and casting herself at my feet, while she buried her head in my lap, 'Ameer Ali! this is my tale of shame—I love you; Allah only knows how my soul burns for you! I will be your slave for ever; whither you go, thither will I follow; whoever you are, and whatever you are, I am yours, and yours only; but I shall die without you. Alas! why did you come to me?'

CHAPTER XXIV

And where now were all my resolutions? By Allah, Sahib, I had forgotten all—home, wife, children—I thought not of them, but I drank deeply of love, wild, passionate, burning love, from her eyes, and I caressed her as though she were mine own. There we sat, and though guilt was in my soul, and it accused me of infidelity to my oft repeated vows, I could not tear myself away from her, and I suffered her caresses in return, though they often struck to my heart like the blows of a sharp knife. Hours passed thus—I thought not of them; she seated at my feet, and I with my hands entwined in her long silken hair, and gazing at her face of such loveliness, that never had my wildest dreams pictured anything like it. Zora was beautiful, Azima was even more so, but Shurfun surpassed them both in as great a degree as they excelled any of their sex I had ever seen. Fain would she have had me stay with her: fain would she, the temptress, have then and there separated me from my band, and led me with herself, whither she cared not, so I was with her and she with me. Wealth, she said, she had in abundance, and we could fly to some undiscoverable spot, where we should pass years in bliss together, and where she would, by communication with her family, procure such money from time to time as would enable us to live in affluence.

'Ameer Ali,' said she, 'you are young, you are unknown, you have to fight your way to fame upon a bare pittance, and for this will you risk your precious life, when I offer you everything I possess, and swear that I am your slave? Ah, you will not, you cannot now leave me to perish in despair, and die of unrequited love! Speak, my soul you will not leave me?'

Wretch, and perjured that I was, I swore to obey her wishes. Sahib, it was a sore temptation, and it overcame me.

At last I tore myself away from her, but not till I had sworn by her head and eyes to return the following day, when being more calm we might arrange our plans for the future.

I returned to my little tent, and there in the agony of my soul I rolled on the ground. I raved, I refused to eat, and was as one bereft of sense; I spoke rudely to Peer Khan, who having been called by my attendant came to comfort me; and I was almost on the point of driving my dagger to my heart to end a life, which though a splendid prospect was open to it, could never afterwards be aught than one of guilty misery. But the passion reached its height; and as a thunder-cloud, which after a burst of internal commotion, after its deep peal has gone forth and it has ejected the lightning from its bosom, gradually pours its pent-up flood of waters to soothe and refresh the earth, so did mine eyes now rain tears, and they calmed me. I can now ask and take advice, thought I, and Peer Khan, who is fondly attached to me, will give it as he would to a brother.

I sent for him, and after apologizing for my rudeness, said he would find the cause of it in the relation I would give of the last few hours. I told him all, and awaited his answer. My heart was relieved of a load of oppressive thought, and I was the better for it.

He pondered long ere he spoke; at last he said:

'Meer Sahib, this is a difficult business indeed, and I hardly know what to advise; go to her tomorrow; be a man, and give not way to this boyish passion, which ill suits you; try to persuade her that you cannot do as she wishes; speak to her kindly, yet firmly, of her home, of her relatives, and of the guilt which must cleave to you both from the connexion she proposes. Tell her you have a wife and two children, and if she is a true woman she will be fired with jealousy, and will quarrel with you; do you then become irritated in your turn, and leave her to go her own way, and find some one who may not be so scrupulous, and may take advantage of her blind passions. And if all this fail, if no words of yours can drive these foolish ideas from her brain, we have only to make a long march in some unknown direction and at once be quit of her. I know the paths through the jungles, and by them, difficult as they are, we can easily reach Berar, where she will never again hear of us.'

I thanked him cordially for his advice; and that part of it which related to Azima and my children struck forcibly on my heart. I was as yet, thanks to the protection of the Prophet, pure, and by his aid I would remain so. I determined I would urge my previous ties to her so forcibly, and I would depict my love for my wife in such colours, that she should at once reject me.

Full of these resolutions I once more obeyed her summons, sent me by her slave, and followed the girl; and as we had made a long march of twelve coss, it was now late in the day. I need not again tell you Sahib, of all her love for me, which she now poured forth without check or reserve. She had fairly cast away all shame, and would hear of nothing I could represent as to the consequences of our connexion with her family. I had only now one resource, and as a man in alarm for his life fires the train of a mine, so did I, hurriedly and perhaps incoherently, mention my wife and children. The effect was, as Peer Khan had expected, instantaneous. She had been sitting at my feet, listening to my objections, and playfully reasoning with me against them; but at these words, she suddenly started to her feet, and drew her noble figure up to its full height, while her eyes flashed, as she smoothed back her flowing hair from her brow; the veins of her forehead and neck swelled, and she was terrible to look on. I confess I quailed beneath the glances of scorn she cast on me.

'Man!' she cried at length, 'ah, vile and faithless wretch, say, did I hear thee aright? Dare to say again that thou hast a wife and children! What dirt hast thou eaten?'

It was my time, and my good resolutions came to my aid; I rose, and confronted her with a look as proud and unflinching as her own.

'Yes, Shurfun,' I said, 'I have spoken the truth; one as beautiful as thou art believes me faithful, and faithful I will remain to her; long I reasoned with thee, and hadst thou not been carried away, and thy good feelings deadened, by an idle and sudden passion, thou hadst heard my words, and submitted to them, for the sake of thy family and hitherto untarnished honour. For my unfortunate share in this matter, may Allah forgive me! Lady, it was thy maddening beauty which caused me to err; but he has strengthened my heart, and again I implore thee to hear the words of friendship, and be thyself again.'

How can I tell you, Sahib, of her despair, and the bitterness of her expressions, as she upbraided me with my deceit! I deserved them all, and not a word did I answer in return. I could not, and I dared not approach her, lest my heart should again yield to her blandishments, for I felt that a kind word or action would renew them, and cause her to forget the past; and it was pitiable to see her as she now sat on the ground, moaning and rocking herself to and fro, while at intervals she tore her hair and beat her breasts in her agony of spirit.

'Leave me!' she said at last. 'Ah Ameer Ali, thou hast broken a heart which could have loved thee for ever. I do not complain: it is the will of Allah that the only man I could ever have loved and honoured should deceive me, and I submit. Shurfun is not yet reduced so low that she could put up with the second place in any man's heart, were he the monarch of Delhi itself. Go! the sight of you is painful to my soul; and may Allah forgive us both!'

I left her. I hastened to Peer Khan, and related the whole to him, and he was delighted.

'Now,' said he, 'to make the matter sure, let us retrace our steps; it is not attended with any risk, for we can put up anywhere, and we need not visit the village we before halted at; we have no hope of booty at Nagpur, and if you like we can penetrate, as I said before, into Berar, and return by Khandesh, which was our original idea.'

'I agree,' said I; 'this woman must be avoided at every risk. To save appearances she must go on to Nagpur with her people, and we shall, by following your advice, avoid her altogether.'

Accordingly the next morning, instead of pursuing the road we had taken, we turned back and after a few hours' travel halted at a small village, a few coss distant from the one we had left. But little had I calculated on that woman's love and wild passions. Before the day was half spent, we saw her palankeen, attended by her men, advancing towards the village by the way we had come. What was to be done? I was for an instant flight into the wild jungles by which we were surrounded, and where she would soon have lost all traces of us. But Peer Khan and Motee would not hear of it.

'It would be cowardly,' said they; 'there is no occasion thus to run before a woman; and why should we expose ourselves to dangers from wild beasts, and the unhealthiness of the forest, on her account? And,' added Motee, 'if she follow us now, depend upon it is not on your account, but because she is now determined to go to her home as quickly as possible.'

'It may be so,' said I; 'whatever her plans may be they will not influence my determinations.' Yet my mind misgave me that she would again follow us, and a short time proved that my suspicions were right. The slave came by stealth to my tent, disguised as a seller of milk, and I followed her, for I knew not why her mistress had sent for me, and why she now sought me after our last meeting.

I reached her presence, and again we were alone. I armed myself against her blandishments, and determined to oppose them with scorn, that she might again quarrel with me, and leave me for ever. I cannot relate to you, Sahib, all that passed between us; at one time she was all love, seeking to throw herself into my arms, and beseeching me to have pity on her, for she felt that her reputation was gone, in words that would have moved a heart of stone; at another, violently upbraiding me for my perfidy, and bidding me begone from her sight; yet each time as I turned to depart, she would prevent me, and again implore me to listen and agree to her proposals.

At last I could bear with her no longer. I was provoked with her importunities, and vexed at my own irresolute conduct. I bade her farewell, and was quitting the shed, where she had put up for the day, when she screamed to me to come back. I returned.

'Shurfun,' said I, 'this is foolishness, and the conduct of children; why should we thus torment each other? You have heard my determination; and could you offer me the throne of Delhi, I might share it with you, but my heart would be hers who now possesses it, and you would live a torment to yourself and me. Jealousy even now possesses your heart, and what would not that passion become when you were in intercourse with the object you even now hate, and whom you could not separate from me?'

'I care not for your words,' said she; 'I care not for the consequences: I have set my life and my fame on the issue of this—and refuse me at your peril! As for your wife, I hate her not. Does not our law allow you four wives? Is it not so written in the blessed Koran? You cannot deny it. Even I, who am a woman, know it. I would love Azima as a sister, and your children for your sake; and can you refuse wealth and a future life of distinction for them? Oh, man, are you bereft of sense? See, I speak to you calmly, and reason with you as I would were I your sister.'

'I would to Allah thou wert my sister,' I said; 'I could love thee fondly as a sister, but never, never can I consent to this unhallowed and disgraceful union. Yes, Shurfun, disgraceful! Disguise it with all thy flattering and sweet words, yet it is disgraceful. Go therefore, I beseech you, to your home, and in after years I will send my Azima to see you, and she shall pray for blessings on the noble woman who preserved her husband to her.'

She sat silent for some time; but the fire was not quenched within her; it burst forth with increased violence, when I vainly thought that my temperate words had quenched it for ever. Again she bade me go, but it was sullenly, and I left her.'

I had not been an hour in my tent when the slave again came to me. But perhaps, Sahib, you are tired of my minuteness in describing all my interviews with the Moghulanee?

No, said I, Ameer Ali: I suppose you have some object in it, therefore go on.

Well then, resumed the Thug, the slave came to me, and I was alone.

'For the love of Allah,' said she, 'Meer Sahib, do something for my poor mistress. Ever since you left her she has been in a kind of stupor, and has hardly spoken. She just now told me to go and purchase a quantity of opium for her; and when I refused, and fell at her feet, imploring her to recall her words, she spoke angrily to me, and said, if I did not go, she would go herself. So I have purchased it; but alas! I know its fatal use, and you alone can save her. Come quickly then, and speak a kind word to her; I have heard all that has passed, and you have behaved like a man of honour; but since you cannot persuade her to forget you and relinquish her intentions, at least for the time fall in with her humour, and agree to accompany her, on the promise that she will not seek to see you on the road; and say that when you reach her Jagheer you will have your marriage duly solemnized. Oh, do this for her sake! You said you could love her as a sister, and this would be the conduct of a brother.'

'Well,' said I, 'since the matter has come to this issue, that her life or death is in my hands, I consent;' and I arose, and went with her.

Oh, with what joy the unhappy girl received me! Long she hung upon my bosom, and blessed me as her preserver, and kissed her slave when she related what she had said to me, and that I had agreed to her wishes. 'It is to save your precious life,' I cried, 'that I thus expose myself to the sneers and taunts of my friends and your own: think on the sacrifice I make in losing their love, and you will behave cautiously and decently on the road; we need not meet—nay we must not, the temptation would be too strong for us both; but I swear by your head and eyes I will not leave you, and you shall travel in our company.'

The slave had gone out, and she drew towards me. 'Beware,' said she, 'how you deceive me, for I know your secret, and if you are unfaithful I will expose it; your life is in my hands, and you know it.'

'What secret?' cried I in alarm. 'What can you mean?'

'I know that you are a Thug,' she said in a low and determined voice; 'my slave has discovered you, and a thousand circumstances impress the belief that you are one upon my mind—your men, the way you encamp, the ceremonies my slave has seen your men performing, and the freedom with which you go forward or return at your pleasure. All these are conclusive, and I bid you beware! for nothing that you can say will persuade me to the contrary; you have even now the property of those you have killed in your camp—you cannot deny it, your looks confirm my words.'

I inwardly cursed the prying curiosity of the slave, and feared she had discovered us through one of our men with whom I had seen her conversing, and I determined to destroy him. But I had now fairly met my match, and though abashed for a moment, I replied to her:

'Then Shurfun, since you have discovered us, I have no alternative, we must be united, I to save my life and the lives of my men, you to save your own. It is a fearful tie which binds us, but it cannot be broken.'

'I thought so,' she said; 'fool that I was not to have urged this before! I might have saved myself the agony which I have endured. Now go; I will hear of you from day to day, and it may be that we shall have an opportunity of conversing unobserved. Now I am sure of you, and my mind is at ease.'

I left her, but my thoughts were in a whirl; she had discovered us, and by the rules of our profession I could not conceal it from my associates. Allah! Allah! to what would the communication I must make to them lead! Alas, I dreaded to think—yet it must be done.

A long time I deliberated with myself whether I should expose the truth to my associates, and fain would I not have done so; but the peril we were in was so imminent, and the lives of my fifty brave fellows were so completely at the mercy of a woman, that I could not overlook the strict rules of my profession. I knew that it could only lead to one alternative; but it was her fate, and it could not be avoided either by her or me.

As I expected, the fatal mandate went forth among us. My men were astonished and terrified at the information Shurfun possessed, and after a very brief consultation her fate was determined on. Sahib, you will think the worse of me for this, but what could be done? We could not leave her, she would have alarmed the villagers, and they would have pursued us. True, they could have done but little against us there; but they would have dogged us through the jungles, and at last have watched their opportunity and seized us. Our next care was to endeavour to find out the person from whom she had gained the information, and I mentioned the name of him with whom I had seen the slave conversing. Sahib, as I did it, his face bore the evidence of conscious guilt. He was a young man but little known to any of us, and was one of the Lughas. He had accompanied Peer Khan in his last expedition, and behaved well, so well as to induce him to allow his accompanying us; but by this act he had forfeited everything, and it was but too plain that he had been seduced by the wiles of that intriguing and artful slave.

Observing his altered looks, I at once accused him of treachery; and my accusation was re-echoed by the voices of the band.

'He must die!' cried one and all; 'we could never carry on our work with the knowledge that there was one treacherous person with us; and it is the rule of our order too. Who ever spared a traitor?'

'Miserable wretch,' said I to him, 'why hast thou done this? Why has thou been unfaithful to thine oath and the salt thou hast eaten? Didst thou not know the penalty? Hast thou not heard of hundreds of instances of treachery, and was ever one pardoned? Unhappy man! thou sayest nothing for thyself, and the sentence must be passed upon thee. Shame, that the wiles of a wretched slave should so far have led thee from thy duty, and exposed us all to peril!'

'Jemadar,' said he rising. 'I have sinned, and my hour is come. I ask not for mercy, for I know too well that it cannot be shown me; let me die by the hands of my own people, and I am content; and if my fate be a warning to them. I am satisfied. I was pure in my honour till I met that slave; she told me that you were to marry her mistress, and that you had told her who you were. I thought it true, and I conversed with her on the secrets of our band; I boasted to her of the deeds we had done, and she consented to be mine whenever we could meet with a fitting opportunity. Fool that I was, I was deceived; yet I offer this as no palliation for my offence. Let therefore Goordut kill me; his is a sure hand, and he will not fail in his duty.'

Goordut, the chief of the lughas, stepped forward. 'Forgive me your death,' said he to the fated wretch; 'I have no enmity against you, but this is my duty, and I must do it.'

'I forgive you,' he replied. 'Let your hand be firm; I shall offer no resistance, nor struggle; let my death-pain be short.'

Goordut looked to me for the signal—I gave it, and in another instant his victim had expiated his crime by death; he suffered passively, and Goordut's hand never trembled. The body was taken from among us and interred; and henceforward we had no treachery among us, nor did I ever meet with another instance, save one, and that was successful; you shall hear of it hereafter.

There but remained to allot to the different members of the band their separate places in the ensuing catastrophe; and this done, I felt that I had acted as a good Thug, and that a misplaced pity had not influenced me during the transactions of the day.

Strange was it, Sahib, that Shurfun, knowing who we were, should not, when she had discovered it, at once have fled from us! How she, a woman unused to and unacquainted with deeds of blood, could have borne to look on, nay more to have caressed and loved, one a murderer by profession, whose hand was raised against the whole human race, is more than I have ever been able to understand: I can only say it was her fate. She might, she ought to have avoided me; in every principle of human conduct, her love for me was wicked and without shame, and a virtuous woman would have died before she had ever allowed it to possess her bosom. She might have cast me off when she said she would, and when her resolution was made to see me no more; but her blind passion led her on into the net fate had spread for her, and she was unable to avoid it, as you or I shall be to die, Sahib, when our hour comes.

We started in company with her the next morning. I was determined I would take no active part in her death, for I could not bear the thought of lifting my hand against one whose caresses I had allowed, and whose kisses were, I may say, still warm upon my lips. Motee and Peer Khan were allotted to her, and one of her attendants was my share. But hers was a large party; she had eight bearers, four sepoys as her guards, and her slave rode on a pony, which was led by another servant. In all therefore they were fifteen individuals, and to make sure, thirty-five of my best men were to fall on them whenever we should meet a fitting place. I knew one, a wild spot it was, where the jungle was almost a forest, and where for miles on either side there was no human habitation; and I intended, for greater security, to lead the party by a path which I had discovered on our way down, and which led into the thickest part of the jungle, where I knew our deadly work would be sure of no interruption.

We reached the spot where the road diverged which I intended to take, and after much opposition on the part of her bearers, I succeeded in persuading them to follow me, by telling them, both that the road was a short one, and that there was a stream of water which crossed it, whereas on the main track there was none.

We gained the small rivulet, and I dismounted; my band surrounded their unsuspecting victims, and eagerly awaited the signal; but I wished to spare Shurfun the sight of the dead which she would be exposed to were she not the first to fall. I went to her palankeen, and asked her to get out and partake of some refreshment I had brought with me; she objected at first, as she would have to expose herself to the rash gaze of my men; but I told her I had put a cloth against a tree, that it was but a few steps off, and that veiled as she was, no one would see her, 'Your slave is there already,' said I; 'so come, she is preparing our meal, the first we have ever eaten together.'

She stepped out cautiously, closely muffled in a sheet, so that she saw not those who were with me, the palankeen too concealed her person, and as she arose from her sitting posture, the rumal of Motee was around her, and she died instantly. Peer Khan held her hands, and the moment her breath was gone, he put the body into the palankeen and shut the door.

'Now thus much is done,' said he, 'we must finish the rest, and that quickly; they are all off their guard, and washing and drinking in the stream; the men are at their posts. Bismilla! give the jhirnee!'

I sought my place and gave it: my own share was quickly done, and the rest too; but one or two were unskilful, and the shrieks of the unfortunate but too guilty slave, among the rest, smote on my ear, and caused a pang to shoot to my heart at the thought that they had all died for the wretched caprice of a wicked woman. I could not bear to look at Shurfun—the sight of her beautiful features would have overpowered me. I saw the lughas bear her away, but I followed not. Her palankeen was broken into pieces and buried with her.

Wretch! cried I: ah, Ameer Ali, hadst thou no pity, no remorse, for one so young and so lovely?

I might have felt it, Sahib, but the fate of him who had died the day before was too fresh in my mind to allow me to show it: that might have been mine had I done so. Besides, can you deny that it was her fate? And, above all, had I not eaten the goor of the Tupounee?

CHAPTER XXV

AFTER all had been completed, we travelled on until we reached a small and wretched village, some coss from the scene of our late adventure, where, after the customary sacrifice of goor, the considerable booty we had gained was produced and distributed. There soon arose a discussion as to our future proceedings. Some advised that we should return and go on to Nagpur—many indeed were for this, and I also inclined to it—but Peer Khan gave better counsel, saying that, by our thus going backwards and forwards on the same road, we should certainly be suspected and perhaps attacked; and that to expose ourselves to this, was not to be put in comparison with any chance of booty: he advised that we should make the best of our way toward Ellichpur, avoiding that town, and keeping near the hills, until we got out of the jurisdiction of Sulabat Khan, who, if he heard of us, would assuredly suspect us of the death of the Nawab Subzee Khan, who had been his guest, and whose fate was generally known over the country and attributed with justice to Thugs. After some further deliberation we all agreed to his plan, and the next day, leaving the high-road, we struck into a jungle-track and pursued it; and I was heartily glad, after some days of weary travel, when, arriving at the pass near the deserted temples of Mookhtagherry, we saw the wide valley of Berar stretched out before us, covered with the still green and luxuriant crops of jowaree.

For some days previous I had had shiverings and pains all over my body, and my mind was restless and ill at ease. In spite of my efforts to throw them off, horrible dreams haunted me at night, and the figure of Shurfun constantly presented itself to my fancy—now in the fullness of her beauty, and now changed and distorted as she must have been in death; while at one time she was pouring out her tale of love to me, and at another upbraiding me with her fate. I had mentioned this to my companions, and many were the ceremonies which they performed over me to drive away the evil spirits which Motee declared had possessed me. But they were of no avail, and on the morning we reached the top of the pass I was so ill that I was obliged to be supported on my horse.

What was to be done? To go into Ellichpur was to run into the tiger's mouth, and all seemed to be at a loss whither to proceed. However, on clearing the mouth of the glen through which the road ran, some of the men discerned a large village a very short way off, and came back with the welcome intelligence. I was sitting, or rather lying, at a miserable Goand hamlet on the road; and when I heard their news I remembered the village they spoke of, which I had passed the morning we left Ellichpur with Subzee Khan, though I had forgotten its name. Thither therefore, I begged they would carry me, and placing me upon my good horse, I was soon there, and made as comfortable as circumstances would admit of in the empty shop of a bunnia. But the fever raged within me; my whole frame was at first convulsed with violent shiverings, which were succeeded by intense burnings. I remember no more of that day, nor indeed of many days after, for I lay insensible, and my spirit hovered between life and death.

The first words I recollect after that terrible time were from my faithful attendant.

'Shookr khoda!' he exclaimed; 'at last he has opened his eyes!' and he ran and called Peer Khan and others to me.

'Where am I?' I faintly asked, for in the violence of the fever I had forgotten everything.

'Shookr khoda!' again exclaimed all; 'he speaks at last!'

I again repeated my question, and it was answered by Peer Khan.

'Why, do you not remember?' said he; 'here you are in the good village of Surrusgaum, within three coss of Ellichpur; and now that you have spoken all will be right, you will soon recover; but we have been sadly anxious about you, for a worthy Mussulman, who is a Hakim, said only yesterday that you would die, and bade us prepare for your burial: however he was wrong, and Inshallah! you will soon see yourself at the head of your brave fellows again.'

'Alas, Khan, I fear not,' said I, 'for I am weak and helpless, and your staying with me here only delays you to little purpose. Leave me to my fate, and if it is the will of Allah that I should recover, I will rejoin you at our home. I feel that I should be only a useless clog on your movements; for if I even get over this fever, I shall not be able to sit on my horse for many a day.'

'Forsake you, Meer Sahib—never!' exclaimed all who were sitting round me. 'Who will bury you if you die? Or who will tend you if you recover? What words are these? Are you not our brother, and more, our leader? and what would become of us if we left you?'

'Well, my friends?' said I, deeply affected by their kindness, 'since you prefer the bedside of a sick man to roaming in the wide and open country, even be it so; a few days will end your suspense, and either you will have to bury me here, or, if it be the pleasure of Allah, I shall once more lead you to new enterprises.'

'But you must be silent,' said Peer Khan, 'for the Hakim said so, and told us if you roused at all to send him word, as he had prepared some medicine for you, which he would administer, and hoped it would hasten your recovery. I will go and tell him the good news.'

In a short time the Khan returned, accompanied by an old and venerable person, who, after feeling my head and body, turned to the Khan and declared that my state was satisfactory. 'But,' said he, 'as the fever proceeded from cold, which is still in his stomach, we must give him the medicine I spoke of: I have prepared it, and, being compounded of heating drugs, it will soon expel the cold, induce perspiration, and, Inshallah! tomorrow he will be a different being, though he will be weak for some time to come.'

The draught was prepared, and, though nauseous in the extreme, I swallowed it, and by his directions covered myself with quilts and horsecloths. I was quickly in a profuse perspiration; and when the Hakim, who sat by my side all the time, thought I had been long enough under this treatment, he withdrew the coverings one by one, and taking my wet clothes from me I soon fell into a sound and refreshing sleep, from which I did not awake till the next morning's sun was shining on my eyelids.

I felt so much refreshed when I awoke that I arose, but my head swam round and I fell. I did not essay to repeat the exertion; but I was well; I felt that I had thrown off the disease, and I was thankful. Soon I had an inclination to eat, and after a slight meal of kicheree I was indeed a different being.

Two days more restored me to convalescence, and I heartily wished to be again on the road toward home; but travelling on horseback was out of the question, as I could only walk a few steps with assistance; so, as Peer Khan volunteered his services, I despatched him to Ellichpur to endeavour to hire a palankeen or doolie with bearers, to carry me a few stages, or as long as I should find them necessary.

He returned with them, and the next day, having remunerated the good Hakim, I gladly set out once again in company with my gallant fellows.

We took the best road to Burhanpur, that through the valley of Berar and close to the hills; and when we reached the old town of Julgaum, I felt myself so strong that I dismissed the palankeen and once more mounted my good horse.

A joyful and inspiriting thing it is, Sahib, to mount one's horse after a long and painful illness, and to feel once more the bounds of the generous animal under you, as though he too rejoiced at his master's recovery. He was, like myself, in high spirits, and I never enjoyed a ride so much as I did on that morning; the cool breeze fanned my thinned cheek as I rode along, now humouring my horse by allowing him to bound and caracole as he pleased, now exercising him on the plain, and again rejoining my band as they walked merrily along, apparently under the influence of the same joy as myself, and rejoicing to see me once more at their head.

We met with no adventure till we reached Burhanpur, where we arrived on the tenth day after leaving the village at which I had been so near dying: indeed we sought none. We found good quarters in one of the old sarais in the town, and I was determined to stay there until we met with something to lead us on. Accordingly, men were daily sent into the different bazaars; but seven days passed in idleness, and I began seriously to think that the death of Shurfun, which, though an inevitable deed, was against my faithful promises, had caused me to forfeit the protection of our patroness; in other words, I feared my good fortune had deserted me, and for once I proposed a grand sacrifice to Devi, and that the omens should be consulted, in order to afford us some clue to our future proceedings.

It was done, and the omens were good—'Propitious to a degree!' said Motee, who was our conductor in these matters; 'we shall have good bunij soon, or these would never have been vouchsafed to us.'

But another day passed, and still the sothas reported nothing. The day after, about noon, Motee came to me. 'You may know,' said he, 'that this place from its wealth, is frequented by rokurraes, or treasure-carriers, who bring money from Bombay, and take it into Malwa to purchase opium.'

'I do,' said I; 'what of that? I heard as much from my father, who bade me return this way in the hope of picking up some of them.'

'Then,' said he, 'I wish you to come with me, you and Peer Khan; you have both sharp eyes, and I am much mistaken if I have not discovered eight of them. I have killed others of their tribe before now, and I think I am not wrong when I say that these are some also.'

'Good,' I replied, 'I will come;' and accompanied by Peer Khan and Motee we set forth to examine the men whom the latter had spoken of.

In an empty shop we found them. Wary as these people are, it was highly necessary that we should not excite their suspicion; so we hurriedly passed them, concealing our faces in our handkerchiefs; yet from the casual glance I threw at them I was certain, from their sturdy forms and the one camel they had with them, as well as from a kind of restless and suspicious bearing, that they were the men we were in search of. This was just the season too; they would be bearing treasure to make advances to the poppy cultivators in Malwa, as the seed of the plant would not be sown for another month at least.

I was satisfied; yet how to ensure their company I knew not, and many schemes passed through my mind before I could determine on anything: at length I formed one, as I sat with my companions on a flight of steps leading down to the river, and whither we often resorted to enjoy the fresh breezes and pure air from the noble river which flowed beneath us.

'I have been thinking,' said I, 'what we are to do to secure these fellows; you know they are proverbially wary.'

Both nodded assent.

'Well,' I continued, 'what think you of the following scheme? You and I, Peer Khan, will pretend to be travellers; we will go now to our sarai, throw dust and mud over our horses and dirty our clothes, and, taking two men and a pony heavily laden with us, we will go round the city, enter by the gate under the old palace, and pretending to be weary halt close to them; we shall easily be able to worm ourselves into their confidence, and will then accompany them. You, Motee, I will leave in charge of the band, and send you word what road we are to take. You must be guided by circumstances, and contrive to let the men overtake me by twos and threes; some must go on before, so that we may come up to them; and in this manner, though the band will be scattered, yet Inshallah! in a few marches we shall muster strong enough to do the work. We can keep up a communication with each other, so that when the business is done we can assemble, and then hurry forward to our home. But on no account must you be more than a stage behind us; and you must contrive to reach our halting-place a short time after we have left it. Now say, my friends, will this plan do? Or can you advise any other more practicable? If so, speak.'

'It is excellent,' cried both, 'and had wisdom for its father. No time ought to be lost.'

We returned to our sarai, and towards the afternoon two as travel-stained and weary travellers in appearance as ever came off a long and fatiguing march were seen to enter the south gate of Burhanpur and traverse the bazaars in search of shelter. These were myself and Peer Khan, attended by my good lad Junglee and two other Thugs. We passed and re-passed the shed, which was a large one, in which the rokurreas were; and feigning to have been denied room everywhere that we had applied, I at last rode up to them, and addressed myself to the most respectable among them, a fine tall fellow, with huge whiskers and mustachios.

'Yaro!' said I, 'you seem to be travellers as well as ourselves, and, for the love of Allah, allow us a little room to spread our carpets. Here you have seen us pass backwards and forwards for many times, and yet there is not a soul who will say to us: Dismount and refresh yourselves. Nay, we have been refused admittance into many empty places. May their owners' sisters be defiled!'

'Go to the sarai,' said the man; 'there is room there, and you will be comfortable.'

'Indeed,' said I, 'we have tried it already, and it is full; some forty or fifty fellows were in it, who bade us begone in no measured terms; and, in truth, we liked not their appearance, having some valuables about us. They looked very like thieves or Dacoos—did they not, brother?' said I, turning to Peer Khan.

'Ay, indeed,' said he; 'who knows, if we had put up among them, whether we should not have had our throats cut? It was the mercy of Allah,' continued he, looking up devoutly, 'that the place was full, or, weary as we are, we should have been right glad to have rested ourselves anywhere, for indeed I can hardly sit on my horse.'

'You see,' said I, 'how we are situated. Hindus though you be, you will not refuse us. The evening is drawing in, and we have ridden all day; a slight meal is all that we can hope to get, and then sleep will be welcome.'

'Well,' said the fellow, 'it will be uncivil to turn you away, so alight; and,' cried he to one of his companions, 'do you, Doorjun, and some others move the camel's saddles and those bags nearer this way, and there will room for these Bhula admis.'

As they were being moved I heard money chink.

We dismounted, and in a short time our horses were rubbed down, and a meal prepared, for we had fasted that day on purpose. When we had eaten it, behold us seated in conversation with the rokurreas; and having already possessed ourselves of their intended route, we agreed to accompany them for mutual security, and in short were on as good terms with them as if we had travelled hitherto together. Our appearance, our good horses, and arms assured them that we were soldiers, for I had told them we were in the service of Holkar, returning from Poona, where we had been on a mission to the Peshwa, and bearing with us not only despatches, but some hoondees of large amount. In proof of this I pulled forth a bundle of papers from my inner vest, and touching my head and eyes with them, praised the munificence of Bajee Rao, and extolled the friendly terms he was on with Holkar.

This was my master-stroke; the idea had occurred to me when I was at the sarai, and I had hastily collected a bundle of waste-papers and accounts, made them up into a packet, directed it to Holkar, and sealed it with my own seal, which was as large as that of any prince in the country.

After agreeing on our stage for the morrow, which was distant eight coss, they went to sleep, with the exception of two, who sat guarding the treasure with drawn swords, and all believing that they were in company with an unknown great personage.

Before I lay down to rest I despatched Junglee with the information to Motee. I spoke to him openly in Ramasi, and he set off on his errand.

'That is a queer language,' said the Jemadar of the rokurreas; 'what is it?'

''Tis Telegu,' said I carelessly. 'I picked the lad up at Hyderabad two years ago for a small sum, and he is my slave; he understands our Hindi, but does not speak it.'

Perhaps it was unwise to have done it, but I spoke in so careless a manner that they concluded I had sent him out on some casual errand. Indeed, I told him to buy some tobacco and pān on his way back, and as the sari was not far from where we were, the time occupied in his going to it would not exceed that of an ordinary errand.

He returned with the pān and tobacco, and told me they were ready, but that the majority would remain the next day, and that seven of the best under Goordut were then about to depart; the rest, leaving one of their number as a scout in the village we were to halt at, would push on as far as they could beyond.

I was satisfied, and so sure did I feel of the success of this adventure that I would have wagered all I possessed that I killed the rokurreas in three days. We started the next morning, and for two days saw none of our men; however Peer Khan augered well from it, saying the fellows were up to their work, and would appear in good time, and that if they came too soon our companions would take the alarm and be off.

On the fourth day one of our companions appeared; we overtook him on the road, and as I lagged purposely in the rear, I learned from him that Goordut and his remaining men were in advance of us one march, and that some would join us that day and the rest the next.

This was as it should be. Four men joined us at the village we encamped at; and as we were now nine to eight, I began to think on the probability of putting them to death by violence—I mean, attacking them with our swords on any opportunity which might offer. But it was dangerous, as they were individually stouter men than we were, good hands at their weapons, and as watchful as cats. In the day, therefore, we had a consultation; we met in a field of jowaree, which concealed us, and there we discussed the affair. Peer Khan proposed to send one of the men back for Motee and the rest, to tell them to pass us in the night without stopping, and to allow us to overtake them early in the morning; and as soon as the two parties were mingled together, in passing each other, that I should give the jhirnee. Sahib, they did not hesitate; one and all pledged themselves to follow me, and die with me should it be their fate. We dispersed, and rejoined our associates. The evening was spent in singing and playing on the sitar, on which two of the rokurreas and some of my men were adepts; and we retired to rest at a late hour, fully prepared to do our work well and bravely on the morrow.

And the morrow came, and the sun rose in splendour; we set

out soon afterwards, for the rokurreas would not travel before it had risen, for fear of surprise from thieves or Dacoos, who generally fall on travellers in the dark.

Somewhat to my mortification, two of the rokurreas mounted the camel they had with them, saying their feet were cracked and sore and they could not walk. This disconcerted me for a moment, for I thought they had suspected us, and I knew that most, if not all, the treasure was laden upon it. But I affected no surprise, and was determined, if they showed the least symptoms of flight, to wound the camel, and thereby prevent its getting away from us by the great speed I knew it possessed, for they had put it to its utmost the day before to show me that it could outstrip a horse.

We travelled along until mid-day, and the fatigue and heat made us glad to dismount at a stream which crossed the road. I thought it would be a good opportunity to fall on them, but I was disappointed; they all kept together, and I was then satisfied that they half suspected our intentions; but I could not delay the attack long, and was determined to make it under any circumstances, for the rapid rate at which the rokurreas travelled was exhausting my men, who had much ado to keep up with them.

By the merest good luck, about a coss after we left the nullah, we entered on a rough and stony track, which diminished the speed of the camel, whose feet were hurt by the stones, and he picked his way cautiously, though I saw the men on his back used every exertion to urge him on. This slowness enabled my men to take their places, and we continued to proceed a short distance, but ready at any moment for the onset. I wished to get as near the camel as I could, in order to prevent its escape; but the road became worse, our pace still slower, and I was satisfied it could not be urged quicker. We were at this time all in a group, and I saw that the time had come. How my heart beat! not with fear, Sahib, but with excitement—excitement like that of a gambler who has risked his all on a stake, and who with clenched hands, set teeth, and half-drawn breath watches the turn of the cowries, which is either to ruin him or better his fortunes.

Peer Khan threw a glance towards me: one of the rokurreas was trudging along at his horse's shoulders, another was at the same place near mine; and the fellows on the camel, with their backs turned towards us, were singing merrily one of the wild lays of the Rajpus, in which from time to time they were joined in chorus by those on foot, and by some of my men who knew the words. Junglee was close behind the camel leading my pony, and the others in the rear, but all in their places. I cast but one look behind to see that they were so, and being satisfied I gave the jhirnee—'Junglee pāni lao!' I cried with a loud voice.

The swords of my party flashed brightly from their scabbards, and in an instant were buried deeply in the bodies of their victims and crimsoned with gore. As for myself, I had cloven the skull of the fellow beneath me, and my sword sticking in the wound escaped from my hand as he fell; I threw myself from my horse to recover it, and only then saw the camel prostrate on the ground, moaning terribly; the men upon it had fallen with it, but both had gained their legs: one had thrown himself upon Junglee, and the poor lad waged an unequal combat with him; the other rushed on me with his sword uplifted. Sahib, I thought my end was come, but I had time to disengage my shield from my back, and held it before me in defence, while I tugged in very desperation at my weapon.

Praise be to Allah! it yielded to my great exertion, and we were on equal terms. I have before told you of my skill as a swordsman, but I had met my match in the rokurrea: he, though all his men were lying around him save one— who having sorely wounded my poor attendant, was now closely pressed by Peer Khan and another—was as cool and wary as myself. We fought well, and for a long time the contest was equal; we were both out of breath, and our shields hacked with the repeated blows we had each caught on them; at last, as my foot slipped on a stone, he made a stroke at my head: the blow was weak from his exhausted state, or it would have ended me: it cut through my turban, and slightly wounded my head.

I did not fall, though I was somewhat stunned by the stroke; he might have taken advantage of the moment, yet he negelected it. Maddened by the thought of defeat, I rushed on him, and by the violence of my attack forced him backward: at last, he too slipped as he retreated, and lost his balance; he raised his sword wildly in the air to recover himself, but I did not lose my opportunity as he had done; my blow descended with its full force, increased by a sudden leap I made towards him, and he fell to the earth cloven through the neck and shoulder—he was dead almost ere he fell. A moment I gazed on the features of the brave Rajput, and then sought my poor lad, from whom the life-blood was fast ebbing away; his wound was also in the neck, and the blood rushing into his throat was choking him.

I tried to staunch it with my waistband, but ineffectually; it relieved him for a moment, and he asked for water. A leathern bag containing some had been tied to the camel by one of the men, and I put the mouth of it to his lips; he drank a little, and sat up, supported by Goordut.

'I am killed,' said he, 'Jemadar—I die—my own blood chokes me: I cannot recover. Do not leave my body to be eaten my the beasts, but bury it. That fellow,' continued he after a short interval, and pointing to one of the dead, 'that fellow's sword killed me. I cut the hind sinews of the camel's leg, and it fell; I thought they would both be stunned, but he got up and attacked me, and I was no match for him. All the rest of you were engaged, or you would have helped me. But it was my fate to die, and I felt it yesterday, the bitterness of death then passed over me, but now I am content; the pain will soon be over.'

Here he sunk insensible, and we stood around him weeping, for he was an affectionate lad, and we all loved him as a brother. But he recovered again slightly, though the rattle was in his throat, and the blood hardly allowed him to speak.

'My mother!' he said faintly, 'Jemadar, my mother! You know her and my little sister. They will starve now—but you will protect them for poor Junglee's sake?' And he strove to bend his head on my hand, as though to supplicate my assistance for them.

'Fear not,' said I, 'they shall be well cared for; and while Ameer Ali lives they shall know no want.' But I could hardly speak for weeping, for I knew the old woman, and many were the prayers she made for his safe return as she confided him to my care. Alas! how should we be able to tell her his fate!

The poor boy was satisfied with my words; he would fain have replied to them, and his lips moved; but a torrent of blood checked his utterance, and raising his dull and glazed eyes to mine, he bowed his head on my hand, and died in the effort. 'Now,' said I to the assembled Thugs, 'I here swear to one thing, and ye are none of mine unless ye agree to it. I swear that whatever share would have come to this poor lad, it shall be doubled for his mother: as yet we know not what it is, but, whatever it be, it shall be doubled.'

'We agree,' cried all; 'nay, every man of us will add to it what he can; had Junglee not hamstrung the camel, which none of us thought of doing, it might, nay would, have escaped: for we saw its speed yesterday, and the two good Rajputs who were on it would have carried it off.'

'Ye are my own brothers for this good promise,' I said; 'and now some of you dig a grave for the poor lad. We must unload that beast, and strip the bodies. For myself, I am in some pain, and will wash my head and tie up the cut: so set about your work quickly.'

The camel still lay groaning; they tried to raise it up, but in vain; the stroke had divided the sinew above the hock, and it could not raise itself; so one of the men cut its throat, and ended its pain. The bags of treasure were transferred to my pony and Peer Khan's horse and mine, and every man also filled his waistband, so that we were enabled to carry it all off. We took the swords of the Rajputs; but everything else, and their bodies, were dragged into the jungle to some distance, and hastily covered with earth and stones. The bloody earth on the scene of the conflict was collected and thrown away, and in a very short time nothing remained to mark the spot but the carcass of the camel, which we could not dispose of; and leaving the usual marks for the guidance of Motee and his party, we continued our march on the main road.

Ah, how great was our joy when, before we reached the stage we were to encamp at, and as we sat at the edge of a stream washing ourselves, we saw, on the brow of a rising-ground we had just passed, our party coming-up!. They ran towards us in breathless anxiety and hope.

Motee was first, and he threw himself into my arms. 'We hastened on,' he said, 'from the last stage, hoping to overtake you in time; and when we saw the dead camel, how great was our suspense till we could find you! We saw the traces of the conflict, and some blood which had escaped your notice—which I have removed—and that added to our anxiety; but Devi be praised! we have found you at last, and you are all safe. Is it not so?'

'Not quite,' I said, 'we have lost poor Junglee, who was killed in the fight: and I am wounded; but 'tis only a slight cut, and a few days will heal it.'

Some of the treasure was instantly distributed to the other ponies; and encamping outside the village, when we reached it, after the accustomed sacrifice, I had my small tent pitched, and all the treasure was conveyed to it. One by one the bags were opened, and glorious indeed was the booty—well worth the risk we had encountered! It consisted of dollars, gold mohurs, and rupees, to the value of sixty thousand rupees in all; and there were also six strings of large pearls in a small box, sewn up in wax-cloth, which could not be worth less than ten thousand more. I need not describe our joy: we had comfort, nay affluence, before us for years, and every one sat and gazed at the heap of treasure in silent thankfulness. Finally, it was all collected and put into bags, which I sealed with my own seal.

We now hurried to our home, for we sought no adventure, nor needed any: only two unfortunate wretches, who insisted on joining us, were killed, and in less than a month we were within three marches of our village. I despatched a man in advance to give notice of our approach; and, Allah! how my heart beat with love and fond anxiety to see Azima, and to press once more my children to my heart, after all the perils I had encountered! how intense was my anxiety to reach my own threshold, when I saw the well-known grove appear in view, the spot from whence I had departed so full of hope, and the walls and white musjid of the village peeping from amidst the trees by which they were surrounded! I urged my horse into a gallop, and I saw my father and Moedeen approaching to meet me, to give me the *istukbal,* the welcome of return; but, as I neared them, they hung their heads, and advanced with slow and mournful steps. A sudden pang shot through my heart. I threw myself from my horse, and ran towards them. My father was weeping.

'Speak, for the sake of Allah!' I cried. 'What can this be? Oh say the worst at once, and tell me—is Azmia dead? This suspense will kill me.'

A few words only the old man spake, as he told me that my child, my beautiful boy, was dead!

And Ameer Ali wept.

CHAPTER XXVI

ALTHOUGH the mind would ordinarily reject sympathy with the joys or sorrows of a murderer like Ameer Ali, one so deeply stained with crime of the most revolting nature, yet for the moment I was moved to see, that after the lapse of nearly twenty years, by his account, the simple mention of the death of his favourite child could so much effect him, even to tears, and they were genuine. I leave other to speculate on the peculiar frame of the Thug's mind,. how this one feeling of tenderness escaped being choked by the rank guilt that had sprung up around it, and will pursue my relation of his adventures.

Sahib, he said, why should I now trouble you with an account of my miserable meeting with my loved Azima? You can picture it to yourself. Our souls had been bound up in that boy, and it was long ere we could bring ourselves to submit to the blow which the hand of Allah had inflicted. But the poignancy of the grief passed away, and our girl, growing up in beauty, occupied our thoughts and engaged our care and attention.

Some time after we returned, my father one day came to me, and with concern on his countenance declared there was a rumour that we were suspected, and that he thought our village was no longer a safe abode for us. We could risk nothing; there might or might not be truth in the report, but it was our duty to secure a safe asylum: and accordingly he and I set out to make a tour of the different states as yet independent of the English, and to find out whether any of their rulers would allow us a residence on payment of a fixed tribute, such as our fraternity had used to pay in Sindia's government when our village belonged to that prince. We accordingly departed, and after visiting many rulers in Bundelkund, (for we were averse to going further from our home) we were received by the Rajah of Jhalone, and were introduced to him by Ganesha Jemadar, who was under his protection, and who made him handsome returns from the booty he collected for his friendly conduct.

Our negotiation was a long one: the Rajah was fearful for some time of the consequences of harbouring us, or pretended to be so in order to enhance the favour he was conferring; but we distributed bribes plentifully to his attendants and confidential servants, and at last succeeded in our object. We were to pay a tax of three hundred rupees a year to l
present him with anything rare or valuable we

and, to preserve appearances, my father agreed to farm three villages situated a short distance from his capital. The whole concluded by our presenting to him one of the strings of pearls we had taken on the last expedition, my own beautiful sword, and other articles, valued at nearly five thousand rupees. When we were thus mutually satisfied, my father and some of the men remained behind, while I and the rest returned to our village, to bring away our families.

I confess I left our home with regret; many, many happy days had been passed there, and we were beloved by the villagers, to whom we had endeared ourselves by our inoffensive conduct. We were now to seek a new country, and form new ties and connexions—a disagreeable matter under any circumstances. But my father's wisdom had saved us. The information the English officers had obtained—Allah only knows how—was correct. In a very few months after we were settled in our new abode, we heard that the whole Purgunna of Murnae had been attacked, village by village. Many of the best and bravest of the Thugs had died defending their homes; the survivors had fled, routed and utterly disorganized, and had taken refuge with those who had made previous settlements as we had done.

Nearly three years passed quietly, and unmarked by anything which I can recall to my memory. I had no more children, and my daughter was growing up a model of beauty and grace. I was happy, and never should have dreamed of leaving home, had it not been for the bad faith of the Rajah, and one unfortunate season of drought; by the former we were obliged to pay five thousand rupees, which he demanded under threats of discovering us; and by the latter we lost considerably in the villages we farmed, which were now seven in number, and for which he obliged us to pay the full amount of revenue. These sums seriously diminished our resources; and I began to look about me for men, to compose a band to go in search of more plunder. But they were not easily collected, for my own men had dispersed to distant parts of the country, and could not be brought together save at great expense and sacrifice of time.

Just at this period it was rumoured through the country that Cheetoo and other Pindari chiefs of note would assemble their forces after the rains, at the festival of the Dussehra, and had planned an expedition of greater magnitude than any ever before undertaken; an expedition which was sure to enrich all its members, and strike terror into the English government. The idea suited me exactly; I was a soldier by inclination, if not by profession; and I thought, if I could join any of the durras with a few choice men, well mounted, we might make as good a thing of it as if we went out on an expedition of our own. The latter scheme, moreover, promised no success, for the roads would be infested by straggling parties of Pindaris, who were well known to spare neither travellers nor Thugs; they looked on the last indeed with great enmity.

Accordingly I set to work to make my preparations. Peer Khan and Motee still remained near us, and when I disclosed my plans to them, they entered into them with great readiness and alacrity. They had enough money to mount themselves well, and after a short absence returned fully equipped for the journey. I had told them to look out for a few really fine fellows to accompany us, whom they brought; but our united means would not allow of our purchasing horses for them, and on foot they would be of no use. In debating on our dilemma, an idea occurred to me that the Rajah would perhaps lend or sell the horses, on the promise of after and double payment. I had heard of such things, and I determined to try what could be done.

To my great joy the Rajah consented, and with less difficulty than I had anticipated, for I had become a great favourite with him. I was allowed to take five horses from his stables, which were valued at three hundred rupees each, with their saddles and accoutrements, and this sum was to be doubled in case we returned successful. The Rajah indeed thanked me for the hint I had given him, and many others obtained horses on the same terms, on giving security for the performance of the conditions under which they took them.

My final arrangements were soon completed. We were all armed and accoutred in the handsomest manner we could afford; and a better mounted or more gallant-looking little party never set out in quest of adventure than I and my seven associates. Before we started we consulted the omens, which were favourable, and we performed all the ceremonies of departure exactly as if we had been going on an expedition of Thuggee.

In due time we arrived at Nemawur, the residence of Cheetoo. Here were collected men from every part of Hindustan, as various in their tribes as they were in their dresses, arms, and accoutrements. The country round Nemawur was full of them, and the town itself appeared a moving mass of human beings, attracted by the hope of active service, and above all of plunder. We lost no time in presenting ourselves at the durbar of the chief, and were graciously received by him. I opened our conference in the usual manner, by presenting the hilt of my sword as a nuzzur; and having dressed myself in my richest clothes, I was instantly welcomed as if I had been a Sirdar of rank, and had the command, not of seven men, but of as many hundreds.

Cheetoo was a fine looking-man, and a gallant leader. He ought to have died on the field of battle, instead of in the miserable maner he did. No man that ever led a Lubhur was juster in the division of plunder; no one was ever more attentive to the wants and complaints of those under him than was Cheetoo Pindari. It was this which gained him so many followers, while his personal activity and hardihood stimulated his soldiers to exertion and emulation. Nothing could tire him; often have I seen him after a long and weary march, when it was as much as most of us could do to sit on our horses, dash out to the front and exercise his noble steed, which bore him gallantly, as though he were only returning from a morning's ride of a few miles.

Cheetoo was, as I said, struck with my appearance, as I introduced myself as a poor Syud of Jhalone, desirous of serving under him in his ensuing campaign.

'Oh,' said he, 'from Jhalone! you have travelled far, my friend; but nevertheless you are welcome, as every brave cavalier is who brings a good horse and a willing heart to the service of Cheetoo. You know my conditions of service; I give no pay, but as much plunder as your own activity can procure: the people will tell you what my share of it is; and I look to your honesty, for your face belies you if you are a rogue.'

'I know the conditions,' said I, 'and will accept them; but I have brought a few friends with me who are desirous of sharing my fortunes, and, if it be the pleasure of the Huzoor, I will bring them.'

'Surely,' he replied; 'but now I am engaged: meet me with your men at the place of assembly in the evening, and I will see them and your horses; for the station I shall allot you in the durra depends on their fitness.'

I made my obeisance and retired. I had made the acquaintance of one of Cheetoo's Sirdars, a man by name Ghuffoor Khan, a perfect savage in appearance and deportment, a fellow who had Pindari written on his face, and had served with much distinction in the durras of Dost Mahomed and Kureem Khan. He had introduced me to Cheetoo, and now, as he accompanied me from the durbar, he gave me instructions how I was to proceed.

'You will meet us,' he said, 'on the plain beyond the town, and see that all your horses look well, that your men are well dressed and armed, and I will venture to declare that you are all placed in my division, which has the honour of leading, and is the first for fighting and for plunder. I shall be glad to have you, and I will try whether I cannot get you the command of a hundred or two of my own risala. We want leaders, and from your appearance I judge that you will do justice to my patronage.'

'It is the very thing I have ever wished for,' I said; 'and if you will but favour me, I will do my utmost to please you. It is true I have as yet seen no service, but that is easily learned when the heart is willing.'

We separated, and I hastened to my men to get them in readiness for the inspection of our new chief. Our horses had now rested from the fatigue of the journey, and were in high condition: our arms were cleaned and sharpened. We provided ourselves with the long spear which is peculiar to the Pindaris, and of which thousands were on sale; and at the appointed hour I led my little band to the place, where some hundred horsemen were already assembled. I had dressed myself in the armour of Subzee Khan, which was a magnificent suit; and my noble horse, as he bounded and caracoled with me, seemed proud of his rider, and glad that he had at last got into a scene suited to his fiery spirit. Peer Khan and Motee were also striking figures, and nearly as well mounted as I was; and the rest were as good, if not better, than the majority of those who were now assembled.

'Keep all together,' said I to them; 'do not straggle, or our party will appear more insignificant than it really is. When you see the chief coming, watch my movements and follow me.'

Long before sunset Cheetoo issued from the town, accompanied by as gallant a company as could well be imagined. The leaders of the different durras were all around him, each surpassing the other in the richness and martial air of his dress, his arms, and the trappings of his horse. Before him, making his horse leap and bound in a wonderful manner, rode Ghuffoor Khan, clad in chain-armour, which glittered in the red rays of the setting sun. No one equalled him in appearance, though many were noble-looking cavaliers; and no one appeared to manage his steed with the ease and grace that he did.

'That is the man!' I cried with enthusiasm to Peer Khan; 'that is the man we are to serve under; is he not a gallant fellow? Now follow me.' And I gave my impatient horse the rein, and dashing onwards was in an instant at the side of Cheetoo, accompanied by my men. I dropped my spear to the ground, as I threw my horse back on his haunches close to him, and making an obeisance down to my saddle-bow, said that I had brought my men as he had directed, and awaited his orders.

Cheetoo checked his horse, and for a moment surveyed me with delight.

'You are a fine young fellow,' he said at length, 'and your men are excellently mounted. I would there were as many hundreds of you as you have companions. However, something may be done. What say you, Ghuffoor Khan, will the Meer Sahib serve with you? And have you a few hundred men to put under him?'

'May I be your sacrifice!' cried the Khan, ''tis the very thing your servant would have proposed. I liked the Meer Sahib from the moment I saw him, and now that he is properly dressed, by Allah! he is a very Rustom, and the only fit companion for himself (forgive my insolence) that Ghuffoor Khan sees.'

'Then be it so,' said Cheetoo; 'take him with you, and see that you treat him kindly.'

'Come,' cried the Khan to me, 'come then, Meer Sahib, take a tilting-spear from one of those fellows; here is a rare piece of ground, and I must see whether you are master of your weapon.'

'I fear not,' said I; 'I know little about the spear. On foot and with the sword I should not fear the best man of the army; nevertheless, to please you, I will try.'

I took the spear, a long light bamboo, with a large stuffed ball of cotton at the end of it, from which depended a number of small streamers of red cloth, and following Ghuffoor Khan I dashed forwards into the plain.

We pursued each other alternately, now advancing to the attack, now retreating, amidst the plaudits of the assembled horsemen, who looked on with curiosity to see how an utter stranger would behave against the most accomplished cavalier of the army. For a long time neither of us had any advantage over the other; our horses were admirably trained, and neither allowed the other to approach within reach of the spear-thrust. This was the great nicety of the tilt, and cries of 'Shabash! Shabash!' resounded at every baffling turn or successful escape from a meditated blow. At last the Khan touched me; it was but a graze, which I received on my arm, having delayed for an instant to turn my horse, and he cried out that he had won.

'I own it,' said I, as our horses stood panting for breath, 'for I am, as you know, a novice at the use of the weapon; yet if you will give me another trial, I will again cross spears with you, and see if I have not better luck.'

'Good!' cried he, laughing; 'but look out, for I warn you I shall not be merciful; a sharp blow on the ribs of a young hand teaches him his vulnerable point, and causes him to be careful ever after.'

'Come on,' cried I; 'if I can I will return the compliment.'

We again took a large circle, and at a good canter approached each other till we were nearly within spear's length. The Khan was as good as his word, and made several desperate lunges at me. I avoided them, however, by the quickness of my horse, and I plainly saw that he could by no endeavour approach near enough to me to strike a decisive blow. His horse too, being fatter, was more blown than my own; and, after allowing him to weary it still more for some time in a vain pursuit of me, I suddenly changed my position and became his assailant. I believe I was more cool and wary than he was, for he appeared vexed that a stranger should be on such equal terms with him at his favourite exercise; he did not parry my lunges with the same precision as in the first encounter, when, notwithstanding all my efforts to touch him, he avoided and laughed at me. Still I had not touched him; and growing weary of my close pursuit, he endeavoured to turn again and become the assailant; but whether his horse was slow in wheeling round, or whether I was too near to allow of his avoiding the blow, I know not; but as he endeavoured to cross behind me, I wheeled my horse suddenly, struck my heels into his sides, and as he gave his accustomed bound of some yards, struck my spear full on the broad chest of the Khan, who was somewhat stunned by the blow. A loud shout from those around us proclaimed my victory, and the Khan himself, though abashed at his defeat, was one of the loudest in my praises to the chief himself.

'By Allah!' said he, 'thou art no stranger at this work, Meer Sahib; thou hast played me a trick.'

'I swear by your beard and the Koran that I have not, Khan,' I cried; 'it was the result of chance. Allah knows that two days ago I had never had a spear in my hand. I only observed what you did when you hit me, and to my good horse I owe my fortune. But it was all chance, and though I prize the victory, yet I regret that such a chance should have hurt you.'

'Nay, I am not hurt, Syud,' he replied, 'and I bear these things with good humour; but if you are as good a hand with the sword as you promise to be with the spear, there will not be a man in the camp to stand before you.'

'It would be boastful in me to challenge any one,' said I, 'seeing that I am a stranger among you; yet if the noble Cheetoo wishes to try me, I will essay what I can do tomorrow.'

'Good, good!' cried all; and Cheetoo himself, vastly pleased with the result of my encounter with Ghuffoor Khan, bade me present myself early at his residence, where he would invite a few good swordsmen to attend and see us exercise.

CHAPTER XXVII

The next afternoon we were all assembled on a small plain outside the town; Cheetoo had spread his carpet after the manner of a Pindari, and sat with his chiefs around him, promising by his demeanour to be an eager spectator of the encounter. He was remarkably civil to me, and asked me to sit by him until a few men, who were ready, had displayed their dexterity and prowess. On the signal being given by him, two stout Rajputs leaped into the circle and clattered their sticks on each other's shield for some time without either touching the other.

'Does this please you?' said Cheetoo to me. 'Those fellows are good hands, you see, at their weapons: neither would have drawn blood had they had swords in their hands.'

'They are expert enough,' said I, 'but methinks they have played together before and know each other's ways; they make a great show, but if I may be pardoned, I think neither has much real skill. If my lord wishes I will try either of them.'

'Take care you are not overmatched,' said he; 'I would not have your fair fame sullied. You have interested me much in your behalf.'

'Do not fear for me,' I replied; 'I will do my best.'

I stripped myself to my trowsers, and girding a handkerchief tightly about my waist, I stepped into the circle, where one of the men, who had now rested from his first encounter, awaited me. I took a stick and a small shield made of basket work from Peer Khan, who had brought them, and advanced to the centre. There were murmurs among the assembly that I was overmatched, for they contrasted my slight form with the tall and brawny one of my antagonist; but I was not to be deterred by this. I knew my skill, and that mere personal strength would avail but little against it.

'How is it to be?' said I to the Rajput. 'Does the first fair blow decide between us?'

'Certainly,' he replied. 'I shall strike hard, so be on your guard.'

'Good,' said I: 'now take your post.'

He did. He retired to one edge of the circle and advanced on me leisurely, now stooping and leaning his shield-arm on his knee as he rested a moment to survey me, and now circling round me, first rising on one leg and then on the other, and waving his stick in the air.

I stood perfectly still and in a careless attitude, but well on my guard, for I knew that I should hazard something in moving after him. It was evident to me he did not expect this, for he seemed for a moment irresolute, but at last he rushed on me with two or three bounds, and aimed a blow at my head. I was perfectly prepared, for I knew his mode of attack; I received the blow on my shield, caught the stick under it, and rained such a shower of blows on his undefended person as completely astonished him. The assembly rang with plaudits, and the other Rajput stepped forward and saluted me.

'You have had but short work with my friend Bheem Singh,' said he; 'but now you must try me.'

'I am ready,' I replied; 'so get to your post.'

I had now an antagonist worthy of me; he knew my system of play, and verily I thought myself for the moment engaged with my old instructor; but I had used to vanquish him, and I did not fear the man before me. We were soon hotly engaged: he was as cool and wary as myself, and after a long conflict, in which neither had the advantage, we rested awhile, both out of breath.

'Enough, enough!' cried Cheetoo; 'you have both done bravely; neither has won, and you had better let the matter stand as it is.'

'Not so, Khodawund,' said I; 'let us finish it; one of us must win, and my friend here desires as much as myself to see which of us is the better man. Is it not so?'

'Ay,' said the fellow laughingly, 'the Nawab Sahib knows that no one as yet has overcome me; but I have fairly met my match: and who ever taught you was a good master, and has had a disciple worthy of him.'

'As you will,' said Cheetoo, 'only play in good humour; let no feud grow out of it.'

We both saluted him, and assured him we could not quarrel, and that whoever was victor must entertain a high respect for his opponent. And to it we set again, as we had now recovered our breath: victory for a long time hovered between us, now inclining to the one and now to the other; we had both lost our footing once or twice, and the spectators would have had us leave off, but excited as we were it was impossible—we stopped not for their exclamations. I was put to my last shifts to avoid the well-directed blows of the Rajput; he had better wind than I, and this obliged me to alter my mode of play: hitherto I had attacked him, I now only warded off his cuts, but watched my opportunity. In his eagerness, thinking by a succession of blows he could beat down my guard, he exposed his side, and my stick descended on his ribs with a sound which was heard by all, and with a force which fairly took away his breath.

'Fairly won!' cried Cheetoo; 'fairly and bravely won! Ramdeen Singh, thou has lost, but it is no disgrace to thee.'

The Rajput laughed, and I was glad he bore the defeat so

good-humouredly, for I had expected the contrary; he allowed that he had been vanquished, and cried out to all that in had been a fair encounter, and that he had used the utmost of his skill.

I was delighted with the noble fellow, and addressed Cheetoo himself.

'I crave a boon, Khodawund, and if I may hope to have it granted, I will speak.'

'Say on,' he replied; 'I will grant it readily.'

'Then,' said I, 'let this brave fellow be placed under me. By your favour, a stranger has been entrusted with the command of part of the Harawul (advance-guard), and I would have both these Rajputs with me, and be allowed to entrust fifty men to the one and twenty-five to the other.'

'Good,' said Cheetoo, 'let it be so; and do you, Ghuffoor Khan, look to it that it is done: these are the men who will serve us in the time of need.'

A few days more and I was fairly installed into my new charge. Fortune had favoured me far above my expectations, and I saw nought before me but a career of distinction under my new master. True, I was no longer a leader on my own responsibility, but the rank I held was honourable, and perhaps far above my deserts.

Our time passed in the camp in the manner I have related. In the mornings I was a constant attendant upon Cheetoo, who rarely allowed me to leave his person during his inspection of the constantly arriving new adventurers; and the evenings closed with feats of strength and trials of skill, in which I sustained the reputation I had begun with.

At last the festival of the Dussehra arrived, and it was held with great pomp and show. A grand review of all the assembled adventurers was held, a muster taken, and it was reported that five thousand good horsemen were present; and this number, with their followers, and those indifferently mounted, was augmented to nearly eight thousand—a gallant band, ready to do the bidding of their chief, and to carry war and devastation into the countries before them.

It was planned that we should separate into two bodies soon after passing the Nurbudda, penetrate as far as the Kistna river to the south, and should we find that fordable, then press on as far south as we could, without exposing ourselves to encounters with the regular armies of the Feringhees, which we were assured, although at present innactive, could speedily be sent in pursuit of us. Accordingly, as the morning broke, the whole camp was in motion; and a noble sight it was to see durra after durra defile before their chief, and hurry onwards at a rapid pace. Boats had been provided at the Nurbudda, which we crossed the same day, and took up our ground near the town of Hindia, on its southern bank.

At this point the army seperated. I remained with my division and Cheetoo, and we pushed on the day after, taking a direction to the westward, so as to come upon the river Tapti, up the valley of which we were to proceed till we should reach the territories of the Rajah of Nagpur, with whom a treaty had been previously made to allow us a free and unmolested passage through his dominions, on the condition that they were not to be plundered. The other division, under Syud Bheekoo, a leader of note, and only second to Cheetoo, took a direction to the eastward, along the bank of the Nurbudda, until they reached the grand road to Nagpur, by which it was their intention to travel.

Meanwhile we proceeded by rapid marches; for we were eager to reach the scene of our operations, as our money was running short, and without plunder we should starve. We heard that there was a small detachment of regular troops under Major Fraser watching our movements; but our spies told us they were few in number, and we were under no apprehension of an attack from them: it was reported that they did not exceed three hundred men, and we vainly thought they would not dare to face as many thousands. But we had not sufficiently estimated their bravery. We knew they were upwards of fifteen coss distant from us, and what infantry could make that march and attack a body of horse like ours?

They did however attack us. We had arrived at our ground near a village on the Tapti, and some were cooking their morning meal, others lounging idly about the camp or lying at full length on their saddle-cloths, when the alarm was given that the Feringhees were upon us. The scene of confusion which ensued is indescribable. Men hurried hither and thither; anything like organization was past all hope: each as he could gain his horse, threw himself upon it and fled for his life: not a man stood. In vain I entreated those with me to rally, and make a charge on the small body of red-coats which was now drawn up in line close to our camp, and was pouring volley after volley amongst us with destructive precision. Not a man would hear me, and though my own Thugs and a few of my division swore they would die if I were to lead them on, I saw no chance of success; and as one or two of my men had fallen near me, we too at length turned our horses' heads and fled. We were not pursued, though there were some horsemen with the infantry, who, had they not been arrant cowards, would have charged after and engaged us.

Our surprise and rout was complete, and if the enemy had had a larger body of infantry, or any good cavalry with them to have followed us, we might have bid adieu to all hopes of future plunder, and most likely should have taken our way to our respective homes and abandoned the expedition. As it was, however, we found we had not lost more than a hundred men, and three days afterwards we were again reunited and in as good spirits as ever.

At length we debouched by almost untrodden paths from the hills to the eastward of Ellichpur, and from among the dense jungles I had before traversed, after the affair with the Moghulance. We entered the territories of the Nizam near the river Wurda, which we crossed, and in one march of nearly twenty-five coss reached Amraoti, which it appeared had been the object of our leader from the first. I have once before described its riches and prosperity, and it was then far richer than it is now.

As we rushed along, like the flood of a mighty river, every village on our route was instantly deserted by its inhabitants and left to our mercy. They were one by one ransacked, and in some of the largest much booty was obtained. I was fortunate in leading the advance-guard on this day, and well do I remember the excitement of the moment, as we passed the last defile in the hills, and rushed in a body into the plain. Well do I remember waving my sword to my companions—whose numbers were now swelled to nearly five hundred splendid fellows, often increased by parties from the rear—as I showed them the broad plains of Berar, and told them that we had unlimited power to plunder as we listed.

Ghuffoor Khan envied me that day; he had been detained with Cheetoo, who remained with the main body, while my own harawul was increased, in order that I might advance and surround Amraoti. On we dashed! The few villages we surprised were quickly laid under contribution; and rupees and gold and silver ornaments were tendered, almost without our asking, by their terrified inhabitants. As we proceeded, the news that we were coming had spread through every village, and thousands of people were seen flying from their homes; while a few only remained in each, with an offering to me accompanied by entreaties not to burn their villages. Nor did I; though from the pillars of smoke which not long afterwards arose in every direction behind us, I too justly thought the main body had been less merciful than we had. We reached Amraoti towards evening. There were but few soldiers to guard this important post, and they had fled on the news of our approach; we therefore entered the town unopposed.

I directed my course to the main street, where I knew I should find the principal sahoukars; and, after stationing parties of my men at each end and at the different outlets, I rode into the middle of the chouke, or market-place, and dismounted among the leading men of the town, who had a carpet spread, and were prepared, as they said, to do us honour. But few words of greeting passed, for ours was no cordial visit, and each party was bent on driving the hardest bargain.

'Come, gentlemen,' said I, after listening some time to their protestations of poverty, 'this is mere fooling. You have offered a lakh of rupees; do you think the noble Cheetoo will be satisfied with this? I swear by the Koran he will not, and you had better at once be reasonable and listen to my words. The whole Lubhur will be here before it is dark, and if any of you will take the trouble to ascend one of your tall houses, or one of the bastions, you will see how Pindaris mark their progress. Many a fine village behind me has not now a roof or tree standing, and your good town will assuredly share the same fate if you trifle with us; and not only will it be burned, but your property will be handed over to the tender mercies of my men—ay, and your wives and daughters also; so I give you fair warning. Go therefore, be wise, consult among yourselves, and before the shadow of this tree has lengthened the measure of my sword, (and I laid it on the ground) bring me an answer worthy of your name for wisdom, and liberal withal; beyond that time I give you not a moment; your houses are close at hand, and Inshallah! we will help ourselves.'

'Well spoken!' cried all the men who were around me; 'but, Meer Sahib, why not help ourselves at once? These stingy merchants can have no idea of the wants of men of honour like us, who have a long journey before us.'

'You shall hear what they say,' replied I; 'meanwhile let us be quiet and orderly, and let none of you interrupt their consultations, or offer violence to any of the townspeople.'

The time had nearly elapsed, and the hilt of my sword was all that remained in the sunlight. The council of the merchants was, from all appearances, as far from a decision as ever, to judge from their angry debate, and the unsettled and anxious expression of their countenances.

Eagerly I watched the increasing shadow, as from time to time I called to them that the period allowed had nearly elapsed; at last the bright hilt of my sword glittered no longer, and I took it up amidst a shout from my men. The merchants saw my action and again advanced in a body towards me.

'Sit down, Meer Sahib,' said the fattest of them, who appeared to be the chief, 'let us talk over this matter calmly and deliberately. That business is always unsatisfactory which is done in a hurry, and with heated minds.'

'No!' I exclaimed, 'I will not: standing as I am, I will hear what you have to say. Remember, when I draw my sword the plunder begins, and though I have some influence over these brave fellows while they expect a reasonable offer from you, yet the instant they are disappointed my power ends, and I will not answer for any of your lives.'

'Come aside with me for a moment,' said the chief merchant;

'I would speak with you apart; you need fear no treachery from a sahoukar.'

We all laughed heartily. 'No, no,' said I, 'I fear nought, and will come. And do you, my good fellows,' I added, turning to my men, 'see that none of these worthy persons escape.'

'Well,' said I, when we had gone a few paces from the group, 'what would you say? Be quick; my men are impatient, and your houses and shops are temptingly near.'

'Listen then,' replied he; 'you are a leader, and by your conduct doubtless have the influence you appear to have. You have not more than five hundred men with you; we offer you therefore ten thousand rupees as your own share, one thousand to each of your sirdars, and one hundred a-piece to your men; this will be nearly a lakh of rupees, and we will take our chance with the main body. What do you say? be quick and tell me, for the money is at hand, and can be easily distributed before the main body comes up.'

I pondered awhile; I knew Cheetoo would make his own terms, and I did not see any harm in getting as much as I could of the spoil before he came. I knew also that he expected ten lakhs, and would get it by fair means or foul.

'Listen again,' said the sahoukar; 'you are in advance; you have only to take your money and push on, and any village before you will shelter you for the night; what will Cheekoo know of it?'

'Nay,' said I, 'here we remain; after a march of twenty-five coss, we are in no humour to proceed; but I will take my men outside the town on the instant payment of one lakh of rupees; —remember, one third of what we get goes to the chief, and our share after all is not much.'

'Agreed,' said he; 'now come to your men, and persuade them to be quiet: they will not get so much by violence as by treating us well.'

We returned to the group we had left, and I unfolded to them the proposition which had been made to me; it was welcomed with a loud shout which made the air ring, and was then succeeded by loud cries for the money.

The sum had evidently been collected previously, for in a few moments a line of men, heavily laden with bags of rupees, issued from a lane close to where we were sitting. Daffa by daffa of the Pindaris, each headed by its own daffadar, was brought up to the spot; each man received his hundred rupees, each leader his thousand, which were stowed away in the bags of their saddles.

'You have not cared for yourself, Meer Sahib,' said Peer Khan; 'you have taken nothing.'

'Oh, do not fear for me,' I replied; 'I have got my share; the bag does not look large, but it holds gold.'

His eyes brightened. 'That is right,' he said; 'the others must not know of it.'

'Not a syllable; it is known only to you and myself. Now we must take care these rascals commit no excess; they seem half in the humour to run riot in the town.'

'They seem content,' he replied; 'at least I for one am. By Allah! Meer Sahib, this is rare work; a thousand rupees in a morning's ride is better than our own profession, though we have been lucky in our time.'

'Choop!' said I, 'silence! This is no time for our secrets. Away with you! See that the men take up ground before the town. I will remain here with some others, and see what becomes of the place when Cheetoo arrives.'

One by one the Pindaris left me, except a few who stayed by my desire; and our business at an end, I sat down and awaited Cheetoo's arrival.

'What do you think he will ask?' said my fat friend to me.

'I know not,' I answered; 'but you had better be liberal at once, or he will sack your town, and you know what Pindaris are; they have few scruples, and some of you may be tortured.'

A shudder ran through the assembly at the thought of the torture, and I saw I had made a hit. 'Yes,' I continued, 'there are such things as korlas, and your fat backs will soon be laid open; besides there are fellows who are rare hands at tying up fingers and hitting them on the ends, which is not agreeable I should think—also at mixing compositions for those bags to be tied over your mouths. I have heard of even still worse contrivances to persuade obstinate sahoukars, but ye are wise men—ye will be warned.'

'Say at once, Meer Sahib,' said another of the merchants who had not yet spoken, 'say what we should offer, and how many Pindaris are there? we have heard there are five thousand.'

'Somewhat below the mark, Sethji,' said I; 'we are little under ten thousand, I think; however, you will see the lubhur, and judge for yourselves. As for the sum, I should say, in the first place, a lakh of rupees for Cheetoo himself—I know he expects as much; then there are three sirdars, Heeroo, Ghuffoor Khan, and Rajun—fifty thousand apiece; then each minor leader and duffadar a thousand, and every good Pindari a hundred. Say, have I spoken well?'

'Bhugwan protect us!' cried one and all, 'we are ruined and dead men. Why this would be at least eight lakhs of rupees; where are we to get such a sum? We are ruined, and you had better kill us at once.'

'No, no, my good friends, not so,' said I. 'All the world knows that Amraoti is the richest town in the country, ay, richer than Hyderabad itself, and that the money may be counted, not by lakhs, but by crores; so talk not to Cheetoo of your poverty, for he will presently prove whether you lie or not.'

'I tell you all,' said the fat sahoukar, 'the worthy Meer Sahib speaks the truth. Bhugwan has sent his gurdee (calamity), and we must be resigned to our fate. Better far is it to give the uttermost farthing, than to see our wives and daughters dishonoured before our eyes.'

'Good!' cried I; 'now you speak like wise men, and I will give you further advice. Cheetoo is a great man, and loves to be paid honour, as indeed is due to him; so also do the other leaders. Now get your pān, utr, and spices, make up a proper tray of them, bring a few handsome shawls, and as he takes his seat, one of you throw a pair of the best over his shoulders and those of the other chiefs, and lay your nuzzurs before him as you would before Sikundur Jah himself. Inshallah! you will find favour in his sight, and where you would have to pay ten lakhs you will get off with half the sum, and save your town besides.'

'By Gunja! 'tis well said!' cried several. 'Meer Sahib, you are a kind friend and give good advice.'

'Again,' said I, 'let none of you have long faces, but all look as if you were rejoiced at his coming. Be none of you alarmed before you have cause. Pay you must, and therefore do it with as good a grace as you can.'

The assembly drank in my words, as I by turns advised and alarmed them, in order to keep up the spirit I had infused; and in this manner the time passed until the dusk of evening, when, by the noise of the tread of many horses' feet and the firing of matchlocks, we were assured of the approach of the main body.'

'Now stick by us,' cried the sahoukars as they crowded round me; 'you are our friend and must present us: we will not be afraid.' But their words belied them, for the teeth of one and all were chattering with fear, and their cheeks blanched at the thoughts of confronting the Pindari chief.

Cheetoo came, and riding into the chouke, surrounded by a crowd of wild-looking figures, the effect of whose appearance was materially increased by the dusk of the evening, his titles were screamed out by a dozen mouths, each vying with the other in exaggeration of his powers.

The group of Sahoukars, headed by me, advanced towards him; and the head merchant, rubbing his forehead on the chief's stirrup, implored him to alight and refresh himself, adding that a zeafut had been prepared, and all were desirous of presenting their nuzzurs. I seconded the request, and he exclaimed, 'Surely I know that voice; whose, in the name of Shatan, is it?'

'That of your slave Ameer Ali,' said I.

'Oh, then all is right,' he cried; 'and thou too hast turned sahoukar. How is this, Meer Sahib?'

'May I be your sacrifice, Nawab!' said I; 'I have but mingled with these worthy persons, because they declared they should be annihilated at the sight of the splendour of your appearance. I did but console them and keep up their spirits till my lord arrived.'

'Thou hast done well,' said Cheetoo. 'Is everything prepared?'

'All,' cried the sahoukars; 'if the noble Cheetoo will but alight, we are prepared to do him honour.'

He alighted, and, led by the hand by the chief merchant, he was conducted into an adjoining house, which belonged to one of the merchants, and where a clean white floorcloth had been spread, and a musnud placed. The room too was well lighted. Cheetoo took his seat, and looked around him with evident gratification; savage as his countenance was, it now wore a smile of triumph, yet mixed with an expression of extreme pleasure.

'These are civilised people,' said he to Rajun, his favourite, who was close to him. 'I little expected this: did you?'

'Indeed no,' said he; 'I thought we should have had to cut our way into the town. Depend on it, this is Ameer Ali's doing.'

'Likely enough,' said Cheetoo; 'he is a gentleman, and knows how a gentleman ought to be received. But for him it is most probable these swine would have shut themselves up in their houses, and given us the trouble of pulling them out. But see—what are they about?'

I was nudged by the sahoukar, who, whispering, implored me to ask Cheetoo to accept their nuzzur. 'Five hundred rupees for you if he takes it!' again he whispered as I pretended to hesitate.

'Agreed,' said I; 'I will revenge myself if it is not paid.'

'By Gunga! by my Junwa!' again said he most earnestly, 'nay, I will double it. Speak for us, good Meer Sahib, are you not our friend and our brother?'

'What are those sons of asses talking to you about?' cried Cheetoo. 'Why don't they speak out?'

'Khodawund!' I said, 'the terror of your name has preceded you'—and he smiled grimly,—'and your appearance is in every way so imposing and surpassing the accounts these men have heard, that by Allah! they are dumb; and though they would fain lay a nuzzur at your feet, befitting your high rank, they have not words to express their desires, and have begged your slave to inform my lord of them.'

'Kabool, Kabool! I agree,' cried Cheetoo; 'let the trays be brought. Verily a nuzzur from the sahoukars of Amraoti ought to be worth seeing.'

Fifteen trays were brought in, covered with rich velvet coverings, and set down before the musnud; one by one their covers were removed, and indeed it was a goodly sight! Dates, pistachio nuts, sweetmeats, and sugar-candy filled four; the rest contained cloths of various kinds, European and Indian, muslins, chintzes, rich turbans, and Benares brocades. It was a nuzzur fit for a prince, and Cheetoo was delighted.

'Now,' said I to the sahoukar, 'this is a happy moment; where are the shawls and the ashruffees? Have a stout heart, and throw the shawls over him, as you would over one of your own tribe at a marriage.'

The sahoukar took the shawls from an attendant, and putting five ashruffees upon them, advanced to the feet of Cheetoo; and having made the tusleemât, or three obeisances, he presented the gold, and unfolding the shawls, which were very splendid, dexterously enveloped the chief's person in them, and then retreating, stood with his hands folded on his breast in an attitude of respectful humility.

CHAPTER XXVIII

CHEETOO was evidently flattered by the distinction with which he had been received, and as he examined the beautiful shawls which now enveloped his person, a grim smile of delight lighted up his coarse features.

'These men have sense,' said he to Ghuffoor Khan, 'and are evidently accustomed to the visits of persons of quality. We little expected this civility, and in truth it is most acceptable after our long ride; but they have forgotten you.'

'Not so, noble Cheetoo,' cried the sahoukar, advancing with several pairs of shawls over his arm; 'we are not forgetful of our distinguished guests'; and he threw a pair over each of the chiefs, which they received with complacency.

'Let the room be cleared,' cried Cheetoo; 'we have business with these worthy gentlemen, which I have sworn to do before we touch any refreshment.'

It was quickly done, and there only remained our leaders and the sahoukars, who huddled together like wild fowl on the approach of a hawk.

'Come forward,' said Cheetoo to them; 'come and sit near us; we would speak to you.' They all arose, and, as they were directed, seated themselves in respectful attitudes on the edge of the musnud.

'Now,' continued Cheetoo, 'you are doubtless aware of our object. We want money, and money we will have, by fair means or foul; if ye are wise, ye will pay me handsomely to be rid of me and my people, who are savage fellows. I desire not to harm you, and on your own heads be it, if any disaster befalls you. Say, therefore, how much are ye prepared to give?'

'Truly,' said the sahoukar, my friend, who was the spokesman, 'we have been duly advised of your Highness's coming; and as a proof that we did not dread you, you see us here, and we have done our poor ability to welcome so distinguished a person. We have also received good counsel from your servant the Meer Sahib; and agreeably by his instructions we have drawn up a list of a few trifles and some ready money which we are desirous of laying at the feet of your Highness.' And the sahoukar handed to him a paper written in Persian.

'This is unintelligible to me, for I am no munshi: but can any of you read, brothers?' asked Cheetoo of the other leaders.

'Not a word, not a letter,' cried one and all; 'none of us knows one letter from another.'

'I can send for a munshi,' said the sahoukar; 'one is in attendance.'

'If I am permitted,' said I, 'I will read the list: I may be able to make it out.'

'Ha! thou art a clerk as well as a good soldier,' cried Cheetoo, laughing. 'Well, take the paper, and let us hear our good fortune.'

'First then,' said I, after I had glanced over the document, 'this paper sets forth, that the sahoukars and others of the market-town of Amraoti, in council assembled, having heard of the near approach of the mighty Cheetoo and his army, and being desirous of approaching his feet with a small tribute of respect, have put down the following articles and sums of ready money, which are prepared and ready for his acceptance—on no condition save that they may find favour in his sight, and be the humble means of insuring his clemency to others.'

'Good!' said Cheetoo. 'Now get thee to the marrow of the matter as speedily as may be, for my stomach craves food, and I doubt not these worthy gentlemen's families have prepared a repast for me.'

'It is ready, noble Cheetoo,' cried the sahoukar; 'and if the order is given, it will be set out; but the food of us poor Hindus would be tasteless to my lord, and therefore we have had the repast cooked by the best Bawurchees of the town.'

'Silence!' cried the chief; 'speak when you are allowed to do so: we are in no humour to be interrupted.'

The sahoukar shrank back intimidated, and raising my voice I proceeded.

'The first item, Protector of the Poor!' cried I, 'is a sum of fifty thousand rupees for yourself.'

'Is that all?' cried he, his brow contracting.

'Stay,' said I, 'more follows.' 'A tray of choice jewels, gold and silver, valued at fifteen thousand rupees, and three trays of shawls and brocades for my lord's Muhal, valued at ten thousand rupees: in all, seventy-five thousand rupees. Secondly, a sum of ten thousand rupees to each leader of rank, of whom we learn from the worthy Syud, Ameer Ali, there are three: a tray of jewels to each, of five thousand rupees, and three trays, each valued at five thousand rupees, and three trays, each valued at five thousand more; in all, twenty thousand rupees each".'

'Go on!' cried Cheetoo; 'you have not done yet, I suppose?'

'No,' said I, glancing down the paper; 'there is more following. "Thirdly, a sum of one thousand rupees to each daffadar: we are uninformed of their number, but we have supposed thirty".'

'Good!' cried Cheetoo; 'what more?'

'"Fourthly, the sum of fifty-rupees to each deserving person, to be given at the discretion of the mighty Cheetoo; by report we hear there are four thousand. Also food, grain, and forage for as many days as the army may remain with us." This is all,' said I; 'what are my lord's orders?'

'The list is well enough,' said Cheetoo; 'but they are wrong in some particulars: first, there are fifty duffadars, are there not, Ghuffoor Khan?'

'There are,' he replied; 'I told them off myself.'

'Put that down, Meer Sahib,' said Cheetoo. 'Again, there are five thousand good Pindaris; am I not right?'

'True again,' cried all the leaders; 'were they not counted at Nemawur?'

This was a lie; there were hardly four thousand, for nearly half the lubhur had gone off in a different direction from the Nurbudda; but it signified little; for Cheetoo, I knew, was determined to make the best terms he could with the sahoukars.

'Put down five thousand,' said Cheetoo; 'and now see how much you have got.'

I hastily arranged the amount, and read the paper to him. 'First,' said I, 'there is your Highness's share, seventy-five thousand rupees; secondly, on account of the leaders, sixty thousand rupees; then the fifty daffadars, each man a thousand, fifty thousand rupees; lastly, five thousand men, each forty, two hundred thousand. And the sum of the whole is three lakhs and eighty-five thousand rupees.'

'And,' said Cheetoo to Ghuffoor Khan, 'the horses' shoes must be worn out, I think? we require new ones.'

'Certainly,' cried the Khan, with a merry grin.

'Put down fifteen thousand rupees for the horse-shoes; this, Meer Sahib, will make the sum an even four lakhs; and gentlemen,' continued he to the sahoukars, 'I must trouble you to pay with as little delay as possible, or we must help ourselves.'

There was a hurried conference for a few moments among the sahoukars, and a few angry words passed among them; but they were wise; my fat friend rose, and making a lowly obeisance, declared the money was at hand, and should be brought immediately.

'Good!' cried Cheetoo; 'now let me have my dinner, and do you all see that the duffadars are present at this house by tomorrow's dawn, to receive their shares and those of their men.

The chiefs separated, and I was preparing to leave the room with them, when Cheetoo called me back; 'Come and take your dinner with me,' said he; 'I doubt not your friends the sahoukars have prepared enough for us two.'

I obeyed the order, and seated myself at the edge of the musnud. The dinner was soon brought, and a choice repast it was. We did justice to it, for in truth our travel had sharpened our appetites. These satisfied, and inhaling the fragrant smoke of our pipes, Cheetoo asked me how I had managed to bring about so advantageous a reception as he had met with. I related the whole to him, suppressing however the fact that I had secured for myself so large a sum as ten thousand rupees; for had I disclosed that, he would presently have helped himself to half of it at least. Peer Khan was the only person who knew of it, and to him alone was I determined to entrust it.

He was delighted; he had, I knew, determined to raise a large sum, and I had purposely exaggerated his probable demand to the sahoukars. 'You see, Meer Sahib,' said he, 'by your excellent conduct I have secured first, seventy-five thousand rupees; and what is over, after every proper Pindari has got his forty rupees, will make the sum pretty near a lakh; which is, you will say, a good beginning.'

'May your prosperity increase, noble Cheetoo,' said I; 'if your slave can help you to a few more sums like the present, he will only feel himself too happy, and too honoured by distinction like the present.'

'And for yourself, Meer Sahib?'

'I have not got much,' said I; 'perhaps I might have arrogated to myself the distinction of one of the leaders, but I refrained: they gave me five thousand rupees however, and I am satisfied.'

'Nay,' said Cheetoo; 'it was too little, my friend, and I advise you to get as much as you can next time. And as you have behaved so well in this instance at the head of the advance-party, I will give it into your command in future, and must satisfy Ghuffoor Khan as well as I can; he is a good soldier, but a thick-headed fellow, who is always for helping himself, and setting fire to towns and villages, by which we seldom get half as much, especially from these rich places, as we could do by a little management and a few soft words.'

'May your condescension increase, Nawab!' cried I; 'your servant, Inshallah! will never disappoint you.'

I took leave of him soon afterwards, and joined the sahoukars, who were sitting below counting the money, which lay in large heaps on the floor. They received me joyfully, and expressed in forcible language how much they were indebted to me for my active interference in their behalf. They would have pressed on me the five hundred rupees they had promised when I presented them to Cheetoo, but I refused it.

'No,' said I; 'if I have done you service, and I think I have, I will not sell my good offices. You have dealt as well by me as I have by you, so the balance is even; all I pray of you is, to let me have my money in gold bars, which I can easily conceal, except a few hundred rupees for present expenses.'

'It is granted,' said the sahoukar; and I had shortly afterwards the gold in my possession; and taking a few of the sahoukars' men to guard me, I bent my way to the camp, the bright fires of which sparkled through the darkness on the plain beyond the town, revealing many a wild group which huddled round them to warm themselves from the effects of the almost chilling night breeze. I was soon at my little tent, which consisted of a cloth stretched over three spears, two of which were stuck into the ground, and another tied across them as a ridge pole; and assisted by Peer Khan, I put the gold into the bags I had had made in the flaps of my saddle, and sewe l them over. I was ten housand rupees richer in one night!

'This is grand work,' said Peer Khan; 'here we have had no trouble; and if we go on at this rate, we shall return far richer than after the toil and risk of a hurdred Thuggee expeditions.'

'I am to have the advance-guard always,' said I; 'and it shall be my own fault if we do not always secure a good share; for my part, I have forsworn Thuggee, as long as there is a Pindhari chief to erect his standard.'

By dawn the next morning I was with Cheetoo. The sahoukars had collected the whole of the money, by subscriptions among themselves and collections from the town; and the whole was distributed fairly, I must say, among the Pindaris. Each daffadar bore away the share of his daffa, and they knew too well the risk they would run if they defrauded any man of his just due.

A few hours elapsed, and after a hurried meal, every man was on his horse, and the lubhur departed to seek fresh plunder in the country before them. Yet before he set out, Cheetoo promised, in consequence of the ready payment of the sum he received, that in every future expedition he might undertake, the town of Amraoti should be exempted from contributions; and he kept his word.

Onwards we dashed! I, at the head of my band, who had now implicit confidence in me, caracoled along on my gallant horse, with a heart as light and happy as the unlimited freedom of action I possessed could make it. No thought of care intruded, and I was spared the pain of seeing the villages we passed through (from each of which we levied as much as we could, which was instantly laden on the Shootur camels that accompanied us) burned or plundered, and the inoffensive inhabitants subjected to the cruel tortures of the men in the rear, who were often disappointed of booty.

We halted at Karinjah: a few soldiers who were in the town made a feeble defence, and wounded a few of my men as we rushed into the place; but they were soon killed or dispersed; and, as a warning to others, the village was given up to sack and ruin. I could never bear the sight of wanton cruelty, and I repaired to my place in the camp; shortly afterwards I could see, from the bright blaze which rose from different parts of the village almost simultaneously against the clear grey evening sky, that it was doomed to destruction. Rapidly the fire spread, while the shouts of the Pindaris engaged in their horrid work, and the screams of the inhabitants—those of the women were fearfully shrill and distinct—made a fit accompaniment. But it was a work in which the Pindaris delighted; order, which never existed save when there was no excitement, was completely at an end, and any attempt to have checked the mad riot which was going on would have been attended most likely with death to the interferer. My own Thugs, too, sat around me, for a Thug is not savage, and they had no inclination to join in the excesses.

We sat in silence, but our attention was soon arrested by the figure of a man dragging along a girl, who resisted to the utmost of her power, but who was evidently nearly exhausted. I rushed forward to her rescue, and my eyes fell on the person of Ghuffoor Khan, his savage features exaggerated in their ferocious expression by lust and the scene he had been engaged in.

'Ha!' cried he, 'Meer Sahib, is that you? here have I been working like a true Pindari, and have brought off something worth having; look at her, man! Is she not a Peri? A Houri? The fool, her mother, must needs oppose me when I got into their house, but I silenced her with a thrust of my sword, and lo! here is her fair daughter, a worthy mate for a prince. Speak, my pretty one, art not thou honoured at the prospect of the embraces of Ghuffoor Khan?'

By Allah! Sahib I could have killed him, and it would have been an easy matter to have done so, as he stood unprepared. I had half drawn my sword from its scabbard, but I returned it: I made an inward determination as to his fate, and I kept it. I vainly endeavoured to induce him to give up the girl and let her go, but he laughed in my face, and dragged her off. She would fain had fled from him, and attempted to do so, but he pursued and caught her, for her tender feet were cut by the rough ground, and I lost sight of them both in the quickly closing darkness. Miserable girl! She was a Brahmin's daughter, and was spared the degradation of seeing the light of another day, and the misery of returning to her desolate home polluted and an outcast. Ghuffoor Khan told me in the morning, with a hellish laugh, that he had murdered her, as she tried to possess herself of his dagger, to plunge it into her own heart. 'I spared her the trouble,' he said.

Gradually the fire lessened in its fury, as there remained but few houses unconsumed, but the Pindaris were still at their wild and horrible work, as the shrieks borne to us on the night wind too well testified. I had heard that these excesses were sometimes committed, but I had formed no idea of their terrible reality. A thousand times I formed the resolution to quit the lubhur and return to my home; but again the thought, that a few straggling horsemen, who could give no proper account of themselves, would be immediately taken for Pindaris, and sacrificed by the now infuriated people of the country—this, and, I must add, a restless desire for further adventures, caused me to dismiss it from my mind. It began to rain too, and we all huddled together in my little tent, and passed a weary night, till the morning broke. Then we were again in motion, and the ill-fated town of Karinjah, now a heap of smouldering ruins, was soon far behind us.

We passed Mungrool; and beyond the town, now in the broad daylight, I had an opportunity of seeing the spot where my first victim had fallen. I had thought that the place where he fell was in a large and dense jungle, so at least it appeared that night in the moonlight—but it was not so; the rivulet was the same as when we had passed it, and I stood once more on the very spot where the sahoukar had fallen! A thin belt of bushes fringed the stream, and Peer Khan pointed with a significant gesture a little higher up than the place at which we crossed. It was the *bhil* where they were buried, and it now seemed a fearfully insecure spot for the concealment of our victims,—so close to the road, and apparently so thinly screened from observation. Yet many years had now passed since they were deposited in their last resting-place, and a succession of rainy seasons had either washed away their remains, or covered them still deeper with sand.

We passed the spot too where our bands had encamped and separated; and before me was now a new country, though it little differed in character from that we had already traversed.

We halted at Basim, and I greatly feared a repetition of the scenes of the past night; but the men were, to my astonishment, quiet and orderly; and a handsome contribution levied in the town in all probability saved it. From hence, in five marches, we reached Nandair on the Godavery, a rich town, and one which promised as large a supply to our army as we had got at Amraoti. We had feared the news of our approach would have reached it, and that the sahoukars and wealthy inhabitants would have fled; but it was not so: they were completely surprised and at our mercy, for not a single soldier worth mentioning was there to guard the place.

I will not weary you with a repetition of almost the same tale; suffice it to say, that one lakh and a half of rupees were collected and paid to the army, and I got for my own share nearly three thousand rupees, some jewels, and a pair of shawls. The town was not destroyed; indeed that would have been impossible, as the houses were substantial ones, with terraced roofs; but the suburbs suffered, and the huts of the unfortunate weavers were sacked for the fine cloths for which the place is famous—nor in vain, for half the army the next day appeared in new turbans and waistbands.

The river was not fordable, and there was but one boat; we therefore pushed along the northern bank, till we reached Gunga Khair, where we were told there were boats and a more convenient ferry: nor were we disappointed. We crossed with ease during the day on which we arrived opposite the place, the men swimming their horses across, and the plunder and baggage being brought over by the boats. A few hundred men attempted to defend the town, but it was carried by forcing open the gate, and plundered.

From hence we penetrated southward. Beeder, Bhalkee, the fine and flourishing town of Hoomnabad (a second Amraoti) were severally plundered, or laid under heavy contributions; while every village which lay in our route was sacked, and too often burned and destroyed. From Hoomnabad I led three hundred men to Kullianee, a few coss distant; but we found the alarm had been given, and that all the rich inhabitants had taken refuge in the fort, which is a very strong one, and to us was impregnable. Such was the dread we inspired, however, that the defenders of it remained quietly within it, and allowed us to keep possession of the town till the next morning, when we rejoined the main body.

We descended by a pass in the hills to the village of Chincholee, which was of course plundered, and we followed a direct southwardly route, burning and plundering every place in our way, till the broad and deep stream of the Krishna effectually opposed our further progress. Here the Lubhur halted for some days; forage was plentiful, every one was loaded with money, and we enjoyed ourselves in our encampment as true Pindaris. Dancing-girls were seized from all parts of the surrounding country, though no violence was ever offered to them, and they amused us with their songs and performances, and left us when we were again put in motion, well satisfied and well rewarded, and regretting that they could not accompany us.

Cheetoo was wrong to have halted, for the alarm that Pindaris were out had flown through the country, and in our march towards Koolburgah we got no plunder worth mentioning. Koolburgah we found garrisoned and prepared for our reception; so relinquishing our designs upon Sholapoor and the rich towns of Barsee and Wyrag, we struck off in the direction of Bheer, Pyetun and Aurungabad, hoping to surprise the latter, though we feared it would be well garrisoned.

But I was determined to surprise Barsee and Wyrag if I could, and I laid my proposals for the expedition before Cheetoo. He readily acceeded to my request, at which Ghuffoor Khan was extremely savage; and taking with me three hundred men, the best I could select, and dividing them into duffas under my own Thugs, I left the main body at the town of Allund, and dashed on towards Toljapur, from whence there is a pass into the low country.

Wyrang was our next aim, and we were successful. Our force was supposed to be a risala of Mahratta horse who were known to be in the district, and we were allowed to enter the town unopposed. We sacked it, and got a large booty, for there was no time for a proposal of contribution; indeed I thought not of that alternative, nor could I restrain my men after their long march. Here we heard that the risala we had been mistaken for was at Barsee, and as that place lay in our direct road to Bheer, where we were to join the main body, I was obliged to give up my intention of proceeding through it; there was also a large body of the Nizam's horse at Purendah, and I feared that we might be cut off. An instant return by the road we had come was our only alternative; and after a few hours' rest we were again in our saddles, and travelling as fast as we could urge our horses towards Toljapur.

Here we rested a day to refresh ourselves, and after that, pushing on, we overtook the main body at Bheer, where they were encamped. I had been baffled in part of my design, yet Cheetoo received with great complacency ten thousand rupees in money, and nearly the same amount in jewels, which I presented to him in full durbar as the results of my enterprise; for this he invested me with a dress of honour, and presented me with a good horse from among his own.

Bheer was sacked, and given up to rapine and excess for two whole days; and when we left it scarcely a rag remained to the miserable inhabitants. It was piteous to see them raking together a few posts of wood, many of them half burned, and erecting wretched hovels, which they covered with green boughs, to screen themselves from the cold winds of the night. They suffered the ravage of their town passively, for there were no soldiers to protect it; and what could they have done against a well-armed and savage horde like ours?

Pyetun, on the Godavery, shared the same fate; and though many of the rich inhabitants had fled for refuge to Aurungabad, yet enough remained for our purpose. I need not follow our track much further with minuteness; suffice it therefore to say, that we passed the Adjuntah Ghat, not however without being closely pressed by some troops of the Feringhees: but we eluded them by a rapid march or two, and after a vain attempt on Boorhanpoor, we struck off to the right by the valley of the Taptee, and in a few days were safely returned to the camp at Nemawur.

In little more than three months we had traversed the richest part of the broad territory of the Nizam; we had eluded his troops and those of the Feringhees, and laughed at their beards; we had plundered his richest towns with impunity, and we had returned, with scarcely the loss of a man, laden with plunder of enormous value. So rich was it, that the sahoukars of Nemawur, after purchasing all they could from us, were unable to find further funds to buy up the whole; and merchants from Oujjain and Indore, and all the neighbouring large cities, were sent for to our rich market.

In due time all had been purchased, and every man prepared to return as quickly as he could to his home, with the proceeds of his booty. I need not say how my heart bounded at the prospect of again seeing mine, and laying at my Azima's feet the wealth I had acquired, nor the pleasure she would experience in hearing me recount the wild adventures I had gone through. I accordingly purchased all the gold I could, as also did my men; and hiring two swift camels, I loaded them with it and the valuable cloths we had received for our own use, and was ready for a rapid march to Jhalone.

Inured as we were to the fatigues of long and severe marches, and our horses also, not a day passed but fifteen or twenty coss were travelled, and at this rate we were not long in reaching our home. Blessed be Allah! we did reach it, and glad was my heart once again to see the groves of Jhalone after my weary pilgrimage. No notice had we been able to give of our approach, and I alighted at the door of my own house unattended and alone, covered with dust, and worn by fatigue and exposure to the fierce heat of the sun. My servants scarcely knew me; but when I was recognised, the glad tidings of my return flew from mouth to mouth. I waited not even to quench my raging thirst before I was again in the embrace of Azima, my own loved one, and peril was once more forgotten.

We assembled in the evening; and as the pockets of our saddles were one by one unripped, and their contents heaped on the floor before us, a glorious pile indeed met our view of lumps of gold and silver, the produce of the jewels we had seized, which we had melted down as we got them. There were a few strings of pearls, one of which I laid aside for the Rajah; and the whole was then weighed, valued, and distributed.

CHAPTER XXIX

THREE years passed in inactivity. My father and myself were in high favour, at least so we thought, with the Rajah, who protected us and bestowed flattering marks of kindness upon us. Our revenue business was increased, we had now the management of a large tract of country, and I believe we gave satisfaction to the people as well as to their prince. The revenue was never in arrear; and many persons from distant parts of the country, hearing of our mild and equitable mode of government, came and settled with us in our villages. Our perquisites as revenue-collectors yielded a handsome income, and we lived happy and tranquilly. Still a restless spirit was within me; I heard of the successes of various bands of Thugs in different directions: men came and boasted of their exploits, and again I longed to be at the head of my gallant fellows, and to roam awhile striking terror into the country.

'Tis true I had gained the highest rank I could; I possessed fame; not a Jemadar or Subadar of Thugs could compare his actions with mine; but I thought there was more to be gained, and that I had only to propose an expedition, to be joined by a larger number of Thugs than had collected together for many years.

I have before mentioned to you the name of Ganesha Jemadar; he was always with us when not on the road, envying our quiet and respectable mode of life, which he could not attain by any means, though he left none untried. He bribed all the Rajah's court, nay the Rajah himself, to procure employment; but there was something so harsh and forbidding in his aspect, and so uncouth were his manners, that he did not succeed in what he so much longed for.

He came in despair to us, and after rating in no measured terms the conduct of the Rajah and his officers, said that he was determined again to take to the road, for there alone he found occupation and amusement. He pressed me to accompany and join him, pictured in strong terms the booty we should gain and the glory we should win; and after many demurs and objections on my part, I finally agreed. Notice was given out to all the Thugs of that part of the country, that an expedition of great magnitude would be undertaken after the ensuing Dussehra.

Accustomed as Azima had become to my temporary absences, after the period of quiet I had passed with her, she now did not oppose my leaving her, as she had done before. She thought it was some mercantile speculation which led me from home, and, as you may believe, I did not undeceive her.

Rejoiced at the prospect of again serving under me, all my old band, and many more, flocked to the place of rendezvous, which was at some distance from Jhalone. Ganesha had upwards of a hundred followers; and, finally, on the day of the Dussehra, the usual ceremonies were concluded in the presence of upwards of three hundred Thugs, than whom a finer or more experienced band were never gathered under any leader.

Some were for trying a new line of road, and for penetrating into Gujerat through Rajputana. This question was fairly discussed in a general assembly, and opinions being much balanced between that route and our old one by Saugor and Jolpur to Nagpur, the matter was referred to the decision of the omens. They were consulted as I have before described; and as they decidedly pointed to the south, no further doubt could be entertained upon the subject, and again we moved on in our old direction.

We had proceeded nearly as far as Saugor, with but indifferent success considering our large body, having only killed fourteen travellers, and got but little booty; when one night, as my father and myself, with a few others, sat in our little tent, we heard the *ekarea*—that most dreadful of all omens to a Thug. The ekarea is the short sharp bark or call of the jackal, uttered in the first watch of the night: in itself there is something peculiarly melancholy and appalling, but to a Thug the sound is one of horror. In an instant all conversation was at an end, and we gazed on each other in consternation and alarm. No one spoke, we all listened intently; it might be repeated, which would be worse than ever. It was; the sharp short bark was again heard, and there was but little time for deliberation: all started to their feet.

'We must return instantly,' said my father. 'Bhowani is unpropitious, or danger threatens; at any rate, to go on is impossible, for marked you not the sound came from the very direction of tomorrow's march?'

All agreed that it did, and were unanimous in their desire to return. Still I could not divine why the bark of a jackel should change the determination of three hundred men, and I ventured to say that I was sure it was some mistake, and that even if it was not, we ought to proceed, since the omens had been so propitious at the commencement. 'Why!' said I to my father, 'were they not so? Have we not worshipped the pickaxe every seventh day according to the law? Have we not performed all the necessary ceremonies on the death of every traveller?'

'That is all true,' said my father; 'but it is madness to think of proceeding. Foolish boy! you have never known a reverse, thanks to your good fortune, and the excellent advice by which you have been guided; but beware how you disregard omens—it will one day lead you to destruction. As to this matter, the designs of Bhowani are inscrutable, and she must be obeyed.'

Other Thugs too had heard the ekarea, and many came in a clamorous body to the tent, begging either to be allowed to disperse, or to be led back to Jhalone.

Any words of mine would have been useless, for the whole band seemed infected by superstitious fear; I therefore held my peace. Our encampment was broken up instantly, and late as it was, we that night retrograded a few coss on the road by which we had come; no fresh omen of favour was vouchsafed to us, and we retraced our steps to Jhalone, disappointed, wearied and dispirited. A month passed in idleness; but having formed my determination again to take to the road, I was not to be put off, and again I assembled my men and sought for omens. They were favourable, and I heartily prayed to Bhowani that they might not deceive us again into a fruitless expedition. They pointed too to a different direction, that of the west, and we knew that between Bombay and Indore, and indeed through all parts of Malwa, large treasures were constantly passing. We accordingly left our home—one hundred and twenty Thugs under myself and Peer Khan, who still stuck to me. Ganesha had gone off in a different direction—whither I knew not; his presence was always hateful to me; why, I could not tell, and I could but ill disguise the feelings I entertained towards him.

It was too long an expedition for my father to undertake, and accordingly he stayed at our village. We met with no adventures worth recording, Sahib, on our road to Bombay, for thither we were determined to proceed in quest of plunder. But when I say this, you must not think that we were idle. Thirty-one travellers died by our hands; several escaped us, the omens being against their destruction; and, finally, we reached Bombay, with about four thousand rupees worth of plunder—enough to enable us to live respectably. In Bombay we put up in the large bazaar which is without the fort; and although, from the danger of detection, we could not keep together, yet a constant communication was kept up among us, and every man held himself in readiness to start in any direction on a moment's warning. I had appointed too a rendezvous, the town of Tannah, which being close to the continent is a place where travellers congregate in large numbers previous to passing over.

I saw the sea! Day after day I went down to its edge, and gazed on its magnificence. I used to lie on the grass of the plain before the fort, and pass hours in a sort of dreamy ecstacy, looking on its varying aspect— like that of a beautiful women, now all smiles, and again agitated by the passions of love—or listening to its monotonous and sullen roar, as wave after wave bowed its crest, and broke into sparkling foam on the white sand.

I was lying thus one day, about the seventh after our arrival, meditating on our inactive life, and had almost determined to depart the next day. when a respectable-looking man came up to me.

'Salaam, Alickoom!' said he; 'you are evidently a stranger, for your dress and carriage bespeak you to be an inhabitant of Hindustan. I have watched you for two days coming to this spot and gazing on the sea; have you never seen it before?'

'Never,' replied I; 'my home is, as you say, far inland, and in Hindustan; you have thus guessed rightly: and to me, a stranger, can it be otherwise than that I should be struck with a sight so novel and so overpowering as this expanse of water is, which seems to melt into the sky?'

'The tones of your voice are music in my ears,' said the stranger; 'I have heard many from my country (for that is also Hindustan), but never any which reminded me so strongly of my own home as yours. May I ask your village?'

'I lived formerly in Murnae, in the Sindouse Pergunna,' said I, 'but now reside in Jhalone.'

'Murnae?' cried the man in astonishment; but he lowered his voice as he aid, 'Ah, I remember now; 'tis on the borders of Sindia's country, and belongs to him.'

'Not now,' said I: 'the Feringhees have had it ceded to them, and they possess it.'

'But,' said the man, changing the topic, 'you love to look on the sea; have you ever been on its surface? Have you visited the ships you may have seen moored before the town?'

'I have not,' replied I; 'I several times determined to go, but my heart failed me when I saw the frail boat which should take me. Besides, I am a stranger; no one would have admitted me were I to have gone to them.'

'Will you accompany me?' said the man. 'I have an idle day before me, and shall be glad to pass it in your company.'

I gladly assented, and we took our way to a stone pier which ran into the sea on the outside of the fort.

I could not divine with whom I had thus scraped an acquaintance; all the peons on the Bunder (for so the pier was called) paid the greatest respect to my new friend; all made low obeisances to him, and a scramble ensued among the owners of the small boats which were tied to the landing-place, for the honour of conveying us to the shipping.

He selected one however, and pushing off, we were on the bosom of the ocean. I confess I was afraid; though Jhalone was not far from the Jumna I had never seen that river, nor had I ever seen a boat before my arrival at Bombay. Now each succeeding wave, as we descended from the top of the last one, appeared as though it would roll over us; but the men were fearless and experienced, and after a few qualms I was reconciled to our situation. We rowed, for the wind was against us, close round several of the ships which lay at anchor; and at last ascended, with the permission of a Feringhee officer who was on board, the side of an immense ship, which my friend told me was one of war and belonged to the king of England. After looking over the upper part, a small gratuity of two rupees to a sailor enabled us to proceed below to see the guns. I was astonished at their size, and at the exactness with which everything was fitted; the ropes even were twisted down into coils, like huge snakes sleeping, and the whole was a picture of neatness and cleanliness which I little expected to have seen. But these matters, Sahib, are doubtless familiar to you, so I will pass them over. We returned to the shore with a fair wind, and as the boatmen spread a small sail, we danced merrily along over the swelling waters.

I was about to separate from my companion, and again protested my sense of his kindness, when he stopped me.

'No, Meer Sahib,' said he, 'I must have further converse with you. I am much mistaken if you are not what I was once, and am still whenever I can seize an opportunity.'

I stared at him. Could he be a Thug? If he was not, he would not understand our words of recognition; if he was, I should be right. I did not hesitate.

'Ali Khan Bhaee Salaam[1]!' said I, gazing intently at him.

'Salaam Aliekoom!' cried he. It was enough—he also was a Thug.

'Those words I have not heard for many a year,' said he; 'they remind me of my early days, and the goor of the Tupounee.'

'Then you have eaten it?' said I.

'I have,' replied the man.

'Enough,' cried I; 'I have met with a friend; but who you are I am as yet ignorant.'

'Have you not ever heard of Soobhan Khan Jemadar?' he asked. 'You say you came from Murnae: surely I must be remembered there?'

'I have,' answered I, 'those who knew you have believed you dead. How is it that you are here, and a person of authority?'

'I will tell you hereafter of my situation, but at present I have many questions to ask of you—and first, is my good friend Ismail Jemadar alive?'

'My father!' said I, 'surely he is; the good old man has attained a fine age, and is well.'

'Shookr Khoda!' cried he; 'but you said he was your father; surely he had no children—he was not even married when I left.'

'Ah,' said I, 'so it might have been then, but here am I to speak for myself.'

[1] Literally, 'Salutation to Ali Khan, my brother.' This is the phrase of recognition by which Thugs are able to make themselves known to each other in all parts of India.

'And Hussein, his and my friend, does he too live?'

'Alas, no; he died two years ago, full of age and honour.' I have not mentioned this event to you, Sahib, but it had taken place soon after I returned from my Phindari expedition.

He continued to ask after many of his old friends, and at last inquired how many men I had with me. I told him, and he was somewhat astonished at their number.

'Well,' said he, 'you are here, and it will be hard if I cannot find some work for you. I have told you I am a Thug, and have been so from my youth; my father and ancestors were Thugs before me. But, many years ago, I came here as the servant of a sahoukar of Indore. I liked the place, and not long after got employment as a government peon, in the service of the English. They have been kind and generous masters to me; I have served them well, and have risen by degrees to the rank I now hold, which is that of Jemadar. Why I left my station as a Jemadar of Thugs is perhaps unknown to you?'

I replied that I did not know.

'It was in consequence of a foolish quarrel with your father. We were on an expidition, and I thought he assumed too much; we were both young men, of fiery blood—we had a sharp altercation, and drew our swords: he was my superior, and I feared that he would condemn me to death. I fled, entered the service of the sahoukar as one of his escort from Indore, and you see what I am. Yet I have never forsaken the Thugs whenever I have met with them. I am too old to seek adventures myself; but I put the young and active in the way of them, and thus have kept up my connexion with them. My acquaintance has been with the Thugs of the Dukhun, and I have headed one or two expeditions towards Poona, when I could get leave of absence for a while from my duties; but when I could not do this, I have secured bands of travellers for my associates, and they have been successful.'

Thus conversing, we reached his house; it was not far from where I was residing; and as he told me afterwards, he had discovered who we were, and had followed me from place to place, until he got an opportunity of speaking with me unobserved. From this time, as you may believe, Sahib, we were sworn friends. I listened to his details of roguery (for rogue he was in his heart) with great interest, and I accompanied him several times to the durbar of the gentleman with whom his duties were connected. He was evidently a person well thought of, and as far as his office was concerned, that of keeping the peace, was zealous and active. Still there was something forbidding to me in the way he now followed his profession of a Thug; and as we became more intimately acquainted, he unfolded to me his plans and operations. I cannot tell you, Sahib, of their extent. He introduced me to the Jemadars of Dukhun Thugs who scoured the roads to Poona, to Nassuk, to Sholapur, and Hyderabad; to others from Gujerat, who were engaged in that part of the country—but all under his control, and from all of whom he exacted a high rate of tribute as the price of the information he was able to give them, as to the despatch of treasures in various directions by the sahoukars and merchants of Bombay.

I had remained with him a week, and our stock of money was sensibly diminishing. What was to be done? He had promised assistance in giving me information of the despatch of treasure in our direction, and I had hitherto waited in expectation that he would fulfil his promise. I was tired too of Bombay; the season was advancing, and I hardly thought we should reach Jhalone before the setting-in of the rains. I therefore went to him, and frankly told him our money was running short, and that in a place like Bombay, where my men were exposed to so many temptations, they could not be expected to keep what they had; I was therefore anxious to depart, and if he could give me no hope of any speedy booty, that I should set off in two days, and take my chance on the road.

'My plans are not quite matured in your direction,' said he. 'I have heard that one of the greatest traders to Indore and Malwa is about to send no less than two lakhs of rupees thither. I know that the rokurreas are hired; but as yet I cannot say whether they carry hoondees or money. Three days ought to determine this, and in the meantime, as you want money, a thousand rupees are at your service, which you can repay me, with interest, at three per cent. per month, on your arrival at Jhalone. I will trust to your good faith as the son of my old friend.'

'I am obliged to you,' replied I; 'but the money is not quite so necessary as I said. I believe every man has some twenty or thirty rupees in his possession; but it was to prevent their spending this that I spoke to you as I did. Only say that within a week we may start, and my men will be careful.'

'Certainly, before a week's time; come to me tomorrow evening after prayer-time, and you shall have further news about your bunij.'

The interest-eating rascal! said I, as I left him. He a true believer! Not a rupee of his money will I touch, the kafir! A Thug to take interest from a Thug—who ever heard of it? I became intimate with a Dukhun Jemadar who was waiting for bunij, who told me that he ground the Thugs unmercifully, threatened to denounce them if they ever demurred, and got from them double the share he would have been entitled to had he shared the risk and danger on the road.

'But,' said the Jemadar, 'there is no doing without him, much as he oppresses us; he throws the most valuable booty into our hands, which we never could get scent of by ourselves; he has a number of Thugs who are his servants, and whom he pays liberally to get him information; he possesses the confidence of the sahoukars, as he assists them to smuggle; they pay him too for a kind word now and then with the Sahib-logue. In fine, he is paid both by them and us, and he contrives to sell all our valuable plunder.'

'Then his receipts must be enormous.'

'They are,' said the Jemadar, 'and we all grudge them to him; but still he protects us, and we could not do without him.'

'Has he ever been treacherous?' I asked; for, by Allah! I was inclined to mistrust the rascal.

'There are some stories of the kind,' he replied, 'but in the main he is to be trusted. Still, as I said, if he were not, we could do nothing without him; he knows every Jemadar of the Dukhun, and could if he chose blow up the whole system tomorrow; but it does not suit his interest to do so, and we are all his slaves.'

'Long may ye continue to be so!' cried I to Peer Khan when he had left me; 'but as for us, brother, 'tis the last time he will catch us here. What say you?'

'Certainly,' said Peer Khan; 'these fellows are never to be trusted; they exist everywhere, in all shapes; they are zemindars and patels of villages; they are fakirs and bhuttearas; they are goosaens, sahoukars, servants, and mutsuddees; nay, the Rajah of Jhalone is one himself. They are an evil 't is true, but we could not do without them.'

'I have done so as yet,' said I, 'and, by Allah! I will never trust one of them.'

'May you never have occasion, Meer Sahib.' And the conversation dropped.

I went as I had promised, and found Soobhan Khan in high glee. 'I have secured the bunij,' said he. 'Are you ready?'

'I am. What are your orders?'

'Listen,' he replied. 'I was right in saying the sum was two lakhs. Contrary to my expectations the sum is in gold and silver and jewels; there are about ten thousand rupees in hoondees (bills), but that is all. Now before I tell you more, we must make our bargain.'

'Speak,' cried I; 'I am ready to give anything in reason.'

'Ay, you are my old friend's son, so I must not treat you as I do the others I associate with,' said he; 'from them I get a third of the whole, but from you I ask only a fifth. A fifth will be twenty thousand rupees. Will you give it?'

'With pleasure,' said I; 'directly I get the money, and reach Jhalone, I will purchase a hoondee on Bombay, and send it to you.'

'Capital!' cried he; 'you are a man I like to deal with. Now give me a promise under your seal that I shall have the money, and I will detail the plan to you. The paper is a mere matter of form, and I am methodical.'

I wrote the paper and handed it to him, having sealed it with my seal; he folded it carefully up, and tucked it into a fold of his turban.

'Now we are all right, Meer Sahib. This treasure goes under the escort of fifteen Rokurreas; they have three camels, and will be disguised as soldiers, going from Poona to Indore. I know the sahoukars who send it; I have spoken with the rokurreas; and to ensure your being unsuspected by them, here is a pass written in Persian and Mahratta, signed and sealed by the English officers of customs here. It represents you as persons who have come from Benares in charge of goods for a sahoukar, by name Hurreedas, and directs that no one shall molest you on your return. The men who brought the goods are still here, and likely to remain till the end of the rains. Their leader's name is Futih Mahomed, so Futih Mahomed you must be if you please; he too is about your own age and appearance, and thus you will be better able to personate him. You see I have laid a good plan, and I leave all the rest to your own judgement. Make the best of your way to Nassuk; wait there four days, and on the fifth you will see your bunij, if you keep a proper look out. Now go, make your preparations, and may Bhowani send you success. Remember Soobhan Khan, and return as speedily as you like; I have no doubt I shall have found fresh work for you.'

'You may depend on me, Khan Sahib,' said I; 'I will not be long away from you. Your plan is an admirable one; and Inshallah! your twenty thousand rupees are as safe to you as though you even now had them in your possession.'

'Remember me with many kind words to your father, Ameer Ali,' continued he; 'would he come thus far to see an old friend, and forgive him for the past?'

'Of that I have but little hope,' said I; 'he is old and infirm, and never leaves his village: but he shall write to you.'

'Enough, enough,' said the Khan; 'I have much to accuse myself of in the past; but 'tis a long time ago, and he has most likely forgotten my foolish conduct.'

I left him, but made an inward determination to be guided entirely by my father's counsel as to whether one cowrie of the twenty thousand rupees should be paid or not. 'And,' said Peer Khan afterwards, 'twenty thousand rupees—the old villain! He get it! Ah Meer Sahib, we shall be the brothers of owls and jackasses if he ever sees one rupee!'

The next morning we were on our return to Jhalone, and we halted between Bombay and Tannah for the day. Our pass was of much use, for it was respected and obeyed; and the day after we passed Tannah and the different revenue guard-houses without interruption.

CHAPTER XXX

'SHOOKR Khoda!' cried Peer Khan, as he rushed into my presence on the fourth day after we had arrived at Nassuk; 'Soobhan Khan was right—they are come!'

'Are you sure, Khan?'

'Certain,' he replied; 'the description we had of them tallies with what I have seen in every point. Come and see yourself; there are the camels and the men disguised. But I could have sworn, had I met them anywhere, that they were rokurreas; they have the air and bearing of the tribe.'

'Enough,' said I, 'you cannot be deceived. They do not know we are here, and we will do the same as we did at Burhanpur. Get the men ready; we will go round the town, travel a coss or two, and enter by the same gate they did: we will then put up in the bazaar with them.'

We were all shortly in motion, and, as I had planned, after going round the outside of the town we entered it on the other side, and were soon in our new quarters in the bazaar. Travellers soon get acquainted: the shop I chose adjoined the one they occupied, and I had quickly scraped an acquaintance with the Jemadar of the rokurreas.

Narrayun Das, for that was his name, was a tall and very powerful man; he had small twinkling eyes, and long straight eyebrows, which, by binding his turban tightly over his temples, he had drawn up in diagonal lines to either side, and this imparted to them a very peculiar expression: long mustachios, which were twisted out to each side, and thick bushy whiskers; his whole appearance proved him to be an experienced rokurrea and one to whom deceit and stratagem were familiar. I shall have a cunning hand to deal with here, thought I, as I scanned his features; no common pretences will go down with him; but have him I must and will, ay, and his two lakhs also. Two lakhs! it is worth an effort were he Rustam himself. Yet he was not slow in forming an acquaintance with me. Our salutations passed in due form, and after we had all cooked our morning meal, and sat down on our carpets, we soon entered into familiar conversation.

'A pretty business Bajee Rao has made of it,' said he, as I had asked him the news from Poona. 'The coward! had he but put himself at the head of his army when the fight took place at Kirkee, he might have annihilated the Feringhees.'

'And do you wish that he had?' said I.

'Certainly; what do we know of them? While they confined themselves to the fort of Bombay it was all very well; but now, little by little they have advanced, until they have upset the Mahratta empire, and are in a fair way to take it.'

'But,' said I, 'Bajee Rao has a good army, all the country is his own, and surely he will do something. The Mahrattas are good soldiers, and he has leaders of renown with him.'

'He will do nothing, Meer Sahib; he will run from place to place, and his army may fight if they can or will. The cowardly wretch has not the soul of a flea.'

'Well, Jemadar, to me it matters little; I have forsworn soldiering, and find that I can get a good livelihood by escorting treasure and goods. I am just come from Benares, and the sahoukar who employed me has sent me for more, which I am to bring down to him.'

'Ah!' cried he, 'so you are in that line. Well, it is a good one if you have plenty of men, but a sorely troublesome and difficult one if you have few. I speak from experience, for I am in the same business myself. I have been lucky, but my poor brother was otherwise; he fell by the hands of thieves between here and Indore; we heard of him from Burhanpur, but beyond that we could get no tidings of him.'

'Strange!' said I: 'I never heard of thieves on the road, though my kafila would have been worth plundering. But now I am under the protection of the Sahib-logue, I care not; they will soon have all the country, and there will be no danger in another year.'

'Under the protection of the Feringhees! how do you mean? I thought you said you served a sahoukar.'

'So I do,' I replied; 'but to ensure my safe return his friend Soobhan Khan got me this pass;' and I pulled out the document, which I had carefully folded up in wax-cloth, and showed it to him.

'You are fortunate, Meer Sahib, and particularly in knowing Soobhan Khan, who is a worthy man and deservedly respected. But you said that you had given up soldiering; in this you have been wise; far preferable is it to gain an honourable livelihood than be marched in all directions, with but little pay, and hard fighting for that. With whom have you served?'

'You must not tell any one,' said I; 'for every man who has served the man I have would desire it to be a secret, and perhaps the knowledge of my former life might be against my present interests. I served under Cheetoo Pindari, and led three thousand of his best horse.'

'Under Cheetoo!' cried the Jemadar; 'this is most strange; and you are not joking?'

'I am not, I swear by your head; I dare say I could find some papers to convince you of the fact if you doubt it. But, as I said, I do not like to tell any one.'

'You need not fear me,' said he, 'I am as close as a rokurrea, and you know the saying is proverbial; but there is nothing to be ashamed of, Meer Sahib; as for being a Pindari, the best in the land were with him; and a gallant army they were when the first lubhur assembled at Nemawur.'

'Then you were there?'

'I was. I brought some treasure from Indore and Ujjain to the sahoukars at Nemawur, and saw the whole of the preparations for the campaign; and Bhugwan knows I was so taken with the appearance of the whole, that could I have got a horse, I verily believe I should have turned Pindari myself. They say every man filled his saddle with gold and pearls.'

'We were lucky enough,' said I, 'especially in the first expedition. Had you come to Nemawur before the second had set out, you would have heard of me; I had a good name and a high rank. In the first I was nobody, and gained Cheetoo's favour solely because I was a better swordsman than any in his camp.'

'Then I have heard of you,' said the man; 'but surely you cannot be that Syud Ameer Ali who was only second to Ghuffoor Khan?'

'I am the very person, and no other,' I replied; 'true, my rank is fallen, but whose has not? Cheetoo is dead; Ghuffoor Khan has disappeared, and is supposed to have gone to Hyderabad; Syud Bheekoo is God knows where; and Shekh Dulla still roams about the hills between Burhanpur and Ellichpur, with a price set on his head. No one knew much of me; I had enough of being a Pindari after the second foray, and got to my home at Jhalone as soon as I could. If the others had been wise, they would have sought their safety as I did.'

'Yes,' said the Jemadar, 'Cheetoo's was a sad fate—he deserved a better: but they say the Sahib-logue offered him a Jagheer—is this true?'

'So I have heard,' said I; 'fool that he was, he would not accept it; but no wonder, his whole soul was bound up in his plans for driving out the Feringhees. He thought the Mahrattas would beat them; and when they had gained the first victory, he was to have joined them with fifteen thousand horse, and become a great commander.'

'A strange history,' said the man, 'and you have told me more than I ever knew before. Had the Peshwa and the Rajah of Nagpur played their parts as well as Cheetoo, all would have gone right; but it is useless to think of them, and I suppose we must make up our minds to our new masters. Now, however, you and I, Meer Sahib, must not separate. I am going to Indore for some treasure, and your best way lies through it; I will keep with you, for your party is a large one, and, to tell you the truth, I don't like passing those jungles by the Sindwah Ghat with my own. The Bheels are taking advantage of the present disturbances to be all in arms. Bands of deserters from the Peshwa traverse the country in all directions, helping themselves to what they can. So we will keep together, if you like, for mutual protection.'

'I shall be glad to do so,' said I; 'though I have nothing to lose, except two or three thousand rupees, and whoever comes to take them will get more blows than money.'

'And I have still less,' said he; 'only enough to pay my expenses and feed my camels; but I am no great hand at fighting, and am not mounted as you are, to run from danger.'

But the heavily laden pack-saddles belied his words. I was not to be deceived, and felt as sure that the coveted treasure was there as that the Rokurrea who guarded it was before me.

We shortly afterwards separated; and when I was alone with Peer Khan I told him what I had said, and how I had deceived the rokurrea. A long and hearty laugh we had over it.

'But I fear for you, Meer Sahib,' said he. 'Compare his power and your own slight frame. You must risk nothing now.'

I laughed. 'His power, Khan!' I said, 'what is it to that of many who have fallen under my hand before now? Besides, he is the brother of the rokurrea we killed beyond Burhanpur, and he must be mine at all hazards. I would not miss this adventure for thousands.'

'I will tell you what,' said Peer Khan, 'it will never do to kill them so far from Indore; let us get them as near to the city as possible, and we shall be the nearer our own home. This matter will cause a stir, and we had better not risk anything.'

'Well, be it as you will. I had intended to have killed them near Burhanpur, and then to have turned off directly into the hills; we should never be followed.'

'Ay, and risk Shekh Dulla and his party, who are out?' said Peer Khan; 'that would never do. He would plunder us; and as he knows us, would most likely serve us as Cheetoo did the poor fellows who were caught.'

'Astaffur Allah!' cried I, shuddering, 'God forbid! no, your plan is the best. We will entice them out of the towns before we have gone many marches, and then they are our own when and wherever we please.'

I pass over our journey, Sahib; all journeys are alike devoid of interest, and only one routine of dusty roads, parching sun, (for the rokurreas would not travel by night) bad food, and discomfort of all kinds. My men behaved admirably. No one could have told, from the broad patois they spoke, that they were aught but what they represented themselves to be—Benares-walas, and Bhojpurees; they looked as stupid a set of owls as could well be collected together; but they played their parts, to a man, with the extreme caution and cunning on which rested the success of our enterprise.

After all, Sahib, cannot you now understand the excitement which possesses the soul of a Thug in his pursuit of men? Cannot you feel with us, as you hear my story, and follow us in my recital? Here had we kept company with these rokurreas for twenty days; we had become intimate; they told of their adventures, we told ours; the evenings passed in singing or telling tales, until one by one we sunk down wearied upon our carpets. Cannot you appreciate the intense interest with which we watched their every movement, nay every word which fell from them, and our alarms, as sometimes our minds misgave us that we were suspected? Yet still we stuck to them through everything, they were never lost sight of for a moment, and, above all, their minds were kept happy.

As to their leader, he was delighted with me. My accounts of my adventures as a Pindari, the plunder we had got, the towns we had burned and sacked, all were to him interesting, and day by day I told him of new exploits. He used to sit, and the rest of his men too, listening with unfeigned pleasure to the accounts which I and Peer Khan gave. Cunning as they were, at heart they were honest and simple, and they readily believed all we told them.

But their time had drawn near. Indore was five marches further, and delay was now impracticable and useless; besides, to ensure their safe arrival, I knew they had determined on going thirty coss in one march, and my men could not keep up with these hardy fellows. Come what will,' said I to Peer Khan, 'they die tomorrow night.'

The time came. We were sitting, as usual, under the same noble tamarind trees, one by one we had sung our song or related our adventures; and who could have guessed, had he seen us thus engaged, that a work of death was to ensue? Every tongue was employed, and the hearty laugh which broke at time from one or other of the assembly, showed how light and merry were our hearts—we, at the certainty of our success; the roukerreas, at the thought that the peril of the road was past, and that their large amount of treasure would reach its destination in safety; there was not a grave face among us.

'There,' cried the Jemadar of the rokurreas, 'there is the moon; when she has risen over the trees yonder we will bid you farewell, kind Meer Sahib; we have been happy in your company, and free from alarms and danger. Bhugwan grant that we may hereafter journey in company, and as safely as we have done!'

The Thugs had taken their places; to each rokurrea were four stout men allotted, and I marvelled that they should have thus allowed themselves to be separated from each other. But they had not suspected; who *could* have done so?

The moon rose majestically above the distant trees; her full, round, and yellow orb cast a mellow light upon our group. The rokurreas rose with one accord, and each turned to the men he was near to give them his parting benediction and salutation.

'Nay,' said I, 'we part not thus, Narrayun Das; let us separate as friends; receive my embrace; we are friends and brothers by profession.' We embraced, and before the others could press forward to salute me, I gave the jhirnee: 'Pān lao!' I exclaimed.

It was enough: the jemadar fell beneath my own handkerchief, and a few shrieks and groans told the rest—all had died.

'Haste ye, my good fellows!' cried I to the lughas; 'quick with your work, the camels are ready, and a few hours will see us safe from pursuit, though indeed none is to be apprehended from this small place.'

The bodies were stripped; every fellow had a heavy humeanah, besides what was laden on the camels. We stopped not to count our money, but hastened on when the interment was finished; and only tarrying for a few moments at the next village we came to, to purchase the goor for the Tupounee, we found ourselves in the morning nearly twenty coss from the scene of our last night's adventure.

We halted till the evening, and again pushed on, but by a different road; and leaving Indore about fifteen coss to the right, we directed our course to a small village named Dehalpur. From this, leaving Ujjain also to the right, we hastened on, always travelling by night on acount of the extreme heat of the weather, and by way of Bahadurgurh and Aorcha, we reached Jhalone in safety. No alarm had we but one. The revenue officers on the frontier of Holkar's dominions insisted on knowing who we were, and what we had with us; and so strict were their inquiries, that, had it not been for the English pass I had with me, we must have been suspected and apprehended. But, thanks to Soobham Khan, it was not questioned; as Futih Mahomed I passed free. A duty, or rather an exaction, of fifty rupees was levied on the treasure, and a fresh pass given to us, by which we escaped further questioning and detention. Who can describe my father's joy at seeing the treasure! The old man was in ecstasy: he kissed me, he embraced me, called me by every endearing name, and extolled my conduct in glowing terms to Ganesha, who happened to be with him. It was easy to see, however, that to that worthy they might well have been spared. Jealously possessed him, which he could ill disguise; and I verily believe, had he dared, that he would have informed the Rajah of the treasure we had secured. In the memory of the oldest Thug no such booty had ever been gained, and I was classed by the Thugs with Jhora Naeck and Kuduk Bunwaree, fabled votaries of Bhowani, of whom stories were told which, though implicitly believed by our fraternity, I never credited. But it was enough for me. I had never met a reverse; and every Thug of Hindustan, I verily believe, only thought he must join me to secure to himself a booty which would support him for years.

I have forgotten, however, to mention to you an incident which befell us at Bahadugurh. We were encamped outside the town, and late in the evening we saw a body of men, whom we at first took to be Thugs, coming towards our camp.

'Who can they be?' said I to Peer Khan; 'they look like Thugs, yet it is late for any party to be out.'

'Some straggling party, I suppose,' said he; 'I will go and see.'

He went, and returned with the leader of the party. I had purposely kept in my little tent, in order that my face might not be seen in case they were strangers; and to conceal it effectually, I tied a handkerchief over my mouth and chin.

'Salaam Aleikoom!' said a gruff voice, as a man with Peer Khan entered the tent.

'You are welcome, friend,' said I; 'sit down.' He was evidently weary with travel, and seated himself slowly.

'Your name?' said I; 'and who are you?'

'My name?' replied the man, 'is well known, I dare say, to most people, and they are afraid of it. I am called Lall Khan, or familiarly Lalloo.'

'I have not heard it before,' said I; 'but who are you and your men?'

'Oh, we are free traders, who help ourselves to what we can get with a strong hand.'

Some wandering Pindaris, thought I; and I asked him if they were such.

'Not exactly,' said he; 'we are Dacoos.'

'Worse and worse,' said I laughing; 'and I suppose you are from Delhi?'

'Ay,' replied he, 'even so; we know you, though you do not know us. We know you to be Thugs by your encampment—but never fear us—brethren should not interfere with each other; we have different ways of helping ourselves to spoil, but what matter? We are brothers in a general sense of the word.'

'Good, we are; and if I can help you, say so.'

'In no wise,' said he, 'but to give us room among ye for the night; we will be off early, if you do not go the same road.'

'Room ye shall have, Khan, till the moon rises, and food too, but after that we are off; we travel northwards. And where are you going?'

'To Hyderabad,' said the man. 'No one suspects Dacoos to be out at this time of the year, and we shall have the whole road to ourselves; we shall return after the rains, about the Dusseira, by the Nagpur road. Now we are going by Bhopal and Burhanpur.'

'Well,' said I, 'you have taken a good line; the road from Burhanpur to Hyderabad is a good one, and you will be in Sikundur Jah's country, where no one asks questions about the people who are left on the highways. I wish you good luck, and my friends will look after your comforts; you must excuse me, as I am in pain from a swelled face and toothache.'

'Salaam'; said he, as he departed: 'If you were going instead of returning, we might get good plunder in company; we Dacoos are rare hands at rough work.'

I had spoken in a disguised voice, and it was impossible he could recognise me again if he met me. I did this for an object which occurred to me at the moment, as you shall learn hereafter. I mentioned this meeting to my father. 'What hinders us,' said I, 'from meeting them as they come up? They will be laden with spoil, and will be an easy prey. Brave and reckless as they are, they have no wit, and will never find us out.'

'I don't know that,' said my father; 'they are not so stupid as you think; I know much of them, have killed some of them, and they were cunning enough. However, I see nothing objectionable in your plan; and at any rate it will furnish excuse for a new expedition.'

'Ay,' said Ganesha, who was present, 'let us go: I long to see the Meer Sahib act. We hear so much of him, that, by Bhowani, perhaps an unlucky old Thug like myself may pick up something new. Will you let me come also?'

'Certainly,' said I; 'but you will see no more than you know already; lucky I have been, but you know my pretensions to knowledge are very small, and I have never boasted of them. To my perception the whole art consists in having a smooth tongue in one's head; and a man who is a good bhuttote rarely makes a good sotha.'

'Yet you are both, Meer Sahib,' said Ganesha, with a malicious grin; 'and your men will follow you to the death.'

'So they will,' said I; 'for I am kind and considerate to them, and reward them handsomely.'

This stung him to the quick; for he was a rough bully, and, though perhaps one of the best bhuttotes then living, was no hand at inveigling travellers; and as he always persisted in being a sotha himself, he was notoriously unlucky; but few men too would serve under him. He was preparing to retort sharply, when my father stopped him.

'Let him alone,' said he; 'he is a proud boy, and bickerings among us lead to no good: you must not think on what he has said.'

'Nay, Ismail,' said he, with the air of an offended child, 'I care not what he says: pride will have its fall, and I may live to see it.'

I was very angry, but there was no use in saying more. Had we been alone he should have answered for it.

So you see, Sahib, out of a trifling incident a new expedition was determined on. We all prayed it might be more favourable than the former one which was planned in that direction, and I confess that my success in the last had strengthened my faith in the efficacy of the omens, though as yet by no means established it. Experience, they say, is always bought at a costly price, and I had to buy mine, though the time was not yet come.

But Soobhan Khan, who was he? said I to Ameer Ali; and did you pay him his price of blood?

Not a cowrie of it, said Ameer Ali; but you shall hear. I asked my father who he was, and detailed the whole of my adventures with him; he remembered the man the instant I spoke of him.

'The rascal!' cried my father; 'and is he so rich and honoured, the son of a vile woman? To think that he should be in such a situation, the scoundrel! But the deeds of Allah are inscrutable. Listen, my son, to his story, which can be told in a few words.

'He and I were Jemadars together. I never liked him, and he had a bad reputation; he was never a good bhuttote, for the fellow was an arrant coward, but he was a capital sotha, and his smooth tongue gained him more bunij than we could gain by straightforward work. Well, many years ago we joined together, he to be Sotha, and I to manage the other work. We had killed a large body of travellers near Jaipur, for we had a numerous gang. Two were sahoukars, and the booty was large. Among it were some pearls and precious stones; they were given over to his party as their share, and he said he would go to Indore to sell them; but I had lent him nearly a thousand rupees at different times, when he had no money to make advances to men to induce them to serve under him, and I pressed him for some of the pearls, which I wanted for my wife, in payment of the money. This was late one night, after we had divided the spoil; he said he would give me them in the morning, when I could pick out the strings I liked best; and he spoke so willingly, that I, fool as I was, never doubted him. That night he absconded, and I never heard of him till this extraordinary account of yours. Pay him-' continued my father; 'not the value of a broken cowrie shall he ever get; in any other man I might have pardoned it, but in him the conduct was ingratitude in the highest degree; for had I not assisted and upheld him, he would have been neglected and have starved.'

This then was the secret of Soobhan Khan's wealth; he must have sold his pearls one by one, as he had hinted to me that he had traded in them, and raised himself by bribery to the state he was in. Of course I neither sent him his money as I had promised, nor wrote him a line to say that I had arrived safely at Jhalone. I destroyed his pass too, as it might have led to detection.

CHAPTER XXXI

I HAVE told you of my popularity among the Thugs; and when it became known that a new expedition was planned, and would set out after the Dussehra, so many men offered themselves, that I was obliged to reject numbers, and select those whom I knew, from experience and character, would be likely to behave best. Among them were a few who were excellent musicians and singers. I had before, on many occasions, felt the want of such men, to amuse travellers with whom I had fallen in; and these were particularly acceptable to me at the present time, as the expedition was a large one; and the country being quieter and more settled than it had been for some years, we were assured that the roads would be full of persons of rank and consequence travelling to and from their homes. In order that our band might have the greater appearance of respectability, I begged of my father to accompany us, for his venerable appearance and polished manners would, I was certain, do more to ensure us success than all our most cunning stratagems.

Nor was I neglectful of the Rajah; from time to time I visited his durbar, and was always received with the greatest civility and attention, as indeed I deserved; for not only was I a good servant to him, but as numbers of Thugs had settled around me in different villages, the revenue they paid for his protection and connivance at our work amounted to a handsome sum yearly; and I need not say it was punctually paid, for upon this mainly depended our concealment. In the last expedition, however, I had pleaded poverty on my return, and though I could have well spared five thousand rupees from my own share, I was content with presenting as my nuzzur a gun I had purchased in Bombay for two hundred rupees, and a small string of pearls which I had found among the treasure of the rokurreas; and he seemed satisfied; but it was merely the feigned content which precedes a violent outbreak of discontent or passion. He was our bitter, deadly enemy, though he cloaked his designs under the garb of friendship, and was gradually perfecting his schemes for our destruction.

We set out. Azima, poor soul, never dreamed of what we were: it was enough for her to know that every expedition brought her new ornaments and better clothes, and enabled her to live in a higher and more expensive manner. She knew too that, with increased wealth, she could look for a higher alliance for our daughter, our only child; and she had even now received proposals of marriage for her, some of which were in every way advantageous, and with persons unconnected with our profession, of which I was glad; for knowing full well that one mischance, or one traitor among us, would hurl me at once from my prosperity, I was desirous of marrying her to some one who could protect her, and be free from any dangers similar to those I was myself exposed to.

I however bade Azima wait, because (as I told her) the journey I was about to undertake would be infallibly prosperous, and a fresh addition to our already ample means would enable us to have the marriage ceremony performed in a manner fitting or perhaps exceeding our pretensions. She readily acceded to my request; for if there be one thing more than another about which a matron of Hindustan is solicitous, it is the marriage of her child; not as regards happiness I must own, though perhaps there may be a lurking wish that she may be happy; but the main matter is that her clothes shall be of the best and richest materials, her jewels many and of value, and the whole of the establishment which she takes to her new lord of the most substantial description; that they may last her for years, and procure for her mother the goodwill of the female members of her husband's family. Nothing is productive of more quarrels among the females than that anything should appear indifferent; remarks are made, and reproaches are bandied about between the united families, and out of these soon grows an enmity which never cools. Many a marriage, which promised well at its outset, has been marred in its joyous termination by fault being found with the equipments of the bride, which are always submitted for inspection to her female relations before they become her own property for ever.

But I am digressing, and must return to my own adventures. We left Jhalone as before, upwards of three hundred Thugs, under my father, Ganesha, Peer Khan, and myself. We gave out along the road that we were servants of the Nizam, and were returning to our service at Hyderabad after our periodical leave of absence: this was necessary, for our numbers without it would have provoked suspicion.

Never shall I forget the first matter we took in hand; not that there was anything remarkable in the destruction of four men, but it was attended by a sad result, which damped the spirits of the party for many days afterwards, and from which *one* never recovered.

Peer Khan had a nephew, a boy of about ten years old, a noble little fellow, beautiful in his features, and intelligent beyond his years. As you may imagine, he was a great favourite among us all, and I had repeatedly asked Peer Khan to allow me to adopt him as my son, to supply the place of the child I had lost: but he would not hear of it, for the child was the son of a beloved sister who was dead; the boy's father had also died about two years before, and Peer Khan had taken him to his home, and loved him as his own.

The little fellow rode a spirited pony which I had given him, was always in the van of the party, and amused us by his mimic feats of horsemanship and by his intelligent prattle: he could never be kept behind; and when the time came that the four men were to meet their fate, we had given him in charge to those who brought up the rear, with strict orders that on no account was he to be permitted to come on after us. Yet all our precautions were of no avail—how could they be, when what followed had evidently been written in his destiny?

I had just given the jhirnee, and the four miserable men were writhing in the agonies of death, one of them too was shrieking, when, Ya Allah! who should come galloping up but Alum Khan, the boy I have mentioned. His first exclamation was of triumph that he had caught us; but how can I tell the look of horror to which his countenance was instantly changed when he saw what was going on! His eyes became fixed, and were wide open, his tongue cleaved to the roof of his mouth, he uttered no sound, but clasped his hands in agony; and before I could dismount, or even Peer Khan, who was superintending the work, he had fallen from his pony insensible.

'What shall we do?' cried I to Peer Khan, as we raised him up and strove to comfort him. 'Speak to him; a word from you may arouse him.'

'My child, my child!' cried Peer Khan, in accents of terror and misery; 'oh speak to me! one word only: you are killing your parent. Ya Allah!' continued he, raising his hands to heaven, 'grant that this swoon may pass away, and that he may speak; I will feed a hundred fakirs in thy name, O merciful Prophet! if thou wilt but intercede and grant my prayer.' But it was of no avail; the poor boy lay senseless, though his eyes were fixed and staring, and not a word could he utter. The Thugs too had left the dead, and were all around us. There was a rivulet close by, in which the bhil had been prepared; I thought of water, and bid one of the men run for some. It was brought, and I poured it into his mouth. 'He revives—his lips move!' cried Peer Khan in an ecstasy of delight—'he speaks!'

And the poor boy did speak.

'Where am I, uncle?' said he in a faint voice. 'Where am I? What have I seen?'

And he passed his hands over his eyes.

'Nothing, nothing,' cried his uncle; 'you have fallen from your pony, that is all; you should not ride so hard, my child; you might have been killed.'

'No, no,' said the boy; 'I did not fall. I saw—Allah, save me!

save me, uncle! Oh look at their eyes and faces—there they lie—oh kill me, I cannot bear it!—I shall die!'

Unhappy child! he had again seen their faces; we had never thought of the dead; one of the bodies lay close to us, the distorted features grinning horribly, and it had fallen against a bank, so that he saw it sitting half upright—a dreadful spectacle for a child.

'Take it away, take it away!' he shouted in his infant voice. 'I shall die—oh, bury me! I shall never forget the face and the eyes; they will be ever before me!'

'Away with them!' cried I; and as I turned again to the child, he had sunk on his face in the sand of the road, and was endeavouring to hide himself in it—he was in strong convulsions.

'Allah! Allah! what shall I do?' cried Peer Khan. 'Oh, Meer Sahib, by your soul, by your mother's honour, do something. Save that child, and I will be your slave till the end of my days; I will serve you on my knees: I will be your menial.'

'What can be done?' said I. 'All we can do is to say with him, and comfort him when the paroxysm is past. He will revive soon and forget all.'

Poor boy, how he strove in his convulsions! he could not speak intelligibly, he foamed at the mouth, his lips grew livid and contracted; his eyes, when he opened them, seemed sunk into his head. I had never seen such terror before, nor could I have believed that is would have had such an effect on any one.

We carried him to the edge of the stream, and by dint of bathing his face, and forcing water into his mouth, he partly revived. He had just opened his eyes again, when by a miserable chance they fell upon one of the turbans of the dead men, with which I had been wiping his face. It had instantaneous effect on him; his screams broke out afresh, nothing could console him, and we were in dreadful alarm about him. What to do we knew not; we were far away from any human habitation, and even had we been near one we dared not have called in any hakim to see him, for his incoherent ravings would have too truly exposed our doings. We sat by the boy in fearful apprehensions that every throe and convulsion would cause his death; at last we raised him up, and placed him on his pony, and had succeeded in conveying him about a coss while he was in a state of insensibility; but it was of no avail. Again he awoke from his temporary unconsciousness, and we were obliged to take him down, and lay him on a bank at the side of the road, while we fanned his face and endeavoured to compose him.

But he was greatly reduced in strength, his moans were feebler and feebler, and though he now opened his eyes and gazed calmly around him, it was but too plain to us that the delicate flower had been blighted, and was fast withering under the terror which possessed him. Peer Khan was in a dreadful state; he raved, he entreated, he prayed; he knelt down beside the poor sufferer, and bedewed his face with his tears, which were fast falling; but no mercy was shown him. We sat thus till long past midday; numerous travellers passed us, all commiserating the child's state of suffering; but they shook their heads as they left us, with a firm conviction that he must die.

And he did die! towards evening the pure spirit fled from the suffering body, and we were left alone in the wild waste with the dead.

'It is of no use lamenting now,' said I to Peer Khan, as he sat, his hands clasped in anguish, rocking himself to and fro, and moaning and sobbing as though his spirit would break. 'It is of no use, brother, the boy is dead, and we must carry the body on to the stage, which is not very far distant.'

'Do as you will,' he replied: 'as for me, my heart is broken; I shall never look up again. He was the life of my soul, and without him what shall I do? What shall I do?'

But we raised the body up, and at times carrying it, at others placing it before us on our horses, we conveyed it to the camp. Our absence had been known, but as its cause,was also known, none of the Thugs had come out to meet us. We laid down our sad burden in my tent, a grave was quickly dug, and it was buried by torch-light, amidst the tears and lamentations of the whole band, for the boy was beloved by all.

Peer Khan came to me in the dead of the night, and awoke me from a restless slumber, in which the dreams of the sad scene had fearfully mingled. I was glad that he had come, but not for what followed.

'Meer Sahib,' said he, after a long silence, 'I am not what I was —I never shall be again; I am broken in spirit, and am no longer fit for my profession. My fate too points against it, and after this dreadful catastrophe I should be useless to you; permit me therefore to depart. You see I am calm and composed, and I do not say what I now urge on you in passion or grief; therefore let me depart. I will go to my home, and in solitude endeavour to make the remainder of my life acceptable to Allah, who has visited me with this affliction. Nor will it be long ere the earth covers me; I feel that this blow has shaken me to my soul, and it will bow me down to the grave.'

I saw it was useless to argue with him: his features were stamped with despair, and to contravene a man's fate is impossible. It is the will of Allah, and what mortal can oppose it? It must have its course.

'Go,' said I, 'Peer Khan; may peace be with you, and the blessing of the Prophet! I feel for you—I shall grieve with you; but if, in after times, your inclination leads you to join me, I need not say how gladly I shall avail myself of your services. We have been friends and brothers, and we part such, I hope, after years of a sincere and mutual affection.'

He could not reply to me—he wrung my hands, while the big tears rolled from his eyes over his manly features: he made attempts to address me, but the words stuck in his throat; and at length throwing himself at my feet, he kissed them, and embraced my knees: he then arose, and after gazing on me for a moment, with features working under the effects of suppressed emotion, he rushed from my presence for ever—ay, for ever! When we returned to Jhalone he was dead: his grief had killed him!

He had been more to me than any of my other companions, and deeply I sorrowed over his untimely fate.

I said this event threw a gloom over our party, which did not pass away for many days; but gradually the men assumed their wonted cheerfulness, and again the song, the jest, and the tale were heard in our merry and light hearted camp. Nor was the more serious part of our object neglected. Within a march or two of Jabalpur, we had heard that a munshi, stated to be a man of great wealth, was travelling before us to Nagpur, and we had made an effort to overtake him. We effected this a march from Jabalpur, on the Nagpur side, and were now entering on our best ground; I say our best, as there were but few inhabitants in that miserable country.

We overtook the munshi, but had it not been that we were neary three hundred Thugs in number, we should has hesitated to attack so large a party as his. He had two good-sized tents, horses, camels, a palankeen and bearers, and servants, and we deliberated long over the matter.

The omens however, having been consulted, were found to be favourable, and therefore we hesitated no longer, but laid our plans to effect an object which promised so much plunder.

We encamped close to the munshi for two days; of course this led to intercourse: hearing that we were respectable persons, he sent to my father and myself to come to him on the second evening, and we went. We spent a pleasant evening with him, for he was a man of extensive information, and amused us with many anecdotes and accounts of the Feringhees, of whom he spoke in terms of the highest praise, and undeceived us as to many particulars we had heard of them, and materially removed many of our prejudices against them. I respected them more from what he said than I had ever done before; for though every one acknowledged they were good and brave soldiers, it was said that they were vicious, and debauched, and drunken. At one or two questions of mine the munshi laughed immoderately. I asked him once why the Europeans eat with knives and forks, and spoons, instead of with their fingers, which God had given them.

'Yes,' said my father, 'old as I am I have never been able to find this out. Tell us, for you know, as you have yourself seen them eat.'

Tell me what you have heard,' said the munshi, 'and I will give you an answer.'

'It appears so extraordinary,' said I, 'that I can hardly believe it; for why should not all men be the same? Nevertheless, I have heard, and from what I thought to be good authority, that their finger-nails contain poison, and therefore they dare not risk the chance of their drawing blood, nay more, of touching their food.'

How he laughed! I thought he would never have ended; and I felt nettled that my remark should have given rise to such immoderate mirth. I could hear too, from the tittering behind the division of the tent, that the women were also provoked to merriment at my expense. At last he said—

'No, no, Meer Sahib, this is folly. Who could have told you such a lie? What if their skins be white and their faces ruddy, are they not the same flesh and blood as we are? They eat with spoons and knives because it is the custom of their country, and because they do not like to soil their hands; besides, their style of cookery is different to ours; for instance, they roast half a sheep and eat it, and how could they do so without the implements they use?'

'I confess my ignorance,' said I, 'and am ashamed to put any more questions to you about them, so shall believe henceforward that all I have heard are lies.' Yet I longed at the same time to ask some more about their drinking scenes, and the meaning of the words, Hip! hip! hip! which I fully believed to be of mystic import.

It was late when we separated, but before we did so we agreed to travel in company, and to pass our evenings together. This was what we wanted; our success was inevitable should we succeed in getting him on one or two marches further, as the villager there knew us, were our friends, and for a small consideration would keep themselves to their houses, and allow us to do what we liked. I have not mentioned this before, Sahib, for you very well know that it is the case. We have friends wherever we go; we bribe all we can, and have our agents in every part of the country in the disguise of fakirs or merchants. Some zemindars fear us, others bully us, and extort large sums from us, but they are generally faithful. In the Nizam's country particularly we are well aided. Many of the zemindars have Thugs in regular pay, whom they have been in the habit of sending out on the road: some are content with a certain sum a year; others, who fear so close a connexion with us, now and then pretend to arrest us, and get as much as they can; and as there is no police of any kind, they are not afraid of their dealings being brought to light. I myself know but little of how these matters are managed there—but I have heard from others, and in particular from Motee, who led a gang of Thugs for some years all over the Huzaar's dominions; he told me, that so long as he paid the patels of villages, the zemindars, and the revenue-servants handsomely, he had no obstruction; that hundreds of others did the same, and practised their profession so openly, that they often never took the trouble of burying the bodies of those they destroyed. But to my story.

We reached the village we wished to gain—a miserable hamlet called Biseynee; but the Patel was in our interest, and a present of twenty rupees now and then, with sometimes a new turban, gained us his silence and cooperation. I had purchased for the worthy Patel a handsome turban and waistband, and had prepared for him a number of other articles, one of which was an English pistol, which he had sent word by a Thug that I was to purchase for him. As soon as I arrived, I went into the village to him, and in his own house tied the turban on his head, presented him with the gifts I had prepared, and added a purse of twenty rupees.

'Ha!' said he, 'what now, Meer Sahib? you are not used to be so liberal. What bunij have you that you are come with it to my poor place, to give it a worse name than it has already?'

'Oh none,' said I carelessly, 'you know I have not been this way for some years, and these are to prove that I have not forgotten you.'

'Thanks for your kindness; may your condescension increase,' said he; 'but the bunij, Meer Sahib? You are a cunning gentleman: I know you of old. Who is he in the tents yonder and why have so many Thugs collected here? You cannot conceal your designs from me.'

'Nor do I wish it,' said I; 'but remember our old compact.'

'I do, I do,' said he hurriedly: 'but times are changed, and with them my masters. Know you not that this country belongs to the Sahib-logue?'

'And what of that, Patelji?' said I; 'what difference does it make?'

'None,' he replied, 'to me; but you have not seen the horsemen?'

'What horsemen?' cried I.

'Six,' said he, 'and a Daffadar. My poor village it seems has a bad name for thieves, and they have sent a party here to guard it. Allah help us, and keep the bread in our mouths!'

'And the Daffadar, what is he like?'

'He is a Hindu,' said the Patel, 'and a Bhojpuree; he is called Hittah Singh; his men too are all of his tribe.'

'Bhojpurees!' said I; 'then I dare say they are Thugs. What Bhojpuree was ever an honest man?'

'No, they are not Thugs, Meer Sahib, for I have tried them with the pass-word. But between you and me, I think my friend

Hittah Singh only wants an opportunity to be as great a rascal as I am myself—may Allah pardon me!'

'I have no doubt of it,' said I. 'Where is he?'

'Shall I call him?'

'Do so,' said I. 'If I cannot persuade him, I will bully him, and if the worst comes to the worst, you know we are more than three hundred to six, and they would have but little chance.'

'True, Meer Sahib; but no violence I pray; have some consideration for my good name. If the Europeans heard of violence having been done, they would turn me out of my place.'

'And you would turn Thug I suppose. But quick Patelji, call the man here.'

He was absent for a short time, and returned with a short mean-looking fellow, and I could plainly see that rascal was written on his countenance. You know the old proverb— 'Chor ke daree men Tinka' (there is always a straw in a thief's beard). Salutations were exchanged, and I came to the point at once.

'Look you, Daffadar Sahib,' said I to him, 'you may have guessed what we are?' He nodded assent. 'This is good,' I continued, ' as perhaps you may have guessed at our object.'

'Partly,' said he; 'but what do I know about you?'

'Exactly,' said I, 'the very thing I want; you need know nothing and you will have nothing to tell if you are ever asked. Take my advice, and remain quietly within your village, and if the earth turns upside down you are not to stir out. For this you shall be well paid. But if you molest us, remember we are three hundred to seven—fearful odds, my friend.'

'Nay, I am wise,' said he; 'what Bhojpuree is not? Nor do I wish to interfere. Do what you like; neither I nor my men will stir a foot.'

'Can you depend on them?' said I: 'can they be close?'

'As close as you wish them to be, Jemadar; but we must be paid.'

'Certainly,' said I; 'I would not have it otherwise: but the reward depends on what we get.'

'Say two hundred rupees,' said the fellow; 'it is worth your while.'

'Well, it is a bargain, Daffadar,' I replied, 'and the Patel is witness. And now I will give you further advice; that you are to know nothing and see nothing, if even the lord Sahib were to ask you. You are to know only that travellers came and departed, and you kept no account of them.'

'Of course,' said the fellow; 'I know this of old. I have met parties of your people in my own country, and have no reason to be dissatisfied with them: they have always behaved like men of honour, and kept their words with me.'

'Then we are agreed?' said I.

'Certainly: you will see nought of us, and I will come to you at night for my money.'

'You had better come now, Daffadar, as I think we shall move on after it is all over.'

'Do you go, Patelji; it would not look well for me to go with the Syud Sahib. Do you go and bring the money.'

'Come then,' said I, 'we are losing time.'

'Shall you return soon?' asked the Daffadar of me.

'I know not,' I replied; 'but it is probable: At any rate, as this country always produces good booty for us, you will see us here pretty often.'

'The oftener the better,' said he; 'and I must continue to keep my station here; it would be hard to lose such good friends. You, Patelji, can help me to a few low-caste rascals from time to time, to send in as thieves we have caught.'

'Certainly,' said the Patel, 'there are plenty of Gonds and Dhers in the country; every one knows they are thieves; and if they may not immediately have committed any robberies, they have been engaged in them some time or other, so it is all the same. I will get you a few from time to time as you want them.'

I could not help laughing heartily at the cool manner in which this was proposed and accepted. But it was the truth, and I know that it was, and is now, a matter of every-day occurrence. Many a Daffadar of police has won a good name with his officers in this way, and for one guilty man he has seized a dozen innocent people. Who cares about Mangs and Dhers? they are always villains and robbers.

CHAPTER XXXII

'THAT is a bhula admi (a respectable man)' said I to the Patel, as he walked to our camp, 'he suits my purpose exactly.'

'He has been on the look-out for some of you,' said he, 'for a long time. We have never spoken openly on the subject, but he has hinted as much many times. And I suspect he chose this post, if he had any choice in the matter, because he was likely to meet Thugs here. If you pay him well, he will help you materially.'

'Do you think I have given enough?' said I.

'Quite,' he replied; 'I don't think he expected you would agree to so much.'

'It is certainly a large sum,' said I, 'but it is the first, and the money is well spent.'

'But you have forgotten me, Meer Sahib: am I not to partake of your bounty?'

'Of course Patelji. What I brought was only a trifle, I have more for you in the camp; you shall have your share.'

'How much, Meer Sahib? I want money; my rents are in arrears and I am in distress.'

'Thirty rupees,' said I.

'Make it fifty, I beseech you. You know not in what a strait I am; I cannot borrow the money, and you have been sent by Allah for my deliverance.'

'Well,' said I, 'you shall have it, but on one condition. We may not be on the road when some people whom we are looking out for pass this place: they are Dacoos; they have some tattoos with them, and great wealth. If they pass either way, you must send them after us with a letter.'

'I will send my own sons, well-mounted,' replied he; 'they will easily find you out, and you may depend on me. Where will these fellows come from?'

'They have gone to Hyderabad now,' said I, 'and will return by Nagpur. If we meet them, all very well; but they may escape us.'

'They shall not, by Allah!' said the Patel. 'I will watch for them myself, and if you get them I shall hope for a handsome present.'

'I will not forget you. But here we are at the camp; take care no one sees the money as you carry it away.'

'Trust an old hand for that,' said he with a knowing wink. 'I must go after I have got it to the Munshi, who has sent for me about fodder for his horses. I should like to see him too—to see a man whose breath is in his nostrils. And he has a wife too.'

'Yes,' said I, 'there is no getting her out of the way, so she must die, which is a pity. He has a child also, about four years old, which I want myself; he is a pretty boy, and I have no son to bless me; he will never know the difference between me and his father after a few days.'

I paid the money and dismissed him. Ganesha came to me. 'I have been looking at the ground,' said he, 'and there is a hole near the munshi's tent which has been dug for some purpose or other, apparently the commencement of a well; it will save us the trouble of digging; the earth lies close to it, and will only have to be filled in.'

'Have the lughas seen it?' said I.

'Yes,' he replied, 'I took one with me; he says it is the very thing.'

'Now, Ganesha,' said I, 'how shall me manage?'

'Oh, do you take the tent work, and leave the rest to me; I will settle all outside. You have a smooth tongue, and the munshi is alone; I will be close at hand in case of anything going wrong; but I do not apprehend anything.'

'Nor I either. None of the sayses or camel-men must escape: there are many of them.'

'Sixteen in all; I have counted them: let me see—eight bearers, two camel-men—one of them has a wife—two khitmutgars, one female servant, and four sayses: how many is that?'

'Eighteen,' said I.

'Ah, well, it does not matter; towards evening I will surround the whole; most of them will be listening to the songs, and the rest we must overpower in the best way we can. The night will be dark too, which is in our favour.'

The evening came. My father and I went to the munshi's, but after the evening prayer time; he had his son on his knee, and a noble little fellow he was. How I shall love that boy! said I inwardly, as I looked on his fair and beautiful features and expressive eyes: he came to me readily and I fondled him, and displayed to his admiring eyes my beautiful sword and dagger. Azima too will love him, thought I, and he will supply the place of our daughter when she is married and gone from us.

'You have no children?' said the munshi; 'or perhaps I ought not to ask, you may have lost them: your brow darkens at the question.'

'One,' replied I, 'a daughter. A son, the counterpart of the Sahib-zada, it pleased Allah to take from me when he was about his age.'

'It is indeed his will,' said the munshi; 'there is no striving against fate. This boy is my only offspring; for many years I had been married, and my case was somewhat like that of the Sultan in the "Story of the Parrot;" grey hairs were coming, and I despaired, but at last Allah was gracious and you see the boy.'

'Allah grant he may live a hundred years, and be prosperous,' said I. 'I have no hope myself.'

We conversed together for some time, and on a message being given from without, I said, 'You have been so pleased with the singing of some of my men, Munshi Sahib, that they have arranged a little masque, after the manner of the Byroopeas, which they are anxious to perform before you. It will be absurd enough I dare say, yet it will serve to pass the evening, and your son too may be amused.'

'By all means,' said he; 'anything in the jungle is acceptable; but for your company, Meer Sahib, we should have had a dull march. I will prepare those within, so pray call in the performers.'

The men came, six stout fellows dressed fantastically, two of them as women, with sitars and drums in their hands; they personated a body of Goosaeens, and danced and sung in a ridiculous manner. Where they had learned their parts I know not, but the whole was well done, and the munshi's little son laughed immoderately. As we had expected, the whole of the munshi's people gathered round the tent, which was open on one side, to admit of their seeing the Tumasha; and I observed with secret exultation that every man had two or three Thugs close to him, and one in particular behind each of them. All was ready as I thought, and I was about to give the signal, when one of the Thugs called to me that I was wanted without. What it could be I knew not, but excusing myself for a moment I went out.

'What shall we do?' said Ganesha to me in a voice full of alarm and apprehension: 'Meer Sahib, the Feringhees are upon us!'

'The Feringhees!'

'Yes,' he replied; 'and what can we do? This good bunij will escape us. Of course the munshi will join them, and we may then as well think of strangling the king of Delhi as of getting him.'

'But how,' said I, 'how are the Feringhees upon us? Have you seen them?'

'No,' said Ganesha, 'but I have seen their people. A long string of camels have just arrived with I know not how many red-coated sepoys to guard them—my curse be on them all!'

'And where are they?'

'Why, they are gone into the village. They wanted this ground, but I told them I would not give it up; that the munshi was a gentleman of rank, and could not be disturbed, and that there was better ground on the other side of the village.'

'Then never fear,' said I; 'the work must be done immediately. I will go in and give the jhirnee; and if any of those prying rascals the Lascars come about us, you know what to do. But I fear not; the Patel will help us, and Hittah Singh too, and there need be no great noise.'

'Good,' said Ganesha; 'but be quick, Meer Sahib, I shall be in a torment of apprehension until the whole are fairly under the ground.'

I left him, and carelessly playing with my rumal, again entered the tent.

'What is it?' asked the munshi.

'Oh nothing,' I replied; 'only some Sahiblogues' tents which have arrived. Their servants wanted this ground to encamp on, but seeing us here, the Lascars have taken them to the other side of the village. The troops will be here early tomorrow.'

'That will suit me exactly,' said he; 'I will stay with them, and bid you gentlemen farewell; but that is no reason why we should be the less merry. I warrant these good fellows have another song or two in store. Have you?' he asked of them.

'A hundred,' replied one of them; 'but perhaps the next will be rather a noisy one.'

'Never mind,' said he, 'play on; you shall have as good a reward as I can afford to bestow.'

I waited till the noise was at its height to give the jhirnee, yet I had not the opportunity I wished for. The munshi sat with his back to the kanât, and to get behind him was impossible; one of the Thugs saw my embarrassment, and relieved it, by begging him to rise and advance a few paces.

'What are they going to do?' asked he.

'I know not,' I replied, 'but you had as well comply.'

He arose, and I slipped behind him. 'Now!' I shouted; 'bring the pān!' and my hand was on the munshi's neck. One wild shriek he gave and fell.

His wife had been looking on through a hole in the kanât; she had seen the work, and rushed out into the midst of us, wih her boy in her arms. I shall never forget her—never: I shall never forget her wild look and her screams. I tore the boy from her arms, and left her in the midst of the Thugs; I ran out into the air, and the first person I met was Ganesha, his face flushed with triumph, which I saw by the glare of the torches from the tent.

'All is done!' cried he; 'they have all fallen. Two I killed myself. Where are the lughas? we must be quick.'

He ran on; and I stood in the open space before the tent. Parties of Thugs passed rapidly to and fro, bearing the bodies of the dead, which were one by one thrown into the hole. But the singing and music went on as merrily as ever, and looking into the tent I saw my father sitting in the place which had been occupied by the ill-fated munshi.

My little charge was crying terribly, imploring me, in tones and words that would have moved any one's heart but mine, to take him to his mother. I soothed him as well as I could, and was going to my tent; but curiosity impelled me to return, and see the hole in which the business of interment was going on. I went to the edge; Ganesha was standing by it encouraging the lughas; he saw the boy in my arms.

'What folly is this, Meer Sahib?' said he, 'you are not going to spare that boy, when we are even now in such danger! — it will be madness. Give him to me; I will silence the crying wretch, and send him with his parents.'

'Never!' cried I; 'the boy is mine; you may have all the spoil, but give him up to death I will not. Have I not lost a son, and is it not lawful to adopt a child of this age.'

'Madness! madness!' cried Ganesha, 'the boy must die. Are you a fool, Meer Sahib, to risk such a chance?'

'He will never find out the difference between us and his parents,' said I; 'and I will not be interfered with.'

'Fool!' said Ganesha, setting his teeth, 'I spared a child once, and will never spare another; I have sworn it on the pickaxe.'

'I care not for a thousand oaths,' I cried; 'the boy is mine, and you had better not oppose me if you wish to avoid a quarrel;' and I was going away. He caught me by the arm.

'Let me go,' I exclaimed, and I felt for my dagger, 'or by Allah! I will strike this steel into you.'

'Boy,' cried he, 'you are mad; I fear you not—talk of daggers to others than Ganesha; he has seen too much of you to fear you. Give me the child I say, his cries will alarm the sepoys.'

I felt for my dagger or a sword, but I had left them in the tent; I tried if pity could move him.

'Have you no compassion?' I said more gently; 'Ganesha, have you no pity for a child? Can you bear to kill him?'

I was off my guard, and he saw his opportunity. Quicker than thought he had rudely snatched the child from my arms, and as he hurled him into the pit, he cried scornfully, 'Pity! no, I know it not. Now go and cry, Meer Sahib, for the loss of your plaything.'

I started forward, and leaned over the edge of the hole, which was being rapidly filled; the poor boy lay senseless and dead at the bottom—one shriek alone had escaped him, as he was dashed with passionate force into it. I gazed for an instant, to satisfy myself that he was dead, and some of the earth which was being thrown in hid him almost instantly from my view.

I turned to Ganesha in savage anger.

'Dog!' cried I, 'and son of a dog! you shall answer for this. Had I my sword now with me, I would cut you in two pieces.'

'An idle threat, and one befitting what I have heard of you, said he. 'Go, Meer Sahib, you are a boy and a fool: I do not fear you.'

Stony-hearted villain, he had destroyed my son. Situated as I was, I could then do nothing, but I was determined to have my revenge: and I took it too. I mentioned what had occurred to my father and to three of my intimate associates: they were determined to stick by me whenever I chose to attack Ganesha, and would fain have done so the next day; but this did not suit me, though his words rankled in my heart, and the deed he had done made me hate him more than ever.

We stayed on the ground that night; the palankeen had been broken in pieces and thrown into the hole, but my father personated the munshi the next morning as we rode through the camp of the Feringhees, which had been pitched so near us, that indeed I have often wondered they heard not the cries of the party as we despatched them. But we had taken good precautions. The noise of the drums, and the confusion occasioned by letting loose two of the munshi's horses, which were here and there pursued by a number of Thugs, shouting and screaming after them, had drowned the cries of our victims, and we had effected the whole without suspicion. Our good friends, the Patel and the Daffadar, had kept the sepoys in conversation, and they had not noticed the noise, beyond hazarding a passing remark as to its cause.

Again therefore, we were on the road. We had not got all the booty we expected, it did not indeed amount to three thousand rupees, and we earnestly looked out for the Dacoos, who were we hoped to be our next bunij. We went on to Nagpur, and sold the munshi's camels and horses. Here the gang divided; one part under a jemadar named Emom Buksh took our old road towards Amraoti, and through the valley of Berar to Khandesh and Burhanpur; the rest of us returned by the road we had come, after staying four days in the city of Nagpur.

On our second or third march homewards we overtook the Dacoos. They had been seen by our spies the moment we entered the village we had encamped at; and as much caution was requisite in managing them, my father at once proposed to be alone the Sotha, or inveigler.

'I shall feign to be a Hindu,' said he; 'these rascals will suspect me if I go by my own name, and indeed they would know me. I will be a Rajput Jemadar, come from Hyderabad, and you shall see I have not forgotten my old trade.'

Accordingly he painted his forehead and breast after the fashion of the Hindus, covered his eyes with wood-ashes, put on a waistcloth and dress he borrowed from one of the men, and attended by another went into the village.

How anxiously I expected his return! I feared he would fail in his mission, but Ganesha was confident. 'He never fails,' said he to me; 'he is one of Bhowani's own favourites; nothing he ever did failed. Would that I had his luck!'

But he was absent so long, that I became apprehensive for his safety, and was on the point of setting out to gain tidings of him, when to my great joy I saw him approaching. I ran to meet him.

'What news?' cried I; 'oh, my father, my liver has been burnt during your absence. Why did you stay so long?'

'Never mind, my son,' said he, when he had dismounted, 'you would have been wrong to come after me. But ah, the owls! I have entrapped them,—they are ours.'

'Ul-humd-ul-illa!' cried I, 'this is rare news; but how did you manage it?'

'Why,' replied he, 'it was done easily enough, though I feared for my success when I saw that one of the Dacoos was a fellow I had known a long time ago; however he did not recognise me, thanks to my white beard and these marks of the infidels: he never thought I was Ismail Thug. I sat and conversed with their leader, who told me very gravely he was a servant of the English going to Hindustan on leave of absence. I said I was one also, and had come from Jalna, where I was a collector of duties on spirits. We then became intimate, and agreed to travel together; and by Allah! if the omens are good, they shall die tomorrow. Delay is useless with these fellows, for they evidently think (from the signs I saw them making among themselves, which are known to me) that we are certain bunij to them, and if we do not attack them they will fall upon us.'

'We shall need good hands,' said I; 'and I will take the leader.'

'I will be a bhuttote also,' said Ganesha; 'I never killed a Daccoo. Are they stout fellows?'

'Very,' answered my father; 'but like all their tribe they are heavily armed, and can do but little against us, if we manage properly.'

'We had better fall on them with our swords,' I observed.

'Not so, my son; but we will surround them, and if there is not a good opportunity, the men can use their weapons.'

We were soon agreed on this point; and in the morning the Dacoos joined us as we moved round the village into the main road. They were twenty-five in number, stout, but heavy-looking men, armed to the teeth, with their heads enveloped in folds of cloth. They had with them thirteen tatoos heavily laden; and it was well they had this encumbrance, as it served to separate them, as each tatoo required a man to drive it. Had they kept in a body, we could have made but little impression on them, and dared hardly to have attacked them.

'Now look out!' said my father to the men; 'if you see them leaving their beasts and collecting in twos and threes, fall on them at once, or they will attack us: they know well enough who we are, though they pretend they do not.'

We journeyed on in company: after I had ridden for some distance I dismounted, and walking beside the leader I entered into conversation with him. He did not recognise me, and very gravely began telling me how he had met with Thugs on his way down; how he had fought with and overpowered a large band,

and carried off their plunder, amounting to some thousand rupees.

I could have struck him on the mouth with my shoe, but I refrained: yet it was enough to have provoked me, being so barefaced a lie. Still I applauded his bravery, and he continued: 'Yes, Meer Sahib, these Thugs are the greatest villains unhung; I praise the Prophet that I have gained some information about them, which I will give to my masters the Europeans. The fool of a Thug, or rather one of his people, told me they belonged to Jhalone; I am going that way, and if I do not tell the Rajah of their being in this city, call me an owl and a father of jackasses. I expect too he will reward me handsomely.'

Ay, you will tell him, thought I; but you must get there first, my friend. Mashallah! words are one thing, but deeds are another.

We trudged on till we came in sight of two trees on the road, on which travellers hung bits of rag as offerings to the guardian saint of the place. I saw very plainly that this was their bhil; one by one they began to forsake their tattoos and collect. More delay on our part would have been fatal, and my father saw this. He was as prompt as I could have desired: he had seen their movements, and just as I had disengaged my rumal from my waist, he gave the jhirnee. Eleven of the Dacoos fell at the same moment, the leader by my hand. I had my rumal round his throat, and before I gave the fatal wrench, I shouted in his ear that I was Ameer Ali, the leader of the Thugs he had met, and that *then* I had sworn to kill him, and had done it. The rest were cut down with swords: my men were prepared, they were not, and were heavily encumbered. We threw the bodies as they were into the jungle, and pushed on, laughing heartily, and in the highest spirits at the issue of our adventure. The booty too was good—thirteen thousand rupees worth of gold, silver, and ready money met our admiring eyes, when the packages of the loaded tattoos were opened for our inspection.

Well, Sahib, we had proceeded as far as Sehora on our return, when we fell in with a great European who was also travelling. We did not fear him, but on the contrary determined to keep with him, because we well knew that he had many travellers in his train who profited by the protection of his troops; so we divided into two parties, one under myself and my father, the other under Ganesha. I need not follow the adventure further, for it differed not from the rest; suffice it to say, that after a few marches a large party of travellers had joined with us. We left the high road to proceed by footpaths through the jungles, and near the village of Shikarpur we selected the bhil. The place was a favourite one, and well known to our party. The travellers fell, twenty-nine men, some women and children; all were buried in one grave, for the spot where they were killed was a desolate one. The deed was done in the night, but by the light of as fair a moon as ever shone on us. One child I saved from the general slaughter; Ganesha was not present to oppose me; and though the boy was a Hindu, yet I determined to adopt him as my own, and to bring him up in the holy faith I professed myself, and this would enhance the merit of having spared him. But when his mother died, I could not force him away from the body; he clung to it, young as he was, with frantic force: he screamed and kicked whenever I attempted to lay hold of him, and bit me in the arms and hands. I thought, if the body was removed from his sight, he would be quiet and submit to his fate; but no—when it was gone, he grew worse and worse; nothing would pacify or tranquillize him, and I fairly grew impatient and angry. I drew my sword, and threatened him, but he was insensible to his danger; he reviled me, he spat at me with a child's virulence. I once more raised him up in my arms, but it was of no use; he seized my ear in his teeth and bit till the blood came. In the agony of the pain and in my rage I knew not what I did. Sahib, how shall I tell you what followed? It was the worst act of my life but one, which I have yet to tell you of.

You killed him, I suppose, Ameer Ali, said I.

Yes, Sahib. I killed him; but oh, how did I do it! It was the devil's work, not mine. I never was cruel. but now the Shitan possessed me.

Here Ameer Ali put his hands to his eyes, and finding my heart sicken, I begged him to refrain from reciting the dreadful particulars. After a pause he continued—

Wretch that I was, I did this. No one was near to me but the Thug who held my horse, and even he was horror-struck, and uttered a loud scream of terror. I silenced him, and leaving the mangled body, I mounted my horse and galloped after my party.

We were in full march on the third day after this happened, when we saw a body of horsemen coming after us. My mind misgave me when I observed them, and I hastened to collect the straggling Thugs, and form them into a close body, in case the horsemen should prove to be enemies, or make any hostile demonstration. On they came, shouting and abusing us in every term of vile reproach their tongues could utter. There were about forty of them; and I verily believe that, had I not been at the head of the band, they would have fled as one man: however I cheered them up, and was determined to show a good front in my retreat. I knew there was a village in our interest within a few coss, which possessed a worthy Patel like him I have told you of; and that if we could but reach it, we might man the walls and towers, and bid defiance to our pursuers.

'Be not afraid,' cried I to my men; 'let the best of ye come behind with me, and we will stop these marauding rascals. I know they are Pindaris, and the veriest cowards in existence. Only be firm; you who have matchlocks take good aim, and when they are near enough, every one mark his man, and see if as many saddles are not emptied.'

On they came; fortunately the road was narrow, and had thick thorny brushwood on each side of it, so that they could not pass us. They were within speaking distance, and I shouted.

'Are ye friends or enemies? If the former, keep behind us; if enemies, begone, in the name of the Prophet, or ye are likely to meet a sharp reception.'

'Stop!' shouted the leader of the party, 'who among you is leader? I would speak to him.'

'I am leader,' said I; 'come out alone and I will meet you; but if any of ye stir, by Allah we will fire on you.'

The fellow advanced, and seeing that none followed him, I rode out in front of my men. 'If there is treachery,' said I to them, 'fire; never mind me.'

'Jemadar,' said the man, 'our Thakoor has sent for you, you may possibly have guessed why. You had better come: you will only have to pay a fine and will be released; I swear this to you on the faith of a Rajput.'

'I will neither trust you nor your master,' said I; 'you are a parcel of vagabond Pindaris; I laugh at you and spit on your beards. If you want us, come and take us; but of our own accord we come not. Are we fools? Are we asses? Oh, man! art *thou* one to talk thus? Go back to him that sent thee, and say, the man is yet unborn who will take Ameer Ali Thug, so long as he has a weapon in his hand, or a few gallant fellows by his side. Have you no shame to deliver such a message?'

He made no answer, but urged his horse and cut at me with his sword. Fool! he did not think that a Thug could fight, and still less that he had engaged one whom no one had ever yet defeated. I caught the blow on my shield, and returned it on his head as he passed me;—the fellow fell from his horse a dead man.

My own men set up a shout and discharged their matchlocks; one horseman and a horse fell wounded, and struggled in the dust. Had only my own good companions in the Pindaris affairs been with me, I would have charged them and put them to flight, but I could do nothing alone. We had checked them however, and retired slowly, followed by the troop, who kept out of shot, but evidently waiting for a piece of level and fair ground to charge us. In this way we retreated till the welcome walls of the village whither I had directed the main body appeared to our view. We redoubled our efforts to gain the shelter they would afford us, and the men were in some disorder as we passed over a level plain in front of the village: they were beginning to run, but I checked them.

'For the love of Allah!' cried I, 'keep together and have brave hearts; so long as we are firm they will not dare to come near us, but if once we separate we are lost. See, even now they are preparing to charge, as a hawk stoops on his quarry.'

And down they came; thundering along, brandishing their spears, and reviling us: some of my men fled at their utmost speed to the gate, but most of them stood. Again I dashed at one of our enemies and wounded him, but the odds were against us; one of my own men fell, pierced through the breast to the backbone by a spear; another was wounded; but they could not take further advantage of us. Those who had fled, joined by others of my men and some villagers, headed by my brave old father, issued from the gate; which the horsemen seeing, they drew off, and we got within the village in safety. They kept hovering about till midday, but out of the reach of our shot; and soon after noon they all departed, and we saw no more of them. We had to pay for our shelter handsomely however, for the Patel shut the gates of his village and declared we should not pass out without having paid him a thousand rupees. I was for attacking him, plundering his village, and burning it after the Pindari fashion, and we could have done it easily. But my father would not hear of it: 'The country would rise on us,' he said; 'and besides, it would ill requite the Patel's hospitality and protection, even though we had to pay for it.' So he paid the money; and after a thousand protestations of mutual goodwill, we left the village in the evening, intending to push on as far as we could, to be beyond the reach of pursuit.

We pursued our route. Ganesha too had been fortunate; he had decoyed a large body of travellers, consisting of a Jemadar who had lost an arm, and his family, with some others, along the bypaths in another direction, and he had killed them all.

You know, Sahib, that it is forbidden to us to kill persons who may in any way be deformed. I was amused afterwards to hear of the deliberations made upon the Jemadar's fate by Ganesha and his gang: he told them to me himself when we met.

'Some, indeed most of the men,' said he 'hesitated as to whether he should be strangled or not. There was no means of separating him from the party, and they said the whole ought to be abandoned on his account, as he had lost an arm, and therefore was not a fit sacrifice to Bhowani. I replied that he was not deformed, that if he had lost an arm, he had one once, and the losing of it was not the work of Allah but of man, and that when he died he would appear in the form in which he had been created; therefore he was not forbidden, but was true bunij; and I asked them how they would show their faces to you and to their brethren at the rendezvous with no deed to boast of, and, more than all, no plunder. I prevailed; the whole were strangled; the Jemadar by my own hand, for no one else would touch him, despite of all I said to convince them there was no harm in it.'

We were now somewhat at a loss for a route, or whither to go.

The omens were consulted at Saugor, which was our place of rendezvous; and as they pointed to the northward, we struck off the high-road to the north at Saugor, and took that to Seronje. But my father returned to Jhalone. We divided into two bodies, each a day's march from the other, for we were fearful of being suspected if we travelled in large numbers; and since the Europeans had got a footing in the country, we found that we were asked more questions at the different posts and guards than we had used to be. Besides, large bodies of travellers had disappeared in various directions, and the authorities were suspicious and inquisitive to a degree. However, now with bullying, now with bribes, we contrived to pass on, leaving our fruit as we went in many a sly place, which the Choukedars never suspected: and although we got no large booty, yet scarcely a day passed but one, or two, or more travellers met their deaths at our hands.

It was at the village of Ekléra, in Holkar's dominions, (alas! I shall never forget it) that our sothas brought us word they had secured a small party of travellers, who were about to proceed to a village a few coss distant. Of course our men told them of the danger of travelling alone, of the alarms there were of Thugs, and begged of them to accompany our large party for safety, which had collected for the same purpose, and they consented. The sothas offered to introduce them to me as the leader of the Kafila; and accordingly, at sunset, one of them returned to the bazaar, and brought two of the men to me. I received them cordially, repeated the same stories as my men had done, and frightened them quite sufficiently for my purpose.

'Listen,' said one; 'though I have never seen a Thug, nor know of any existing in this part, yet that they have been here there is no doubt. My wife's father was killed by them.'

'How!' said I; 'it is horrible to think on; how did this happen? Know you aught of the particulars?'

'No,' replied he, 'none but what I have heard from others. I was a boy at the time, but the old men of the village know them well, and often speak of them even to this day. I will introduce you to my father-in-law as I justly call him, and he shall tell you the tale himself. Mashallah! he tells it with much spirit, and 'tis worth hearing.'

I confess I was interested; why I should have been so at a common tale of Thuggee was more than I can imagine. I rose and followed the man to his house, determined to hear the whole story from his father-in-law's mouth.

I have said it was yet day; the sun was setting and the village was a scene of bustle and noise, as is always the case in an evening; the herds which had been out to graze were pouring in at the gates, raising clouds of dust, through which the walls were but dimly seen. Yet still as I advanced I fancied them familiar to me; I imagined I knew the names of different places near them—

one in particular, the abode of a fakir, around which was a small garden. I almost started when I approached it, for it seemed like the face of a familiar friend one meets after a long absence, when one hesitates to accost him by name, though almost assured of its identity. But in spite of my desire to know the name of the garden I walked on, for it would not have suited my purpose to have appeared to recognize any object, having represented myself to be an utter stranger. As we passed through the gate, objects more and more familiar to my eyes, presented themselves—the bazaar, the little Mosque, the Kotwal's Chowree, the temple of Mahadeo. I could have named them all, and one house in particular—my heart leaped within me as I passed it. There was nothing remarkable in it; but it seemed unaccountably fresh to me—as though I had but left it yesterday.

Still I walked on silently, and my companion did not notice the agitation and surprise which must have been depicted on my features. We reached the house, a respectable one in appearance; and desiring me to be seated, he left me, to bring the old man of whom he had spoken. When he entered, Allah! Allah! I could have called him too by name, though his features were shrunken and withered. I was almost about to exclaim Rheim Khan! but I checked myself, and as he was presented to me under another name, Futih Mahomed Khan, I was silent.

The whole, after this, thought I, must be a wild dream, or I may have visited the place in my wanderings, perhaps stayed a few days at it, and it is thus familiar to me. After some desultory conversation my new friend stated what he had told me, and requested his father-in-law to relate the story of Peer Khan with all its particulars.

CHAPTER XXXIII

THE old man returned my salutations cordially; and when we were fairly seated, and the hookah had passed round, he related the sad history of the parents of the girl he had adopted. His version of the tale differed little from that of my new acquaintance; and indeed the whole affair appeared to have been as successful a piece of Thuggee as I had ever listened to. I wonder who they were, thought I; I will mention the story to my father; perhaps he may have heard of it, and can give me some clue to the boy whose fate is buried in uncertainty. Yet the lad may even now be among us; and as this thought flashed across my mind, a half conviction forced itself upon me that I was the man! But I checked it—it was a foolish thought, such as one harbours sometimes upon the slightest cause, and dismisses after a moment's reflection.

'And you never heard aught of them afterwards, nor of the boy?' I asked.

'Never,' said the old man; 'never; years have passed since then, and the lad, if he lives, is about your own age. Meer Sahib; and—Ya Allah!' cried he, gazing on me, as a gust of wind caused the lamp to flare towards me, 'those features are familiar to me!—speak, man! thou art not the son of him who was murdered?'

I confess that his earnest gaze and manner, with my previous convictions that the village was familiar to me, almost overpowered me; but I was too old an adept in deceit to be long staggered by a suspicion which he had no means of confirming, and I replied carelessly and with a laugh, 'No, no, that cannot be; my father still lives, though my mother is dead; indeed I have but little remembrance of her. Besides we are pure Syuds by descent, and reside in a distant country, and you spoke of your old friend as a Pathan.'

'It cannot be, then,' said the old man, turning away with an air of disappointment; 'yet the resemblance is very striking, and I pray you, Meer Sahib, to pardon an old man's mistake; it may be that my eyes are failing me. Yet look at him, my son, and say does he not resemble *her*?'

'He does so certainly,' replied the other, 'and I was struck with the similarity of features when I first saw him; but it must be imaginary, or it is perhaps one of those unaccountable resemblances which one often sees without being able to discover any cause why it should exist.'

'But you spoke of a coin,' said I, 'which you hold to be possessed of peculiar virtues.'

'I did, Meer Sahib, and my father will tell you that I have not overrated its efficacy.'

'Nor has he,' said the other; 'many charms have I seen, but none equal to it: when around the neck of a wearer, no evil comes to her no disease attacks her, and the eye of the malevolent or envious rests in vain upon her. Assuredly it possesses wonderful virtues, for if it is ever absent from her, she suffers from disease, or is unquiet in mind.'

'Allah ke Qoodrut!' I exclaimed; 'it is the work of God. Such charms are indeed precious, and lucky is the possessor of them. I had once a son—he became the victim of an evil glance, cast by a fakir to whom alms were denied; he cursed my house, and the boy pined and died. I was absent from my home, and you may judge, sirs, of my agony when I arrived and learned my boy was dead. I have never been blessed with another; but a girl still survives, upon whom every care is lavished, and no charm is offered for sale by the wandering fakirs, Moslem or Hindu, but it is eagerly purchased, and hung around her neck. In this manner I have spent much money, but as yet without effect; for my child is delicate, and afflicted with dreams which disturb her rest and disquiet her gentle spirit; and I would to Allah I could become the possessor of some charm similar to the one you mention.'

'Keep a stout heart, Meer Sahib,' said the old man; 'you have bought your experience with sorrow, to be sure, yet a constant attention to the wants of the holy wanderers will no doubt have its effect in the end, and their prayers will be offered for the health of your child and her long life.'

'May Allah listen to them!' said I fervently, for my heart was then with my child and my loved wife.

I arose to take my leave and as my new friend insisted on accompanying me to our camp, we walked thither.

'You will be ready, then, at the first dawn,' observed I; 'we travel early for the sake of the cool morning air, and my companions bestir themselves as soon as the first blush of light spreads over the east.'

'Depend on me,' said he, 'I will not keep you waiting: we have a long stage before us.'

He left me. I will have the charm, thought I, as I lay down to rest; my child shall be protected by its extraordinary virtue, and there will be an end of the constant searchings for amulets, which do no good, and cost much money: besides I could not bring Azima a gift she would prize more highly, better far in her eyes than strings of pearls or costly jewels. Thus musing, my thoughts wandered to my home: my treasures were before me in imagination, and I compared this my wild and exciting life with the peaceful moments I enjoyed when I was there with them—Azima lying beside me, and our child amusing us with her innocent gambols. The contrast was forcible, and appealed to my best feelings.

I fell asleep; nor did I wake until the bustle of preparation for the journey warned me that it was time to rise. Having performed my ablutions, I repeated the morning prayer and thanksgivings, and issuing from my little tent, I saw the band was in readiness to move on; but my new acquaintance and his family were as yet not with us.

'Shall we move on?' asked Laloo—who was now my confidant being the second of the bhuttotes—as I stood near my horse, preparing to mount.

'Not yet,' said I; 'I expect some bunij from the village; they promised not to be late, yet the day advances. Send some one to hurry them.'

'Ay, our friends of last night, I suppose, Meer Sahib? Of course we will wait for them, and I will send a fellow to quicken them: know you how many there will be to deal with?'

'Not I,' I replied; 'there are a man and his wife, but how many more I know not.'

Our messenger returned almost immediately. 'They come,' said he; 'I had not reached the village gate when I saw them issue forth.'

'And how many are there?' I asked.

'There are two women on ponies, one old one on foot, and three men armed with sword and matchlock.'

The village party soon approached us, and salutations were exchanged; we stayed not, but pushed on at as rapid a pace as allowed the villagers to keep up with us; and we travelled thus to the end of the stage. I saw no likely place for the deed on our way, for the country was thickly peopled and the villages were close to each other. But I heard with inward satisfaction from my acquaintance that the next march was through a lonely tract, and I was urged by him to be on the alert and careful, for that robbers were plentiful, and we might be attacked.

They rested in our camp that day and night. I watched eagerly to see, if it were possible, the face of the woman who bore the prize I so eagerly coveted, but I could not discern it; she was strictly secluded, or if she moved out of the temporary screen her husband had erected, she was enveloped in a thick wrapper, which defied my utmost attempts to discover her countenance. But she was *mine*, and I gloried in the thought that ere another day should pass over me, she would have fallen under my hand, and the charm would be mine also. You, Sahib, will perhaps wonder at my eagerness to possess it; but you know us not if you do. What mother is there in Hindustan, ay, or father, who does not covet a potent charm against the evil eye for his child or for his wife, far more than riches nay the commonest necessaries or comforts of life? A child falls sick, the glance of some one is declared to have rested on it, ceremonies are performed without number, pepper is burned, mustard-seed placed in the room, and other things done which you would laugh at were I to relate them all; and hence comes the necessity of charms. Holy men are besought to give them, and are paid for them highly: fakirs are implored to pronounce mystic words over the suffering infant; and women will sell anything they possess, even their jewels, to purchase an amulet which is said to be efficacious. Sahib, I had lost one child; another, my sole offspring, was constantly ailing, and we were tormented by a thousand miserable anticipations regarding her. Within my reach was a sovereign remedy for all—so at least I firmly believed; car. you wonder my eagerness, my impatience to possess it?

Laloo came to me, and him the chief of the Belhas. 'We are to go on. I suppose, as soon as we can?' said the latter.

'Certainly,' replied I; 'I hear the road lies through a lonely tract, which commences a few coss from here. See that you choose a good place, and that the grave will hold six bodies.'

'Jo hookum!' rejoined the fellow; 'I will start by sunset. I suppose the nearer to this the place is selected, consistently with security, the better?'

'Certainly,' said I. 'Go; you have your leave.'

Midnight arrived: we had arisen and proceeded about three coss on our way; we had passed every village, and entered on the desolate tract I have mentioned. The hot night wind still sighed over the waste, and through the thorny bushes by which it was thinly covered. No sound broke the silence, save a shrill neigh from one of our baggage ponies at intervals, or the wild and melancholy note of the plover as it piped its song to its mate, and was answered again from afar. Once or twice the half shriek, half howl of a hyæna might be heard, and so like was the cry to that of a wretch under the knife of an assassin, that my blood curdled in my veins as the sound thrilled through me. I rode on, first of the party, eagerly looking for the Belha, who should give me the welcome intelligence that the grave was ready, and that we were secure from interruption; nor had I long to wait for this. At a turning in the road I saw the trusty messenger seated; and as he espied me and arose, I hastened to meet him.

'Bhil manjeh?' I asked in our slang lanuage.

'Manjeh,' was the reply: "tis ready Meer Sahib.'

'And how far, Gopal?'

'Scarcely a cannon-shot from hence, a dry nullah with a sandy bed crosses the road; and a tributary streamlet's course, between high and narrow banks, was the best place we could find.'

'Good,' said I, 'you are always careful; now keep near me, and hold my horse when I dismount: I have a share in this affair which I would not trust to another.'

I slackened my horse's pace, and the party soon overtook me. I stopped as they came up, and dismounted.

'A plague on these roads of yours, Khan,' said I to my acquaintance; 'my horse has lost a shoe, and his foot is somewhat tender; so I will walk a coss or two to ease him of my weight. Surely there cannot be much more of this stony track.'

'Not much; a coss or two perhaps; we ought to be near a dry nullah, if I am not mistaken, and from thence the next village is a coss and a half; after that the road is good.'

'Let the Meer Sahib ride on my tattoo,' said a voice like music: 'I am cramped and stiff, and shall be glad to walk awhile.'

It was that of my victim! she who was to die under my hand ere a quarter of an hour elapsed.

'No, no, Khan,' said I, 'that must not be; I am soldier enough to walk when I have no horse. Mashallah! my limbs are strong and supple, and I would not mind trying you at a long stage.'

'As you will, Meer Sahib, but you have only to say the word, and she dismounts. Allah knows 'tis a small recompense for your safe protection over this dreary tract, which never man yet passed but with fear and apprehension. The nullah too, we shall reach it soon—they say many a brave fellow's blood has moistened its sand.'

I saw the woman shudder at her husband's speech and I checked him.

'Shame on you, Khan!' said I; 'think who hears you: women's ears not fitted to listen to tales of blood, save when they are of a battlefield, and of scenes in which honour is gained and fame won at the sword's point. Here you are safe; no rascally Dacoo would dare to meddle with a kafila like ours, and we shall pass the nullah as we have those behind us, without a thought of its dangers or what has happened in it. But what was that?' I eagerly asked, as something crossed our path close to my feet.

'Nothing, but a hare,' said the Khan; 'some prowling jackel has scared her from her form, and she seeks another hiding-place.'

'A hare!' I repeated, the current of my blood seeming to be suddenly arrested, as I thought on the fearful omen to a Thug—one that could not be disregarded, or, if disregarded, was certain to be followed by the most dire calamities, nothing less than death or long imprisonment.

'Yes, Meer Sahib, a hare: what of it?'

'Nothing,' replied I; 'nothing—we have an old superstition about it in my country—but 'tis an old woman's tale, I dare say.'

I paced on in silence. Ya Allah! what a conflict was raging in my heart! I have told you I disregarded omens: I cared not for them, only as they were the soul of Thuggee as far as my men were concerned; and to humour them I feigned to be particular in their observance. But my soul quailed when I was put to the proof. Every tale I had heard of the vengeance of Bhowani at a conscious neglect of her commands and omens flashed in rapid succession across my mind—how one had died, eaten by worms;

another been overtaken by what the world called justice; how another had lost his wife or children—and I too had yet a child! I say I quailed in mental terror for awhile; but mine was a stout heart, a noble spirit; and it roused at my call. Away with such idle tales, fit only to be bugbears to children! said I mentally; Ameer Ali is not to be frightened by them. And to lose the charm —the object of my anxiety, when almost within my grasp! I laughed aloud.

'You are merry, Meer Sahib,' cried Laloo, who I saw was at his place; 'tell us your thoughts, that we may laugh too; and by Allah! we need it, for a more unsainted country I never saw.'

''Twas but a thought,' said I. 'Know you where my hookah is?'

'I do not,' he replied, 'but I will call for it.' And the word was passed by those who followed us for it to be brought.

This was the preparatory signal. Every one heard it and took his post. The place could not be far, and with my last words had passed away every chance of life to our companions.

Nor was it far off; a few moments' walking brought us to the brink of the nullah. I first descended into it, and disengaged my rumal. I was ready; one by one the others followed me, and we were now in the middle of the dry and sandy bed, mingled together, the victims and their destroyers. I saw the time was come, and I gave the jhirnee.

They fell—ay all! and almost at the same time. There was no sound, no cry; all that I heard was a faint gurgling noise from the husband of the woman, who had writhed in her death-agony under my fatal gripe; a few convulsive throes and she was dead! I tore away the bodice which covered her bosom; I thrust my hands into it, and groped upon the still warm breast for the prize I had so earnestly longed for. I found it tied to a silk cord— which defied my utmost efforts to break; but I unsheathed my dagger and cut it, and I hugged the treasure to my heart in a frenzy of exultation. One look at the face, thought I, and the lughas may do their work; and I gazed on it. It was beautiful, very beautiful; but the expression and the eyes—Sahib! why did I look at it? I might have spared myself years of torment had I not done so. That face, of all that I have ever seen in death, haunts me still, and will ever haunt me, sleeping or waking.

Not that it had any particular effect on me then. No, it was afterwards, as you shall hear, and when I had discovered what I had done. Yes, she was beautiful, fair as my own Azima, as delicate and faultless in form. The lughas shall not behold these beauties, thought I, nor could I listen to their coarse remarks; so I covered up the bosom, folded the body decently in the sheet which had been around her, and sat down by it to await their coming.

'How, Jemadar Sahib!' said Gopal, as he came up to me, 'have you not stripped the body? But let me do so; yonder sheet is worth two rupees.'

'Let it alone!' cried I; 'touch her not; she is too fair for the like of you to look on. And hark ye, my friend, let her be buried as you see her now. Whatever the others may say, tell them that it is my order; and for your own share, you shall have a new sheet when we reach Jhalone.'

I went with him to where the grave had been dug, between the high and narrow banks of a small watercourse; it was deep, and already contained some bodies. I saw that of the fair girl laid carefully down over them, and I prevented their mutilating it with their knives as they had done the others. I waited till all had been finished, and the grave covered in; and collecting my scattered party we pursued our journey. It was well we had been so expeditious, for scarcely half a coss from the spot we met a large party of travellers, who, confident in their numbers, had pushed on by night as we had done. Short greetings were exchanged between us, a few inquiries as to the road, whether water was to be had, and where, and we passed on.

Our booty was small enough, as you may conceive: about forty rupees, a few changes of raiment, the tattoo of the deceased, and the few and simple ornaments of the women, worth perhaps a hundred rupees, were all we got. But I had the real prize, worth in my eyes thousands of rupees. No one knew I had it, and I kept it hung round my own neck, and close to my heart. A thousand times I took it out and gazed at it; there was something about it which had a mysterious effect on me: many times I thought I had seen it before, and I fancied its old and battered surface was familiar to me. But my mind gave me no clue to the idea and I attributed the effect I have described to the influence of the charm itself, and I was assured of its potency. How Azima will prize it! thought I—in itself valueless, yet a treasure in her eyes and mine, for it will protect our child, and many an envious eye is upon her.

We were still far from Jhalone, and the season admitted of further wanderings; but I was sated. Strange to say, I no longer thirsted for adventure; and though it came, and men were delivered into our hands, yet I sought not for them. Those we destroyed were casual travellers who joined our party, and whose destruction was unavoidable.

CHAPTER XXXIV

Now therefore we had no inducements to tarry away from our homes; we needed no fresh adventure to enrich us, and we pushed on to Jhalone. We reached it in safety, and again I clasped Azima to my heart, and rejoiced to see that my child was well, and with a girl's eagerness looking forward to the time when her marriage ceremony was to take place. My father too was well, and had reached Jhalone without any adventure worth recording, so at least he told me.

Months passed at my home without care and in peace. Alas! now that I think on it, I can only compare the course of that time to the gentle stream of a river, which as it winds among peaceful scenes and between green and flowery banks, ruffled only by the soft winds playing over its bosom, is suddenly arrested, dashed among rocks, and its current changed to turmoil and furious contention with its stony opposers. I saw no mark of my future lot, no warning was given to me; destruction came upon me in one fell swoop, and I was overwhelmed—I and mine! But for that stroke of fortune I had lived till now an honest and gentle life, for I abandoned Thuggee; and the more I experienced of the soothing pleasures of my home, the more I became estranged from my habits of wandering and of plunder and destruction. Nor was the least urgent reason in the meditated change of my life, that I dreaded every day more and more that some unlucky chance would reveal to Azima the dreadful trade I followed. I could paint to myself the effect it would have on her loving and gentle disposition, and the prostration of every faculty of her existence, under the shock of knowing that I was a murderer; and often, as she lay upon my heart in the dead of night, these thoughts have come so thick on me, that, could her soul have held any mysterious communion with mine, she would have recoiled in horror from my embrace and fled from me for ever. And these fancies recurred so frequently and forcibly that sometimes I almost thought them a warning of coming evil, and I had fully determined to remove my abode and my wealth to Delhi after my daughter's marriage, there to reside for the remainder of the days which might be allotted to me.

I have said months passed without incident; I should have mentioned that an English gentleman some time after my arrival came to Jhalone; and in the many conferences he held in secret with the Rajah, we were given to understand that a treaty of some kind or other had been made, and that he had placed himself under the protection of the English Government. I thought not of it; yet even then a system was working silently yet surely which for a time struck at the power and confederacy of the Thugs—a blow as severe, nay more so, as being more lasting, than they had yet experienced.

The Englishman had left Jhalone some time, and his visit was nearly forgotten by us; my daughter's marriage had begun, and everything was rejoicing in my house. About noon one day one of the Rajah's hurkaras came with a message that he required my presence and my father's in the Durbar on particular business. In vain was it that I excused myself on the plea of the marriage ceremony. The messanger would take no excuse; and at last, seeing no alternative, we girded our loins and accompanied the hurkara.

We were ushered through the various courts to the Dewan Khana, where the Rajah sat in Durbar, surrounded by his mutsuddees and soldiers. Leaving our shoes at the entrance, we were as usual advancing towards his Guddee to make the customary salutations, when a sudden rush was made upon us from both sides of the hall, and we were at once seized and disarmed. In vain I struggled with my captors, in vain I attempted to shake them off by the most strenuous exertions: it was useless; I was surrounded and overpowered, my turban was torn rudely from my head, and my arms were bound so tightly with it that I thought the blood would have burst from under my nails. I desisted at last, and remained passive in the hands of the soldiers. Seeing me quiet, the Rajah addressed me.

'Ah, Ameer Ali,' said he; 'what is this I hear of thee, that thou art a Thug, a common murderer? Can this be true of one who was looked up to in Jhalone as a merchant and a respectable man? What hast thou to say? Speak, man, and prove if thou canst to me that the accusations I hear against thee are false.'

'Rajah,' said I, 'I know not who hath poisoned thy mind against me or mine; is there any one in your city who can speak one word against me? Have I not been fair and honourable in my dealings with all, and with thyself too? Have not I managed villages and brought them to prosperity from desolation; and can any one, young or old, in this Durbar say that I have ever wronged him, or defrauded him of a fraction? Rajah, none can say this; and therefore why am I and my old father thus disgraced in the eyes of the city, and torn from our houses in the midst of the rejoicings of marriage?'

'*I* accuse thee not,' said the Rajah, 'Bhugwan alone knows whether what I hear is the truth or not; but witnesses are many against thee and the old man; let them speak, and we will afterwards decide in your case. Bring them forth!' cried he to an attendant; 'one by one let them give their evidence before these unhappy men—we desire no secrecy.'

There was a moment's pause in the assembly, and every eye—a hundred eyes—were upon us. I looked to my father, to see the effect this situation had on him; but I read no hope in the glance he threw on me; his energy had deserted him, and he looked like a convicted felon long before he was so in reality; he returned my anxious and meaning glances by a stare of stupid apathy or extreme fear—I know not which; and it was pitiable to behold him, for his venerable and respectable appearance but ill assorted with the disgraceful situation he was in. I turned away from him to look at the man who entered, and then I felt that my doom was sealed. I have never mentioned him, but he had been connected with our gang from the first as a tilha, or scout, and had afterwards assisted as a bhuttote on many occasions. His name was Sooruj; he had accompanied me on all my first expeditions, and knew every particular of my career, and, until I became a Pindari, described every event with minuteness and fidelity. He offered to point out the spots upon which travellers had been destroyed, declared the amount of booty we had gained on many occasions, and ended by denouncing both my father and myself as the greatest leaders in Bundelkhund, and as cruel and remorseless Thugs: He dared me to disprove his words, and indeed I quailed under his accusations; for they were true, and truth searches the heart and overwhelms the guilty. But against my father he was the most bitter. 'Look on him, Rajah!' cried he; 'look on this hoary wretch; one would think that, old as he is, he would have ceased to deprive his fellow-creatures of life; that he would have spent the remainder of his days in propitiating Bhowani by sacrifices, and his own Prophet by prayers! yet it has not been so. Within these two months he has returned from an expedition laden with spoil, and the last man he strangled was one of thine own subjects, O Rajah!—one who was respected and beloved here, and whose bereaved family will rue this day that I have declared his fate in your Durbar.'

'One of my subjects!' cried the Rajah; 'thou canst not mean it. Speak! and let not fear prevent your disclosing the truth.

'Fear! Rajah, I know it not. If I feared him, that old man, should I have dared to speak as I have done? Listen; you knew Jeswunt Mul, one of the most respectable of the shroffs of Jhalone?'

'Knew him, O messenger of ill-tidings! Jeswunt Mull is not dead?'

'Ask *him,*' said the man hoarsely; 'or stay, ask the other man you have here; let him be brought forward, he will tell the tale; I saw it not. But Jeswunt Mul will never speak more, and let those who believe the good man safe at Saugor shave their mustachios and mourn, for he will never more be seen. Yes, he is dead, and *that* old man looked on while he writhed out his last agony under the rumal of the bhuttote.' And he pointed at my father, while he regarded him with a look of grim and revengeful pleasure.

There was a general shudder through the assembly, as the deep tones of the informer's voice fell on the ears of those who heard it; and 'Jeswunt Mul dead!' was repeated by many in an incredulous tone as they drew into knots and whispered together. Nor was the Rajah himself least struck by the melancholy information. He sat on his musnud in silence, though it could be seen by the working of his features how much he was affected. But he aroused himself at last.

'Thou didst not then see this murder?' said he to the informer.

'I did not, Maha Rajah; but send for Bodhee, he will relate the particulars.'

Bodhee! thought I, then there is indeed no hope. Until his name was mentioned, I had a faint idea that the accusation might be a fabricated one; especially as I had heard nothing of the sahoukar's fate from my father: but Bodhee had been with him, and he was the chief of the lughas, and it was more than probable that he had dug the grave for the victim.

'Let Bodhee be brought forward!' cried the Rajah.

He came; his fetters clanked as he moved, and it was not until he had advanced into the midst of the Durbar that he beheld my father and myself bound as criminals. The sight staggered him, and well it might; he had been trusted by us, raised to the rank he held by my father, and ever treated by him as a son, though he was of a different faith to ours. His face was convulsed by his emotions—they might have been those of a faithful heart struggling against ingratitude; and I looked with a breathless anxiety to the first words which should fall from him. But before he spoke the Rajah addressed him.

'Miserable wretch!' said he, 'your life has been spared on the condition that you speak the truth, and reveal, without reservation of a single circumstance, every deed of murder you have been engaged in: this has been promised you by the English, and you have now to prove that you will perform your engagement. If you do perform it—well; if not, though the English are your protectors, I swear to you that you shall be dragged to death by my elephants ere a ghurree of time has passed over you. Bid the elephant be brought!' cried he to an attendant, 'and see that the chains are ready: by Gunga! there will be work for him ere long. And now,' continued he to the approver, 'knowest thou aught of the death of Jeswunt Mul of this town—he who used to manage my private affairs, or if he indeed be dead? Speak, and remember that truth alone can save you.'

There was a breathless silence; my father gazed at the informer with an intense anxiety; it was evident to me that he thought one word from him would seal his fate for ever, or that, should he deny the deed, he would escape. Earnestly, imploringly he looked at him, and the informer was well nigh overcome; he trembled in every limb, and the big drops of sweat stood out on his face, while the veins of his forehead swelled almost to bursting.

'Speak, Bodhee!' said my father in a hollow voice—yet still he smiled—'speak, and tell the Rajah that his poor servant Ismail is not guilty of this deed.'

'Silence!' exclaimed the Rajah; 'gag him if he attempts to utter a word to influence the informer; we will do justice in this matter; and you, Meer Sahib (turning to a respectable-looking person who was seated near him) you shall be able to tell the Sahib-logue that justice can be done in the Durbar of Jhalone. Bring up the elephant!' he cried to the attendants; 'and do you, Bodhee, look your last on the earth and sky, for by Gunga I swear thou art nigh to death if thou deceivest me. I read it in thy face that this matter is known to thee.'

But still Bodhee hesitated: there was evidently a struggle within him whether he should die in defence of his old protector, or betray him to save his own life. For a moment the former feeling prevailed; he turned to the Rajah, and said distinctly and firmly, 'May I be your sacrifice, Maha Rajah! I know nothing of this matter: of other murders I can tell you, but I know naught of this.'

'He lies!' said the other approver; 'he was with Ismail Jemadar; he is afraid to speak out, and has lied to you, O Prince.'

'You hear him,' cried the Rajah to Bodhee; 'you hear what your fellow Thug says; yet, much as you have deserved death, I give you a few moments more: the shadow of the verandah is now close on my musnud—till it reaches it thou shalt live—beyond it, one finger's breadth, and you die!'

There was not an eye in the crowd that was not fixed on the advancing shadow; barely a hand's breadth of light remained, and the Thug gazed on it as though he were fascinated by the eye of a tiger. My father! oh he was fearful to look on; his eyes were glazed—his lips were tightened across his teeth—fear, agony was depicted in his countenance in stronger lines than I had ever before seen. I could not look on him—his face was altered, and his usual bland expression had been usurped by that I have described. I felt sick, I could have died I thought; and would that I *had* died, to have been spared what followed!

'Fool!' cried the other approver, 'will you sacrifice your life for those who will be instantly put to death?' He spoke in Ramasi.

The words rallied the man to whom he addressed them, and they saved him.

'Pardon, pardon!' he cried; 'O mighty Prince, I have told lies.

Jeswunt Mul is indeed dead; these hands dug his grave and bore his yet warm body to it.'

'Ai Bhugwan! Ai Seeta-ram!' cried the Rajah, 'and is it even so? My poor friend, and art thou dead?' and for a moment or two he wept. 'This is womanly,' said he, rallying himself. 'Proceed, O kumbukht! let me know all, and what share *he* had in it.'

'We met the sahoukar at ———,' said the Thug. 'Ismail well knew that if we were all seen by him he would suspect us, so he sent the greater part of the band out of the village, and prevailed upon Jeswunt Mul to come and sleep in our camp, instead of remaining where he was; he went to the village and brought him away himself, else he would not have come. The grave was dug long before he arrived, and he had not been an hour with us after the sun had set, when he was strangled in the Jemadar's presence by two bhuttotes, and his two servants shared the same fate. I buried them all. The sahoukar's pony we sold the next day for twenty-five rupees; and we got but little else, for he had no money but in hoondees, which we burned.'

'Enough, enough!' said the Rajah; 'this is ample proof.'

'Nay, if your greatness requires more proof, I can give you some now,' continued the approver: 'look at the Jemadar's hand; he wears on it a ring he took from the body himself, and it may be recognised even by you, Maha Rajah.'

My heart sunk within me at this new and desperate stroke of fortune. I saw the ring torn from my father's finger; all examined it: a sahoukar who was in the assembly declared it to have belonged to Jeswunt Mul, and, more than all, his name was engraven on its inner surface.

'Enough!' again cried the Rajah, 'I know it myself; I could have sworn to that diamond among a thousand. Away with him! chain him to the elephant, let him be dragged through the town, and proclamation made that he was a Thug.'

'Stay,' cried the Syud, who had not as yet spoken, 'he may have something to urge in his defence; ask him and hear him.'

'Speak!' cried the Rajah to my miserable father; 'speak, O kumbukht!'

And then my father's proud spirit broke out. With the certainty of death before his eyes he quailed not. While hope remained for life, he had clung to it as every man will; and when I had expected a grovelling entreaty for his life to be spared, from his previous demeanour, he asked it not, but gloried in the cause for which he died.

'Yes,' said he drawing himself, up, while his eye glistened proudly. 'I scorn to die with a lie upon my lips. I killed Jeswunt Mul because he was a villain, as you are, Rajah! Because he employed Thugs, and would not reward them, but wrung from them every rupee he could, as you do. I have murdered hundreds of men because they were given into my hands by Allah, but I never destroyed one with the satisfaction I did your friend. Ay, you were friends and brothers in guilt, and you know it. My life! I care not for it. What has an old man to do with life? His enjoyments are gone, his existence is a burthen to him. A short time and nature would have claimed me; you have anticipated the period. Yet, O Rajah, Bhowani will question you for this deed—for the destruction of her votary. By blood be on your head, and the curse of a dying man be with you! You have deceived me, robbed me, shared my spoils, taken the produce of murder—nay, be not impatient, you know it is the truth, and that Allah, who is the judge of all, knows it also. He will cast your portion in Jehanum, as a kafir; and Bhowani will rejoice that the destroyer of her votary writhes in the torments of the damned.'

'Gag him! strike the kafir's mouth with a shoe!' roared the Rajah in a fury, more like that of a beast than a man, as he foamed at the mouth; 'away with him! and let his son look on his dying agony.'

And they dragged us both forth; I should not say my father, for his step was firm. I struggled against my tormentors, but it availed me not. 'One word, my father!' cried I to him as we were brought near each other; 'wilt thou not speak to thy son?'

He turned his head, and a tear stood in his eye. 'I leave thee, Ameer Ali; but thou knowest a believer's Paradise, and the joys which await him—the seventy virgins and everlasting youth. Thou are not my son, but I have loved thee as one, and may Allah keep thee!'

'No more!' cried the rough soldiers, striking him on the mouth, and dragging him forward.

'Revenge me!' exclaimed my father in Ramasi; 'tell the English of that monster's conduct to us, and when he is torn from his seat of pride, my soul will be happy in Paradise.'

He spoke no more; I was held forcibly, so that I saw the end of that butchery. They secured him by a chain round his loins to the fore-foot of the elephant, and they tied his hands behind him, so that he could not save himself by clinging to it. He still continued repeating the Kulma; but now all was ready—the Mahout drove his ankoos into the head of the noble beast, which uttering a loud scream dashed forward. A few steps, and my father's soul must have been in Paradise!

Note.—The Rajah of Jhalone died from an inveterate leprosy, which all Thugs declare to have broken out soon after the death of the Thug in the manner described, and that it was a judgement upon him sent by Bhowani.

CHAPTER XXXV

SAHIB, can I describe to you the passions which then burned in my heart? I cannot. A thousand thoughts whirled through my brain, till I thought myself mad; perhaps I was. Revenge for my father was uppermost; and oh that I could have got loose: by Allah! unarmed as I was, methinks I could have sprung on the Rajah and strangled him. But resistance was unavailing; the more I struggled, the tighter my arms were bound, until they swelled so that the pain became excruciating, and I was well nigh sunk under it. I suffered my guards to lead me away from the Durbar: I was thrust into a vile hole, and at last my arms were bound.

That day—Allah, how it passed! Men gazed at me in my cage as though I had been a tiger, and mocked and derided me. The boys of the town hooted me, and thrust sticks at me through the iron gratings. One and all reviled me in the most opprobious terms they could devise—me! the respectable, nay the wealthy, to whom they had bowed before me, when I basked in the sunshine of the Rajah's favour—but I was degraded now. Alas! my dreams my forebodings had come to pass—they had been indefinite shadows—this was the reality. Allah! Allah! I raved, I called upon Azima's name, I implored those who still lingered about my prison to fly and bring me news of her, and to comfort her; and I cursed them when they derided me, and mocked my cries. Azima, the name that might not have been breathed by mortal out of the precincts of my zenana, became a word in the mouths of the rabble, and they jested on it, they loaded it with obscene abuse, and I heard it all. In vain I strove to stop my ears—it provoked them the more; they shouted it close to the iron bars, and spat at me. Night came, and I was left in my loneliness. I should have been in her fond embrace—now I shared the company of the rat, the lizard, and the scorpion. It was in vain that I courted sleep, to steep my senses in a temporary oblivion of their misery, my frame was too strong, and my anguish too great, for it to come to me. I wrestled with my agony, but I overcame it not, and I had to drink the bitter cup to the dregs. At last the morning broke; I performed the Namaz: the dust of the floor served me instead of sand or water for my ablutions. Water I had none; I had begged for it, for my mouth was parched and dry with anxiety yet no one gave it. Again the court was filled; old and young, women and children, all come to look at the Syud—to look at Ameer Ali the Thug—to deride him, and torment him!

But I was now sullen; like a tiger, when his first rage, after he has been entrapped, has subsided, I cowered into the corner of my cell, and covered my face with my waistband, nor heeded their savage unfeeling mirth, nor the bitter words they poured out against me. In vain was it that I now and then looked around to see whether one kind pitying glance rested on me. Alas! not one; every face was familiar to me, but the eyes never spoke a brutal satisfaction at my sufferings, or turned on me with the cold leaden stare of indifference. I tried to speak several times, but every murmur was hailed with shouts from the rabble before me, and my throat was parched and my tongue swelled from raging thirst.

The whole day passed—I had no food, no water. It was in the height of the burning season, and I who had been pampered with luxuries, who in my own abode should have drunk of refreshing sherbets, prepared by Azima, was denied a drop of water to cool my burning throat. In vain I implored those nearest to me, in words that would have moved aught but hearts of stone, to intercede with the Jemadar who guarded my prison to allow me a draught of the pure element. I might as well have spoken to the scorching blast that whistled into my cage, bringing with it clouds of dust, which were increased by the unfeeling boys when they saw I shrank from them. Thus the day passed: evening came, and still no water, no relief, no inquiry into my condition. Had I been placed there to die? And no sooner had the thought flashed across my mind than I brooded over it. Yes, I was to die! to expire of thirst and hunger; and then, oh how I envied my father's fate! his was a quick transition from the sorrows and suffering he had undergone during one short hour, to Paradise and the houris.

And from evening, night. I had watched the declining sun, till its last fiery and scorching beams fell no longer on my prison-floor —I watched the reddened west until no glare remained, and one by one the stars shone out dimly through the thick and heated air—and I thought I should see the blessed day no more, for I was sick and exhausted even to death. I lay me down and moaned, in my agony of spirit and of body, and at last sleep came to my relief. For a time all was oblivion; but horrible dreams began to crowd my prison with unsightly shapes and harrowing visions; my life passed as though in review before me, and the features of many I had strangled rose up in fierce mockery against me—faces with protruding tongues and eyes even as I had left them strangled.

Why describe them to you, Sahib? Why detain you with a description of the horrors of the scenes which rose to my distempered fancy, and at last woke me, burning as though a fire raged in my bowels and would not be quenched? But morning broke at last, and the cool air once more played over my heated and fevered frame, and refreshed me. Yet I was still in agony;—who can describe the sufferings of thirst? Hunger I felt not; thirst consumed me, and dried up my bowels. How anxiously and impatiently I looked for the first man who should enter the court where my prison was! One came, he passed through and heeded not my piteous cries: another and another; none looked on me, and again I thought I was to die. Another came; I called, and he turned to regard me. He was one that I knew, one who had eaten of my bread and my salt, and had been employed about my house, and he had pity; he had a remembrance of what I had done for him: he came, and looked on me. I spoke to him, and he started, for my voice was hollow, and thin and hoarse. 'Water!' cried I, 'for the sake of the blessed Prophet, for the sake of your mother, one drop of water! I have tasted none since I was confined.'

'Alas!' said he in a low tone, 'how can it be, Meer Sahib? The Rajah has threatened any one with death who speaks to you or brings you food.'

Again I implored; and I who had been his master, prostrated myself on the ground and rubbed my forehead in the dust. He was moved—he had pity and went to fetch some; fortunately no one saw him and he brought a small earthen pot full, which I drank as though it had been that of the well of Paradise. Again and again he took it and refilled it; and last he left me, but not before he had promised to visit me in the night, bring me a cake of bread if he could, and, more than all, news of Azima and of my house.

The next day passed, and I had no food. I treasured up the water which had been left with me, and sipped it now and then; but by nightfall again I was in torment. Yet I had hopes, for I knew that the young man would not deceive me; he had sworn by his mother's head to bring me food, and he could not break his oath.

And he came. I had sat watching, with that anxiety which can only be known by those who have been in a situation like mine, listening to every distant footfall, to every noise, as though it were the step of him I looked for. I have said he came; he was muffled in a blanket, and had stolen in unobserved by the lazy sentinel at the gate; he brought me food, and a few coarse cakes, and an earthenware pot of milk. 'Eat!' said he in a low tone; 'I will sit here, and will tell you the news you bade me inquire for afterwards.' I was ravenous, and I ate; coarse bread, such as I should have loathed three days before, was now a luxury, sweet and grateful; I ate it, drank the milk, and was thankful; and I called him and blessed him for his venturous daring, and for his gratitude to one who could no longer do him a kind turn. 'And the news, Gholam Nubbee? can you tell me aught of *her* and my child?'

'My news is bad, Meer Sahib, and I am the unwilling messenger of tidings which will grieve your soul and add to your misery.'

'Say on,' said I: 'tell me the worst; tell me she is dead, and you will only say what my soul has forewarned me of.'

He paused for awhile. 'You must know it sooner or later, Meer Sahib—she is dead.'

'And my child?'

'She is with the good mullah who protected your wife when she had no longer a house to cover her, and who performed the last rites of our faith to her when she was dead.'

'No home!' cried I; 'they did not drive her forth?'

'They did, Meer Sahib. The Rajah sent soldiers, your house was stript of everything, and your gold and silver, they say, was a prize he little expected; your wife and child were turned into the street, with only the clothes they had upon their persons. But to her it little mattered, for I have heard she never spoke from the time she knew of your father's fate and the cause of your imprisonment. They say she sat in stupor, like a breathing corpse, without speaking a word to say where her pain was.'

'Enough!' said I, 'go; may Allah keep you! I would now be alone, for grief sits heavy on me.'

Then she was dead—my Azima, my beloved!—she for whom I had loved as a man can only love once—she was dead; she had known that I was a Thug, and that had killed her. It was well—better far that she should have died, than lingered on to be scoffed at and insulted as the wife of one who was now a convicted murderer. Had she lived I could never have dared to approach her, for she was pure, and I—!

I may say I almost rejoiced at her death, Sahib; I did not grieve as I should have done had the blow fallen on me while I was yet in prosperity—then it would have been hard indeed to bear; but now I was altered, and she was dead, and again I say it was well. Allah in his mercy had taken her from her scene of suffering, almost before she knew to its full extent the horrible reality. And my child too was safe; she was in friendly hands, and the mullah would be a father to her.

The day after the nocturnal visit of my humble friend, food was allowed me; it was scanty to be sure, but still I existed though worn down by sufferings, which I have no words to express, to a shadow of what I was. Three months passed thus, and they appeared to me like years when I looked back on them.

At the end of this time I was taken to the Rajah's Durbar. Few were the words he spoke to me, but those were bitter ones; for he had shared my spoil, taxed me for protection, and, after putting my father to death, he had plundered my home, and his booty was the accumulation of mine for years past. I say my father, and yet he had told me he was not my parent. But what mattered that now? He was dead, and the mystery of my birth, if any had ever existed, was gone with him. What mattered it too who was my father? I was alone in the world; not a tie, save one, bound me to existence. My daughter was with strangers, and in a few years she would forget me—truly I might say I was alone.

I was in the Rajah's Durbar—I had no friend; no one of all those by whom he was surrounded, who had formerly courted me, eaten of my bread, and flattered me that I was yet to rise to greatness under his patronage—not one spoke for me, not one interceded to avert my shame. The Rajah spoke to me.

'Ameer Ali,' said he, 'I had trusted thee, I had thought thee honest (how he lied as he spoke!), I had believed thee a rich and fortunate merchant; but, O man! thou hast deceived me—not me alone, but thousands—thou art a Thug and a murderer. Still, because I have a lingering sentiment of kindness towards thee, I do not seek thy death; justice has been satisfied in the destruction of the hoary villain who made thee what thou art, a wretch upon whose head is the blood of hundreds. Yes, Ameer Ali, I speak truth, and thou knowest it; but though I desire not thy death, yet thou canst not be released without a mark on thy brow that men may know and beware of. Throw him down,' cried he to the attendants, 'and let him be branded!'

They threw me down. Sahib, what could my attenuated and wasted frame do against men who had suffered no misery like mine? I struggled, yet it was unavailing; they held my arms, and legs, and head, and a red-hot pice was pressed upon my forehead; it was held there as it burnt down to the bone, ay my very brain seemed to be scorched and withered by the burning copper. They took it off, and raised me up. Allah! Allah! the agony that I endured—the agony of pain, and, more than that, of shame—to be branded publicly that the world might think me a thief—to have a mark set on my forehead that I must carry to my grave— a mark only set on the vile and on the outcasts from society—Sahib, it was bitter cup to quaff!

'Away with him!' cried the Rajah. 'Release him at the boundary of my territory. And mark me,' he continued, addressing himself to me, 'I have given thee thy life, Ameer Ali; go and be wise; learn by what has happened to be an honest man for the future; and remember, that if ever thou art seen in Jhalone again, or in any of my towns or villages, nothing will be able to save thee from the feet of an elephant.'

He rose and strode out of the Durbar; and in pain and misery, I was conducted in two days to the frontier of his country and unbound. Two rupees were given to me, and again the wide and cruel world was before me. I hurried from my late keepers. I bound my turban over my still burning and aching brow, so that man might not see my shame, and took the road before me. I wandered almost unconscious of anything, save the pain I was suffering, until night fell around me, and I directed my steps to a village, the lights of which were a short distance before me. Exchanging one of my rupees, I sat down at the shop of a bhutteara, and satisfied my craving appetite; there I slept, and when I arose I was refreshed, and again believed myself to be Ameer Ali.

The morning breeze blew fresh on my face as I took my way out of the town; the refreshing rest of the night had invigorated me, and I bounded along with a light heart—yes, with a light heart—for I was free! I had no thought for the past now. It was my fate which had been fulfilled: what had been written in my destiny had come to pass. As I proceeded, a jackass brayed on my right hand, and I hailed the favourable omen with a joy I can feebly express. Yes, great Bhowani, mother of men! cried I aloud, I answer to thy omen; I am ready, and again devoted to thy service. I have sinned against thee; I had wilfully avoided thy warning omens, led me on by an irresistible destiny and by a proud heart. I have been punished, and have bought a dear experience; but henceforward no votary of thine breeding shall excel Ameer Ali in devotion to thee; and therefore, great goddess, vouchsafe the thibao and pilhao. And they were granted; the omen on the right was followed by that on the left, and I felt that I was pardoned, and again accepted as a Thug.

And so you believe, Ameer Ali, said I, that your not observing the omens in the instances you related was the cause of your father's death and your misfortunes?

Assuredly, Sahib; I was a sceptic till then, as I have told you, but I was now no longer one; had I not cause to believe in the truth of the omens? and, had I obeyed them then, should I have the heavy crime I had committed still rooted in my heart? No, no! omens cannot, dare not be disobeyed; and I have never known an instance in which they were, or where a band has been led to destroy a person against the wishes of Bhowani, that they were not all punished by her vengeance, either with domestic misfortune, imprisonment or death. Ask any Thug you know, and he will tell you the same. I never doubted omens afterwards, and have allowed some rich prizes to escape me, fearing they were not completely propitious.

Well, Sahib, to continue. I pressed forward; I again untied my rumal, for that had never quitted my waist, and I welcomed it to my grasp as I should have done the embrace of an old and valued friend. With such omens, thought I, I cannot be unsuccessful; and over any single traveller, where he Rustam himself, I can gain a victory. I had but one rupee and some pice; my clothes were in rags about me, and I must have others before I could venture to associate myself with Thugs, and hope to lead them.

But I travelled long, and met no person alone; and when noon came, and the sun's heat had overcome me, I lay down under a tree by the roadside, near which was a well; and having washed and bathed and said the Namaz, I waited to see what chance would throw in my way. There I sat a long time, but no one passed me, and overcome by fatigue I dropped asleep. I was awakened by a touch from some one, and looking up I beheld a middle-aged Mussulman gazing upon me. I arose rapidly, and returned his

'Salaam Aleikoom' as kindly as he had given it. Fortunately my face remained well wrapt up, and the brand on my forehead could not be seen; he took me to be a traveller like himself, and as he was weary, he sat down and we entered into conversation, such as usually passes between persons situated as we were. After he had been seated for a few minutes, he loosed a small wallet from his shoulder, and opening it displayed some cakes and mango pickle, to which he seemed to be inclined to do ample justice; but seeing that I looked wistfully at them he invited me to join his repast, which I was right glad to do, as I had fasted since the morning. When we had finished our meal, he said to me, 'Meer Sahib, you say there is no water for some coss in the direction I am going; and therefore, if you will kindly watch my clothes and arms, I will bathe in this well.'

'Surely,' I replied; 'I am in no hurry to be gone, and you will not delay me.' As I said it, he began to strip, and taking with him a lotah, he descended the steps of the well, and I soon after heard the splashing of the water as he poured it over himself. Now is my time, thought I; he will be defenceless, and will fall an easy prey; and I prepared my rumal for work.

He soon returned, and began to dress. I loitered near him till I saw him take up his garment and put both arms into the sleeves to draw it over him. It was a capital opportunity, and I closed behind him as if to assist him; he turned to me, and as he had just accomplished his purpose, I had finished mine. The rumal was about his neck, and in a few moments he was dead at my feet! I had no time to lose; so hastily stripping the band from his waist, in which there seemed to be money, I dragged the body to the edge of the well, and threw it in. I then arranged his clothes at the head of the steps, as though he had taken them off to bathe, and left them there; his lotah I left also with them; and taking up his sword and shield, I girded the first to my waist, and the shield to my back, and pursued my way at as quick a pace as I could. No one will imagine he has been murdered, thought I; the clothes on the brink of the well will cause it to be supposed that he died in the water; and I chuckled over my success and strode along joyfully. But, the more to avoid detection, I struck off from the road I was travelling and seeing the groves and white temple of a village at some distance, I bent my steps towards it; there I purchased some goor, and ate the tupounee, as a good Thug ought to do, and after that I opened the humeanah to see what my good fortune had sent me.

And so you murdered the first man who had shown you any kindness after your misfortunes. Oh, Ameer Ali, you are indeed a villain; you ate of his bread and salt, and murdered him! The recompence of a Thug certainly.

But what could I do Sahib? I should have starved most likely had I not killed him. Besides he was the first traveller I met after those good omens; he was neither blind nor lame; assuredly therefore he was bunij. It must have been his fate to die, or I should not have gone to sleep under that tree. Had I met him in the road, I should have hesitated to attack him; indeed unarmed as I was, I dared not have done so. But, as I was saying, I examined the humeanah; I found in it nineteen rupees, a gold nose-ring, and two gold rings for the fingers which were worth at least forty rupees. Ul-humd-ul-illa! I cried, this is rare fortune, here is enough to last me for three months, and to provide me with new clothes; and it will be hard but in that time I find out some of my brethren.

Wandering along the next day, I reached Calpi on the Jumna, and sitting one morning at the shop of a pan seller, some persons stopped at it, and talking among themselves I understood that they were going to Chutterpur. Chutterpur, thought I—what an owl I have been! there must be Thugs there, and I had forgotten it. So I immediately determined if possible to accompany them. I watched them to a bunnia's empty shop, before which, in the street, were tied our tattoos and some bullocks; and without ceremony I told them I had overheard their conversation, that I was also going to the town to which they were journeying, and, if they would allow me and pardon my intrusion, I should be glad to travel in their company, as I was alone, and knew not the road, and was afraid of being robbed.

'Since you are alone, you may come, and welcome,' said the man I addressed. 'But we are going by Bandah, which is not exactly in the direct road to Chutterpur, and our business may detain us there a day or two; if therefore, a delay is of no consequence to you, come with us; you seem to be a soldier, and we are poor merchants who will be glad of your protection.'

Bandah! thought I; another place full of Thugs—at least it used to be. I shall see at any rate, and if I find any, I may then alter my route.

I joined them in the evening, and we reached Bandah in a few days by long marches. Here they declared they would stay four days, so that I had ample time before me to search the place for Thugs, should any reside there. Nor was I disappointed in my hope of meeting them. I was sauntering through the town in the evening of the day we arrived, when I met Hoormut, an old follower of Ganesha; he did not at first recognise me, as may readily be imagined, and when I gave him our token of recognition he stared as though I had been an apparition; however he was soon convinced of my reality, and I accompanied him to his house. The relation of my adventures and mishaps occupied a long time, and after I finished them I naturally asked for an account of my old associate Ganesha. Hoormut declared him to be in misfortune, abandoned by his followers, and that he was wandering with one or two men somewhere in the neighbourhood of Saugor. Next followed questions as to my present plans, and when he heard I was alone and travelling with merchants, it naturally followed that some plan should be undertaken for their destruction.

'Look you, Meer Sahib,' said he, 'I believe I can muster as many as fifteen Thugs, in and near this place. I am not suspected as yet, but the country is getting too hot for us, and we must either quit it or give up Thuggee, which no man, you well know, can do after he has eaten the goor; the others are of the same way of thinking, and we had determined that we would leave this place for good after the rains, and go wherever our fate might lead us.'

We soon afterwards separated for the time, Hoormut promising to collect the men by the next evening. I joined him again by the time appointed, and found the whole assembled. I was received with exultation, for they had wanted a leader in whom they could confide, and mine was a name which, in spite of recent misfortunes, they could look up to. I knew none of them, but they swore on the pickaxe to follow me; Hoormut vouched for their several capabilities and fidelity, and I was satisfied.

Our plan was soon formed: they were to go by two stages to a village they knew, and there wait for my arrival with the merchants. Beyond the village was a favourite bhil of theirs, and they would have everything prepared against our coming up. This being settled, we fixed the next morning (it being Monday and a lucky day) to observe the omens and open the expedition with due form. The omens were declared to be satisfactory, and by noon my new companions had started with their families for their station on the road.

CHAPTER XXXVI

We strangled the merchants at the place we had fixed on, them and their bullock-drivers—nine in all, and yet we were only seventeen Thugs; but we were desperate. In our route we had travelled towards Jhalone, and I could no longer delay my project of proceeding thither, and making over my concealed treasure to the good mullah who had charge of my child. Hoormut volunteered to accompany me; and desiring the remainder of the band to make the best of their way to Calpi, and there to await our arrival, we pushed on to Jhalone.

Considering the risk we ran, in approaching a place where inevitable death awaited me should I be discovered, we did well to disguise ourselves as Gosaeens. We covered our bodies with ashes, matted the hair on our heads with mud, hung gourds at our waist, and in this mean and wretched disguise we entered the town—that spot where I had passed so many years of happiness, where my fairest prospects had been blighted, and the resolutions I had formed of leading a new life and forsaking Thugee rendered alike impracticable and distasteful to me. My emotions on entering the town, and more than all on passing the house where I had resided, were overpowering, but I rallied my heart; I passed through the city, and my friend and myself took up our abode for the day near a well outside the gates which was not far from the spot where I had buried my treasure.

As the evening approached, I strolled towards the trees under which was deposited the sum I had hoarded up to serve me at any time of need. It was a deserted burial-place, overgrown by custard-apple bushes and other brushwood, and the rank grass had sprang up from the frequent rain. My heart beat quick as I approached the spot; my hoard might have been discovered, and if it had been removed my child would be a beggar, dependent upon the charity of strangers; she might even be thrust into the street, to herd with the vile and worthless, when the care of her became irksome or expensive to her present protectors. But, anything, thought I, is better than that she should accompany me, where a life of hardship would be her portion, and where she could not escape the contamination which scenes of guilt and murder would effect in a short time, and from which, alone as I was, I could not protect her.

I reached the tomb in which, by removing a stone, I had placed the vessel containing the money. I hardly dared look at the well-remembered spot, hardly dared attempt to remove the stone; but I did remove it, and, O joy of joys, there was my treasure undisturbed! I hastily seized the earthen vessel, and crawled with it into the thickest of the underwood ere I ventured to open and examine it. I had forgotten what it contained, and the contents surpassed my expectations. I found thirty ashruffees and four small bars of gold, a box containing two strings of pearls of some value and some jewels, and tied up in a rag were some loose stones of value, one of them a diamond of great lustre and beauty. The jewels I determined to keep, as they might be afterwards of use to me, not only from their value, but to enable me to assume the character of a dealer in precious stones, which is always a respectable calling, and for which, in the jewels before me, I had ample stock for trade. I replaced the vessel and its precious contents, which could not have been worth less than a thousand rupees; and I felt my heart lightened of a load, both at seeing my treasure safe, and at the assurance it gave me that by means of it my daughter would be decently provided for. I returned to my companion, who had been anxiously watching my proceedings, and he too rejoiced at my good fortune.

I did not proceed into the town till it was dusk; the gates, I knew, would be open until long after dark, and I went alone to avoid any chance of being remarked. I soon reached the house of the mullah, when, abandoning my character of a Gosaeen, I asked for alms in a lusty voice in the name of Mullah Ali of Hyderabad. Fortunately the old mullah was sitting alone in his verandah; I saw him through the open gate, and advanced rapidly, shutting it behind me. He was engaged in reading his Koran, and was rocking himself to and fro, apparently absorbed in the book before him, so that he did not observe my approach; nor was he aware of my presence till I had prostrated myself before him.

'Punah-i-Khoda!' he exclaimed; 'what is this, a Gosaeen? thou must be mad, good friend: or what seekest thou with the old mullah. Speak, thou has almost frightened me, and disturbed my meditations on the holy volume.'

'Pardon, Mullahji!' I cried; 'you see one before you who has risked his life to speak with you, and you must listen to me for a few moments. I know you well, though you do not recognise me in this disguise.'

'I know thee not, friend,' he said; 'nevertheless, if I can do aught to serve thee, speak; yet it is seldom that the Hindu seeks the house of the priest of the Moslem faith; and I am in astonishment at thy garb and address.'

'Mullah!' I said, 'I would fain speak with thee in absolute secrecy; are we secure from interruption here? Fear me not; I come with good intent, and am not what you think me, but one of thine own faith;' and I repeated the Belief.

'Strange, most strange is this!' said the old man rising; 'I doubt thee not: no one would do the old mullah harm; and so, as thou requirest secrecy, I will but fasten the outer gate and join thee instantly.' He did so, and returned.

'Mullah,' said I, when he was once more seated, and was prying into my face with a look of mingled curiosity and wonder, 'Mullahji! O Wullee Mahomed! dost thou not recognise me?'

'Thy voice is familiar to mine ears,' said the old man, 'yet I remember not thy features. Who art thou?'

'Mine is a name which may hardly be pronounced in Jhalone,' I replied; 'but we are alone. Have you forgotten Ameer Ali?'

'Punah!' exclaimed the mullah, sliding away from me to the edge of his carpet; 'Punah-i-Khoda! do I behold that bad and reckless man?'

'Bad I may be, mullah,' said I quietly, 'and reckless I certainly am; yet I wish thee no harm. You were kind to one I loved —you have my child in your house—it is of them I would speak, not of myself. Tell me, for the sake of Allah, whether my child is well—tell me whether she lives, and I will bless you.' I gasped for breath while he replied, lest I should perchance have to hear of further misfortune.

'This is madness, Ameer Ali,' said he; 'know you not that your father's fate awaits you if you are discovered here?'

'I know, I know all,' said I; 'and I have braved everything. I have sought you despite of my danger—for my heart clove to my child, and I would fain hear of her. Ah, Mullah, think not of what I was, and be merciful to me.'

'Unhappy man!' he cried; 'thy crimes brought with them their own reward; but I will not speak of the past. Know then that thy daughter is well; but she grieves still for thee and for her mother, who Allah in mercy removed from her sufferings before she knew her degradation.'

'Shookhr Khoda!' I exclaimed: 'ah Aallah, thou art merciful even to me. And my child is well, and remembers me?'

'She does, Meer Sahib; she often speaks of you, but we have told her you are dead, and she no longer thinks of you as one whom she may never meet again.'

'And you are right, Mullah,' said I; 'you are wise in having done this. May Allah repay your kindness to a deserted child, for I cannot. I have sought you for a purpose which you must promise to agree to even before I speak it—it is the only request I shall ever make for my child, and from henceforth you will never see my face again, nor hear my name.'

'Speak,' said the mullah; 'I promise nothing, Ameer Ali; thou hast deceived thousands, and the old mullah is no match for thee in deceit.'

'Briefly then,' said I, 'there was a small treasure which I buried in a field here long ago: I have returned and found it safe. It is a trifle, yet it is of no use to me; and I would give it over to you, both as a portion for my daughter when she is married, and as some provision for her until that can be effected.'

'The spoil of the murdered,' said the old man, drawing himself up proudly, 'can never enter the house of the mullah; it would bring a curse with it, and I will have none of it. Keep it yourself, Ameer Ali, and may Allah give you the grace to use it in regaining the honest reputation you have lost.'

'No, no,' cried I; 'the money was my wife's; she had hoarded it up for our child; she brought it with her from the Dukhun, and it has remained as she placed it in the vessel. I swear to you that it is honest money; would I curse my child with the spoil of murders?'

'Swear to me on the Koran that it is, and I will believe you, Ameer Ali, but not else;' and he tendered me the holy book.

I raised it to my lips; I kissed it, and touched my forehead and eyes with it. I swore to what was false—but it was for my child. 'Are you satisfied now?' I asked; 'now that you have humbled me by obliging me to swear?'

'I am,' he replied; 'our trust shall be carefully and religiously kept. Have you the money with you?'

'No,' said I; 'but I will go and return with it instantly. Admit me alone; I will cough at your gate when I arrive.'

I hastened to the spot I have before described; I seized my treasure and returned to the mullah: he was waiting for me at the gate of his house, and we entered it together.

'Here is all I have,' said I pouring out the contents of the vessel on the carpet; 'it is not much, but it is the only portion of my wealth which remains to me.'

'Think not of the past, Meer Sahib; what happened was predestined, and was the will of the All powerful!'

'I have indeed no alternative but to submit, good Mullah. But my time is short, and night advances; ere morning breaks, I must be far away from this, where my associates expect me. One favour I would beg—it is to see my child: one look will be sufficient for my soul to dwell on in after years, for I am assured that it will be the last—you will not deny me?'

'I will not, Meer Sahib; she is now at play with a neighbour's child in the zenana, and if you will follow me I will show her to you. One look must be sufficient for you; after that she is mine, and I will be a father to her. Follow me.'

I did; I followed him through a court-yard to the door of a second, which was the entrance to his zenana. I heard the merry voices of the children, as they played with light and joyful hearts, and I could distinguish the silvery tones of my precious child's voice, so like those of her mother, which were now silent for ever.

'We will not disturb them, Meer Sahib,' said the mullah in a whisper as he pushed open the door gently; 'look in, so that you may not be seen; you will easily distinguish your daughter.'

Yes, she was there, my child, my beautiful child! still delicate and fragile as she had ever been; but her face had a joyous expression, and she was as merry as those by whom she was surrounded. Long, long I gazed, and oh, my heart yearned to rush in, and for the last time to clasp her to my bosom and bless her. But I restrained myself; she would not, could not have recognised me in the disguise I wore, and I should have only needlessly alarmed and terrified her. Yet I put up a fervent prayer to Allah for her protection and happiness, and I tore myself from the spot—dejected, yet satisfied that she still lived and was happy.

'Enough!' said I to the mullah when we regained the outer apartment; 'I now leave you; be kind to my child, and Allah will more than repay you for aught of care and anxiety she may cause you. What I have given you will be ample for a dowry to her in marriage with any person you may select—any one who may be ignorant of her father's shame.'

'I will; and rest assured that wherever you are, whatever your after lot in life may be, you never need give one anxious thought about Meeran; for I again repeat it, if I am now her parent, and she has also found another mother.'

'I believe you,' said I: 'and if ever I am again favoured by fortune, and in a situation to come to you without shame to her, you shall take me to her and present a father to his child: until then you hear not of me again.'

I left him. I had borne up against my feelings. I had struggled against and overcome them as long as I was with him; but as I passed his threshold, the fond love of a parent would not be stifled: I was overcome by bitter grief, and I sat down and wept, for I felt that I had seen my child for the last time—and it was even so; I have never beheld her since, Sahib, nor even been able to get a clue to her fate. May Allah grant she is happy, and knows not of mine. But of this more hereafter.

I wept! Yes, I sat at the threshold of what had been my own home and wept, yet not aloud. My eyes were a fountain of tears, and they welled over their lids, and coursed down my rough visage, and fell hot upon my hands. My memory was busy with the past, that period of bliss when all earthly joy was my portion, and with it wealth and fame. All was gone—gone like the fleeting dream —a mockery, which, gorgeous or blissful as it may be while it possesses the sleeping senses, is broken—even the remembrance of it lost—by awakening to reality. Allah help me! I said in the bitterness of my heart at that moment; I am indeed desolate, and it matters not what becomes of me: I have no hope.

How long I thus sat I know not; but arousing myself by a sudden thought of the danger I was in, I rose up, took one long sad survey of what was once my own, but which was now deserted;

and hurrying away from the spot, I reached the gate as it was about to be shut, and soon afterwards joined my companion.

At length we reached Calpi, where we found the band and their families; and at a council of all assembled, after many plans of proceeding had been discussed and many plans proposed for our final settling-place by the different members, I opened to them one of my own which I had long entertained. It was, to proceed to Lucknow by a boat, which could be easily hired, and to remain there, as it was a city which promised an ample harvest to a Thug; and from the not over-strict character of its government, a more likely one than any other to enable us to pursue our calling with security. The plan was agreed on; and the next morning I betook myself to the Ghaut, to hold communication with the Manjees of the boats, and to strike a bargain for their conveyance of my party.

All was arranged to the satisfaction of my associates; and at the hour appointed, which had been declared a lucky moment by some astrologer employed by the boatmen, the anchor was raised and a fair wind carried us rapidly over the smooth waters.

Day after day passed in this manner, and there was a kind of dreamy pleasure about the voyage which was indescribably grateful to me. Here I had no alarms, no fatiguing journeys, no anxiety; my mind became calm and unruffled, and I was once more at peace.

At Lucknow we lived for some time upon the proceeds of our last booty, and I established a small traffic in precious stones upon those I had brought with me; but it yielded small returns to me, and I only delayed commencing operations till I could fix upon some settled plans. At length I thought I would attempt the same system we had practised so successfully at Hyderabad. No sooner had the idea possessed me than I longed to put it into execution; the more so, as my associates received it with ardour, and seemed strongly convinced of its practicability. We were unknown in that crowded and vicious city, lived in an obscure part, and could never be suspected in our daily perambulations through the bazaars in search of bunij. And so it turned out; we were in great luck for two months, money flowed in upon us, and we had killed upwards of thirty persons, mostly travellers to distant parts, whom we decoyed from the serais. But fortune was against me despite of this cheering commencement, and we did not long enjoy our easy and profitable career.

We had one day taken out of the city a party of seven travellers, we being sixteen Thugs in number. I well remember it was a Friday, an unlucky day at best. Among the Thugs was an old man, one of the old Murnae stock, a capital bhuttote, who had joined us a short time before; he had known my father, and me when a child, and had recognised me in a street in Lucknow, which led to his joining us. We had taken the travellers to a favourite bhil of ours about four coss distant, and were in the act of strangling them—some even lay dead on the ground, and the rest were in their last agonies—when by the merest chance a body of horses, which were on their way from the city to a distant pergunnah, came upon us. We had grown too confident from our frequent successes—it was still far from morning, and we had neglected to place scouts. The horse came upon us unheard and unseen, and, as I have told you, caught us in the very act. Nine of us were seized after a faint resistance; the rest, fortunate men! made their escape. Our hands were bound behind us and we were dragged into the city, objects of wonder and terror to the inhabitants. The bodies were brought in after us: and two of the travellers who had been only half strangled, and were revived by the horsemen, gave so clear an account of our whole proceedings, how we had inveigled them and accompanied them on their march till we attacked them unawares, that no doubt remained of our guilt; and after our brief trial had been concluded before the Kazee, we were cast into prison, to await our fate.

CHAPTER XXXVII

AGAIN I was in prison; and although not in such wretched plight as I had been in at Jhalone, for the cell was roomy and tolerably clean, yet still it was a prison—confinement to my limbs and to my spirit; a conviction which threatened my life hung over me; and as I saw no prospect of escape, I was resigned to die, and to meet my fate like a man and a Thug who had been familiar with death from his childhood. We sat in silence, and my wretched companion, old as he was, clung to the idea of life with a fondness that I felt not. He had no ties on earth to bind him to it; he had never had any, yet he longed to live. I *had* possessed them—they were all broken, and life had no charms for me. I could not say that I wished for death, but I was indifferent to my fate.

A week passed thus—a long, interminable week. In vain was it that I emplored my jailers to relieve me from suspense, to tell me whether I was to live or die: either they knew not, or their hearts were hardened towards me: they would not tell me.

But after the expiration of this period, we were not long ignorant of our sentence. We were informed that seven of our companions had been hanged, as they had been detected in the act of strangling the travellers. But there was no evidence against us so conclusive; the merchants who had escaped the fate of their associates could not swear that we had murdered any of those who had perished; and the horsemen who had captured us knew no more than that we were of the party. If this had been all, we should probably have been released; but one of the miserable men who had been executed, in a vain attempt to preserve his life, confessed his crimes, and by this last stroke of ill fortune we were convicted, and the decree went forth that we were to be imprisoned for life.

Despair seized on my faculties at the announcement of this hard sentence. Death in its most horrible shape would have been courted joyfully by me in preference to it. To linger out years and years in that wretched hole, never to be free again! I could not believe it: I tried to shut out the dreadful reality from my mind, but in vain. I implored that they would lead me to instant execution, that I might be impaled, or blown away from a gun, or hung—anything rather than have my miserable existence protracted in the solitude and suffering of a prison. But my entreaties were laughed at or scorned. I was loaded with a heavy chain, which confined my legs; my companion the same, and we were left to our fate. Still my restless spirit held out to me hopes of escape—hopes that only mocked me: for every plan I formed became utterly impracticable, and this only increased my misery. One day I bethought me of the money I had collected before I was seized. It was hidden and it was not improbable that my hoard had remained undiscovered. With this I fondly hoped I should be enabled to bribe one of my jailers; and the idea comforted me for many days, while I waited for an opportunity to put it into execution.

There was one among the guards of the prison, a young man, who was always kinder in his deportment to us than any of the others. The food he brought us was better, and the water always pure and in a clean vessel. He used to cheer us too sometimes with the hope that our imprisonment would not last so long as had been decreed; and he instanced the cases of several criminals who had been sentenced like us, but who had been released when the memory of their crimes had ceased to occupy the minds of the officers in charge of the prison. He had our clothes washed for us, and did a thousand kind acts—trifles, perhaps but still more than we experienced from any other of his companions.

It was with him, therefore, that I proposed to my fellow-captive to try our long-brooded and cherished scheme of deliverance. The next time it was his turn to attend us, I begged he would come to the cell at night or in the evening, when he would be secure from observation, for that I had something particular to communicate to him. He came in the evening of that day, and seated himself muffled in a dark-coloured blanket, close to the bars of our cell.

'You have something to say, I think,' said he in a low tone, 'and I have done your bidding; I am here.'

'I have, good Meer Sahib,' said I, (for he was also a Syud) 'listen for what I would communicate will be for your benefit, if you will enter into my plans.'

'Say on,' replied the youth; 'you may command my utmost exertions.'

'To be brief then,' I continued, 'you must endeavour to effect our escape.'

'It is impossible,' he said.

'Not so,' cried I; 'nothing is impossible to willing hands and stout hearts. You can manage everything if you will but listen to me. When we were apprehended, we had saved a round sum of money, which is concealed in a spot I can tell you of, if you will be faithful to us. Half of it shall be yours, if you will only aid us.'

'How much is it?' he asked.

'Upwards of five hundred rupees,' said I; 'it was securely hidden and no one can have discovered it. I repeat, half of it shall be yours if you will assist us.'

'How can I?' cried he, in a tone of perplexity; 'how is it possible that you can pass these doors and walls, even were you as free as I am at this moment?'

'Leave that to me,' said I; 'do you accept the offer?'

'I will consider of the matter, and will be here at this time tomorow, to give you a final answer.'

'May Allah send you kind thoughts to the distressed! We shall look for your decision with impatience.'

The next evening he came at the same time, and seated himself as before.

'What would you have me do, Meer Sahib?' he asked; 'I am ready to obey your commands if they are practicable. First, however, I must be secure of the money you have mentioned; I must receive it before I peril my situation, and, more than that, my life in your behalf.'

'Listen then, Meer Sahib,' said I; 'I trust you—you are a Syud, and I also am one; you are not to deceive me, and incur the wrath of Allah.'

'I will not, by the Prophet, whose descendant I am,' said he; 'were the Koran in my hands this moment, I would swear upon it.'

'No, no,' said I, 'do not swear; the word of an honest man is far more binding than an oath. I believe that you are true, and therefore it is that I trust you. First, then, as regards the money; do you remember two old tombs, one of them much broken, which stand near the river's brink over the north side of the city, about a cannon-shot from the wall?'

'I do, perfectly.'

'Ten,' I continued, 'in that broken one is an earthen vessel, containing the money; the vault where of old the body of the person over whom the tomb was erected was deposited, can be opened by removing four stones, which are loose, from the eastern side of it. In the cavity you will find the vessel, and the money is in it. I shall require half for my expenses. Now all I ask you for the present to do in return is, to procure us two small and sharp files and some ghi; and when we have cut through our chains, and one of these bars, I will tell you how you can aid us further.'

'I will perform all you wish,' said the youth; 'and Inshallah! you shall have the files tomorow night by this time, if I find that your statement about the money is true.'

He then left us, and we anxiously and impatiently awaited his coming the next day. Nor did he disappoint us.

'I have come, as you see, Meer Sahib,' he said 'and behold, here are the files for you—they are English, and new and sharp; here too is the ghi. I have fulfilled my promise.'

'And the money?' I asked.

'Without it you would not have seen me tonight, I can tell you, Meer Sahib. I have got it; the amount is five hundred and fifty rupees, and you shall be welcome to your share when you have got out of this hole. And how do you intend to manage this part of your scheme?'

'Are the gates of the prison shut at night?' I asked.

'No,' he replied; 'that is, the gate is shut, but the wicket is always open.'

'And how many men guard it?'

'Only one, Meer Sahib; the rest sleep soundly after midnight.'

'It is well,' said I; 'we can but perish in the attempt; and I for one would gladly die, rather than linger out a wretched existence here.'

'And I also,' said my companion.

'I fear I cannot assist you,' said the man: 'yet stay, suppose you were to attempt your escape when I am on guard. I shall have the last watch tomorrow night.'

'May the blessing of Allah rest on you!' said I; 'you have anticipated my thoughts. We will attempt it then, and may the Prophet aid us! All night we will work at our irons and one of these bars, and tomorrow night we shall be free. Go, kind friend, you do but risk detection in being seen here.'

He left us, and we set to work with a good will to cut the irons on our legs and the bar. All night we worked, and the morning's light saw the iron bar nearly cut through at the top and bottom; to cut it at the top, one of us sat down by turns, while the other standing on his shoulders filed till his arm was tired. Despite of the ghi however, the files made a creaking noise; we tried to prevent this by using them slowly, but in the excitement of the moment this was at times forgotten, for we worked hard for our liberty.

The morning broke and we rested from our labour; one strong shake would have separated the bar, and our irons were so nearly cut through at the ankles and the waist, that a slight wrench would have divided them. Our friend we knew was faithful, for he had proved himself so, and we enjoyed a silent anticipation of our eventual triumph.

'This time tomorrow,' I exclaimed, 'we shall be free, far from Lucknow, and the world again before us, wherein to choose a residence!'

My companion was as full of hope as I was, and we passed most of the morning in debating whither we should go, and calling to mind the names of our former associates who would welcome us and join us in seeking new adventures. It was about noon, I think, that a party of the soldiers of the prison, headed by the Darogha, approached our cell. My heart sunk within me as I saw them coming and the haste with which they advanced towards us increased my alarm and apprehension.

'We are lost!' said I to my companion; 'they have discovered our plans.' He did not reply, but despair was written on his countenance.

The Darogha applied his key to the lock; it was opened, and the whole party rushed in and seized us.

'What new tyranny is this?' I exclaimed; 'what new crime have we committed, that we are again to be ill-treated?'

'Look to their irons!' cried the Darogha to his men.

'You have been busy it seems,' said he to us, when they found them in the state I have described. 'Let me give you a piece of advice; when you next file your irons, either use more ghi or make less noise. Search them well,' continued he to the men; 'see where these instruments are which they have used so cleverly.'

They stripped us stark naked, and the files were found in the bands of our trowsers, through which the string that ties them runs. The Darogha examined them carefully.

'These are new, Meer Sahib, and English. Inshallah! we will find out who supplied you with them. The fellow who has done this assuredly has eaten dirt.'

'We brought them here with us,' said I doggedly. 'Ye were sons of asses that ye did not search us when we entered your den of tyranny.'

'We may be sons of asses,' he replied grinning, 'but we are not such owls as to believe you, O wise and cunning Syud; Thug as you are, we are not going to eat dirt at your hands. Some friend you have had among my men; one is suspected and if these files can help us to trace him—and it is probable enough—he had better say the Kulma, for his head and shoulders will not remain together. But come,' said he to his men, 'our work is only half done; examine every foot of these bars; for my worthy friends here, rely upon it, have not half done their business.'

They obeyed him, and, as you may suppose, soon found the bar which had been cut.

'Enough!' said the Darogha. 'You were a fool, O Meer Sahib, for this wild attempt. Had you been content to bear your deserved imprisonment, mercy might in time have been shown to you; but now, give up all hope; you have forfeited that mercy by your own imprudence, and you will long live to repent it. Bring them along,' said he to his men; 'we must put them into narrower and safer lodgings.'

Ya Allah, Sahib, what a place they led us to! A narrow passage, between two high walls, which but just admitted of a man's passing along it, contained, about half way down, two cells, more like the dens of wild beasts than aught else. They were more strongly grated than the last we had been in, and were not half the size. Far heavier irons than those we had last worn were fastened on our legs by a blacksmith, and we were thrust into our horrible abodes.

'Now,' said the Darogha, 'get out if you can, Meer Sahib. If walls and iron bars can hold you, you are pretty safe here I think.'

They left us, and once more we were cast into the abyss of

despair; nor was there one ray of hope left to cheer our gloomy and wretched thoughts. Here am I to live, here am I to die, thought I, as I surveyed the narrow chamber—I who have roamed for years over the world, I who have never known restraint. Allah! Allah! what have I done that this should be? O Bhowani, hast thou so utterly forsaken Ameer Ali? I cast myself down on the rough floor, and groaned in agony. I could not weep, tears were denied me; they would have soothed my over-burthened soul. A cup of misery was before me, and I was to drain it to the dregs. Hope had fled, and despair had seized and benumbed every faculty of my mind.

Months roled on. Though only a strong grating of iron bars divided me from my old companion, we seldom spoke to each other; at most it was a word, a passing remark hazarded by the one, and scarcely heeded by the other, so absorbed were we in our misery. I ate and drank mechanically, I had no craving for food; and what they gave us to eat was of the coarsest kind. The filth which accumulated in our cells was removed only once a week, and it bred vermin which sorely tormented us. Oh that I could die! I cried a thousand times a day. Alas! my prayer was not granted.

The second year of our captivity passed—the same unvarying rotation of misery—no change, no amelioration of our condition. We existed, but no more; the energies of life were dead within us. I used to think, were I ever released, that I could not bear the rude bustle of the world, that I should even prefer my captivity to its anxieties and cares. It was a foolish thought, for I often yearned for freedom, and occupied my mind with vain thoughts and plans for future action, should any lucky chance give me my liberty; but no ray of hope broke in upon the misery of my dungeon.

I mean to say that my companion, the old Thug, and I never conversed; we did so now and then; we recounted our exploits again and again, and by thus recalling mine to my memory, from the begininING of my career, I stored up in my mind the adventures and vicissitudes I have related to you. One day we had been talking of my father, and his parting words to me, 'I am not your father,' flashed across my thoughts. I mentioned the circumstance to the old Thug, and earnestly requested him to tell me what he knew of Ismail, and of my early state.

'What!' he asked, 'so you know not of it, Meer Sahib? Surely Ismail must have told you all? And yet,' continued he after a pause, 'he would not have done it—he dared not.'

'What can you men,' cried I, 'by saying he dared not? Was I his son, or did he say truly when he declared I was not?'

'He spoke the truth, Meer Sahib. I know your origin, and it is just possible there may be one or two others who do also, and who are still living: one of these is Ganesha.'

'Ganesha!' I exclaimed; 'by Allah! my soul has ever told me that he knew something of me. I have striven in vain to bring any scene in which he was concerned with me to my recollection, and always failed. By your soul, tell me who and what I was!'

''Tis a long tale, Ameer Ali,' said the old man, 'but I will endeavour to remember all I can of it; it is one too which, were you not what you are, would horrify you.'

'My parents were murdered then?' said I, my heart sinking within me. 'I have sometimes thought so, but my conjectures were vague and unsatisfactory.'

'You have guessed truly, Meer Sahib. But listen, my memory is still fresh, and you shall know all.

'Ismail, your father, as he called himself to you, became a Thug under Hussein Jemadar, whom no doubt you remember. I well recollect the day he joined us, at a village not very far from Delhi; I was then a youth, and belonged to the band of which Hussein was one of the best bhuttotes.'

'I know Ismail's history,' said I; 'he related it to me.'

'Then I need not repeat it,' he continued. 'In time Ismail, by his bravery and wisdom, rose far above Hussein and became the Jemadar of a band of thirty Thugs. It is of this time I would speak. We were one day at a village called Eklera, in Malwa, encamped outside the place, in a grove of trees near a well. We had been unlucky for some time before, as it was the season of the rains, when but few travellers are abroad, and we were eagerly looking for bunij.

'Ismail and Ganesha had been into the bazaar and returned with the joyful news that a party was about to set off towards Indore, and that we were to precede them by a march, and halt whenever we thought them secure to us. I and another Thug were directed to watch their movements, while the main body went on. The information was correct, and we dogged them till the third or fourth march, when at a village whose name I forget we found the band halted, and rejoined it. The party consisted of a respectable man and his wife and child, an old woman, and some young men of the village who accompanied them. The man rode a good horse, and his wife travelled in a palankeen. They were your parents, Meer Sahib.'

'Go on,' said I in a hoarse voice; 'my memory seems to follow your narration.' O Sahib! I was fearfully interested and excited.

'Well,' continued he, 'not long after they had arrived, Ismail and Ganesha went into the bazaar, dressed in their best clothes, to scrape an acquaintance with your father, and, as Ismail told us afterwards, this was effected through you; he saw you playing in the streets, gave you some sweet-meats, and afterwards rescued you from the violence of some of the village boys who would have robbed you of them. This led to his speaking with your mother, and eventually to his becoming acquainted with your father. The end of all was, that they agreed to accompany us, and dismissed the young men by whom they had been previously attended. Does your memory aid you now, Meer Sahib, or shall I finish the relation?'

'It does,' said I, 'most vividly as you proceed. But go on; without your assistance, I lose the thread of my sad history.' He resumed.

'Ismail in those days always rode a good horse, as also did Ganesha. He grew fond of you, and you of him, and he used to take you up before him and carry you most part of the march, or till you became fatigued. This went on for some days, but we were approaching Indore, and it was necessary to bring the matter to a close; besides our cupidity was strongly excited by the accounts we heard from Ismail of your father's wealth, as he had told him that he carried a large sum of ready money with him. At last, the bhil was determined. I could show it you now; it was close to a river, and before the party had crossed, the jhirnee was given. We strangled them all. Ganesha killed your mother, the old woman was allotted to me; Ismail had his share also, and I believe it was your father. You had been riding upon Ismail's horse all the morning, at least after the rain had ceased, and when the jhirnee was given you were half across the river; I saw you fall, and as you did not move afterwards, I thought you were killed. You moved however, and Ganesha ran towards you; he threw the rumal about your neck, and was in the act of strangling you when Ismail, who had uttered a cry of despair on seeing Ganesha's action, arrived just in time to prevent his deadly purpose. They had a serious quarrel about you, and even drew their swords; but Ismail prevailed, and led you to where the bodies were lying and being stripped by the lughas. You became frantic when you saw your mother; you clung to her body, and could hardly be torn from it; you raved and cursed us all, but terror overcame you at last, and perhaps pain also for you fainted. Ismail, when the bodies had been disposed of, and the plunder collected, mounted his horse and took you up before him; and turning off the road we travelled in another direction.

'How you ever bore that journey I know not; you were a thin and delicate child, and we all said you would die; but you bore it well, and when we reached a place in the jungle, I was sent to a village for milk, and you drank some. Here again Ismail and Ganesha had a second quarrel about you; Ganesha said you were too old to adopt, that you would remember all that had happened, and that he would strangle you; and the abuse that you poured upon him made him still more savage. Again they drew their swords, and would have fought about you, but we prevented them.

You were taken away by me to a distance; I rubbed your

swollen neck, and Ismail gave you a strong dose of opium, which put you to sleep, and we again resumed our flight.

'Ganesha and he were never cordial friends after that day; they never acted in concert again until, as I heard, in your last expedition; and though they preserved an outward show of civility to each other, their hate was as strong as ever.

'Ismail took you to his home. He was married, but had no children; and as you grew up and improved under his kind and fatherly treatment, he became proud of you, and used often to say to us, that he regretted your father had left your sister behind when he undertook his fatal journey to Indore.'

'My sister!' cried I, in an agony of apprehension.

'Yes, Meer Sahib, your sister. I, for one, heard your father say that he left her behind, as she was too young to be moved. You might get news of her at Eklera, if ever you get out of this cursed hole.'

But he now spoke to one bereft of sense—of any feeling save that of choking, withering, blighting agony. Why did not my heartstrings crack in that moment? Why did I live to drag a load of remorse with me to my grave?

Yet it has even been so. I live, and I have borne my misery as best I could; to most I appear calm and cheerful, but the wound rankles in my heart; and could you but know my sufferings, Sahib, you would perhaps pity me. Not in the daytime is my mind disturbed by the thoughts of the past; it is at night, when all is still around me, and sleep falls not upon my weary eyelids, that I see again before me the form of my unfortunate sister: again I fancy my hands busy with her beautiful neck, and the vile piece of coin for which I killed her seems again in my grasp as I tore it from her warm bosom. Sahib, there is no respite from these hideous thoughts; if I eat opium—which I do in large quantities, to produce a temporary oblivion—I behold the same scene in the dreams which it causes, and it is distorted and exaggerated by the effects of the drug. Nay, this is worse to bear than the simple reality, to which I sometimes become accustomed, until one vision more vivid than its predecessors again plunges me into despair of its ever quitting me.

Sahib, after that fatal relation, I know not what I did for many days. I believe I raved, and they thought me mad, but my mind was strong and not to be overthrown. I recovered, though slowly, and again and again I retraced in my memory the whole of my life till that miserable day on which I murdered my sister! It could have been no other.

I tried in vain to cheat myself into the belief that it was another, but no effort that I made could shake the conviction that it was she. My unaccountable recollection of Eklera—the relation of my father's death by the old man there, his almost recognition of me, and, more than all, the old and worthless coin for which

I destroyed her, and which I now remember perfectly—all were undeniable proofs of my crime; and conviction, though I tried to shut it out, entered into my soul, and abode there. Allah help me I was a wretched being! My hair turned grey, my form and strength wasted, and any one who had seen me before I listened to the old Thug's tale would not have recognised me two months afterwards. A kind of burning fever possessed me; my blood felt hot as it coursed through my veins; and the night, oh, how I dreaded it! I never slept, except by day, when exhausted nature at length claimed some respite. Night after night, for months and months, I either rolled to and fro on my miserable pallet, or sat up and rocked myself, groaning the while in remorse and anguish. No other act of my life rose up in judgment against me—none but they passed from my mind as quickly as they entered it, and my sister was ever before me.

You know the worst, Sahib—think of me as you will, I deserve it. I cannot justify the deed to myself, much less to you; and the only consolation I have—that it was the work of fate, of unerring destiny—is but a weak one, that gives way before the conviction of my own guilt. I must bear my curse, I must wither under it. I pray for death, and as often too pray that I may live, and that my measure of punishment may be allotted to me here, that my soul may not burn in Jehanum. I may now as well bring my history to a close, to the time when, by accepting your boon of life, I became dead to the world.

My old companion died in the fourth year of our captivity. I would fain have had him deny the tale he told me of my father's destruction, but he would not; he was dying when I urged him to do so, and again declared in the most solemn manner that what he had related was true in every particular; and again he referred me to Ganesha, my mother's murderer, for confirmation of the whole.

He died, and I was left to solitude, to utter solitude, which was only broken by the daily visit of my jailer, who brought me food, and attended me during a short walk up and down the passage. This favour alone had I extorted after those years of misery, and it was grateful to me to stretch my cramped limbs, and again to feel the pure air of heaven breathe over my wasted features.

The seventh year had half passed; the Darogha of the jail was dead or had been removed; another supplied his place, and some amelioration of my condition ensued. I was removed from the lonely cell into one near where I had been first confined; it was more spacious and airy, and people passed to and fro before it. I used to watch their motions with interest, and this in some degree diverted my mind from brooding over the past.

In the twelfth year of my imprisonment the old king died, and his successor, the late monarch, ascended the musnud. Many a heart beat quickly and with renewed hope—hope that had almost died within the hearts of those wretches who were immured within the walls, and of mine among the rest. We had heard that it was customary to release all who had been sentenced to perpetual imprisonment; and you can hardly imagine, Sahib, the intense anxiety with which I looked for the time when the mandate should be issued for our release, or when I should no longer dare to hope.

It came at last; after some days of weary expectation, the order reached the Darogha, and it was quickly conveyed to me. I was brought forth, the chains were knocked off my legs, and I was free. Five rupees were given to me, and a suit of coarse clothes in place of those which hung in rags about my person. After more than twelve weary years I issued from those prison walls, and was again thrown upon the world to seek my fortune.

'Beware, Meer Sahib,' said the Darogha, as he presented me with the money, 'beware of following your old profession; you are old, your blood no longer flows as it used, and what you have been you should forget. Go! follow some peaceful calling, and fortune may yet smile upon you.'

I thanked him and departed. I roamed through the city till night-fall, and after satisfying my hunger at the shop of a bhutteara, I begged from him shelter for the night. It was readily granted, and I lay down and enjoyed the first quiet and refreshing sleep I had known for years. I arose with the dawn and went forth —whither I cared not—all places in the wide world seemed alike to me. I knew no one, I could find no one who knew me in that large city, and I felt the desolation of my condition press heavily upon me. What to do, or whither to go, I knew not; but a faint hope that I might discover some of my old associates if I could reach Bundelkhund impelled me to travel thither.

A change in my dress was soon effected. From a Kalundur fakir I purchased a high felt cap and a chequered garment for a small sum; and thus equipped, with a staff in my hand, I left the city by the north gate, and travelled onwards.

It was as I thought; I was never without a meal, though it might be of the coarsest food; and when I reached Jhalone, my stock of money was nearly as large as when I had left Lucknow. I went direct to the house of the Mullah, for my thoughts were ever with my daughter, and my soul yearned to know her fate. Alas! I was disappointed. His house was inhabited by another, whom I knew not, and all he could tell me was that the old man had gone to Delhi he believed some years before, and that he had not heard any tidings of him since. I asked after his daughters, but the man knew nothing of them, except that one he had adopted had been married in Jhalone to a person who resided in a village of the country, but of his name or direction he was ignorant.

I turned away from the door—I dared not pass my own, and I withdrew to an obscure part of the town where there was a small garden in which a fakir usually resided. Him I had known of old, he had eaten of my bread and received my alms, and now I was his equal. He will not recognize me, thought I, in this dress, and changed as I am no one knows me; I will seek him however, and if he is as he used to be I may learn some news of my old friends.

I found the fakir whom I sought; old I had left him, he was now aged and infirm; his garden, which he had always kept with scrupulous neatness, was overgrown with weeds and neglected, and he had barely strength remaining to crawl about the town for the small supply of flour or grain which sufficed for his daily wants. I was much shocked to see him thus, and represented myself to be a wandering Kalundur desirous of remaining in Jhalone, I begged to be allowed to reside and share with him whatever I got. My offer was readily accepted, and there I took up my abode, in the hope that some wandering party of Thugs might pass Jhalone, to whom I could disclose myself.

Gradually I discovered myself to the old man; I led him to speak of old times and of persons by allusion to whom he must know I was a Thug. He did not hesitate to speak of them, and in particular of myself, whose fate he mourned with such true grief that I could control myself no longer; and to his wondering ear I related the whole of my adventures, from the time I had been released by the Rajah, to the period of my taking up my abode with him. And much had I to hear from him in return, much that distressed and grieved me; many of my old companions were dead, others had been seized and executed, and hardly one of the old leaders of Bunkelkhund were in the country or in the exercise of their vocation: new leaders had sprung up, and he spoke in warm terms of a young man named Feringhea, who when I had last seen him was a mere boy.

Four months passed thus. To support the old fakir as well as myself, I was obliged to perambulate the town daily, and I asked and received alms, given in the meanest portions, in the place where my hand had ever been open to the poor. A sad change in my fortune, Sahib! Yet I bore up against it with resignation, if not with fortitude, hoping for better days and new adventures.

New adventures, Ameer Ali! I exclaimed; had not the punishments you received turned your heart from Thuggee?

No, Sahib! cried the Thug with fervour; why should they? Had not my heart become hardened by oppression and misery? They had aroused within me a spirit of revenge against the whole human race; I burned to throw off my wretched disguise and again take to the road—it mattered not whether as a leader or a subordinate, so that I could once more be a Thug. Nor was I old; true, my beard had become grizzled and grey, and care had seamed my countenance with many wrinkles; but I was still strong and powerful, and my hands had not forgotten their cunning. Four months I have said had elapsed, and as no Thugs came near Jhalone, I set off, with a few rupees I had saved from the produce of my daily alms, for Tearee, where I hoped to meet the Brahmin astrologer who had so materially aided me in the affair of the pearl-merchant. His share of that booty had been duly remitted to him immediately on my arrival at Jhalone, and though I had never heard from him afterwards, yet I felt assured that the letter could not have miscarried.

I reached Tearee after many days. I knew that bands of Thugs were abroad, for I saw their fire-places and marks at many villages and upon the roads; but I met with none, to my disappointment, and on my arrival I hastened at once to the temple where I found the Brahmin; and, notwithstanding my misfortunes, I was kindly, nay warmly welcomed. The Brahmin still kept up his connexion with Thugs, and I learned from him to my joy that a band, under a Jemadar named Ramdeen, about twenty in number, had passed through the town only the day before, and were on their road towards the Nerbudda.

'You can easily overtake them, Meer Sahib,' he said; 'and if your old fame as a leader ails in procuring you a welcome reception, a few lines from me may aid you.' And he wrote a note to the Jemadar, informing him who I was, and how I had been connected with him of old. I did not long delay after I had received it, and again set off in search of my future companions. I came up with them on the second day, and warm indeed was the welcome I received; one and all were amazed to see me, whom they had long thought dead. I was clothed in decent raiment by them, admitted as one of their band, and treated as a brother. Truly their kindness was refreshing to my almost withered heart. Ramdeen insisted that I should take an equal rank with him in the band; and after the necessary ceremonies I resumed my rumal, and again ate the goor of the Tupounee.

Sahib, you must by this time be weary of my adventures with travellers, and I met with none during my connexion with Ramdeen's party worthy of relation. We avoided the Company's territories, and kept to those of Sindia; penetrating as far as Burhanpur, and on our return visiting the shrine of Oonkar Manduttee, on the Nerbudda. From this latter place we were fortunate in enticing a party of pilgrims, and a large booty fell into our hands at the bottom of the Jām Ghat, whither we escorted them on their return to Ujjain. Upwards of four hundred rupees was my share of this: so again you see me independent and fortune smiling upon me. But Ramdeen became jealous of me, and of my superior skill and intelligence. We had many quarrels, and at last I left him, and determined, with what I had, to travel to the Dukhun, and to seek my fortune in the Nizam's country, where I knew that Thuggee still flourished unchecked.

But it was fated not to be so. My road from where I left Ramdeen lay through Saugor, and there I met with my old acquaintance Ganesha, at the head of a small band, apparently in wretched plight. I could but ill dissemble my feelings of abhorrence at meeting with him; my own misfortunes and history, and the tale of my companion in imprisonment, were fresh in my recollection; nevertheless I disguised the dislike I felt, though revenge still rankled in my heart, and I would gladly have seized any opportunity to satisfy it. Among his band was a Thug I had known in former days; he was weary of Ganesha, whose temper was not improved by age, and he advised me to put myself at the head of a few men he could point out to me, who would be faithful, and who he thought would prove the nucleus of a large band; for my name was still fresh in the memory of the older Thugs, who would gladly flock to me when they heard I was determined to set up for myself without connexion with others. And he was right; in a few months I was at the head of forty men; and we were fortunate. Taking a new direction we passed through the territories of the Rewah Rajah, returning to our home, which we fixed in a village not far from Hindia, in a wild and unfrequented tract, where we were secure from treachery, and from the operations against the Thugs then being carried on from Saugor.

Two years passed in this manner, and I was content, for I was, as I wished to be, powerful and actively employed. Two seasons we went out and returned laden with plunder, and the name of Ameer Ali was again known and feared. Another season and it shall be my last, said I; I had discovered some clue to my daughter, and thought (vain idea!) if I could only collect a few thousand rupees, that I could dare to seek her, to live near her, and to abandon Thuggee for ever. Why was I thus infatuated? What else could it have been but that inexorable fate forbade it? The destiny which had been marked out for me by Allah I was to fulfill, and I blindly strove against it. The vain purposes of man urge him to pursue some phantom of his imagination, which is never overtaken, but which leads him on often by smooth paths and buoyed up by hope, till he is suddenly precipitated into destruction.

I had planned an expedition on a larger scale than ever, towards Calcutta, and we had sworn to Bhowani to pay our devotions at her shrines of Bindachul and Calcutta; the omens were favourable, and we left our home in joy and high excitement. And what cared I then, though I knew that the English had set a price of five hundred rupees upon me? It was a proof that I was dreaded and feared, and I rejoiced that Ameer Ali, the oppressed and despised for a time, had again emerged from his obscurity, and I braved the danger which threatened me. I was a fool for this, yet it was my destiny that impelled me: and of what avail would have been precautions, even had I taken any?

Saugor lay directly in the route which we proposed taking, and it was here that the greatest danger was to be apprehended. I might have avoided it perhaps, but I trusted to the celerity and secrecy of my movements for a few days until we should pass it; and as my band were unanimous in refusing to change the route after it had been determined on and sanctioned by favourable omens, I undertook to lead them at all hazards. We travelled by night therefore, and avoided all large villages, resting either in waste spots or near miserable hamlets. Nor did we seek for bunij —the danger was too imminent for any time to be lost; and though one or two persons died by our hands, yet this was rather to enable us to eat the goor of the Tupounee, and to perform such ceremonies as were absolutely necessary for the propitiation of our patroness, and our consequent success.

CHAPTER XXXVIII

SAUGOR, I have said, lay directly in our route, and we reached a village close to it on the evening of a day of severe travel. We were fatigued already, but the town was now so close to us that we did not hesitate to push on, and we arrived at the well-known spot shortly after dark. Selecting an empty shed in as lonely a part of the town as we could, we cooked a hasty meal and lay down, determined to rise before dawn and again pursue our journey. One of our number was set to watch ere we retired to rest, and we depended upon him to give us warning should any suspicious person be observed.

The night passed, and I arose, roused my followers, and long before day had dawned we were beyond the gates of the town. 'See,' said I to my friend, 'our much-dreaded danger is past; we are now again on our way, and we shall leave this spot at least ten coss behind us before noon; beyond that there is nothing to fear, and we shall travel with light hearts.' Alas! I spoke as my sanguine hope prompted me to do; but it was not fated to be as we thought. Again treachery had been at work, and when I conceived I possessed a band free from all suspicion, two traitors, as I afterwards heard, had already laid a deep plan for my apprehension.

Already we had lost sight of the town, and before us was a broad, well-beaten road, which I well remembered; yet I feared so public a route, and determined to strike off into a bypath as soon as I could see one which diverged in the direction we were going. We might have proceeded a coss or two perhaps, and the day was now beginning to dawn; a nullah was before us at a short distance, and as none of us had washed before leaving the town, I proposed that we should perform our ablutions there, the better to enable us to sustain the fatigue of the stage before us: my proposal was agreed to, and when we reached the running stream, one and all ungirded their loins and sat down by the water; we had not been engaged thus for more than a few minutes, when a sudden rush was made upon us by a number of horse and foot soldiers, who must have been lying in wait for us on the road we were to travel.

I had left my weapons at some little distance from the water, and my first impulse was to endeavour to possess myself of them; but in this I was foiled. Two of my own men threw themselves upon me and held me, and as I vainly struggled to free myself some foot-soldiers seized me. I was thrown down and bound. The surprise was most complete. A few of my band drew their swords, and some blows were exchanged between them and the party who had come upon us, and a few of my Thugs were wounded; but we were all overpowered, and the whole affair was concluded in less time than it requires to relate it; only a few of my men had escaped.

Bitterly did I upbraid the men who had prevented my getting my weapons. Had I but possessed them Ameer Ali would never have been taken alive; I would have sold my life dearly, Sahib, and sooner than have been seized I would have plunged my sword into my heart, and ended a life which had no charms for me, and which I only wished to prolong to wreak vengeance on mankind, the source of all my misery.

As I reviled them they mocked and jeered at me. 'Where is now your journey to Calcutta, O Meer Sahib?' said one; 'behold, the long travel is saved thee, and thou art returning to Saugor to live in a fine house and to keep company with many old friends who are in it.' 'Yes,' said the other, 'the Jemadar's day is past, and his wit deserted him when he must needs approach the den of the tiger, as if he would not be smelt out! Why didst thou come to Saugor, O Jemadar? Hadst thou forgotten the promise of reward and free pardon which was offered for thy apprehension? Truly we have done a good deed,' said he to the other, 'and the Sahib-logue will be pleased with us.'

But their idle talk was silenced by the leader of the party, who warned them to be careful, and not to boast, lest their expectations should not be realized; and they shrank behind, unable to bear the glances of scorn and contempt which were cast on them by all; by all, I say, for even the soldiers who had seized us cursed the means of their success for having been treacherous and unfaithful to the salt they had eaten.

And thus in bitter agony of spirit, and indulging in vain regrets at my senseless imprudence in approaching Saugor, they led me, bound and guarded, by the road I had just travelled, free then as the morning breeze which played on me. For the third time I was a prisoner, and now I saw no hope: I had retained some on each of the former occasions, but it all vanished now. Then I was young, and a young heart is always buoyant and self-comforting; but the fire of my spirit had long been quenched, and it was only in the wild excitement of a life of continual adventure and unrestrained freedom, when I resembled what I had formerly been, that I rekindled within me. Death too was now before me; for I knew the inexorable laws of the Europeans, and that no mercy was shown to Thugs of any grade —how much less to me for whom a reward had been offered! It was a bitter thought: I should be hung—hung like a dog—I who ought to have died on a battle-field! There death would have been sweet, and followed by an everlasting Paradise. Alas! even this hope deserted me now, and I felt that the load of crime with which my soul was oppressed would weigh me down into hell.

Who can describe the myriad thoughts which crowd into the heart at such a moment? One by one they hurry in, each striving to displace the foregoing—none staying for an instant—till the brain reels under the confusion. It was thus with me. I walked mechanically, surrounded by the soldiers, vainly striving to collect my wandering senses to sustain me in the coming scene, the scene of death, for I verily believed I should be led to instant execution why should the mockery of a trial be given to one so steeped in crime as I was?

A short time after our arrival at the town, I was conducted, closely guarded, to the officer who was employed by the English Government to apprehend Thugs. A tall, noble-looking person he was, and from the severe glance he cast on me I thought my hour was come, and that ere night I should cease to exist. I had prepared myself however for the worst; I saw no pity in his stern countenance, and I confess I trembled when he addressed me.

'So, you are Ameer Ali Jemadar,' said he, 'and at last you are in my power; know you aught of the accusations against you, and wherefore you are here? Read them,' he continued to an attendant munshi, 'read the list which has been drawn up; yonder villain looks as though he would deny them.'

The man unfolded a roll of paper written in Persian, and read a catalogue of crime, of murders, every one of which I knew to be true; a faithful record it was of my past life, with but few omissions. Allah defend me! thought I, there is no hope; yet I still put a bold face on the matter.

'The proof, Sahib Bahadur;' said I, 'you English are praised for your justice, and long as that list of crimes I never before heard of, you will not deny me a fair hearing and the justice you give to thousands.'

'Surely not; whatever your crimes may be, do not fear but that your case shall be inquired into. Call the approvers,' said he to an attendant; 'bring them in one by one, and the Jemadar shall hear what they have told me about him.'

The first man who entered was an old associate of mine in former days, before my misfortunes commenced: he had been with me in the expedition just before my father had been put to death by the Rajah of Jhalone, which I have minutely described to you; and he related the whole, from the murder of the munshi and his child, down to the last event, the destruction of the pearl-merchant. His story took a long time in relating; and the whole was so fresh in my recollection, and he was so exact and true in its details, that I could not answer a word, nor put a single question to shake his testimony. In conclusion he referred the officer to the Rajah of Jhalone for corroboration of the whole, and he appealed to me to declare whether aught he had said was false. 'Not only,' said he, 'do you know, Meer Sahib, that it is all true, but there are others, as well as myself who can speak to these facts; and know, moreover, that many graves have been opened, and the remains of your victims have been disinterred.'

'Say yours as well as mine,' I replied, thrown completely off my guard at last, and nettled by the emphasis he had placed on the words 'your victims.' 'You had as much to do with them as myself; besides, did you not aid that villain Ganesha when I would have saved the child of the munshi?'

'He has confessed!' cried many voices.

'Silence. Silence!' said the officer, 'let no one dare to speak. Do you know, Ameer Ali, what you have said? Are you aware that you have admitted you are a Thug?'

'It is useless now to attempt to recall my words,' said I doggedly; 'make the most of them, for after this you shall wring no more from me; no, not by the most horrible tortures you can inflict.'

The examination however proceeded. Others were brought forward who had known me or had been connected with me in Thuggee, and at last those who had earned the reward of the Government by betraying me. They had been associated with me for the last two years, and they related what I had done, and where the bodies of the murdered were lying. After this was finished, and all the depositions recorded, I was remanded to prison; and the better to secure me, I was not only loaded with irons, but confined in a cell by myself.

After many days, which elapsed without my being sent for, and when I had concluded that my fate was decided, the munshi whom I had seen in the court, with a Jemadar of Nujeeb's and two of the approvers, came to me.

'Ameer Ali,' said the first, 'we are sent by the Sahib Bahadur to tell you of your fate.'

'I can guess it,' said I—'I am to suffer with the rest. Well! many a good Thug has thus died before me, and you shall see that Ameer Ali fears not death.'

'You have guessed rightly,' said the munshi, 'there is no hope for you: your final trial will come in a day or two, and there is such an array of facts against you, and the accounts from the Rajah of Jhalone so entirely agree with the statements of all the approvers, that it is impossible you can escape death: or, if you do escape it, nothing can save you from the Kala Panee.'

'Death!' cried I, 'death at once! Ah, munshi, you have influence with my judges, you can prevent my being sent away over the far sea, never to behold my country more, and to linger out the remnant of my days in a strange land, condemned to work in irons. These hands have never been used to labour; how shall I endure it? death is indeed welcome, compared with the Kala Panee.'

'But why should it be either, Meer Sahib?' asked the Jemadar; 'your life or death is in your own hands: these men will tell you how they are treated by the master they serve, and you may be like them if you are wise.'

'Never!' cried I; 'never shall it be said of Ameer Ali that he betrayed an associate.'

'Listen, Kumbukht!' said the munshi; 'we are not come to use entreaties to one who deserves to die a thousand deaths, to one whose name it a terror to the country; you are in our power, and there is no averting your fate; an alternative is offered, which you may accept or not as you please; no force is used, no arguments shall be wasted on you. Say at once, will you live, and become an approver like the rest—have good clothes to wear and food to eat, and be treated with consideration—or will you die the death of a dog? Speak, my time is precious, and I have no orders to bandy words with you.'

'Accept the terms, Ameer Ali,' said both the approvers, 'do not be a fool, and throw your last chance of life away!'

I mused for a moment: what was life to me? Should it be ever be said that Ameer Ali had become a traitor, and for the sake of a daily pittance of food and the boon of life, had abandoned his profession and assisted to suppress it? No, I would die first, and I told them so. 'Begone!' said I; 'take this message to your employer—that the soul of Ameer Ali is too proud to accept his offer, and that he scorns it. Death has no terrors for him, yet shame, everlasting shame has!'

They left me, and I mused over my lot. I was to die; that was determined. Did I fear death? Not at first; I looked at the transition as one that would lead me to eternal joys—to Paradise—to my father and Azima. But as I thought again and again, other reflections crowded on my spirit: I was to die, but how? Not like a man or a soldier, but like a miserable thief, the scorn of thousands who would exult in my dying struggles; and then I remembered those of the wretch who had been hung before my eyes when Bhudrinath was with me, and I pictured to myself the agony he must have suffered ere life was extinct—the shame of the death—the ignominy which would never leave my memory. All these weighed heavily on me. On the other hand was life—one of servitude it was true, but still it was life; I should be protected, and I might once more perhaps be free, if the Europeans relented towards me, and I did them faithful service.

Thus I debated with myself for many days; at last I was warned that my trial would come on the next day; it was clearly the crisis of my fate, and, I must confess it, the fear of the horrible death of hanging, the dread of the Kala Panee, and the advice of the munshi, caused my resolutions of dying with the rest to give way to a desire of life. Ganesha too crossed my thoughts: I can revenge myself now, thought I, and his death will not lie at my door. I knew too how earnestly his capture was desired, and that I alone could tell where he was to be found, and of his probable lurking-places, in case he ever escaped from us. My determination was made, and I requested that the munshi who had formerly spoken with me on the subject might be sent for. He came, and I told him at once that I was willing to accept the alternative he had offered.

'Ah! you speak like a wise man now,' said he, 'and if you exert yourself in the service you have embraced, and prove yourself faithful and trustworthy, you may rely upon it, indulgences, as far as can be granted to a person in your condition, will be allowed to you hereafter; but you must first deserve them, for with the Europeans nothing goes by favour.'

'I am ready,' I replied; 'point out what I am to do, and you will find that Ameer Ali can be true to the salt he eats.'

'Then come, it is still early, and I will take you at once to the Court, there you will receive your instructions.'

My prison irons were struck off, and a light steel rod with a ring attached to it fastened about my right leg, so that it left me at perfect liberty to walk, but not to run, and I was duly admitted as an approver, under the threat of instant execution in case I ever neglected my duty, failed to give information where I really possessed it, or abused in any way the confidence which had been reposed in me.

'Know you aught of Ganesha?' said the officer to me.

'I do, Sahib Bahadur,' I replied, 'I know him well; you have offered a reward for him as you did for me, and yet you know not that even at this moment he is within a few coss of Saugor.'

'Can you guide my people to him?' he asked. 'Remember, this is the first matter with which you are entrusted, and I need not say that I require you to use your utmost intelligence in it Ganesha is wary, and has hitherto evaded every attempt which has been made to apprehend him.'

'I will undertake it,' I exclaimed. 'It is possible he does not know of my capture; and if you will give me six of your own men, I will disguise them, and pledge myself to bring him to you; and not only him, but Himmut, who is I know with him.'

'Ha!' cried the officer, 'Himmut also! he is as bad as the other.'

'He is as good a Thug,' I replied, 'and more cannot be said. But we lose time; select your men, let them be the bravest and most active you have—their weapons may be needed. I will too ask you for a sword.'

'Impossible,' said he; 'you must go as you are: what if you were to lead my men into destruction?'

I drew myself up proudly. 'Trust me or not as you will—Ameer Ali is no liar, no deceitful villain to the cause he serves. Trust me, and you make me doubly true to your interests; doubt me, and I may doubt you.'

'Thou speakest boldly,' said he, 'and I will trust thee. Let him have his own weapon,' he added to an attendant. 'And now you must begone, Ameer Ali; the men await you without.'

'This instant—food shall not pass my lips till I have taken Ganesha.'

I left him. I found the men, six resolute-looking fellows, well armed; I stripped them of their badges of office, and made them throw dust on their garments so that it would appear they had travelled far. The iron on my leg I secured so that it should make no noise, and not be visible under my trowsers; and I put the party in motion.

It was nearly evening, and avoiding the town I struck at once into the open country. 'If we travel well,' said I to the men, 'we may be up with him by midnight.'

'Where is he?' asked the leader of the party.

'At———; he lives with the Patel there, and passes for a Hindu fakir.'

'By Gunga! I have seen him then,' rejoined the fellow; 'he is tall, and squints, does he not?'

'That is the man,' said I; 'you would hardly have thought of looking for him so near you?'

'No, indeed! had we known it, we might have captured him a week ago.'

'Now you are sure of him,' said I: 'but we must be wary; will you trust me?'

'I will, but beware how you attempt to escape or mislead me.'

'I have a heavy reckoning to settle with Ganesha—he murdered my mother!' was my only reply.

We reached the village in the very dead of night; everything was still, and it was perfectly dark, which aided my purpose, for my companion's face could not be distinguished, and my own approach to the Patel's house would not be noticed. 'Now,' said I to the Nujeeb, 'you alone must accompany me; let the rest of your men stay here: I will bring Ganesha here, and then you must bind him. Do you fear me?' (for he appeared irresolute) 'nay then I will go alone, and tell your master that ye are cowards.'

'That will not do either,' cried the man, 'I must not let you out of my sight; my orders are positive; so go I must; and if I do not return,' said he to his associates, 'do you make the best of your way to Saugor alone, and say that I am murdered.'

I laughed. 'There is no fear,' said I; 'in half an hour or less we shall return: are you ready?'

'I am Meer Sahib; lead on, and remember that my sword is loose in the scabbard. I may die, but thou shalt also.'

'Fool!' said I, 'cannot you trust me?'

'Not yet,' he replied; 'I may do so hereafter.'

'Remember,' I continued, 'that you are neither to speak to Ganesha nor the other, if he is here. I will get them out of the house; after that look well to your weapon. If they attempt to escape, or show suspicion of our real errand, fall on Himmut when I ask you how far it is to Saugor: leave me to deal with Ganesha—we are two to two, and Ganesha is a better swordsman than the other. You will remember this?'

'I will,' he replied; 'I will stick by you—I fear not now, for I see you are faithful.'

A few more steps brought us to the Patel's house, and I called for him by name. 'Jeswunt! Jeswunt! rouse yourself and come out, man. Thou knowest who I am.' I spoke in Ramasi, which I knew he understood. He answered me from within, and soon after I heard the bars and bolts of his door removed, and he came forth wrapped in a sheet. 'Who calls me?' he asked.

'I, your friend Ameer Ali,' I replied; 'where is Ganesha?'

'Asleep, within; why do you ask?'

'And Himmut?'

'Asleep also; what do you want with either? and what bring you here, Meer Sahib, so late, or so early, which you please? we thought you were half way to Calcutta.'

'Ah,' said I, 'that matter has been given up; the Nujeebs were out, and there was risk. But go and rouse Ganesha, I have some work in hand for him, and have no time to lose; it must be finished by daylight.'

'I understand,' said the Patel, 'some bunij, eh?'

'Do not stand chattering there, or your share may be forgotten, Patelji; bring Ganesha to me—or tell him I am here, he will come fast enough.'

He went in. 'Now be ready!' said I to the Nujeeb; 'do as I do, and remember the signal.'

I heard the Patel awaken Ganesha; I heard the growling tones of his voice as he first abused him for rousing him, and afterwards his eager question, 'Ameer Ali here! Ai Bhowani, what can he require of me?' at length his gaunt figure appeared at the doorway. Ya Allah! how my heart bounded within me, and then sickened, so intense was my excitement on beholding him.

'Where art thou, Ameer Ali?' said he; 'I can see nought in this accursed darkness.'

'Here,' said I, 'you will see well enough by and by when your eye is accustomed to it; give me your hand; now descend the step; that is right.' We embraced each other.

'Are you ready for work?' I asked, 'I have only two men with me, and we have picked up some bunij; there will be good spoil too if you will join us—alone we can do nothing—there are four of them.'

'Where?' he asked.

'Yonder, in the lane; I have pretended to come for fire.'

'Who is that with you?'

'A friend; no fear of him, he is one of us.'

'Does he speak Ramasi?'

'Not yet,' said I, 'he is a new hand, but a promising one: but where is Himmut?'

'Within, snoring there, you may even hear him; wait for me a moment, I will go for my sword and shoes, and rouse him up. Four men you said, and we are five; enough, by Bhowani! We will share the spoil.'

'Before you are two hours older; be quick or they may suspect me.'

He went in, and returned in a short time fully equipped; Himmut accompanied him, and we exchanged salutations.

'Now, come along,' said I, 'there is no time to lose.'

'Hark ye!' said Ganesha, 'there is a well in yonder lane, will that do for the bhil?'

'Certainly,' I replied, 'you will see the men directly.' Soon after I had spoken we approached our party.

'Who goes there?' cried one of them.

'A friend—Ameer Ali!'

'Then all is right,' was the reply, and in another instant we had joined them.

'There are your men, seize them!' cried I, throwing myself upon Ganesha with such violence that we fell to the ground together, struggling with deadly hate; but two of the Nujeebs came to my aid, just as Ganesha had succeeded in drawing a small dagger he wore in his girdle, and as I had fortunately seized his hand.

'Bind him hand and foot,' said I, disengaging myself from him, 'and gag him, or he may alarm the village by his cries.' This was done and he was disarmed; a cloth was tied round his mouth, so that he could not speak, and we hurried our prisoners along as fast as the darkness and the roughness of the road would allow.

None of us spoke, nor was it till day had fully dawned that I looked upon Ganesha; then our eyes met, and the furious expression of his face I shall never forget. 'Take the gag from his mouth,' said I to one of the Nujeebs; 'let him speak if he wishes.' It was done.

'You are revenged at last, Ameer Ali,' he said, 'may my curses cleave to you for ever, and the curses of Bhowani fall on you for the destruction of her votary! May the salt you eat be bitter in your mouth, and your food poison to you!'

'Ameen!' said I. 'You have spoken like Ganesha. I am indeed revenged, but the debt is not paid yet—the debt you owe me for my mother's life. Devil! you murdered her.'

'Ay, and would have murdered you, when you were a weak

puling child, but for that fool Ismail; he met his fate, however, and yours is yet in store for you.'

'You will not see it,' said I; 'and when I behold you hung up like a dog I shall be happy.'

'Peace!' exclaimed the leader of the Nujeebs; 'why do you waste words on him, Ameer Ali?'

'Because I am glutting my soul with his sufferings,' I answered; 'and, had I my will, I would stand by and taunt him till the hour of his death. Did he not murder my mother? And, if he had not, should I have murdered my sister? Have I not cause for deep and deadly hate? Yet I will be silent now.'

We reached Saugor, and the delight with which the officer received Ganesha from my hands could not be concealed. 'A deep blow has been struck at Thuggee in the capture of this villain,' said he, 'and thou hast done thy duty well, Ameer Ali.'

From that hour I rose in his confidence and estimation, and I have never forfeited it.

Ganesha's trial came on, and I was the principal witness against him. I told all I knew of the murders he had committed, and others corroborated my statements in the fullest manner. He was sentenced to die.

In vain was it that I entreated to see him before his execution; I wanted to taunt him with his fate, and to embitter his last hours, if anything I could have said might have done so. It was denied me; the officer knew of my purpose, and was too humane to allow it. But I saw him die—him and twenty others—all at the same moment. He saw me too, and cursed me, but his curses were impotent. They all ascended the fatal drop together—refused the polluting touch of the hangman—adjusted the ropes round their own necks—and exclaiming 'Victory to Bhowani!' seized each other's hands, and leaped from the platform into eternity. I watched Ganesha, and I joyed to see that his struggles were protracted beyond those of the others. I was satisfied—he had paid the debt he owed me.

And now, Sahib, after this event, my life became one of dull routine and inactivity. One by one I tracked and apprehended my old associates, till none of them remained at large. The usefulness of my life to you has passed away, and all that I can do is at times to relate the details of some affair I may either have witnessed, or heard from others. Why should I live is a question I often ask myself; why should an existence be continued to me in which I have no enjoyment, no pleasure, no care, not even grief? I have remorse but for one act, and that will never leave me. Yet I must support it until Allah pleases to send the angel to loose the cord which binds my life to the clay it inhabits.

I used often to think on my daughter, but her too I have almost forgotten; yet I should not say forgotten, for I love her with a parent's affection, which will last to the latest moment of my existence. But she is happy, and why should she know of me?

I fear that I have often wearied you by the minute relation of my history; but I have told all, nor concealed from you one thought, one feeling, much less any act which at this distance of time I can remember. Possibly you may have recorded what may prove fearfully interesting to your friends. If it be so, your end is answered; you have given a faithful portrait of a Thug's life, his ceremonies, and his acts; whilst I am proud that the world will know of the deeds and adventures of Ameer Ali, the Thug.

THE END.